Houghton Mifflin
Reading

Teacher's Edition

Grade 1

Surprises

Senior Authors J. David Cooper, John J. Pikulski

Authors Kathryn H. Au, David J. Chard, Gilbert G. Garcia, Claude N. Goldenberg, Phyllis C. Hunter, Marjorie Y. Lipson, Shane Templeton, Sheila W. Valencia, MaryEllen Vogt

Consultants Linda H. Butler, Linnea C. Ehri, Carla B. Ford

HOUGHTON MIFFLIN   BOSTON

LITERATURE REVIEWERS

Consultants: Dr. Adela Artola Allen, Associate Dean, Graduate College, Associate Vice President for Inter-American Relations, University of Arizona, Tucson, AZ; **Dr. Manley Begay,** Co-director of the Harvard Project on American Indian Economic Development, Director of the National Executive Education Program for Native Americans, Harvard University, John F. Kennedy School of Government, Cambridge, MA; **Dr. Nicholas Kannellos,** Director, Arte Publico Press, Director, Recovering the U.S. Hispanic Literacy Heritage Project, University of Houston, TX; **Mildred Lee,** author and former head of Library Services for Sonoma County, Santa Rosa, CA; **Dr. Barbara Moy,** Director of the Office of Communication Arts, Detroit Public Schools, MI; **Norma Naranjo,** Clark County School District, Las Vegas, NV; **Dr. Arlette Ingram Willis,** Associate Professor, Department of Curriculum and Instruction, Division of Language and Literacy, University of Illinois at Urbana-Champaign, IL

Teachers: Shirley Ferguson, Lakota Elementary School, Lakota, ND; **Susan Flanagin,** Mt. Jumbo School, Missoula, MT; **Robin Holland,** Windsor Academy, Columbus, OH; **Maureen Mack,** Lawn Manor Elementary, Oaklawn, IL; **Amy Shisako,** Harding Elementary, El Cerrito, CA; **Deborah Lopez Young,** Navajo Elementary School, Albuquerque, NM

PROGRAM REVIEWERS

Linda Bayer, Jonesboro, GA; **Sheri Blair,** Warner Robins, GA; **Faye Blake,** Jacksonville, FL; **Suzi Boyett,** Sarasota, FL; **Carol Brockhouse,** Madison Schools, Wayne Westland Schools, MI; **Patti Brustad,** Sarasota, FL; **Jan Buckelew,** Venice, FL; **Maureen Carlton,** Barstow, CA; **Karen Cedar,** Gold River, CA; **Karen Ciraulo,** Folsom, CA; **Marcia M. Clark,** Griffin, GA; **Kim S. Coady,** Covington, GA; **Eva Jean Conway,** Valley View School District, IL; **Marilyn Crownover,** Tustin, CA; **Carol Daley,** Sioux Falls, SD; **Jennifer Davison,** West Palm Beach, FL; **Lynne M. DiNardo,** Covington, GA; **Kathy Dover,** Lake City, GA; **Cheryl Dultz,** Citrus Heights, CA; **Debbie Friedman,** Fort Lauderdale, FL; **Anne Gaitor,** Lakeland, GA; **Rebecca S. Gillette,** Saint Marys, GA; **Buffy C. Gray,** Peachtree City, GA; **Merry Guest,** Homestead, FL; **Jo Nan Holbrook,** Lakeland, GA; **Beth Holguin,** San Jose, CA; **Coleen Howard-Whals,** St. Petersburg, FL; **Beverly Hurst,** Jacksonville, FL; **Debra Jackson,** St. Petersburg, FL; **Vickie Jordan,** Centerville, GA; **Cheryl Kellogg,** Panama City, FL; **Karen Landers,** Talladega County, AL; **Barb LeFerrier,** Port Orchard, WA; **Sandi Maness,** Modesto, CA; **Ileana Masud,** Miami, FL; **David Miller,** Cooper City, FL; **Muriel Miller,** Simi Valley, CA; **Walsetta W. Miller,** Macon, GA; **Jean Nielson,** Simi Valley, CA; **Sue Patton,** Brea, CA; **Debbie Peale,** Miami, FL; **Loretta Piggee,** Gary, IN; **Jennifer Rader,** Huntington, CA; **April Raiford,** Columbus, GA; **Cheryl Remash,** Manchester, NH; **Francis Rivera,** Orlando, FL; **Marina Rodriguez,** Hialeah, FL; **Marilynn Rose,** MI; **Kathy Scholtz,** Amesbury, MA; **Kimberly Moulton Schorr,** Columbus, GA; **Linda Schrum,** Orlando, FL; **Sharon Searcy,** Mandarin, FL; **Melba Sims,** Orlando, FL; **Judy Smith,** Titusville, FL; **Bea Tamo,** Huntington, CA; **Dottie Thompson,** Jefferson County, AL; **Dana Vassar,** Winston-Salem, NC; **Beverly Wakefield,** Tarpon Springs, FL; **Joy Walls,** Winston-Salem, NC; **Elaine Warwick,** Williamson County, TN; **Audrey N. Watkins,** Atlanta, GA; **Marti Watson,** Sarasota, FL

Supervisors: Judy Artz, Butler County, OH; **James Bennett,** Elkhart, IN; **Kay Buckner-Seal,** Wayne County, MI; **Charlotte Carr,** Seattle, WA; **Sister Marion Christi,** Archdiocese of Philadelphia, PA; **Alvina Crouse,** Denver, CO; **Peggy DeLapp,** Minneapolis, MN; **Carol Erlandson,** Wayne Township Schools, IN; **Brenda Feeney,** North Kansas City School District, MO; **Winnie Huebsch,** Sheboygan, WI; **Brenda Mickey,** Winston-Salem, NC; **Audrey Miller,** Camden, NJ; **JoAnne Piccolo,** Westminster, CO; **Sarah Rentz,** Baton Rouge, LA; **Kathy Sullivan,** Omaha, NE; **Rosie Washington,** Gary, IN; **Theresa Wishart,** Knox County Public Schools, TN

English Language Learners Reviewers: Maria Arevalos, Pomona, CA; **Lucy Blood,** NV; **Manuel Brenes,** Kalamazoo, MI; **Delight Diehn,** AZ; **Susan Dunlap,** Richmond, CA; **Tim Fornier,** Grand Rapids, MI; **Connie Jimenez,** Los Angeles, CA; **Diane Bonilla Lether,** Pasadena, CA; **Anna Lugo,** Chicago, IL; **Marcos Martel,** Hayward, CA; **Carolyn Mason,** Yakima, WA; **Jackie Pinson,** Moorpark, CA; **Jenaro Rivas,** NJ; **Jerilyn Smith,** Salinas, CA; **Noemi Velazquez,** Jersey City, NJ; **JoAnna Veloz,** NJ; **Dr. Santiago Veve,** Las Vegas, NV

CREDITS

Cover
Cover illustration by Dave Clegg.

Photography
Theme Opener © Ariel Skelley/CORBIS. **T183** © Frans Lanting/Minden Pictures.

Assignment Photography
© HMCo./Michael Indresano.

Illustration
T31 Normand Chartier. **T113** Tom Leonard. All kid art by Tim Johnson.

STUDENT WRITING MODEL FEATURE

Special thanks to the following teachers whose students' compositions appear as Student Writing Models: **Cheryl Claxton,** Florida; **Patricia Kopay,** Delaware; **Susana Llanes,** Michigan; **Joan Rubens,** Delaware; **Nancy Schulten,** Kentucky; **Linda Wallis,** California

Animal Adventures

OBJECTIVES

Phonemic Awareness segmenting phonemes; counting sounds in words

Phonics long *o* (CV, CVC*e*) and long *u* (CVC*e*), final clusters *ft, lk, nt;* long *e* (CV, CVC*e*) and vowel pairs *ee, ea;* vowel pairs *ai, ay*

Reading Strategies phonics/decoding; summarize; question; predict/infer

Comprehension story structure; noting details; making predictions

High-Frequency Words recognize high-frequency words

Fluency build reading fluency

Grammar naming words for people, animals, things, places; naming words for one or more

Writing writing to persuade; answering a comprehension question; writing a summary; process writing: description

Spelling words with long *o;* words with long *e* (*e, ee, ea*); words with *ay*

Vocabulary alphabetical order; fruits and vegetables; rhyming words; expressions of surprise; parts of the body; animal action words

Listening/Speaking/Viewing listening for enjoyment; compare and contrast; viewing to retell; listening to retell; listening for information

Information and Study Skills parts of a book: captions, headings, chapter headings, index

Animal Adventures

CONTENTS

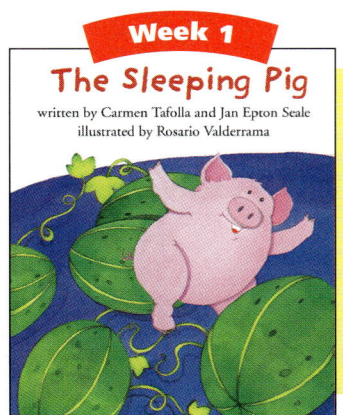

Week 1

The Sleeping Pig

written by Carmen Tafolla and Jan Epton Seale
illustrated by Rosario Valderrama

Fantasy

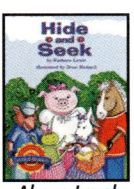

Below Level   *On Level*   *Above Level*   *Language Support*

Writing Process

Theme 6

Week 2

EEK! There's a Mouse in the House

WONG·HERBERT YEE

Fantasy

Below Level

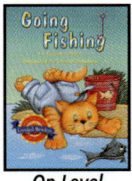
On Level

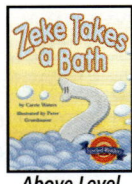
Above Level

Language Support

Week 3

RED-EYED TREE FROG

BY JOY COWLEY · PHOTOGRAPHS BY NIC BISHOP

Nonfiction

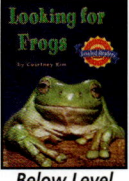
Below Level

On Level

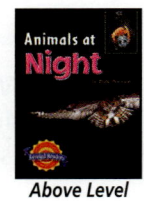
Above Level

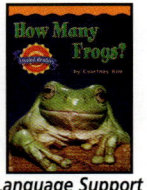
Language Support

Theme Wrap-Up

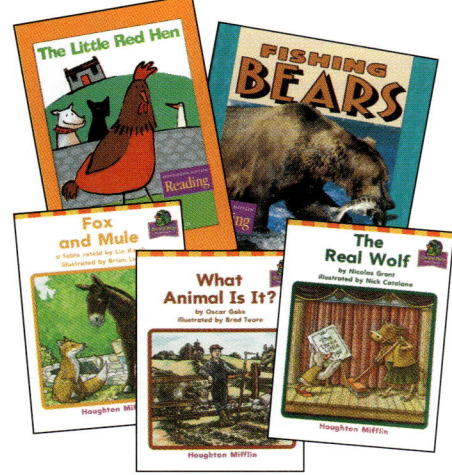

Leveled Theme Paperbacks

Leveled Bibliography

BOOKS FOR INDEPENDENT READING AND FLUENCY BUILDING

TARGET SKILL To build vocabulary and fluency, choose books from this list for children to read outside of class. Suggest that they read for at least twenty minutes a day, either independently or with an adult who provides modeling and guidance.

Key

 Science

 Social Studies

 Multicultural

 Music

 Math

 Classic

 Art

 Career

Classroom Bookshelf

WELL BELOW LEVEL

Mouse at Night
by Nancy Christensen Hall
Orchard 2000 (32p)
While Miss Bumbly sleeps, Mouse enjoys watching TV and cooking in this nearly wordless story.

Bowl Patrol!
by Marilyn Janovitz
North-South 1996 (32p)
Rhyming word pairs tell how a dog protects her water bowl from a spider, a bird, and other creatures.

Catch That Cat!
by Cari Meister
Children's 1999 (24p) also paper
Labeled pictures of a playful cat introduce words that are opposites.

Honey Helps
by Laura Godwin
McElderry 2002 (24p)
Honey the kitten is determined to help Happy the dog bury his bone.

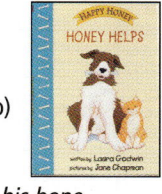

BELOW LEVEL

"I Don't Care!" Said the Bear
by Colin West
Candlewick 1996 (24p) also paper
The only animal a big bear is afraid of is a little mouse in this story with repetitive text.

 Little Lions
by Jim Arnosky
Putnam 1998 (32p)
On a rocky ledge, two mountain lion cubs play under the protection of their mother.

 Get the Ball, Slim
by Marcia Leonard
Millbrook 1998 (32p) also paper
Twin brothers Tim and Jim play ball with their dog Slim.

Pig Parade
by Patricia Hubbell
Random 2003 (32p) also paper
Little Pig is watching a parade when he sees a fire at Wolf's house.

Minerva Louise and the Red Truck
by Janet M. Stoeke
Dial 2002 (32p)
During a ride in the farm truck, the daffy hen Minerva Louise misinterprets what she sees.

ON LEVEL

● **Tiny's Bath**
by Cari Meister
Viking 1998 (32p) also paper
A boy has trouble finding a place big enough to give his huge dog Tiny a bath.

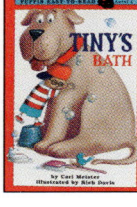

 ● **Every Autumn Comes the Bear**
by Jim Arnosky
Putnam 1993 (32p) also paper
The author describes the bear that shows up every autumn near his home.

Foggy Friday
by Phyllis Root
Candlewick 2001 (24p)
A rooster loses his cock-a-doodle-doo on a foggy morning, and no one on the farm can get out of bed.

 Amazing Animals
by Betsy Franco
Children's 2002 (32p)
Animals have all kinds of amazing abilities, including using their noses as hoses.

The Tail of Little Skunk
by Marsha Diane Arnold
Random 2002 (32p)
Little Skunk worries about what he'll do if Big Bear comes down from the mountain.

Drip, Drop
by Sarah Weeks
Harper 2000 (32p)
A mouse with a leaky roof tries to catch the water in pots, pans, cups, and cans.

ABOVE LEVEL

● ✻ **Annie and the Wild Animals**
by Jan Brett
Houghton 1985 (32p) also paper
Annie tries to befriend a moose, a bear, a wildcat, and other woodland animals.

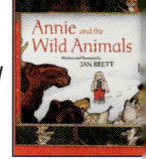

Busy Busy Moose
by Nancy Van Laan
Houghton 2003 (48p)
Moose and his animal friends share adventures throughout the seasons.

● **Henry and Mudge and Annie's Perfect Pet**
by Cynthia Rylant
Simon 2000 (40p)
Henry and his big dog Mudge help cousin Annie pick out a bunny at the pet store.

● = A suggested lesson plan for each of these books is provided in Theme Resources, pages R7, R8, R10, and R11.

✻ = Included in Houghton Mifflin Classroom Bookshelf, Level 1.

Pouncing Bobcats

by Joelle Riley
Lerner 2002 (32p)

A brief photo essay provides information about bobcats and their behavior.

Feeding Time

by Lee Davis
DK 2001 (32p) also paper

African animals eat all kinds of things, including grass, bark, bananas, and termites.

The Case of the Fidgety Fox

by Cynthia Rylant
Greenwillow 2003 (56p)

Crime solvers Bunny Brown and Jack Jones help a bus driver find his missing lucky dice.

BOOKS FOR TEACHER READ ALOUD

Harry the Dirty Dog

by Gene Zion
Harper 1956 (32p) also paper

The classic story features a dog, dirt, and a bath. **Available in Spanish as Harry, el perrito sucio.**

Tops and Bottoms

by Janet Stevens
Harcourt 1995 (32p)

A clever hare outwits a lazy bear in this trickster tale, a Caldecott Honor book.

✶ Young Mouse and Elephant

by Pamela J. Farris
Houghton 1996 (32p)

In an East African folktale, Young Mouse sets out to prove he's stronger than Elephant.

What Do You Do with a Tail Like This?

by S. Jenkins and R. Page
Houghton 2003 (32p)

Animals can do many things with their eyes, ears, noses, feet, and tails.

How Chipmunk Got His Stripes

by Joseph and James Bruchac
Dial 2002 (32p)

Braggart Bear loses a bet to Brown Squirrel in this Native American folktale.

Bow Wow Meow Meow

by Douglas Florian
Harcourt 2003 (56p)

This funny collection of brief poems features all kinds of cats and dogs.

Toestomper and the Bad Butterflies

by Sharleen Collicott
Houghton 2003 (32p)

Trouble follows when Toestomper's cute caterpillars turn into butterflies with attitude.

The Ant and the Grasshopper

by Amy L. Poole
Holiday 2000 (32p)

At the summer palace of the Chinese emperor, a grasshopper plays while the ants prepare for winter.

The Birdwatchers

by Simon James
Candlewick 2002 (32p)

Jess likes Granddad's stories about his adventures birdwatching so much she decides to join him.

Technology

Computer Software Resources

- **Get Set for Reading CD-ROM for** *Animal Adventures*
  Provides background building, vocabulary support, and selection summaries in English and Spanish. Houghton Mifflin Company

- **Curious George® Learns Phonics**
  Provides interactive phonics practice. Houghton Mifflin Company

- **Curious George® Learns to Spell**
  Provides interactive spelling practice. Houghton Mifflin Company

- **The Magic School Bus Explores the World of Animals CD-ROM.** *Microsoft*

- **Animals Alike CD-ROM.** *Heinemann*

Video Cassettes

- **The Hat** *by Jan Brett. Spoken Arts*
- **Anansi Goes Fishing** *by Eric A. Kimmel. Live Oak*
- **The Biggest Bears.** *Big Kids*
- **Tops and Bottoms** *by Janet Stevens. Spoken Arts*
- **A Boy, a Dog, and a Frog** *by Mercer Mayer. Weston Woods*
- **Mouse Around** *by Pat Schories. Weston Woods*

Audio

- **Annie and the Wild Animals** *by Jan Brett. Houghton Mifflin Company*
- **Harry the Dirty Dog** *by Gene Zion. Weston Woods*
- **One Fine Day** *by Nonny Hogrogian. Weston Woods*
- **CD-ROM for** *Animal Adventures*. *Houghton Mifflin Company*

Technology Resources addresses are on page R46.

Education Place®

www.eduplace.com *Log on to Education Place for more activities relating to* Animal Adventures, *including vocabulary support—*
- e • Glossary
- e • WordGame

Book Adventure®

www.bookadventure.org *This Internet reading incentive program provides thousands of titles for children to read.*

Accelerated Reader® Universal CD-ROM

This popular CD-ROM provides practice quizzes for Anthology selections and for many popular children's books.

Theme Skills Overview

Pacing
Approximately 3 weeks

	Week 1
	The Sleeping Pig 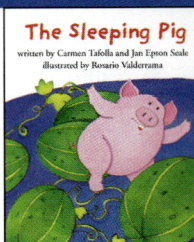 Fantasy pp. T46–T57
Learning to Read **Phonemic Awareness** **Phonics**	🔥 **Segment Phonemes; Count Sounds in Words** 🔥 **Long _o_ (CV, CVCe) and Long _u_ (CVCe)** T 🔥 **Final Clusters _ft, lk, nt_** T **Phonics Review:** Long _i_ (CVCe); Contractions
Comprehension	**Guiding Comprehension** 🔥 **Story Structure** T 🔥 **Summarize** T
Fluency	🔥 **Decodable Text** _Duke's Gift; Legs Gets His Lunch; The Nest_ **Social Studies Link** How to Read a Social Studies Article
Leveled Readers • Fluency Practice • Independent Reading • Lessons and Leveled Practice	**Leveled Readers** _The Huge Carrot_ _Watermelon for Lunch_ _Hide-and-Seek_ _The Carrot_ 
Word Work **Vocabulary** **High-Frequency Words** **Spelling**	🔥 **Alphabetical Order** 🔥 **Fruits and Vegetables** 🔥 **High-Frequency Words:** _by, climb, found, morning, out, shout, show_ T **Words with Long _o_** T
Writing and Oral Language **Writing** **Grammar** **Listening/Speaking/Viewing**	✏️ **A Letter of Persuasion** **Write a Poster** **Writing to Persuade** **Naming Words for People and Animals** T Listening Comprehension Listening: For Enjoyment Listening and Speaking: Compare and Contrast
Cross-Curricular Activities	Classroom Management Activities

T Skill tested on Integrated Theme Test and/or Theme Skills Test

Target Skills

Phonemic Awareness
Phonics
Comprehension
Vocabulary
Fluency

Week 2	Week 3
EEK! There's a Mouse in the House Fantasy pp. T128–T139 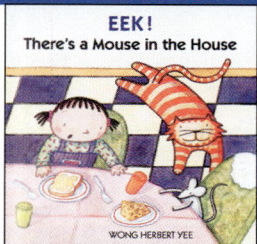	**Red-Eyed Tree Frog** Nonfiction pp. T198–T211 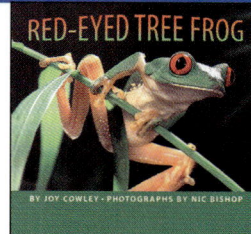

Week 2	Week 3
Segment Phonemes; Count Sounds in Words	**Segment Phonemes;** Count Sounds in Words
Long e (CV, CVCe) T	**Vowel Pairs *ai*, *ay*** T
Vowel Pairs *ee*, *ea* T	
Phonics Review: Long o (CV, CVCe) and Long u (CVCe); Final Clusters ft, lk, nt	**Phonics Review:** Long e (CV, CVCe); Vowel Pairs ee, ea
Guiding Comprehension	**Guiding Comprehension**
Noting Details T	**Making Predictions** T
Question	**Predict/Infer**
Decodable Text	**Decodable Text**
Seal Beach; Pete and Peach; Gram's Huge Meal	Rain Day; Cub's Long Day; Jay's Trip
Math Link How to Read a Pictograph	**Poetry Link** How to Read a Poem

Week 2	Week 3
Leveled Readers 	**Leveled Readers** 
The Feast *Going Fishing* *Zeke Takes a Bath* *Fun and Food to Eat*	*Looking for Frogs* *The Mouse in the Forest* *Animals at Night* *How Many Frogs?*

Week 2	Week 3
Rhyming Words **Expressions of Surprise**	**Parts of the Body** **Animal Action Words**
High-Frequency Words: cow, door, horse, now, table, there, through, wall T	**High-Frequency Words:** been, evening, far, forest, goes, hungry, near, soon T
Words with Long e (e, ee, ea) T	**Words with *ay*** T

Week 2	Week 3
A Class Story **Write a List** **Answering a Comprehension Question** T	**A Class Summary** **Write a Riddle** **Writing a Summary**
Naming Words for Things and Places T	**Naming Words for One or More** T
Listening Comprehension Listening and Speaking: Compare and Contrast Viewing: Retelling	Listening Comprehension Listening: To Retell Listening and Speaking: Listening for Information
Classroom Management Activities	Classroom Management Activities

Additional Theme Resources

- Lesson Plans for Leveled Theme Paperbacks
- Reteaching Lessons
- Challenge/Extension Activities
- Information and Study Skills Lesson
- Word Wall Cards/ Activity Masters
- Music
- Word Lists
- Technology Resources
- Pronunciation Guide

Technology

Education Place®
www.eduplace.com

Log on to Education Place for more activities relating to *Animal Adventures*.

Lesson Planner CD-ROM
Customize your planning for *Animal Adventures* with the Lesson Planner CD-ROM.

Management Routines

Sorting Papers

Encourage children to take an active role in filing and storing work samples to save throughout the year. Label a hanging file folder for each child, and hang the folders alphabetically in a cardboard carton.

- Sort portfolios, journals, and other dated samples of children's work into the folders so the samples will be readily available for parent conferences.
- Teach children how to find their files and store their work independently. This is a hands-on way for children to practice alphabetical order and to learn to be organized.

Teacher's Tip: Practicing ABC's Have children hang their folders, one at a time, as they recite the alphabet slowly. Help each child hang his or her folder alphabetically. If more than one name begins with the same letter, demonstrate how to alphabetize by the second and third letter.

Tips for Centers

Remind children that they should be doing their best to complete the work in the centers. Explain that if they have extra time, they can review their own work and challenge themselves to do even more on a project. Review the following tips for how to work both independently and with small groups.

1. Pay attention when centers are explained.
2. Work hard at each center.
3. Try to solve problems on your own first, or ask friends for help.
4. Plan your time. Try to complete work in each center.
5. Respect your friends.

Instructional Routines

Word Hunts

Have children search Anthologies and other texts to find and list words that have a target phonic element. For example, children might look for words with long e spelled *ee* and *ea*.

- Distribute a piece of paper to each child. Choose a phonic element children have just learned, and have them print the spelling at the top of the paper.
- Have children search through books and magazines for words with that phonic element, and list as many as they can find.
- Have children share their words with the class, pointing to the sound/spelling in them.
- During the course of the year, do hunts for other phonic elements, rhyming words, and word parts such as verb endings, prefixes, and suffixes.

<u>ee</u>	<u>ea</u>
sheep	beach
cheese	bean
free	
tree	

Word-Building Buckets

Materials	2 coffee cans index cards	**Practice Book** punchout letter cards and letter tray

Provide opportunities for children to practice spelling and decoding with this word-building routine.

- In one coffee can, place letter cards for single consonants, clusters, and digraphs. In the other can, place vowels and vowel pairs. Put a letter tray between the two cans.
- Have partners work together to build a word on the tray. They can take turns drawing letter cards from the cans until a word is built.
- Partners can also take turns writing each word they build on an index card.

home

Cross-Curricular Activities

Independent Activities

Assign these activities at any time during the theme while you work with small groups.

Additional Independent Activities

- Challenge/Extension Activities, Theme Resources, pp. R13, R15, R17, R19, R21, R23, R25, R27, R29, R31

- **Classroom Management Handbook,** pp. 122–145

- **Challenge Handbook,** pp. 66–71

- Classroom Management Activities, pp. T26–T27, T108–109, T178–179

Look for more independent activities in the Classroom Management Kit.

Phonics Center
Long Vowel Animals

👥👥👥 Groups	🕐 15 minutes
Objective	Find animals with long vowels in their names.
Materials	chart paper, crayons or markers, animal books and magazines

- Post a large piece of chart paper in the Phonics Center with the heading *Long Vowel Animals*.

- Divide the paper into columns for each vowel.

- As groups rotate through the center, children can look through animal books and help each other add to the chart any animal names that have long vowel sounds.

Long Vowel Animals

A	E	I	O	U
snake	sheep	spider	goat	mule
whale	peacock	tiger	toad	bluebird

Math Center
Build a Zoo

👥 Pairs	🕐 30 minutes
Objective	Build and measure a play zoo.
Materials	plastic zoo animals, even-sized blocks, paper, pencils

Have partners build a block zoo for plastic zoo animals. The zoo should have enough space so that the animals inside are not touching.

- Have children record the number of animals in the zoo and the number of blocks it takes to build the zoo.

- Then have them take away one block to make the zoo smaller. Do all the animals still have enough room? If not, children should take away one of the animals.

- Children continue taking away blocks and animals until only one animal is left. Have them record how many blocks it takes to build a zoo for one animal.

Consider copying and laminating these activities for use in centers.

Writing Center
Favorite Animals

👤 Singles	⏱ 15 minutes
Objective	Write a description of a favorite animal.
Materials	paper, pencil, crayons

Have children write two sentences describing their favorite animal and why they like it. You may wish to post these sentence models in the Writing Center:

- My favorite animal is a _____.
- I like _____s because _____.

If there is extra time, children can illustrate their descriptions.

Science Center
Animal Groups

👤 Singles	⏱ 45 minutes
Objective	Make a booklet that classifies animals by fur, feathers, and scales.
Materials	illustrated animal magazines, paper, pencils, crayons, scissors, glue

Hand out sheets of paper labeled *Fur, Feathers,* and *Scales* to each child. Tell children:

- Look through magazines.
- Find one animal from each category.
- Draw or cut and paste each animal onto the correct page.
- Label each animal with its name.
- Gather your pages into a booklet.
- Make a cover for your book and call it *Animal Groups*.
- Illustrate your cover.

Social Studies Center
Animal Map

👥 Groups	⏱ 20 minutes
Objective	Show on a map where different animals live.
Materials	world map showing continents, plastic animals or animal pictures

- Place a large world map on the table or floor. Make sure the continents are clearly labeled.
- Give children plastic animals or animal pictures and a list that tells the continent on which each animal lives.
- Have children work together to place the animals on the map.

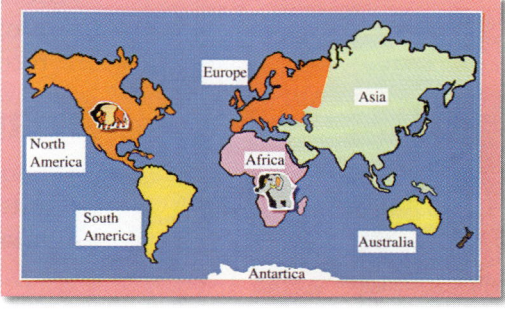

Planning for Assessment

During instruction in Theme 6 . . .

Lexia Phonics
CD-ROM
Quick Phonics Assessment
Houghton Mifflin
Reading

1 SCREENING AND DIAGNOSIS

Screening
- Baseline Group Test
- Emerging Literacy Survey

Diagnosis
- Leveled Reading Passages Assessment Kit
- Phonics/Decoding Screening Test
- Lexia Quick Phonics Assessment CD-ROM

2 MONITORING PROGRESS

Monitoring Student Progress

If . . .	Then . . .
children have difficulty summarizing the selection,	have partners help each other to remember and tell about the important parts of the story.

ONGOING INFORMAL ASSESSMENT
- Guiding Comprehension questions
- Story Retellings
- Comprehension Checks
- Oral Reading/Fluency Checks
- Monitoring Student Progress boxes
- Writing Samples
- Observation Checklists
- Skill lesson applications

END-OF-THEME REVIEW AND TEST PREPARATION

Preparing for Tests
- prepares children for formal assessments by teaching and providing practice for test-taking strategies.

Assessing Student Progress
- provides suggestions for administering formal assessments, information and recommendations for Fluency Assessment, and resources for differentiating instruction.

FORMAL ASSESSMENT
- End-of-Week Skills Checks or Alternative Assessments
- Integrated Theme Tests
- Theme Skills Tests
- Fluency Assessment
- Reading-Writing Workshop

3 MANAGING AND REPORTING

 **Technology**   Record each child's performance on the **Learner Profile® CD-ROM.**

National Test Correlation
Documenting Adequate Yearly Progress

○ SKILLS for *Animal Adventures*	ITBS	Terra Nova (CTBS)	CAT	SAT	MAT
Phonemic Awareness					
• Segmenting Phonemes*	○	○	○	○	○
Phonics					
• Blending Long *o*, *u*, and *e* Words (CVCe)	○	○	○		○
• Vowel Pairs *ee*, *ea*, *ai*, *ay*	○	○	○		○
• Final Clusters *ft*, *lk*, *nt*	○	○	○		○
High-Frequency Words					
• High-Frequency Words			○		○
Comprehension Strategies and Skills					
• Strategies: Summarize; Question*; Predict/Infer*	○	○	○		○
• Skills: Story Structure; Noting Details; Making Predictions	○	○	○	○	○
Vocabulary					
• Vocabulary*	○	○	○	○	○
Spelling					
• Words with Long *o*, Long *e*, and Vowel Pair *ay*	○	○			○
Grammar					
• Common Nouns					
• Singular and Plural Nouns	○		○		
Writing					
• Reading-Writing Workshop: Description					
Listening/Speaking/Viewing					
• Listening Comprehension*	○	○		○	○

*These skills are taught, but not tested, in this theme.

KEY

ITBS Iowa Tests of Basic Skills

Terra Nova (CTBS) Comprehensive Tests of Basic Skills

CAT California Achievement Tests

SAT Stanford Achievement Tests

MAT Metropolitan Achievement Tests

Launching the Theme

Theme **6**

Animal Adventures

Two Feet, Four Feet

I have only two small feet,
But horses, dogs, and cows
  Have four.
I can walk and run with
  Mine.
So why do **they** need any
  More?

by Ilo Orleans

Introducing the Theme: Discussion Options

Read aloud the theme title on Anthology page 129. Ask children to name the kind of animal the children in the photograph are holding.

Read aloud the poem "Two Feet, Four Feet" by Ilo Orleans. Ask these questions:

1 What clue in this poem tells you that a person is speaking?
(The line that reads "I have only two small feet.")

2 Why do you think the animals need four feet?
(Answers will vary.)

Ask children what animals have two feet and what animals have four feet. Then tell children that in this theme, *Animal Adventures,* they will read stories about many kinds of animals.

Using the Read Aloud

Read aloud the Big Book *Two's Company*. After reading the story (see text on page R2), use the following questions to discuss how the story relates to the theme *Animal Adventures*.

1 Which of the animals do you think might have the most exciting adventures? Why?
(Answers will vary.)

2 Do you think animals have more adventures alone or in groups? Why?
(Answers will vary.)

Read aloud for oral language and vocabulary development. Read aloud other stories to help develop children's oral comprehension, vocabulary, and listening skills. You may want to choose other books to read aloud from the Leveled Bibliography on pages T6–T7.

Home Connection

Send home the theme letter for *Animal Adventures* to introduce the theme and suggest home activities. (See **Teacher's Resource Blackline Masters.**)

For other suggestions relating to *Animal Adventures,* see **Home/Community Connections.**

Classroom Management

At any time during the theme, you can assign the independent theme-level activities on Teacher's Edition pages T12–T13 while you give differentiated instruction to small groups.

Additional independent activity centers related to specific selections can be found in the Teacher's Edition.

- Classroom Management Activities, Week 1, pages T26–T27
- Classroom Management Activities, Week 2, pages T108–T109
- Classroom Management Activities, Week 3, pages T178–T179

Monitoring Student Progress

Monitoring Progress

Throughout the theme, monitor children's progress by using the following program features in the Teacher's Edition:

- Guiding comprehension questions
- Literature discussion groups
- Skill lesson applications
- Monitoring Student Progress boxes
- Theme Wrap-Up, pages T244–T246

Lesson Overview

Literature

The Sleeping Pig

written by Carmen Tafolla and Jan Epton Seale
illustrated by Rosario Valderrama

Selection Summary

A bunch of different animals try to help Celina move a sleeping pig from her watermelon patch.

1 Decodable Text

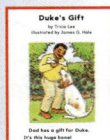  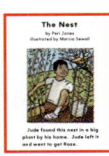

Phonics Library
- *Duke's Gift*
- *Legs Gets His Lunch*
- *The Nest*

2 Background and Vocabulary

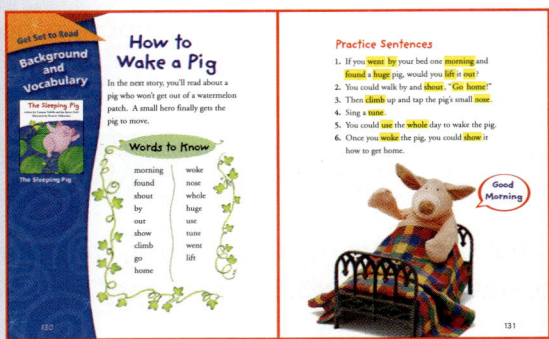

3 Main Selection

The Sleeping Pig
Genre: Fantasy

4 Social Studies

T18

Instructional Support

Planning and Practice

- Planning and classroom management
- Reading and skill instruction
- Plans and activities for reaching all learners

- Newsletters
- Observation Checklists
- Theme Activity Masters
- Alternative Weekly Tests

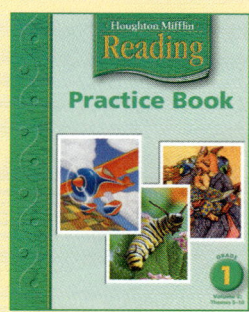

- Independent practice for skills, Level 1.3

- Decodable Text, Books 51–57, Review Books 49–71

- Charts/ Transparencies
- Strategy Posters
- Blackline Masters

Reaching All Learners

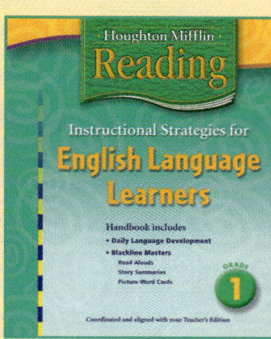 

Coordinated lessons, activities, and projects for additional reading instruction

For
- Classroom Teacher
- Extended Day
- Pull Out
- Resource Teacher
- Reading Specialist

Technology

Audio Selection
The Sleeping Pig

Get Set for Reading CD-ROM
- Background building
- Vocabulary support
- Selection Summary in English and Spanish

Accelerated Reader®
Practice quiz for the selection

www.eduplace.com
Log on to Education Place for more activities related to the selection, including vocabulary support—

- e • **Glossary**
- e • **WordGame**

Leveled Books for Reaching All Learners

Leveled Readers and Leveled Practice

- Independent reading for building fluency
- Topic, comprehension strategy, and vocabulary linked to main selection
- Lessons in Teacher's Edition, pages T84–T87
- Leveled practice for every book

Technology

Leveled Readers
Available on CD

Book Adventure®
Practice quizzes for the Leveled Theme Paperbacks

www.bookadventure.org

● BELOW LEVEL

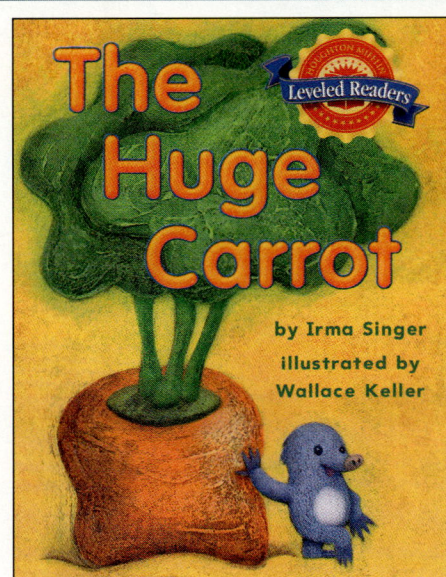

The Huge Carrot
by Irma Singer
illustrated by Wallace Keller

● Below Level Practice

Name

Vocabulary

Write the word from the box below the picture it goes with.

Story Words
mule
carrot
mole
pulls

1. pulls   2. mule

3. carrot   4. mole

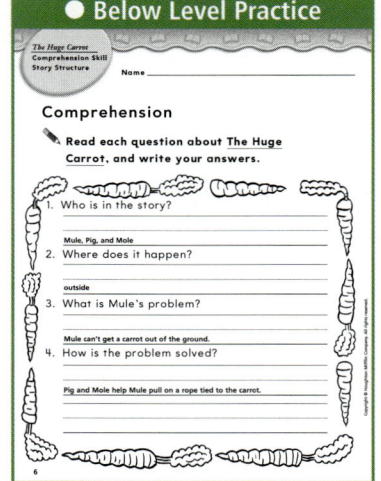

● Below Level Practice

The Huge Carrot
Comprehension Skill
Story Structure

Name

Comprehension

Read each question about The Huge Carrot, and write your answers.

1. Who is in the story?
Mule, Pig, and Mole

2. Where does it happen?
outside

3. What is Mule's problem?
Mule can't get a carrot out of the ground.

4. How is the problem solved?
Pig and Mole help Mule pull on a rope tied to the carrot.

▲ ON LEVEL

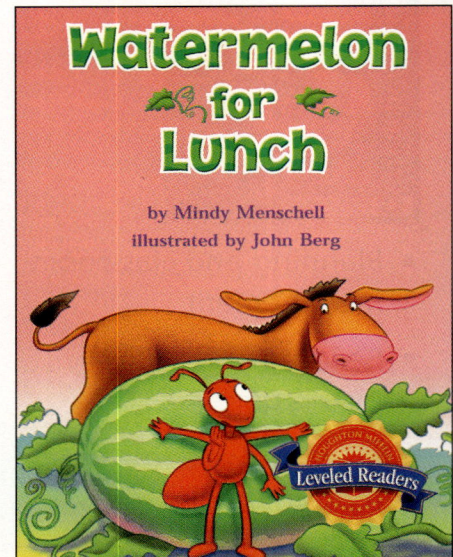

Watermelon for Lunch
by Mindy Menschell
illustrated by John Berg

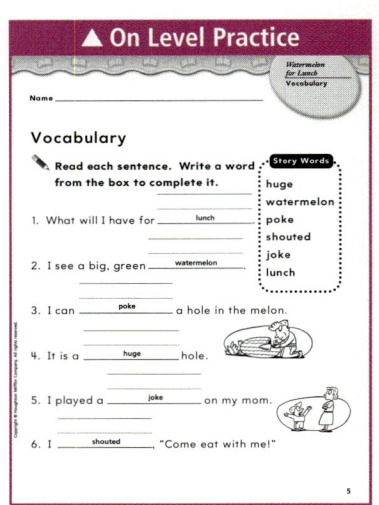

▲ On Level Practice

Name

Vocabulary

Read each sentence. Write a word from the box to complete it.

Story Words
huge
watermelon
poke
shouted
joke
lunch

1. What will I have for _____ lunch
2. I see a big, green _____ watermelon
3. I can _____ poke a hole in the melon.
4. It is a _____ huge hole.
5. I played a _____ joke on my mom.
6. I _____ shouted "Come eat with me!"

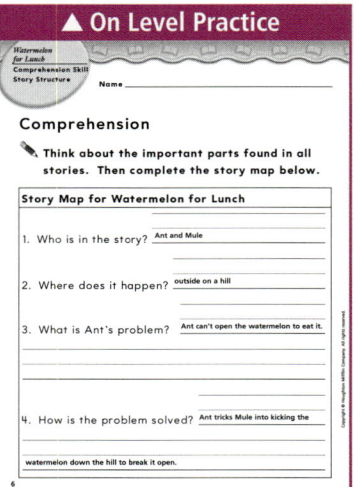

▲ On Level Practice

Watermelon for Lunch
Comprehension Skill
Story Structure

Name

Comprehension

Think about the important parts found in all stories. Then complete the story map below.

Story Map for Watermelon for Lunch

1. Who is in the story? Ant and Mule

2. Where does it happen? outside on a hill

3. What is Ant's problem? Ant can't open the watermelon to eat it.

4. How is the problem solved? Ant tricks Mule into kicking the watermelon down the hill to break it open.

Leveled Theme Paperbacks

- Extended independent reading in theme-related paperbacks
- Lessons in Teacher's Edition, pages R3–R5

■ ABOVE LEVEL

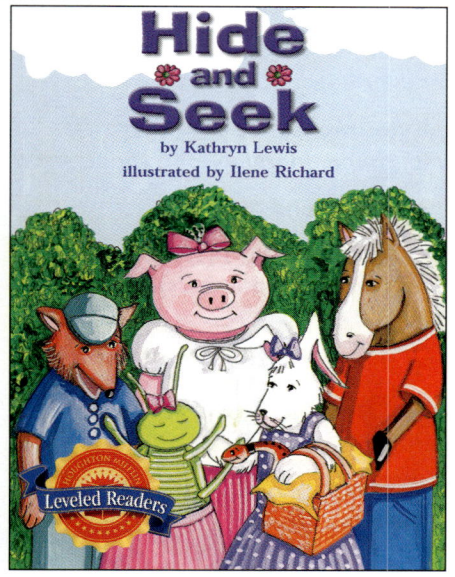

◆ LANGUAGE SUPPORT

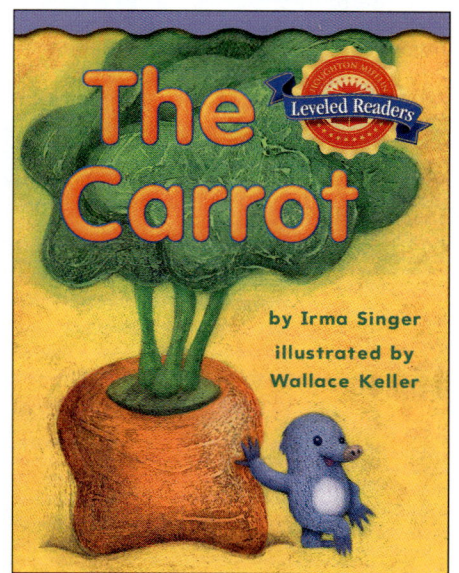

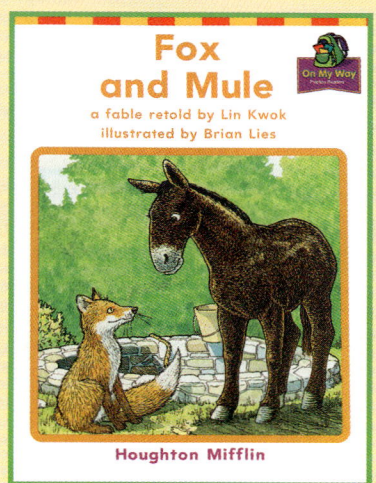

Below Level

On Level

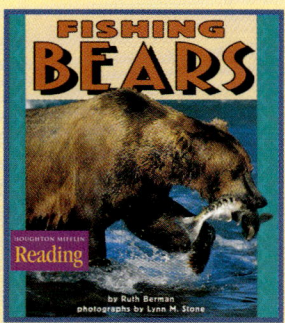

Above Level

■ Above Level Practice

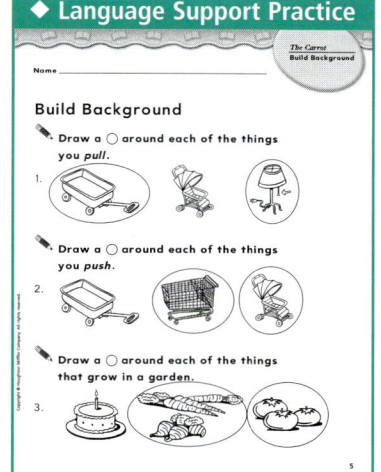

■ Above Level Practice

◆ Language Support Practice

◆ Language Support Practice

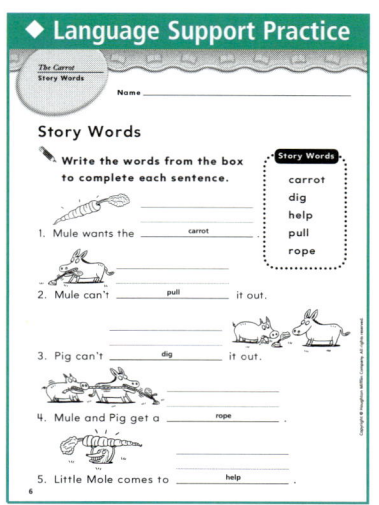

Daily Lesson Plans

 Technology

Lesson Planner CD-ROM allows you to customize the chart below to develop your own lesson plans.

T Skill tested on Integrated Theme Test and/or Theme Skills Test

 80–90 minutes

Learning to Read

Phonemic Awareness
Phonics
Comprehension

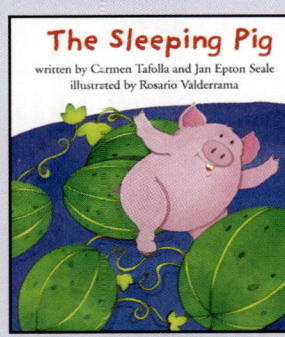
The Sleeping Pig
written by Carmen Tafolla and Jan Epton Seale
illustrated by Rosario Valderrama

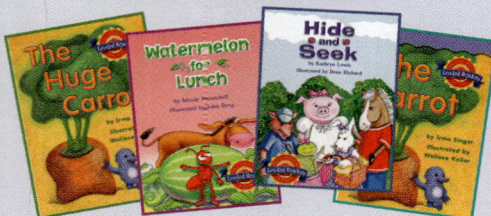

Leveled Readers
• Fluency Practice
• Independent Reading

 20–30 minutes

Word Work

Spelling
Vocabulary and
High-Frequency Words

 20–30 minutes

Writing and Oral Language

Writing
Grammar
Listening/Speaking/Viewing

DAY 1

Daily Routines, T28–T29
Phonics, High-Frequency Words,
Phonemic Awareness,
Independent Reading, Writing

Listening Comprehension, T30–T31
Fox, Alligator, and Rabbit

Phonics, T32–T34
Blending Long *o* Words (CV, CVCe) and Long *u* Words (CVCe) **T**
Final *ft, lk, nt* **T**

Reading Decodable Text, T35–T37
Duke's Gift

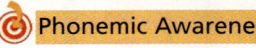 Duke's Gift
by Tricia Lee
illustrated by James G. Hale

Leveled Readers
The Huge Carrot
Watermelon for Lunch
Hide-and-Seek
The Carrot

Lessons and Leveled Practice, T84–T87

Spelling, T38
Words with Long *o* **T**

Vocabulary, T38
Word Wall: Spelling Pattern *-oke*

Daily Language Practice
1. Me and Jake play ball.
   (**Jake** and **I** play ball.)

Shared Writing, T39
A Letter of Persuasion

Listening, T39
For Enjoyment

DAY 2

Daily Routines, T40–T41
Phonics, High-Frequency Words,
Phonemic Awareness,
Independent Reading, Writing

High-Frequency Words, T42–T43
by, climb, found, morning, out, shout, show **T**

Building Background, T44

Story Vocabulary, T45
began, celebrate, coyote, cricket, howl, rabbit, tail, watermelon

Reading the Selection, T46–T57

Comprehension Strategy, T46
Summarize **T**

Comprehension Skill, T46
Story Structure **T**

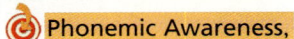 The Sleeping Pig
written by Carmen Tafolla and Jan Epton Seale
illustrated by Rosario Valderrama

Leveled Readers
The Huge Carrot
Watermelon for Lunch
Hide-and-Seek
The Carrot

Lessons and Leveled Practice, T84–T87

Spelling, T58
Practice: Words with Long *o* **T**

Vocabulary, T58
Review: High-Frequency Words **T**

Daily Language Practice
2. that is soe big!
   (**That is so** big!)

Interactive Writing, T59
A Letter of Persuasion

Target Skills of the Week

Phonics Awareness	Segment Phonemes; Count Sounds in Words
Phonics	Blending Long *o* Words (CV, CVCe) and Long *u* Words (CVCe); Final Clusters *ft, lk, nt*
Comprehension	Story Structure, Summarize
Vocabulary	High-Frequency Words; Alphabetical Order; Words That Name Fruits and Vegetables
Fluency	Leveled Readers; Decodable Text: Phonics Library

DAY 3

Daily Routines, T60–T61
Phonics, High-Frequency Words,
Phonemic Awareness,
Independent Reading, Writing

Comprehension Check, T62

Responding, T62

Comprehension Skill, T64–T65
Story Structure **T**

Leveled Readers
The Huge Carrot
Watermelon for Lunch
Hide-and-Seek
The Carrot

Lessons and Leveled Practice, T84–T87

Spelling, T66
Practice: Words with Long *o* **T**

Vocabulary, T66
Alphabetical Order

Daily Language Practice
3. Is this your hom.
(Is this your **home**?)

Writing: Responding, T63
Write a Poster

Grammar, T67
Naming Words for People and Animals **T**

DAY 4

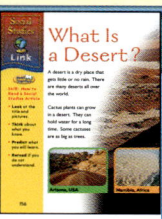

What Is a Desert?

Daily Routines, T68–T69
Phonics, High-Frequency Words,
Phonemic Awareness,
Independent Reading, Writing

Reading the Social Studies Link, T70–T71

Comprehension:
How to Read a Social Studies Article, T70

Phonics Review, T72–T73
Long *i* Words (CVCe)
Contractions

Leveled Readers
The Huge Carrot
Watermelon for Lunch
Hide-and-Seek
The Carrot

Lessons and Leveled Practice, T84–T87

Spelling, T74
Practice: Words with Long *o* **T**

Vocabulary, T74
Words That Name Fruits and Vegetables

Daily Language Practice
4. My noz is cold?
(My **nose** is cold.)

Independent Writing, T75
Writing to Persuade **T**

DAY 5

Daily Routines, T76–T77
Phonics, High-Frequency Words,
Phonemic Awareness,
Independent Reading, Writing

Comprehension: Rereading for Understanding
(Story Structure **T**) T78

Rereading for Fluency, T78

Reading Decodable Text,
T79–T81
The Nest
End-of-the-Week Skills Check

The Nest
by Peri Jones
illustrated by Marcia Sewall

Jude found this nest in a big
plant by his home. Jude left it
and went to get Rose.

13

Leveled Readers
The Huge Carrot
Watermelon for Lunch
Hide-and-Seek
The Carrot

Lessons and Leveled Practice, T84–T87

Spelling, T82
Test: Words with Long *o* **T**

Vocabulary, T82
Review: High-Frequency Words

Daily Language Practice
5. can you goe with me?
(**Can** you **go** with me?)

Independent Writing, T83
Journal Entry

Grammar Review, T83
Naming Words for People and Animals **T**

Listening and Speaking, T83
Compare and Contrast

Managing Flexible Groups

Leveled Instruction and Leveled Practice

	DAY 1	**DAY 2**
WHOLE CLASS	• Daily Routines (TE pp. T28–T29) • Teacher Read Aloud (TE pp. T30–T31) • Phonics (TE pp. T32–T34)	• Daily Routines (TE pp. T40–T41) • High-Frequency Words (TE pp. T42–T43) • Get Set to Read, Strategy and Skill, Purpose Setting (TE pp. T44–T47) *After Reading at Small Group Time* • Wrapping Up (TE p. T57); Comprehension Preview (TE p. T55)
SMALL GROUPS **Extra Support**	**TEACHER-LED** • Phonics Library: *Duke's Gift* (TE pp. T35–T37) • Selected I Love Reading Books: 51–57	**TEACHER-LED** • Anthology selection (T46–T57) • Phonics Library: *Legs Gets His Lunch* (T43) _____ **Partner or Individual Reading** • Read with audio CD of Anthology selection. • **Fluency Practice** Reread Phonics Library: *Duke's Gift* OR I Love Reading Books: 51–57.
On Level	**TEACHER-LED** • Phonics Library: *Duke's Gift* (TE pp. T35–T37)	**TEACHER-LED** • Anthology selection (TE pp. T46–T57) • Phonics Library: *Legs Gets His Lunch* (TE p. T43) • **Fluency Practice** Reread Phonics Library: *Duke's Gift* (TE pp. T35–T37) ✔ OR begin Leveled Reader: On Level (TE p. T85).
Challenge	**Partner or Individual Reading** • Phonics Library: *Duke's Gift* • Little Big Book: *Two's Company* (TE p. R2) OR book from Leveled Bibliography	**Partner or Individual Reading** • Anthology selection • Phonics Library: *Legs Gets His Lunch* • **Fluency Practice** Reread Phonics Library: *Duke's Gift*
English Language Learners	**TEACHER-LED** • Phonics Library: *Duke's Gift* (TE pp. T35–T37) • Selected I Love Reading Books: 51–57	**TEACHER-LED** • Phonics Library: *Legs Gets His Lunch* (TE p. T43) • **Fluency Practice** Reread Phonics Library: *Duke's Gift* (TE pp. T35–T37) ✔ _____ **Partner or Individual Reading** • Read with audio CD of Anthology selection.

Independent Activities

• Get Set for Reading CD-ROM or audio CD of Anthology selection
• Journals: selection notes, questions
• Complete, review **Practice Book** (pp. 53–60, 61–62) and **Leveled Reader Practice Blackline Masters** (TE pp. T84–T87).

✔ **Opportunity to informally assess oral reading rate.**

DAY 3

- Daily Routines (TE pp. T60–T61)

After Reading at Small Group Time
- Responding (TE p. T62)
- Comprehension lesson (TE pp. T64–T65)

TEACHER-LED
- Read Anthology selection aloud to answer Guiding Comprehension. (TE pp. T46–T57)
- **Fluency Practice** Reread Phonics Library: *Legs Gets His Lunch* OR selected I Love Reading Books: 51–57. ✔

Individual Reading
- Reread with audio CD of Anthology selection.
- **Fluency Practice** Reread Phonics Library: *Legs Gets His Lunch* OR complete Leveled Reader: On Level.

TEACHER-LED
- Read aloud from Anthology to answer Guiding Comprehension. (T46–T57) ✔

Partner or Individual Reading
- Leveled Reader (TE p. T86) OR book from Bibliography

TEACHER-LED
- Reread Anthology selection, first half. (TE pp. T46–T51)

Partner or Individual Reading
- Reread Phonics Library: *Legs Gets His Lunch.*
- Selected I Love Reading Books: 51–57

DAY 4

- Daily Routines (TE pp. T68–T69)
- Social Studies Link (TE pp. T70–T71)
- Phonics Review (TE pp. T72–T73)

TEACHER-LED
- Read On My Way Practice Reader. (TE p. R3)
- Begin Leveled Reader: Below Level (TE p. T84) OR book from Leveled Bibliography.
- **Fluency Practice** Reread Phonics Library: *Duke's Gift, Legs Gets His Lunch,* ✔ OR selected I Love Reading Review Books: 51–57.

Partner Reading
- Reread Anthology selection, partners alternating pages.
- **Fluency Practice** Reread Phonics Library: *Duke's Gift, Legs Gets His Lunch,* OR Leveled Reader: On Level (TE p. T85).

TEACHER-LED
- **Fluency Practice** Reread Anthology selection, Link, OR Phonics Library. ✔

Partner or Individual Reading
- Begin Theme Paperback OR book from Bibliography OR reread Little Big Book.

TEACHER-LED
- Reread Anthology sel., last half. (T52–T57)
- Begin Leveled Reader: Language Support (T87) OR On My Way Practice Reader (R3).

Individual Reading
- **Fluency Practice** Phonics Library: *Duke's Gift, Legs Gets His Lunch*

DAY 5

- Daily Routines (TE pp. T76–T77)
- Rereading for Understanding (TE p. T78)
- Responding: Select from activities (TE p. T63)

TEACHER-LED
- Phonics Library: *The Nest* (TE pp. T79–T81)
- Complete Leveled Reader: Below Level (TE p. T84)
- **Fluency Practice** Reread On My Way Practice Reader (TE p. R3), Phonics Library books, OR selected I Love Reading Review Books: 51–57 ✔

TEACHER-LED
- Phonics Library: *The Nest* (T79–T81) AND reread Link. (T70–T71)
- **Fluency Practice** Reread Phonics Library, Anthology, OR Leveled Reader. ✔

Partner or Individual Reading
- Theme Paperback (R4) OR book from Bibliography.

Individual Reading
- Phonics Library: *The Nest*
- Complete Theme Paperback (R5) OR book from Bibliography.
- **Fluency Practice** Reread Anthology selection and Link, Little Big Book, Above Level Theme Paperback, OR Leveled Reader.

TEACHER-LED
- Phonics Library: *The Nest* (TE pp. T79–T81)
- Complete Leveled Reader: Language Support (TE p. T87) OR On My Way Practice Reader (TE p. R3).
- **Fluency Practice** Reread week's Phonics Library books, Anthology selection, OR selected I Love Reading Books: 51–57. ✔

- Reread familiar selections.
- Read trade book from Leveled Bibliography (TE pp. T6–T7).
- Responding activities (TE pp. T62–T63)
- Activities related to *The Sleeping Pig* at Education Place: www.eduplace.com

Turn the page for more independent activities.

Classroom Management

Independent Activities

Assign these activities while you work with small groups.

Differentiated Instruction for Small Groups

- **Handbook for English Language Learners,** pp. 178–187

- **Extra Support Handbook,** pp. 174–183

Independent Activities

- Daily Routines, pp. T29, T41, T61, T69, T77

- Challenge/Extension Activities, pp. R13, R15, R21, R27

- **Classroom Management Handbook,** pp. 122–129

- **Challenge Handbook,** pp. 66–67

Look for more independent activities in the Classroom Management Kit.

Phonics Center

Super Sentences

👥 Pairs	🕐 25 minutes
Objective	Write and illustrate sentences with long *o* and long *u*.
Materials	paper, crayons, pencils

Have children write sentences using words with long *o* and long *u*.

- Partners can brainstorm a list of words with long *o* and long *u*.

- Children use words from their list to write a sentence.

- Provide crayons for children to illustrate their sentences.

- Have children put their pages together to make a book.

Art Center

Paper Bag Puppets

👥 Groups	🕐 30 minutes
Objective	Create paper bag puppets and use them to retell stories.
Materials	paper lunch bags, scissors, glue, crayons, buttons, yarn

Have children make paper bag puppets of a favorite character they read about this week.

- Children decorate a small paper lunch bag to look like a story character.

- Groups can put on a puppet show to retell a story they read this week.

Consider copying and laminating these activities for use in centers.

Writing Center

Dream Clouds

👤 Singles	🕐 15 minutes
Objective	Write about Mrs. Pig's dream.
Materials	white paper, pencil, crayons, scissors

Ask children to think about what Mrs. Pig may have been dreaming as she slept in the watermelon patch.

- Children can draw or trace a cloud onto white paper and cut it out.
- Have them write a sentence on the cloud about Mrs. Pig's dream. They may use this model: *Mrs. Pig had a dream about _____*.
- If there is extra time, children can draw a picture on the cloud to go with their sentence.

You may want to hang the dream clouds up above the Writing Center.

Mrs. Pig had a dream about eating watermelon.

Math Center

Estimating

👤 Singles	🕐 15 minutes
Objective	Estimate numbers of objects.
Materials	fruits and vegetables or math manipulatives in clear plastic jars

Place various fruits and vegetables in the Math Center.

- Children estimate the number of seeds in the fruits and vegetables.
- Have them record their estimates on paper and leave them in a box in the Math Center.
- At the end of the week, cut open the fruit and have children count to see if their estimations were correct.

Rather than using fruits and vegetables, you may choose to place math manipulatives, or other small objects, in a jar and have children estimate the number.

Science Center

Make a Desert

👥 Groups	🕐 30 minutes
Objective	Make a desert sandbox.
Materials	sand, box, paper, crayons, scissors, glue, craft sticks

If you do not have a sand table, put a few inches of sand in a sturdy cardboard box.

- Remind children of the desert animals they read about on Anthology pages 156–159.
- Have children draw desert plants and animals on construction paper and cut them out.
- Children then glue a craft stick onto the back of their drawing and use it to stick their plant or animal into the sandbox.

Desert Sand Box

Day at a Glance
pages T28–T39

Learning to Read

Teacher Read Aloud
Fox, Alligator, and Rabbit

Phonics Instruction
Blending Long *o* Words (CVC*e*)
and Long *u* Words (CVC*e*)
Final Clusters *ft, lk, nt*

Reading Decodable Text
Duke's Gift

• • • • • • • • • • • • • • • • • • •

Leveled Readers, *T84–T87*
- ● *The Huge Carrot*
- ▲ *Watermelon for Lunch*
- ■ *Hide-and-Seek*
- ◆ *The Carrot*

Word Work

Spelling: Words with Long *o*
Vocabulary: Spelling Pattern *-oke*

Writing & Oral Language

Shared Writing: A Letter of Persuasion
Listening: For Enjoyment

Daily Routines

Daily Message

Review skills. Point to each word as you read aloud the Daily Message.

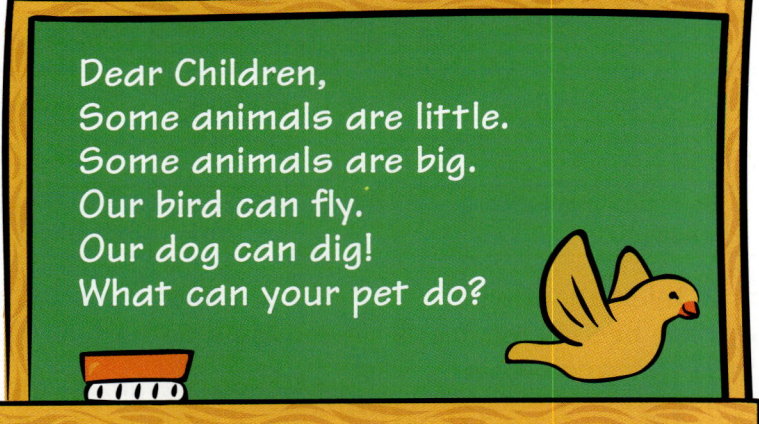

Dear Children,
Some animals are little.
Some animals are big.
Our bird can fly.
Our dog can dig!
What can your pet do?

Have children

- respond to the question;
- circle and read the word that begins with *fl*; *(fly)*
- find the following high-frequency words: *Some, animals, are, little, Our,* and *fly*.

Word Wall

High-Frequency Word Review Briefly review these and other high-frequency words daily. Have children practice reading, chanting, spelling, and writing them.

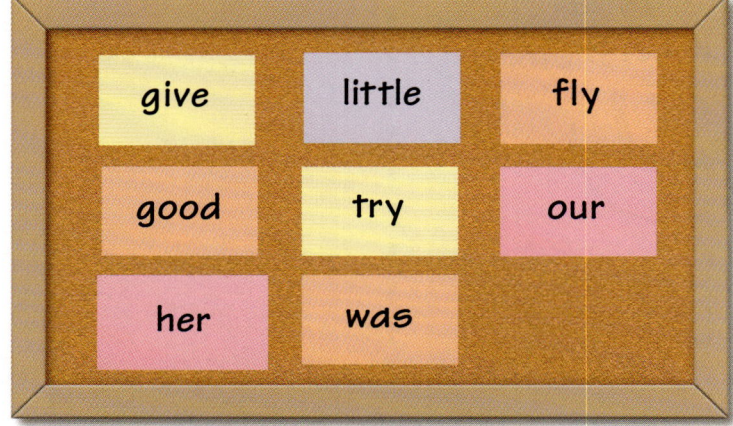

give little fly
good try our
her was

Blackline Master for these Word Wall Cards appears in Theme 5, page R40.

Daily Phonemic Awareness

Segmenting and Counting Phonemes: Clap the Sounds

- One at a time, say the words *froze, stove, left, stunt, broke,* and *tube.*
- Ask children to say the separate sounds. Examples: /f//r//ō//z/ for *froze*; /l//ĕ//f//t/ for *left*.
- Have children clap once for each sound they say and tell you how many times they clapped. Example: After clapping four times for *froze*, children should say "Four!"

Daily Language Practice

Grammar Skill: Using *I* or *me* in Sentences
Write the sentence, read it to children, and have them tell you how to correct it.

Me and Jake play ball.

(**Jake** and **I** play ball.)

 # Daily Writing Prompt

Remind children to write complete sentences, beginning with a capital letter and ending with a punctuation mark when responding to the prompt below or writing on self-selected topics.

- **Write about an adventure you have had.**

One day I went for a walk. A big dog came by. My dog ran and pulled me. We got away from the big dog.

Daily Independent Reading

To increase children's reading fluency, provide a variety of theme-related books for them to read. Here are some suggestions.

- Leveled Bibliography, pages T6–T7

Choose books from this list for children to read, outside class, for at least twenty minutes a day.

- On My Way Practice Reader: *Fox and Mule*
- Little Big Book: *Two's Company*

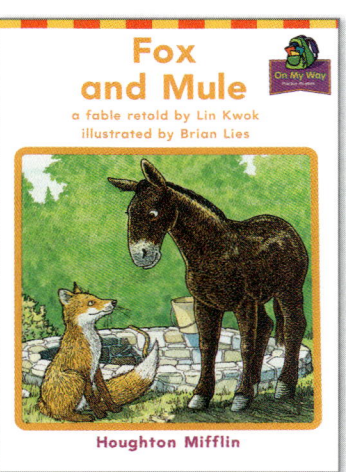

Fox and Mule
a fable retold by Lin Kwok
illustrated by Brian Lies

On My Way Practice Reader

Houghton Mifflin

Listening Comprehension

OBJECTIVES
- Listen to identify the parts of the story.

Building Background

Tell children that you will read a folktale from Jamaica. Explain that some folktales use animals to teach lessons. Have children discuss a time when they asked someone to help them solve a problem.

Fluency Modeling

Explain that as you read, you will model how to read dialogue with humor and expression.

Story Structure

Explain these concepts: A story has characters; the characters often have a problem to solve.

Read the selection aloud. Ask children to listen to find out the problem and how it is solved.

Guiding Comprehension

1. **STORY STRUCTURE** What is the problem in the story? (Rabbit needs to cross the river, but hungry Alligator is blocking the way.)

2. **STORY STRUCTURE** How do the characters solve their problem? (Fox tricks Alligator while Rabbit crosses the river.)

Sing a Song

Children may enjoy singing a song with many animal names. The music and lyrics for "Animal Song" are on page R39.

Teacher Read Aloud

Fox, Alligator, and Rabbit

One day Rabbit was on his way to the market to sell his melons. He needed to cross the river, but Alligator was waiting right in the middle of the water, as hungry as ever. Rabbit went to ask Fox for help. "Fox, you are so clever," said Rabbit. "Will you help me cross the river?"

"If you promise to share some of your melons, I'll show you how to outsmart Alligator. Watch carefully," said Fox and he headed to the river.

Without a doubt, Fox knew things about Alligator that no one else did. For one thing, Fox knew that Alligator was not too bright but thought he was very smart. Secondly, Fox knew that Alligator liked to eat porridge so hot that it could melt the hair right off your head . . . and Alligator loved to watch people eat his fiery porridge. So Fox wasn't too surprised when Alligator invited him to his house for lunch.

When the porridge was ready, Alligator placed a big bowl of it in front of Fox, chuckling to himself as he pictured all the fur melting right off Fox. "Alligator, this porridge is much too cold!" exclaimed Fox. "Why not leave it in the sun to warm up?"

Alligator, thinking the porridge would get even hotter, placed it in the sun. A few hours later, Fox dipped his spoon into the porridge. "Ahhh! Now this is what I call *hot* porridge," said Fox as he gobbled it up.

After lunch, as Fox was crossing the river, Alligator wondered, "How come Fox's porridge was hot, and mine is cold as can be?" Alligator swam after Fox and asked him, but Fox was already on shore.

"I'll tell you tomorrow. See you later, Alligator!" replied Fox.

Imagine Fox's surprise when he saw Rabbit already at the market. "You're not the only smart one," laughed Rabbit. "While you were with Alligator, I brought my melons across the river."

"Well then, if you weren't watching to see how I crossed the river, how are you going to get back home?" asked Fox, and Rabbit stopped his laughing.

OBJECTIVES

- Segment phonemes and count sounds.
- Associate the long *o* sound, /ō/, with the CV and CVC*e* patterns; associate the long *u* sounds, /yōō/ and /ōō/, with the CVC*e* pattern.
- Blend and read words with long *o* (CV, CVC*e*); long *u* (CVC*e*).

Target Skill Trace

Teach	pp. T32–T33
Reteach	p. R12
Review	p. T154
See	*Handbook for English Language Learners*, p. 179; *Extra Support Handbook*, pp. 174, 180

Materials

- **Large Sound/Spelling Cards** *ocean, unicorn*
- **Picture Cards** *cube, flute, globe, hose, mule, nose, note, rope, stone, tube*
- **Blending Routines Card 1**
- teacher-made word cards *bone, cute, go, huge, mule, pole, stove, rule, tube, tune, vote, zone*

Practice Book page 53

Long o

Circle the word that goes with each picture, and write it on the line.

1. (yo-yo / fish / yam) — yo-yo **(1 point)**
2. (bake / broke / clock) — broke **(1)**
3. (hope / mug / hose) — hose **(1)**
4. (cane / cone / drum) — cone **(1)**
5. (hole / home / cluck) — hole **(1)**
6. (rose / room / robe) — robe **(1)**

PHONICS: Blending Long *o* Words (CV, CVC*e*) and Long *u* Words (CVC*e*)

❶ Phonemic Awareness Warm-Up

Model how to segment phonemes and count sounds.

- Segment *joke*: /j//ō//k/. Then clap and count the sounds in *joke*. (3) Repeat with *mule*: /m//yōō//l/. (3)
- Have children repeat each of the following words, say its sounds, and clap and count the sounds: *hop* (/h//ŏ//p/, 3), *hope* (/h//ō//p/, 3), *cut* (/k//ŭ//t/, 3), *cute* (/k//yōō//t/, 3), *go* (/g//ō/, 2), *gift* (/g//ĭ//f//t/, 4), *rule* (/r//ōō//l/, 3), *sent* (/s//ĕ//n//t/, 4), *silk* (/s//ĭ//l//k/, 4), *broke* (/b//r//ō//k/, 4).

❷ Teach Phonics

Connect sounds to letters: *o*, /ō/; *u*, /yōō/, /ōō/.

- Display **Large Sound/Spelling Card** *ocean*. Have children name the picture. Point to the letter *o*. Explain that the /ō/ sound at the beginning of *ocean* and the end of *go* is called the long *o* sound. Have children say /ōōō/ as you point to the letter.
- Display **Picture Card** *hose*. Say /h//ōōō//z/, elongating the /ō/ sound. Explain that the sound /ō/ is in the middle of the word *hose*. Have children repeat *hose* and say the sound they hear in the middle of the word.
- Display **Large Sound/Spelling Card** *unicorn*. Have children name the picture. Point to the letter *u*. Explain that the /yōō/ sound at the beginning of *unicorn* is called the long *u* sound. Have children say /yōō/ as you point to the letter.
- Display **Picture Card** *cube*. Say /k//yōō//b/, emphasizing the /yōō/ sound. Explain that the sound /yōō/ is in the middle of the word *cube*. Have children repeat *cube* and say the /yōō/ sound they hear in the middle of the word. Display **Picture Card** *flute*. Explain that long *u* can also sound like /ōō/, as in *flute*.
- Display and name the remaining **Picture Cards** *globe, mule, nose, note, rope, stone, tube*. Have children repeat each word and tell whether they hear the long *o* or the long *u* sound.

Model how to blend long *o* and long *u* words.

- Write *no* on the board, and read the word. Explain that when a word ends with *o*, the *o* has the long *o* sound. Point to the *o* spelling on the back of **Large Sound/Spelling Card** *ocean*. Using **Blending Routine 1,** model how to blend *no.*

- Write *not* and have children blend it. Have them say the sound for *o* in *not.* Remind them that /ŏ/ is called the short *o* sound.

- Add *e* to *not* to make *note,* and read the word. Point out the *o*-consonant-*e* pattern. Explain that in words with this pattern, the *o* stands for the long *o* sound and the *e* is silent. Point to the *o_e* pattern on **Large Sound/Spelling Card** *ocean.* Model how to blend *note.* Repeat with *cub* and *cube.*

- Model how to blend *rose, Jo, rude, nose, flute, yo-yo, so, globe, chose, woke, robe, poke, doze, prune.*

o
o_e
oa
ow
_oe

u
u_e
_ue
ew

❸ Guided Practice

Check understanding. Distribute the word cards *bone, cute, go, huge, mule, pole, stove, rule, tube, tune, vote, zone.* Have children take turns blending the words.

Connect sounds to spelling and writing. Tell children that you will say a word with the vowel-consonant-*e* pattern, and they are to write the word.

- Say *June.* Have children repeat *June* and then write it. Write *June* on the board, and have children check their work.

- Repeat with *hope, use, go, wrote, spoke, code, tone, cone, Mo, dune, rode, froze, those, slope,* and the sentence *Luke drove home.*

❹ Apply

Assign Practice Book pages 53–56.

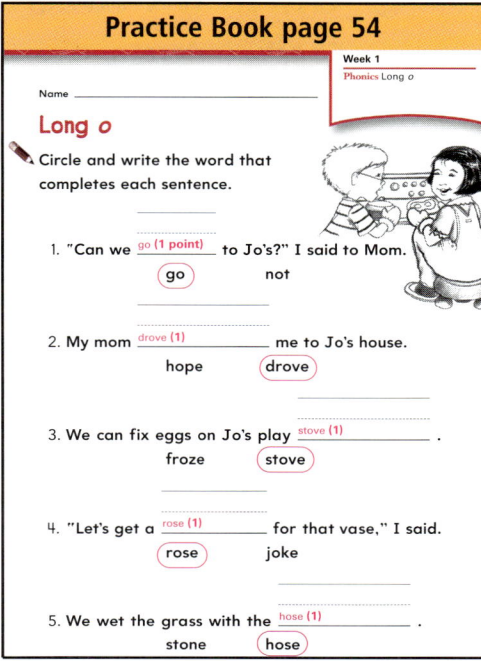

Practice Book page 54

Week 1
Phonics Long *o*

Name _____

Long o

Circle and write the word that completes each sentence.

1. "Can we ___go (1 point)___ to Jo's?" I said to Mom.
   (go)   not

2. My mom ___drove (1)___ me to Jo's house.
   hope   (drove)

3. We can fix eggs on Jo's play ___stove (1)___ .
   froze   (stove)

4. "Let's get a ___rose (1)___ for that vase," I said.
   (rose)   joke

5. We wet the grass with the ___hose (1)___ .
   stone   (hose)

Practice Book page 55

Week 1
Phonics Long *u*

Name _____

Long u

Use the letters in the box to write the word that goes with each picture.

etbu

utec

heug

elutf

ulme

bcue

1. t u b e (1 point)   2. c u t e (1)

3. h u g e (1)   4. f l u t e (1)

5. m u l e (1)   6. c u b e (1)

Practice Book page 56

Week 1
Phonics Long *u*

Name _____

Long u

Write the words from the box to complete the story.

Word Bank

| flute | huge | cute | mule | tune |

The girl plays a ___tune (1 point)___ on the ___flute (1)___ . The ___mule (1)___ kicks its legs. The mule gives the girl a ___huge (1)___ kiss. It's so ___cute (1)___ !

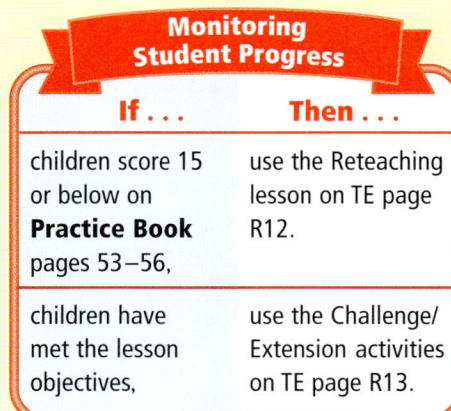

Monitoring Student Progress

If . . .	Then . . .
children score 15 or below on **Practice Book** pages 53–56,	use the Reteaching lesson on TE page R12.
children have met the lesson objectives,	use the Challenge/Extension activities on TE page R13.

OBJECTIVES

- Associate sounds for final *ft, lk,* and *nt* with letters and letter patterns.
- Blend and read words with final *ft, lk, nt.*

Target Skill Trace

Teach	p. T34
Reteach	p. R14
Review	p. T155
See	Handbook for English Language Learners, p. 185; Extra Support Handbook, pp. 175, 181

Materials

- Picture Cards *ant, milk, raft*
- Blending Routines Card 1

Practice Book page 57

Monitoring Student Progress

If . . .	Then . . .
children score 3 or below on **Practice Book** page 57,	use the Reteaching lesson on TE page R14.
children have met the lesson objectives,	use the Challenge/ Extension activities on TE page R15.

INSTRUCTION

 TARGET SKILL

PHONICS: Final Clusters *ft, lk, nt*

❶ Teach Phonics

Connect sounds to letters. Display **Picture Cards** *ant, milk, raft.*

- Say each picture name, and have children repeat it.
- Write the picture name above each card.
- Underline the letters *nt, lk, ft* in the picture names.
- Remind children that sometimes two consonants come together at the end of a word.

Model how to blend words with *ft, lk, nt.*

- Point to *ant.* Tell children that they know the sounds for *n* and *t.* Using **Blending Routine 1,** model how to blend *ant.*
- Repeat with *milk* and *raft.*
- Model how to blend *mint, spent, bunt, shift, bulk, print, rent.*

❷ Guided Practice

Check understanding. Write *ft, lk, nt.* Then call on a child to point to the letters that stand for the last sounds in *bent.* Have the rest of the class raise their hands if they agree. Continue with *soft, elk, paint, craft, sulk, draft, dent, hint, swift, sent.*

Connect sounds to spelling and writing. Tell children that you will say a word that ends with the letters *ft, lk,* or *nt,* and they are to write the word.

- Say *tent,* emphasizing the final sounds. Have children repeat *tent* and then write it. Write *tent* on the board, and have children check their work.
- Repeat with *drift, went, lift, elk, silk, cent, plant, stunt,* and the sentence *Kent left a gift for Rose.*

❸ Apply

Assign Practice Book page 57.

HOUGHTON MIFFLIN
Reading

Decodable Text

Phonics Library

Animal Adventures

Duke's Gift

by Tricia Lee
illustrated by James G. Hale

Dad has a <u>gift</u> for <u>Duke</u>.
It's this <u>huge</u> <u>bone</u>!

5

PHONICS LIBRARY

Reading Decodable Text

Have children preview *Duke's Gift*. Ask them to predict what the story is about.

Model the Phonics/Decoding Strategy. Read the steps of the strategy on **Poster B** and use the strategy to read the story title.

Think Aloud *I see the* u-*consonant-*e *pattern in the first word, so I know that the* u *stands for the long* u *sound and the* e *is silent. I'll blend,* /d/ /ōo/ /k/ /s/, *Duke's. In the second word, I see the letters* G, i, f, t. *I think about the sounds and blend them,* /g/ /ĭ/ /f/ /t/, *Gift. When I put the words together the story title is* Duke's Gift.

Apply the Phonics/Decoding Strategy. Have children read *Duke's Gift*. If necessary, coach them in applying the strategy to words such as *bone*.

- *What are the letters from left to right?* (b, o, n, e)
- *What is the sound for o in words with the o-consonant-e pattern?* (ō)
- *Blend the sounds. What is the word?* (bone)
- *Is bone a word you know? Does it make sense in the sentence?*

Word Key

Decodable words with long *o*, long *u*, final *ft*, *lk*, *nt* ———

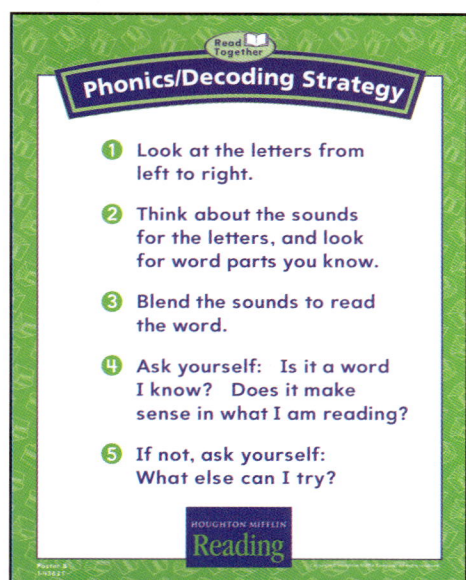

Read Together

Phonics/Decoding Strategy

1. Look at the letters from left to right.
2. Think about the sounds for the letters, and look for word parts you know.
3. Blend the sounds to read the word.
4. Ask yourself: Is it a word I know? Does it make sense in what I am reading?
5. If not, ask yourself: What else can I try?

HOUGHTON MIFFLIN
Reading

Reading Decodable Text **T35**

Duke checks <u>left</u> and right and up and back. He has not got a safe place to hide his huge bone.

6

Duke <u>hunts</u> for the best place to dig. He digs up Dad's five prize <u>rose</u> <u>plants</u>.

7

Oral Language

Discuss these questions with children. Have them answer in complete sentences.

- What gift does Dad give Duke? (Dad gives Duke a bone.)
- What is Duke looking for? (He is looking for a place to hide his bone.)
- Is Dad happy about what Duke does? How do you know? (Dad is not happy. He says "no" and is waving his arms for Duke to stop.)

"No, Duke, no!" yells
Dad. "No more holes."

8

 **Build Fluency**

Model fluent reading.

- Read aloud pages 7 and 8. Then have children read the pages aloud.
- Encourage children to use expression when reading dialogue.
- Repeat the process for the remaining pages.

Have children practice fluent reading. Have partners reread the pages several times until each child can read them aloud effortlessly.

Home Connection

Hand out the take-home version of *Duke's Gift*. Ask children to reread the story with their families. (See the **Phonics Library Blackline Masters.**)

SPELLING & VOCABULARY

WEEK 1

- Write the Basic Words.
- Learn to associate the long *o* sound with the letter *o*.
- Make words with spelling pattern *-oke*.

Materials

- teacher-made word cards *nose, poke*

SPELLING WORDS

Basic

go*	nose*
bone	home*
so	no

Challenge

also	woke*

Forms of these words appear in the literature.

Practice Book page 307

Take-Home Word List	Take-Home Word List
EEK! There's a Mouse in the House	**The Sleeping Pig**
The Long *e* Sound	**The Long *o* Sound**
me	go
see	bone
mean	nose
Spelling Words	**Spelling Words**
1. me	1. go
2. see	2. bone
3. mean	3. so
4. feet	4. nose
5. eat	5. home
6. he	6. no
Challenge Words	**Challenge Words**
1. maybe	1. also
2. sheep	2. woke
Read directions to children.	Read directions to children.
My Study List Add your own spelling words on the back.	**My Study List** Add your own spelling words on...

Take-Home Word List

INSTRUCTION

SPELLING: The Long *o* Sound

❶ Teach the Principle

Pretest Say each underlined word, read the sentence, and repeat the word. Have children write only the underlined word.

Basic Words

1. Can you **go** to the shop?
2. Where did Rusty hide his **bone**?
3. I am **so** mad!
4. My dog has a wet **nose**!
5. Pedro went **home**.
6. The man has **no** hat.

Teach Write the Basic Words, and read them with children. Tell children that in each spelling word, the vowel *o* stands for the /ō/ sound. Point out that some words have the *o*-consonant-*e* spelling pattern, and others have the *o* at the end.

❷ Practice/Apply

Word Card Flaps Display the word card for *nose*. Fold back the *se*, display the word *no*, and have children read the word *no*. Unfold the flap to display the final *se*, and have children read the word *nose*. Ask *What vowel sound do you hear in both words?* (the long *o* sound)

Practice/Homework Assign **Practice Book** page 307, the Take-Home Word List.

INSTRUCTION

TARGET SKILL

VOCABULARY: Spelling Pattern *-oke*

Teach Post the word *poke* on the Word Wall and write it on the board. Erase the *p* in *poke*, and write *j*. Have a child read the word. Point out that *poke* rhymes with *joke*. Continue with *broke, choke, smoke,* and *woke*.

Practice/Apply Have partners write as many words as they can that rhyme with *poke*.

SHARED WRITING:
A Letter of Persuasion

OBJECTIVES
- Contribute sentences to a letter of persuasion.
- Discuss listening for enjoyment.

Materials
- *Fox, Alligator, and Rabbit*, page T30, or another Read Aloud selection from the Leveled Bibliography, pages T6–T7.

Introduce the topic for a letter of persuasion.

- Have children recall the story *Fox, Alligator, and Rabbit*. Point out that Alligator *persuades* Fox to come for lunch.

- Explain that to *persuade* someone means to convince that person to do something.

- Tell children that today they will write a letter from Alligator to Fox. In the letter, Alligator will try to persuade Fox to come to his house for lunch.

- Remind children that a letter has a date, a greeting, a body, a closing, and a signature.

Prompt children to contribute to the letter.

- Begin by writing the date and the greeting *Dear Fox*.

- Continue by writing the topic sentence *Please come to my house for lunch.* Point out that the sentence tells the main idea of the letter.

- Record children's sentences telling about Alligator's delicious porridge.

- Add the closing and Alligator's signature.

- Ask a child to read the letter in Alligator's voice.

- Have children identify the parts of the letter.

Illustrate and display the letter. Have children illustrate the letter, and display it on a bulletin board.

LISTENING:
For Enjoyment

Discuss reasons for listening to stories. Have children brainstorm a list of reasons for listening to stories. Make sure they include listening for enjoyment, or for fun.

Discuss the enjoyment of listening to a story. Ask:

- *Who enjoyed listening to* Fox, Alligator, and Rabbit?

- *What is your favorite part of the story?*

- *Why do you like the story?*

Check children's understanding. Have partners explain why they enjoyed the story and illustrate their favorite part.

DAY 2
week 1

Day at a Glance
pages T40–T59

Learning to Read

High-Frequency Words
Reading Decodable Text
Legs Gets His Lunch
Reading the Anthology
The Sleeping Pig

• • • • • • • • • • • • • • • • • •

Leveled Readers, *T84–T87*

- ● *The Huge Carrot*
- ▲ *Watermelon for Lunch*
- ■ *Hide-and-Seek*
- ◆ *The Carrot*

Word Work

Spelling: Words with Long *o*
Vocabulary: High-Frequency Words

Writing & Oral Language

Interactive Writing: A Letter of Persuasion

Daily Routines

Daily Message

Review phonics and language skills. Point to each word as you read aloud the Daily Message.

> Dear Boys and Girls,
>
>   I really liked the story about the fox, alligator, and rabbit. It made me laugh! _____ forgot one part of the story. Will you help _____ remember how Rabbit got across the river?

Have children

- complete the sentences with *I* or *me*;
- circle the long *i* words; (*I, liked*)
- use their own words to tell how Rabbit got across the river;
- find the following high-frequency words: *Girls, about, one, of, the,* and *you.*

Word Wall

High-Frequency Word Review Briefly review these and other high-frequency words daily. Have children practice reading, chanting, spelling, and writing words from the Word Wall. Have individuals point to words on the Word Wall while the class reads them aloud.

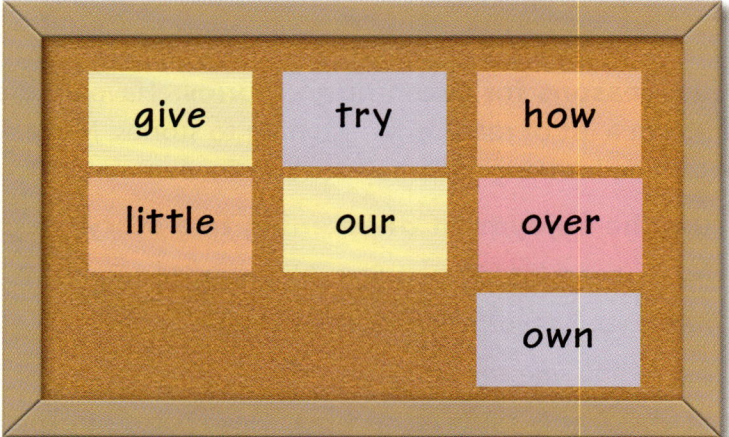

Blackline Masters for these Word Wall Cards appear in Theme 5, pages R39–R40.

Daily Phonemic Awareness

Segmenting and Counting Phonemes: Pennies for Sounds

- Distribute pennies or counters to children.

- One at a time, say the words *flute, cute, globe, use, raft,* and *rose.*

- Ask children to say the separate sounds in each word. Examples: /f/ /l/ /o͞o/ /t/ for *flute*; /yo͞o/ /z/ for *use.*

- Have children put down a penny for each sound they say, forming a horizontal line. Have them count the pennies and tell how many sounds are in the word.

Note For words with the /yo͞o/ (long *u*) sound as in *use,* some children may count two sounds for the vowel.

Daily Language Practice

Grammar Skill: Beginning Sentences with Capital Letters
Spelling Skill: Words with Long *o*
Write the sentence, read it to children, and have them tell you how to correct it.

that is soe big!

(**T**hat is **so** big!)

Daily Writing Prompt

Remind children to write complete sentences when responding to the prompt below. Children may also choose to write on a self-selected topic.

- **Choose an animal character from a story you have read and write about an adventure that the animal has.**

The hermit crab had to get a new shell.

Daily Independent Reading

To increase children's reading fluency, provide a variety of theme-related books for them to read. Here are some suggestions.

- Leveled Bibliography, pages T6–T7

Choose books from this list for children to read, outside class, for at least twenty minutes a day.

- Phonics Library: *Duke's Gift*

- Leveled Readers

- Book Boxes

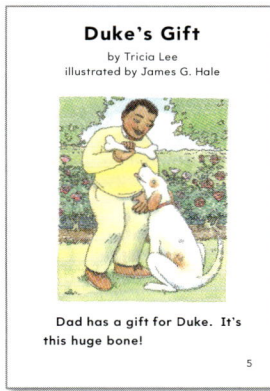

Duke's Gift
by Tricia Lee
illustrated by James G. Hale

Dad has a gift for Duke. It's this huge bone!

5

INSTRUCTION

TARGET SKILL HIGH-FREQUENCY WORDS

1 Teach

Review last week's high-frequency words.

- Point to the words *fly, good, her, little, try,* and *was* on the Word Wall.
- Have children read these words aloud, repeating any words that give them difficulty.

Introduce the new high-frequency words.

- Hold up the Word Wall Card *morning* and read the word aloud.
- Have the class clap and spell *morning* several times: *m-o-r-n-i-n-g, morning!*
- Choose a child to post morning on the New Words section of the Word Wall.
- Repeat the above procedure for the other new high-frequency words, *found, shout, by, out, show,* and *climb.*

Display Chart/Transparency 6–1.

- Have children read the poem with you.
- Call on individuals to read each of the underlined words.
- Have the class try to think of other words that rhyme with the new high-frequency words.

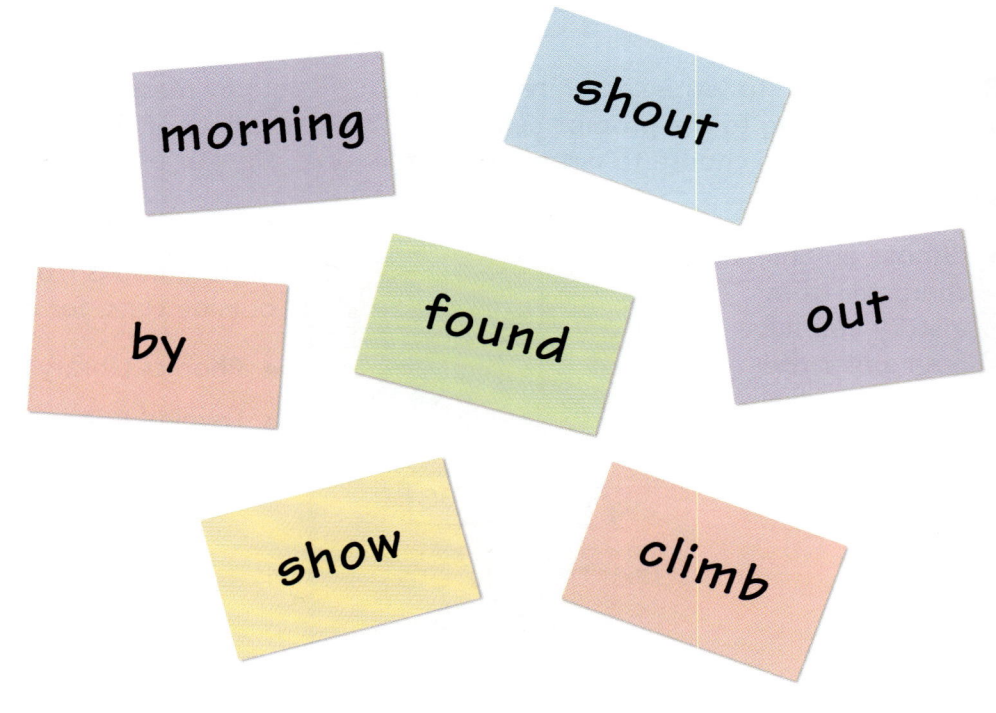

Chart/Transparency 6–1

Get That Cat!

One <u>morning</u>, I went <u>out</u>.

I looked up a tree and gave a <u>shout</u>.

"I <u>found</u> a little cat and it is stuck.

This is not good. What bad luck!"

Mom came and said, "<u>Show</u> that cat to me."

So I took her <u>by</u> the tree.

I said, "Too bad it can not fly.

But I know what I will try.

I will <u>climb</u> up to the cat."

"No," said Mom, "others will do that!"

❷ Guided Practice

Have children read the words in context.

- Have pairs practice reading lines of the poem on **Chart/Transparency 6–1** to one another.
- Tell children to say the new word a little more loudly than the rest of the sentence. Remind them not to shout!

❸ Apply

Assign one or more of the following activities.

- Have children complete **Practice Book** pages 58 and 59 independently, in pairs, or in small groups.
- Have partners practice reading their punch-out word cards to one another.
- Have children read the **Phonics Library** story *Legs Gets His Lunch* independently, with partners, or in small groups.

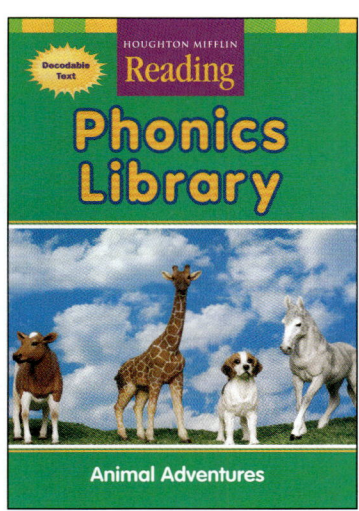

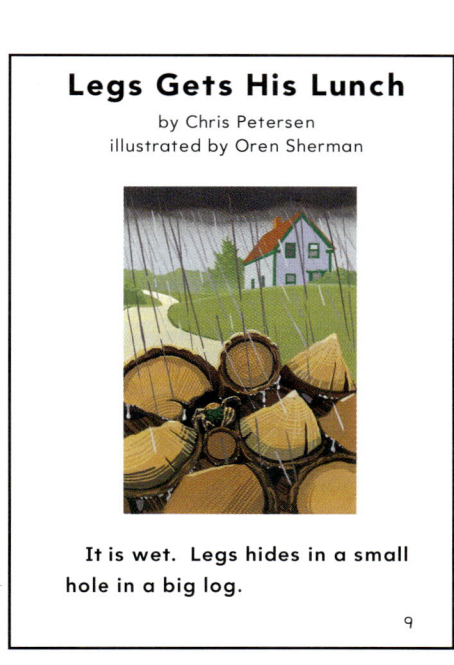

Legs Gets His Lunch
by Chris Petersen
illustrated by Oren Sherman

It is wet. Legs hides in a small hole in a big log.

9

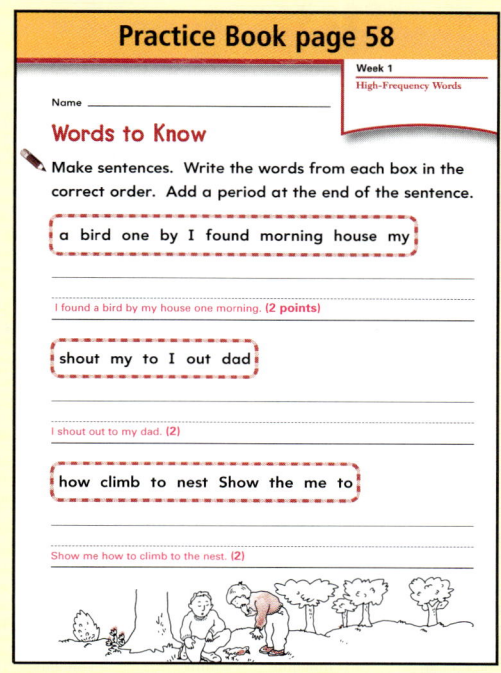

Practice Book page 58

Week 1
High-Frequency Words

Name _____

Words to Know

Make sentences. Write the words from each box in the correct order. Add a period at the end of the sentence.

a bird one by I found morning house my

I found a bird by my house one morning. **(2 points)**

shout my to I out dad

I shout out to my dad. **(2)**

how climb to nest Show the me to

Show me how to climb to the nest. **(2)**

Practice Book page 59

Week 1
High-Frequency Words

Name _____

Words to Know

Read each pair of sentences. Circle the sentence that tells about the picture.

You do not have to shout! **(2 points)**
I know that girl.

I will show you how to ride. (2)
I ate too much!

In the morning, I climb out of bed fast. (2)
Here is my mother.

My room is big.
I found a dime by the swing. (2)

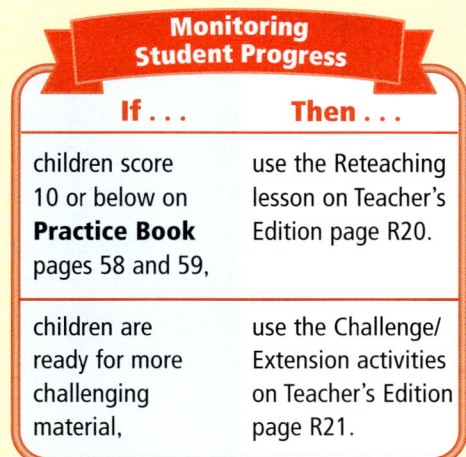

Monitoring Student Progress

If . . .	Then . . .
children score 10 or below on **Practice Book** pages 58 and 59,	use the Reteaching lesson on Teacher's Edition page R20.
children are ready for more challenging material,	use the Challenge/Extension activities on Teacher's Edition page R21.

Building Background

Key Concept: How Watermelons Grow

Together, read the paragraph on Anthology page 130. Then ask children if they know how a watermelon grows. Turn to the picture on Anthology pages 134–135.

- Explain that watermelons grow on the ground in a watermelon patch.
- Point out the leaves and explain that the long, curly stems are called vines.

Reviewing Vocabulary

Words to Know

High-Frequency Words

by	climb	found	morning
out	shout	show	

Words with long o; long u; final consonants ft, lk, nt

go	huge	home	left
lift	mule	nose	tune
use	went	whole	woke

Use "Get Set to Read."

- Read Anthology page 130 together. Remind children that the Words to Know are either words they already know or words that contain sounds they know.
- Read the Practice Sentences together. Ask children what helped them to read each word. Review words or skills as necessary.
- Remind children that these words will appear in the story.

THEME 6: Animal Adventures
(Anthology p. 130)

Background and Vocabulary

The Sleeping Pig
written by Carmen Tafolla and Jan Epton Seale
illustrated by Rosario Valderrama

The Sleeping Pig

How to Wake a Pig

In the next story, you'll read about a pig who won't get out of a watermelon patch. A small hero finally gets the pig to move.

Words to Know

morning	woke
found	nose
shout	whole
by	huge
out	use
show	tune
climb	went
go	lift
home	

130

English Language Learners

Language Development

Beginning/Preproduction Take a story walk. Have children repeat each of the following words after you and help them point to its example in the story illustrations: *pig, coyote, mule, snake, cricket, rabbit, tail, watermelon.*

Early Production and Speech Emergence Ask a question about each of the Story Vocabulary words and have individuals answer orally, repeating the word in their response. Example: *What animal has a* tail*? A dog has a* tail.

Intermediate and Advanced Fluency Have children find an example of each Story Vocabulary word in the story illustrations and discuss what they know about each word.

Practice Sentences

1. If you **went** **by** your bed one **morning** and **found** a **huge** pig, would you **lift** it **out**?
2. You could walk by and **shout**, "**Go** **home**!"
3. Then **climb** up and tap the pig's small **nose**.
4. Sing a **tune**.
5. You could **use** the **whole** day to wake the pig.
6. Once you **woke** the pig, you could **show** it how to get home.

Good Morning

131

Introducing Story Vocabulary

Story Vocabulary

These words support the Key Concept and are important to children's understanding of the selection.

began started to do something

celebrate to have a party because of a special occasion

coyote an animal that looks like a small wolf

cricket a hopping insect; the male makes a chirping sound by rubbing its front wings together

howl a long, loud cry made by a dog, wolf, or coyote

rabbit an animal with long ears, soft fur, and a short tail

tail a thin part that sticks out from the back of an animal's body

watermelon a large green fruit with a sweet, watery, pink inside

 e • Glossary
e • WordGame

Use Chart/Transparency 6–2.

- Read aloud the sentence at the bottom of the page.
- Call on children to name the animals at the celebration.
- Together, read the labels: *coyote, cricket, rabbit, howl, tail, watermelon.*
- Ask children to look for these words as they read, and to use them as they discuss the selection.

Practice Assign **Practice Book** page 60.

Chart/Transparency 6–2

The Animals Celebrate!

howl

cricket

coyote

rabbit

tail

watermelon

TRANSPARENCY 6–2
TEACHER'S EDITION PAGE T45

ANIMAL ADVENTURES Week 1, Day 2
Story Vocabulary *The Sleeping Pig*

ANNOTATED VERSION

The animals **began** to **celebrate** at 2:00.

Practice Book page 60

Name _____

Week 1
Story Vocabulary *The Sleeping Pig*

Story Vocabulary

Read the story. Use the box to help you find and circle some words from **The Sleeping Pig.**

It was fall, so Cricket said, "Let's celebrate!" Coyote let out a howl. Rabbit jumped and twitched his tail up and down.

Then they began to eat a huge watermelon!
(8 points)

Word Bank
began
celebrate
coyote
cricket
howl
rabbit
tail
watermelon

Draw a picture to go with the story.

(4)

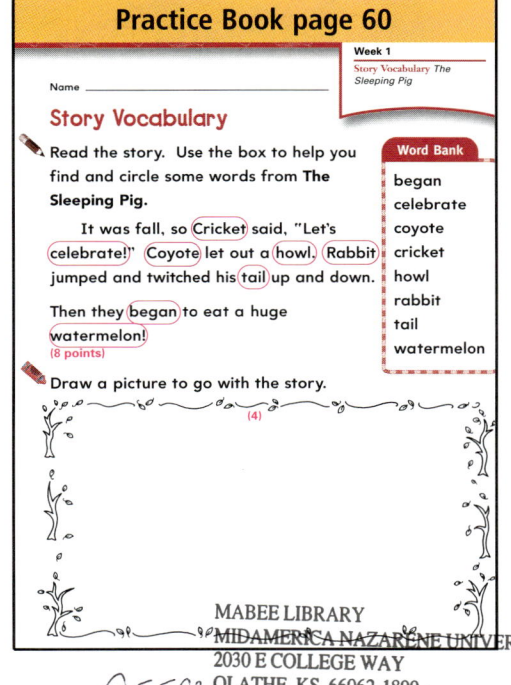

Introducing Vocabulary
(Anthology p. 131)

T45

COMPREHENSION STRATEGY

Summarize

Teacher Modeling Read the title, the authors' and illustrator's names, and the Strategy Focus on Anthology page 133. Then read aloud pages 134–137 and model the Summarize strategy.

Think Aloud *I want to tell the most important parts of what has happened in the story so far. I will say,* Celina found a pig sleeping in the watermelon patch. She shouted, but the pig didn't wake up.

Test Prep Children can quickly summarize a test passage before they answer a question. Thinking about the order of facts or events will help them decide where to look to find the answer.

COMPREHENSION SKILL

Story Structure

Remind children that a story usually has a problem that the characters must solve. After reading aloud pages 134–137, ask children about the story events so far.

- What is the problem? (The pig is sleeping in the watermelon patch.)

- How does Celina try to solve the problem? Does her solution work? (She shouts at the pig. It doesn't work.)

THEME 6: Animal Adventures
(Anthology p. 132)

Read Together

Meet the Authors

Carmen Tafolla

Jan Epton Seale

The authors first wrote this story in Spanish. Carmen Tafolla and Jan Epton Seale both live in Texas. Jan Epton Seale lives near Mexico. Carmen Tafolla has a daughter named Mari.

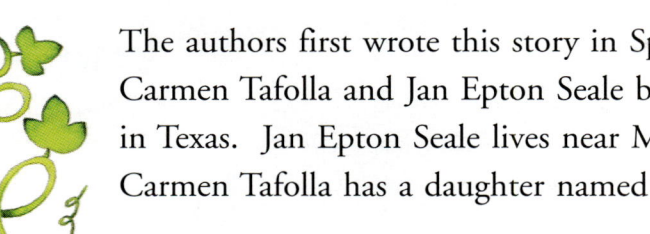

Internet

You can learn more about Carmen Tafolla and Jan Epton Seale at Education Place.
www.eduplace.com/kids

132

English Language Learners

Supporting Comprehension

Write the phrase *watermelon patch* on the board. Say the phrase several times and have children repeat it. Check pronunciation. Explain that a watermelon patch is a place where watermelons grow. Ask children what they call a watermelon in their home languages. Also review the animals the children will encounter in the story.

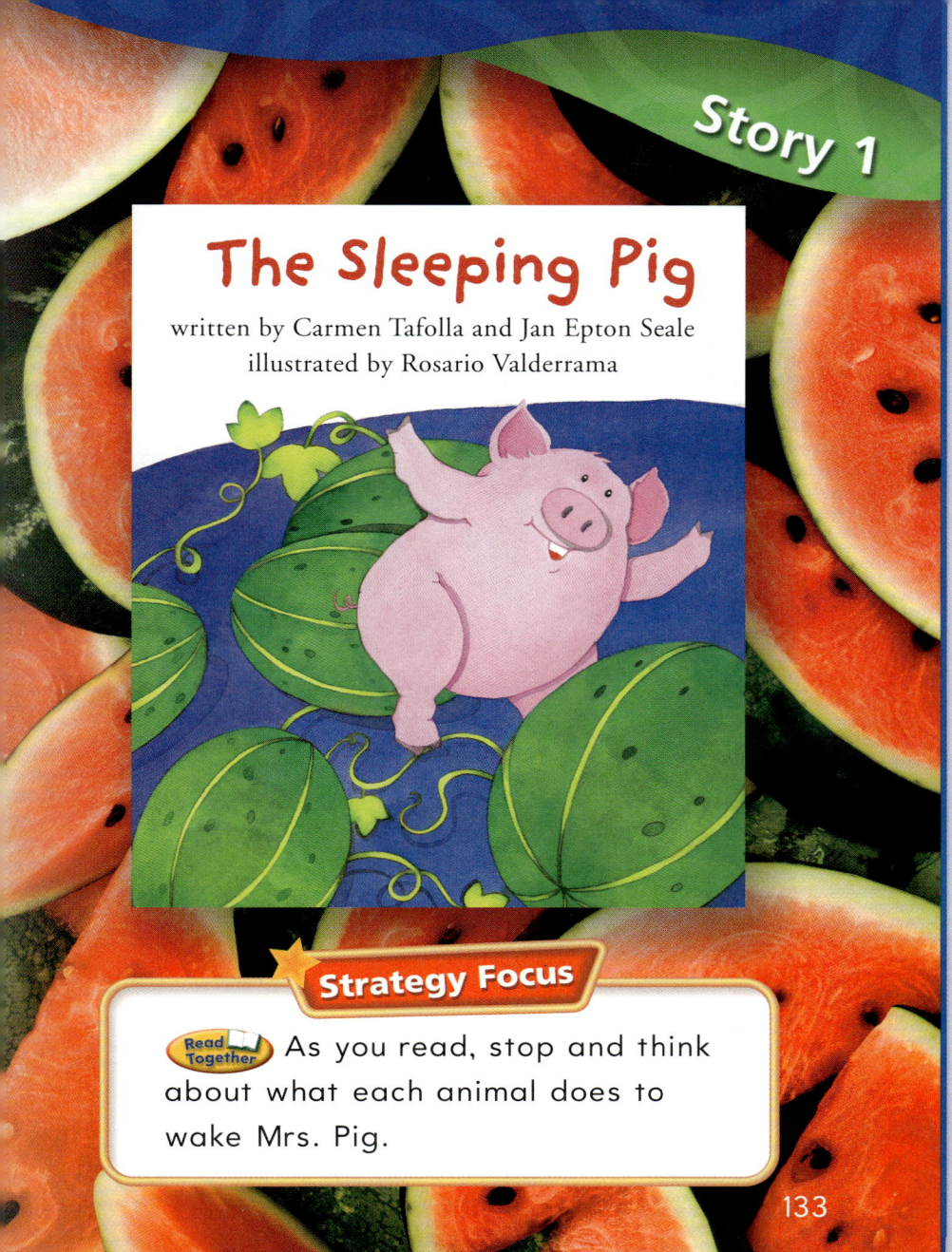

Story 1

The Sleeping Pig

written by Carmen Tafolla and Jan Epton Seale
illustrated by Rosario Valderrama

Strategy Focus

As you read, stop and think about what each animal does to wake Mrs. Pig.

133

Purpose Setting

- Remind children of the story problem they identified earlier. (Celina needs to wake up Mrs. Pig.) Tell them to read to find out what solution works best to solve the problem.

- Remind children to use the Summarize strategy and other strategies as they read.

- Ask children to turn to Responding on Anthology page 154. Read the questions aloud. Encourage children to think about the answers to these questions as they read *The Sleeping Pig*.

Journal ▶ Children can keep track of how the animals try to wake up Mrs. Pig by drawing or writing in their journals.

Extra Support/Intervention

Preview pages 134–141.

pages 134–135 Where is Mrs. Pig? What is she doing?

pages 136–137 Why do you think Celina is shouting?

pages 138–139 What is the Coyote doing?

pages 140–141 This animal is a mule. What other animal do you know that looks like a mule? How will the mule try to move Mrs. Pig?

Preview pages 142–152.

pages 142–145 What animals do you see on these pages? What do they do to try to get Mrs. Pig out of the watermelon patch?

pages 146–149 What could this little cricket do to wake up Mrs. Pig?

pages 150–152 Do you think the cricket solved Celina's problem? How do you know?

Reading the Selection
(Anthology p. 133)   **T47**

> One morning, Celina found a huge pig sleeping in the **watermelon** patch.

READING STRATEGY
Phonics/Decoding

Teacher/Student Modeling Help children use what they know about letters and sounds to decode *sleeping*. First, write *sleep* on the board and underline *sl*. Ask children to say the sounds they know for *s* and *l*. Then remind them that *ee* stands for the long *e* sound. Help them blend all the sounds together, /s/ /l/ /ē/ /p/, and say *sleep*. Then write and say the ending *-ing* and help children blend the whole word, *sleeping*. Repeat with *sulking* on Anthology page 151.

Story Vocabulary

watermelon a large green fruit with a sweet, watery, pink inside

Word Key

Words with long *o*; long *u*; final consonants, *ft, lk, nt* ————

High-Frequency Words ————

Story Vocabulary ▢

THEME 6: Animal Adventures
(Anthology pp. 134–135)

Celina began to shout. "Go home, Mrs. Pig! I wish you would go. You can't rest here in the watermelon patch. I can't pick my watermelons."

But huge Mrs. Pig didn't wake up.

136   137

CRITICAL THINKING
Guiding Comprehension

1 **CAUSE AND EFFECT** Why can't Celina pick the watermelons? (Mrs. Pig is sleeping in the watermelon patch.)

2 **PROBLEM SOLVING** How does Celina try to wake up Mrs. Pig? (She shouts.)

Story Vocabulary

began started to do something

REACHING ALL LEARNERS   **Extra Support/Intervention**

Concepts of Print

Dialogue Have children look at the first four sentences on Anthology page 137. Point out the quotation marks on the page. Remind children that these marks show that a character is talking. Ask children who is talking in this part of the story. Then have children find other dialogue in the story and identify who is talking.

Reading the Selection
(Anthology pp. 136–137)   **T49**

A <mark>coyote</mark> came by and said, "Let me show you how to get Mrs. Pig out of the patch." The coyote began to <mark>howl</mark> and howl.

But huge Mrs. Pig did not wake up.

138   139

CRITICAL THINKING
Guiding Comprehension

3 DRAWING CONCLUSIONS Why do you think Mrs. Pig doesn't wake up when the coyote howls? (Accept all reasonable answers that draw upon children's own knowledge and experiences.)

COMPREHENSION STRATEGY
Summarize

Teacher/Student Modeling Help children to summarize the story so far. Have children think about who has tried to wake up Mrs. Pig. Ask, *What would you tell a friend about what the characters have done so far?*

Story Vocabulary

coyote an animal that looks like a small wolf

howl a long, loud cry made by a dog, wolf, or coyote

REACHING ALL LEARNERS   Extra Support/Intervention

Review pages 134–141.

Before children join in Stop and Think, have them

- take turns modeling the **strategies** they used;
- **summarize** the important parts of the story up to this point.

On Level	Challenge

Literature Discussion

Have small groups discuss the story, using their own questions or prompts from Guiding Comprehension.

THEME 6: Animal Adventures
(Anthology pp. 138–139)

A <u>mule</u> came by and said, "I can make Mrs. Pig <u>climb</u> out of the patch." The mule began to push and push.

But huge Mrs. Pig <u>went</u> on sleeping.

140

141

Stop and Think

Critical Thinking Questions

1. **STORY STRUCTURE** What is the main problem in this story? (Mrs. Pig will not wake up.)

2. **MAKING GENERALIZATIONS** Where do pigs usually sleep? Do you think Mrs. Pig is like most pigs? Why or why not? (Answers will vary.)

Strategies in Action

Have individuals model **Summarize** and any other strategies they used as they read.

Discussion Options

Review Predictions/Purpose Discuss the ways the animals have tried to wake up Mrs. Pig. Have children predict how they think Mrs. Pig will finally wake up in the end.

Share Group Discussions If children discussed the story in groups, have them share their questions and answers.

Extra Support/Intervention

Strategy Modeling: Summarize

Use this example to model the strategy.

This is what has happened so far. The characters try to wake up Mrs. Pig. Celina shouts, the coyote howls, and the mule pushes, but Mrs. Pig still doesn't wake up.

Monitoring Student Progress

If . . .	Then . . .
children have successfully completed the Extra Support activities on page T50,	have them read the rest of the story cooperatively.

Reading the Selection
(Anthology pp. 140–141)

A rabbit came by and said, "I will get Mrs. Pig out of the patch for you." The rabbit began to hop and hop.

But huge Mrs. Pig went on sleeping.

142

143

CRITICAL THINKING
Guiding Comprehension

4 PROBLEM SOLVING Do you think the rabbit's idea for waking up Mrs. Pig is a good one? Why or why not?
(Sample answer: No, it doesn't make Mrs. Pig wake up.)

READING STRATEGY
Phonics/Decoding

Teacher/Student Modeling Write the word *huge* on the board. Underline the *u*-consonant-*e* pattern and remind children that the *u* will have a long vowel sound. Also remind them that the *g* has a soft sound /j/ when followed by *e*. Then have children blend and say the word together, /h/ /ū/ /j/, *huge*. Have children blend other long *u* words from the story: *use* (page 144), *tune* (page 148).

THEME 6: Animal Adventures
(Anthology pp. 142–143)

Story Vocabulary

rabbit an animal with long ears, soft fur, and a short tail

tail a thin part that sticks out from the back of an animal's body

English Language Learners

Supporting Comprehension

Read pages 142–145 aloud. Ask, *Why won't Mrs. Pig wake up? What did the rabbit try to do? What did the snake try to do? Why do you think Mrs. Pig is so sleepy?* Pantomime *sleepy*. If appropriate, encourage children to respond with phrases or complete sentences rather than single words. Listen for the correct use of the present and past forms of verbs.

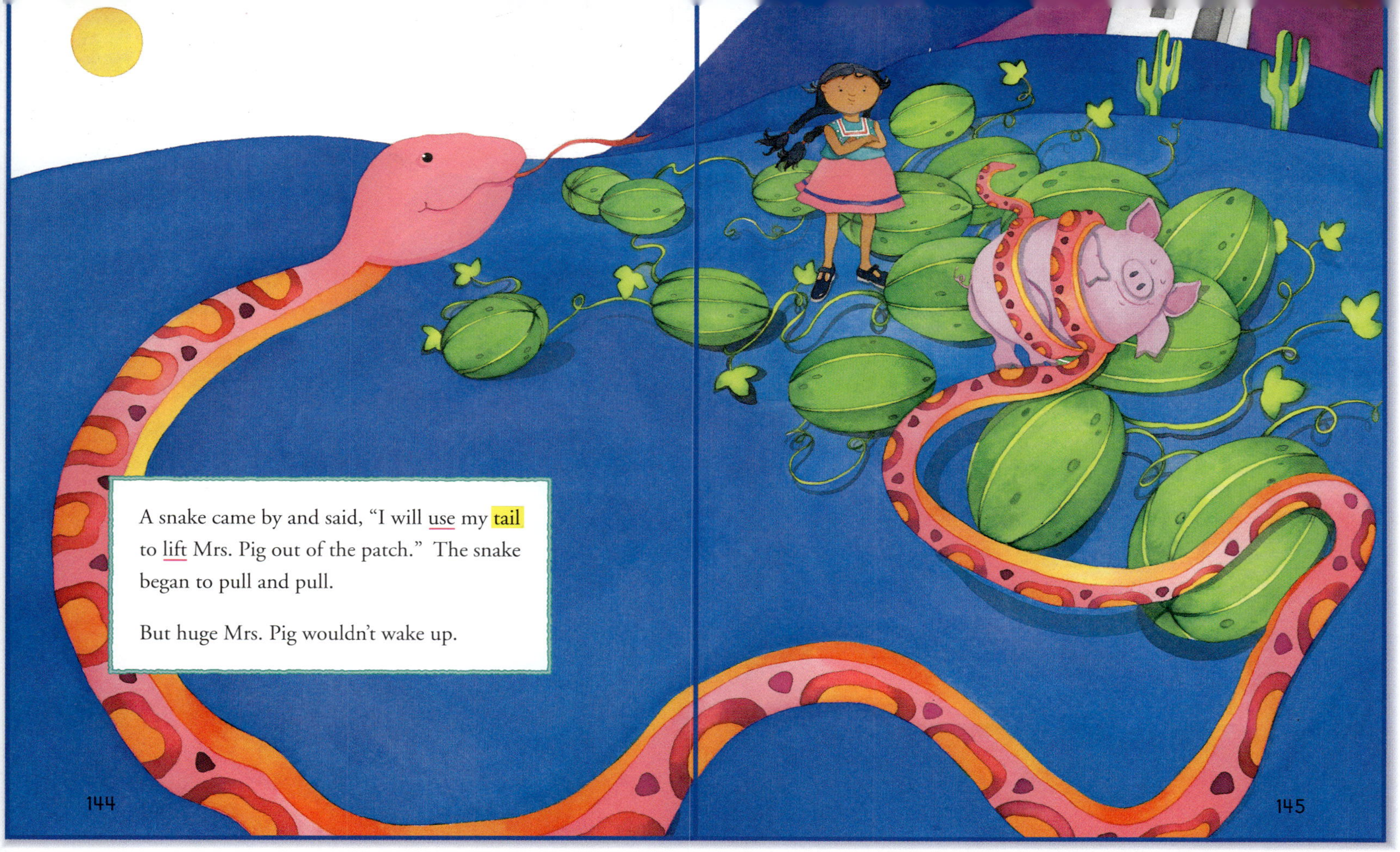

A snake came by and said, "I will <u>use</u> my <mark>tail</mark> to <u>lift</u> Mrs. Pig out of the patch." The snake began to pull and pull.

But huge Mrs. Pig wouldn't wake up.

144

145

CRITICAL THINKING
Guiding Comprehension

5 **COMPARE AND CONTRAST** How are the ways that the snake and the mule try to wake up Mrs. Pig the same? How are they different? (They both try to move Mrs. Pig. The mule tries to push her with its head, but the snake tries to lift and pull her with its tail.)

REACHING ALL LEARNERS

Extra Support/Intervention

Concepts of Print

Dialogue Read Anthology page 144 together. Ask a child to find the quotation marks. Then reread the first sentence and point out the comma after *said*. Explain that writers often tell who is talking before the dialogue begins. There is usually a comma before the dialogue begins.

Reading the Selection
(Anthology pp. 144–145)

T53

Then a cricket came by and said, "I know I am small and Mrs. Pig is huge. But just look at what I can do."

146

147

CRITICAL THINKING
Guiding Comprehension

6 MAKING PREDICTIONS What do you think the cricket will do next? (The cricket will probably try to do something to wake up Mrs. Pig.)

COMPREHENSION STRATEGY
Summarize

Student Modeling Ask children to tell a partner in their own words what has happened on pages 142–147. If they have trouble, allow another child to help them or use the prompt in the Extra Support box on this page.

Story Vocabulary

cricket a hopping insect; the male makes a chirping sound by rubbing its front wings together

REACHING ALL LEARNERS   Extra Support/Intervention

Strategy Modeling: Summarize

Use this example to model the strategy for pages 142–147.

The rabbit tried to wake up Mrs. Pig by hopping. Then the snake tried to lift and pull Mrs. Pig with its tail, but Mrs. Pig kept on sleeping. Now a small cricket has an idea.

The cricket began to sing a <u>tune</u>.
Chirrr-chirrr-chirrr! Di-di-di-di!

148

149

Comprehension Preview

Story Structure

Teach

Review the important parts of a story: setting, or where and when the story takes place; characters; problem; events; and ending.

Practice/Apply

Have children revisit the story pages shown in the chart to identify the different parts of the story.

Target Skill Trace	
▶ **Preview; Teach**	pp. T30, T46, T55; T64–T65
Reteach	p. R26
Review	p. T78

Parts of the Story

setting and problem	pages 134–137
characters and events	pages 134, 138–148
ending	pages 151–152

Mrs. Pig woke up fast. "Yes, it's time to go home," she said with her nose up. "A watermelon patch does not make a good bed." And she left, sulking.

150   151

CRITICAL THINKING
Guiding Comprehension

7 CAUSE AND EFFECT What makes Mrs. Pig finally wake up? (The cricket's tune.)

8 DRAWING CONCLUSIONS Why do you think Mrs. Pig wants to go home? (Possible answer: She wants to keep sleeping and the watermelon patch is not a good place to sleep.)

9 FANTASY AND REALISM Could this story happen in real life? How do you know? (No, real animals can't talk.)

REACHING ALL LEARNERS

Extra Support/Intervention

Selection Review

Before children join in Wrapping Up, have them

- take turns modeling the **strategies** they used;
- **summarize** the important parts of the story.

On Level	Challenge

Literature Discussion

Have small groups discuss the story, using their own questions and questions from Think About the Story on Anthology page 154.

English Language Learners

Supporting Comprehension

Pantomime *woke up fast* and *sulking*. Discuss why Mrs. Pig might be sulking after she is woken up fast.

THEME 6: Animal Adventures
(Anthology pp. 150–151)

Celina thanked the small cricket. Then they ate a <u>whole</u> watermelon to <mark>celebrate!</mark>

152

Meet the Illustrator
Rosario Valderrama

Rosario Valderrama was born in Mexico City. When she draws, she tries to remember the things she loved as a child. She says young artists should try to show their worlds to others.

Internet To find out more about Rosario Valderrama, visit Education Place. **www.eduplace.com/kids**

153

Wrapping Up

Critical Thinking Questions

1. **STORY STRUCTURE** How is Celina's problem finally solved? (The cricket's tune wakes up Mrs. Pig and she leaves the watermelon patch.)

2. **DRAWING CONCLUSIONS** What do you think the authors want readers to learn when they make the smallest creature the one to wake Mrs. Pig? (Possible answer: Even small people and animals can make a difference.)

Strategies in Action

Have individuals model using **Summarize** to retell the story. They can also discuss other strategies they used.

Discussion Options

Review Predictions/Purpose Ask children if they correctly predicted how Mrs. Pig would wake. Discuss why their predictions were or were not accurate.

Share Group Discussions Have children share the results of their literature discussions.

Story Vocabulary

<mark>celebrate</mark> to have a party because of a special occasion

Monitoring Student Progress

If . . .	Then . . .
children have difficulty summarizing the selection,	have partners help each other to remember and tell about the important parts of the story.

Reading the Selection
(Anthology pp. 152–153)

T57

OBJECTIVES

OBJECTIVES

- Spell the Basic Words.
- Complete sentences with the high-frequency words.

Challenge

Matching Words to Definitions

Have children write the Challenge Word that matches each definition.

1. something added (*also*)
2. what you did before getting out of bed (*woke*)

PRACTICE

SPELLING:
Words with Long *o*

Review the principle. Write *no* and *nose* on the board. Have children read the words. Remind them that words ending in *o* or the *o*-consonant-*e* pattern have the long *o* sound.

Practice/Apply Tell children they will play a game called "Oh, No! No O!"

- Have each child fold a piece of paper in half, write *O* above the left column, and write *No O!* above the right column.
- Say *Now I will read a list of words. Write a word with the long* o *sound in the* O *column. Write a word without the long* o *sound in the* No O! *column.*
- Read the words *so, cat, bone, no, pig, home, go,* and *kite.*

REVIEW

VOCABULARY:
High-Frequency Words

Review the words. Read the New Words section of the Word Wall with children. Tell them they will use some of these words to finish sentences.

Practice/Apply Write the first letter of the answer, and read the sentence aloud. After children identify the word, have them clap and spell it.

- (*m*) *Hal got up early this _____.* (*morning*)
- (*f*) *Ann _____ a dime when she was walking to school.* (*found*)
- (*c*) *Maria wanted to _____ up the stairs of the slide.* (*climb*)
- (*b*) *Please finish your work _____ the time you go home.* (*by*)
- (*s or sh*) *Please don't _____. I can hear you if you talk more quietly!* (*shout*)
- (*o*) *Let's go _____ to play.* (*out*)
- (*s or sh*) *Please _____ me how to make a kite.* (*show*)

INTERACTIVE WRITING: A Letter of Persuasion

OBJECTIVES
- Contribute sentences to write a letter of persuasion.
- Participate by writing letters, words, and punctuation.

Discuss the idea for a letter of persuasion.

- Remind children that to *persuade* someone means to convince that person to do something.

- Point out that Rabbit persuades Fox to help him by giving Fox a compliment: "You are the cleverest of all creatures."

- Say that Rabbit might have solved his problem a different way by persuading Alligator to let him cross the river.

- Tell children they will write a letter from Rabbit to Alligator. In the letter, Rabbit will try to persuade Alligator to let him cross the river.

- Remind children that a letter has a date, a greeting, a body, a closing, and a signature.

Prompt children to contribute to the letter.

- Begin by writing the date and the greeting *Dear Alligator*.

- Model how to give a compliment to Alligator.

Think Aloud *I want to give Alligator a compliment to persuade him to let me cross the river. I'll begin by writing* I have heard you are the smartest animal in the river.

- Record children's sentences. Invite them to write familiar letters, words, and punctuation.

- If necessary, finish the letter by writing *Please let me cross the river!*

- Add the closing and Rabbit's signature.

- Ask a child to read the letter aloud in Rabbit's voice.

- Have children identify the parts of the letter.

Illustrate and display the letter. Have children illustrate the letter, and display it on a bulletin board.

Dear Alligator,

    I have heard you are the smartest animal in the river.

Day at a Glance

pages T60–T67

Learning to Read

Responding
Comprehension Instruction
Story Structure

• • • • • • • • • • • • • • • •

Leveled Readers, *T84–T87*
- ● *The Huge Carrot*
- ▲ *Watermelon for Lunch*
- ■ *Hide-and-Seek*
- ◆ *The Carrot*

Word Work

Spelling: Words with Long *o*
Vocabulary: Alphabetical Order

Writing & Oral Language

Writing: Responding
Grammar: Naming Words for People and Animals

Daily Routines

Daily Message

Review phonics and language skills. Point to each word as you read aloud the Daily Message.

Dear Children,

Look at the note I wrote: June can go play a tune on her huge flute! Can you play a tune?

Have children

- respond to the question;
- circle words with long *o* and long *u* sounds; (*note, wrote, go; June, tune, huge, flute, you*)
- find and read the word with the soft *g* sound; (*huge*)
- find and read the following high-frequency words: *Children, Look, the,* and *play.*

Word Wall

High-Frequency Word Review Review these and other high-frequency words by holding up the Word Cards and having children read the word and find it on the Word Wall. Then have children chant the spelling of each word: s-h-o-w *spells* show!

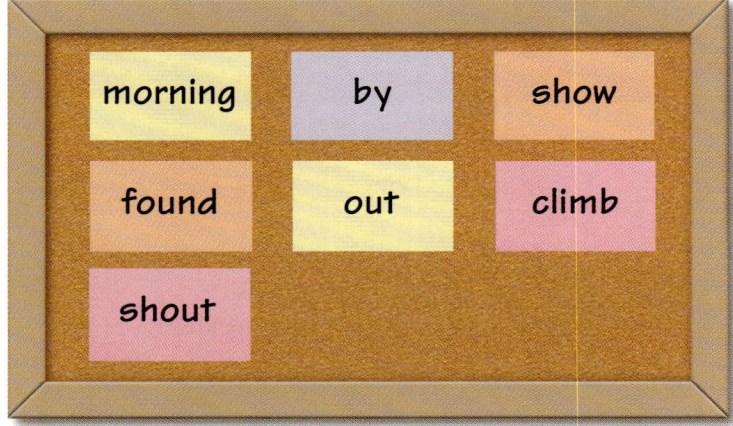

Blackline Master for this week's Word Wall Cards appears on page R33.

Daily Phonemic Awareness

TARGET SKILL

Segmenting and Counting Phonemes: Cheer the Sounds

- Have children form groups and choose leaders.
- Say one of the following words to each group: *robe, mule, tube, bone, slope, cube.*
- Have the group leader begin a cheer with "Give me a _____!" and say the first sound in the word. The group then repeats the sound. After children cheer the remaining sounds of the word in the same way, they end with "What's the word? It's _____!"
- Suggest that children make up a movement for each sound in the word. Ask how many motions they will need to match the number of sounds.
- Continue with new words, giving everyone a chance to be the leader.

Daily Language Practice

Grammar Skill: Which Kind of Sentence?
Spelling Skill: Words with Long *o*
Write the sentence, read it to children, and have them tell you how to correct it.

Is this your hom

(Is this your **home?**)

Daily Writing Prompt

Remind children to write complete sentences, beginning with a capital letter and ending with punctuation as they respond to the prompt below or write on self-selected topics.

- **Write and draw about where you like to sleep.**

I like to sleep in my bed.
My bed is soft.
I let my dog sleep on
my bed, too.

Daily Independent Reading

To increase children's reading fluency, provide a variety of theme-related books for them to read. Here are some suggestions.

- Leveled Bibliography, pages T6–T7

Choose books from this list for children to read, outside class, for at least twenty minutes a day.

- Anthology: *The Sleeping Pig*
- Phonics Library: *Duke's Gift, Legs Gets His Lunch*
- Leveled Readers

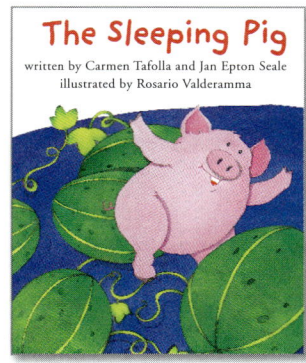

The Sleeping Pig
written by Carmen Tafolla and Jan Epton Seale
illustrated by Rosario Valderamma

Responding

Comprehension Check

Have children reread or finish reading the selection. Then assign **Practice Book** page 61 to assess children's comprehension of the selection.

Think About the Story

Have children discuss or write their answers. Sample answers are provided; accept reasonable responses.

1. **DRAWING CONCLUSIONS** Celina probably felt frustrated or angry because she couldn't pick watermelons while Mrs. Pig was sleeping in the watermelon patch.

2. **PROBLEM SOLVING** The cricket was the only animal who could sing a tune that could wake up Mrs. Pig.

3. **PROBLEM SOLVING** Answers will vary.

4. **Connecting/Comparing** What are some other stories you have listened to or read where characters solve a problem? (Answers will vary.)

THEME 6: Animal Adventures
(Anthology p. 154)

Responding

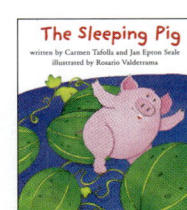

Read Together

The Sleeping Pig
written by Carmen Tafolla and Jan Epton Seale
illustrated by Rosario Valderrama

Think About the Story

1. How did Celina feel when she saw Mrs. Pig?

2. Why was the cricket the only animal who could wake Mrs. Pig?

3. What would you do if you were Celina?

Internet

Print Out Puppets

Print out story character puppets from Education Place to retell the story.

www.eduplace.com/kids

154

Practice Book page 61

Week 1
Comprehension Check *The Sleeping Pig*

Name _____

Who Tried to Wake Up Mrs. Pig?

Draw one animal that helped Celina.

Write about what that animal did.

(5 points)

Social Studies

Make an Award

Make an award for the hero in the story. Write a title for your award.

Explaining

Write a Poster

How would you wake a sleeping pig? Draw a poster and write one sentence. Share your poster with the class.

Tips

- Think about some ways to wake up a pig.
- Make sure that your drawing and your sentence match.

155

Additional Responses

Personal Response Have children share their personal responses to *The Sleeping Pig* orally or in small groups.

Journal ▶ Ask children to write or draw in their journals about a time when they had to solve a problem.

Sing a Song After discussing the story, children may enjoy singing "Little Pig." The music and lyrics are on page R40.

REACHING ALL LEARNERS

Extra Support/Intervention

Writing Support

Before children make their poster, provide them with a sentence starter. Then help children brainstorm ways they could wake up a pig.

> I could wake up the pig by _____.

English Language Learners

Supporting Comprehension

Beginning/Preproduction Have children draw pictures of the animals that tried to wake up Mrs. Pig. Help children label the animals.

Early Production and Speech Emergence Have children draw and label pictures of Celina at the beginning and end of the story. Discuss what changed.

Intermediate and Advanced Fluency Have children finish the sentence, *If I were Celina, I would _____.*

Monitoring Student Progress

Monitoring Student Progress

Student Self-Assessment Have children assess their reading with questions such as

- What were some hard words I figured out on my own?

- How did I know what the problem was in the book?

Responding
(Anthology p. 155)   **T63**

OBJECTIVES

- Identify the parts of a story.
- Identify the problem and solution in a story.
- Complete a story map.

Target Skill Trace

Preview; Teach	pp. T30, T46, T55; T64–T65; Theme 2; Theme 9
Reteach	p. R26
Review	p. T78
See	*Extra Support Handbook*, pp. 176–177, 182–183

INSTRUCTION

COMPREHENSION: Story Structure

① Teach

Discuss the five important parts of story structure.

1. <u>setting</u> where the story takes place

2. <u>characters</u> people or animals the story is about

3. <u>problem</u> something the characters must solve

4. <u>events</u> things that happen as the characters try to solve the problem

5. <u>ending</u> the last event in the story, when the problem is often solved

Modeling Demonstrate how to identify characters and setting. Turn to Anthology pages 134–135.

Think Aloud *I can tell where the story takes place and who some of the characters are on the first two pages of* The Sleeping Pig. *In the pictures I see a girl and a pig in a watermelon patch. I read that the girl is Celina, and a huge pig is sleeping in her watermelon patch. So far, I know that Celina and the pig are characters, and the watermelon patch is where the story takes place.*

Explain that as they read, children should also look for other characters, the problem, events, and ending. Knowing the parts of the story helps readers to understand what they read.

② Guided Practice

Display Chart/Transparency 6–3.

- On the Story Map, fill in the characters and setting that you discussed in the Think Aloud.

- Have children revisit *The Sleeping Pig* to identify other characters, the problem, events, and ending. Then call on children to provide information to complete the Story Map.

- Discuss how the problem in the story was solved.

- Have children use the completed Story Map to retell the story to a partner.

Chart/Transparency 6–3

Story Map

Story Map for _____ The Sleeping Pig

Setting (Where? When?)	a watermelon patch during the day
Characters (Who?)	Celina, Mrs. Pig, and a coyote, rabbit, snake, and cricket
Problem (What is wrong?)	Mrs. Pig is sleeping and won't get out of the watermelon patch.
Events (How does the character try to solve the problem?)	1. Celina shouts. 2. The coyote howls. 3. The rabbit hops. 4. The snake pulls.
Ending (Is the problem solved?)	A cricket sings a tune and wakes Mrs. Pig, who gets up and leaves.

ANIMAL ADVENTURES Week 1, Day 3
Comprehension Story Structure

ANNOTATED VERSION

TRANSPARENCY 6–3
TEACHER'S EDITION PAGE T64

❸ Apply

Choose one or more of these activities.

- Have partners choose another story they have read, complete a story map for it, and use the map to retell the story.
- Assign **Practice Book** page 62.
- Have children apply this skill as they read the **Leveled Readers.** You may also select books from the Leveled Bibliography for this theme (pages T6–T7).

✔️ **Test Prep** Explain that test questions on a story may ask about characters, where and when the story takes place, or what happens. It may be helpful for children to take notes on these elements of story structure as they read.

Leveled Readers and Leveled Practice

Children at all levels apply the comprehension skill as they read their Leveled Readers. See lessons on pages T84–T87.

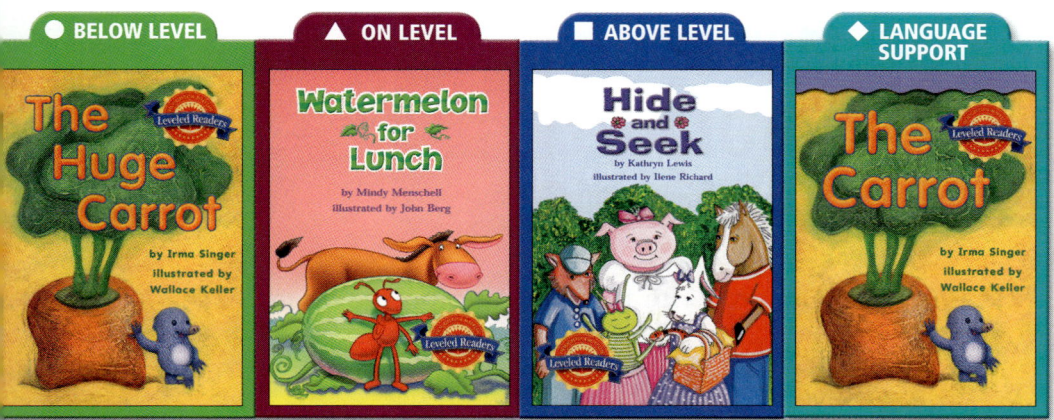

● BELOW LEVEL   ▲ ON LEVEL   ■ ABOVE LEVEL   ◆ LANGUAGE SUPPORT

Reading Traits

As children develop the ability to identify the elements of story structure, they are learning to "read the lines" of a selection. This comprehension skill supports the reading trait **Establishing Comprehension.**

Practice Book page 62

Week 1
Comprehension Story Structure

Name _____

Problems, Problems

✏️ Write two problems the family has in **The Kite.** In the box, draw or write how the problems were solved.

Problems

(4 points)
_____
_____

Solutions

(4)

Monitoring Student Progress

If . . .	Then . . .
children score 6 or below on **Practice Book** page 62,	use the Reteaching lesson on Teacher's Edition page R26.
children have met the lesson objectives,	use the Challenge/ Extension activities on Teacher's Edition page R27.

- Identify Basic Words from their meanings.
- Arrange words in alphabetical order.

Practice Book page 63

Name _____

Week 1
Spelling The Long *o* Sound

The Long *o* Sound

Color the pigs whose words have the long *o* sound.

Spelling Words

| go | bone | so | nose | home | no |

brown
go (1 point)
so (1)
sock
bone (1)
home (1)
nose (1)
no (1)

Write the Spelling Words from the pigs you colored.
The order of words may vary.

1. go   2. so   3. bone

4. nose   5. home   6. no

Practice Book page 65

Name _____

Week 1
Vocabulary Alphabetical Order

ABC Order

Cut out and paste the words in ABC order.

A B C D E F G H I J K L M N O P Q R S T U V W X Y Z

1. could (2 points)

2. fly (2)

3. give (2)

4. shout (2)

give

could

shout

fly

SPELLING: Words with Long *o*

Mystery Words Tell children to guess the mystery words. Explain that each mystery word has the long *o* sound spelled *o*. Read clues one at a time, giving the next clue if children cannot identify the word.

- *This word means "to move from one place to another." It can also mean "to leave." It can also mean "to belong or have a usual place," as in "The books ___ here in the classroom."* (go)

- *This word means "not so." It can mean "a vote against something." It also can mean "not any," as in "You will have ___ music class today."* (no)

- *This word means "very," as in "I am ___ angry at you." It also means "for that reason," as in "It's raining, ___ I'll wear my raincoat." It can mean "also" as in "You like that book and ___ do I."* (so)

Practice/Homework Assign **Practice Book** page 63.

TARGET SKILL VOCABULARY: Alphabetical Order

Words in Order Write the following on the board:

a b c d e f g h i j k l m n o p q r s t u v w x y z

coyote   mule   snake

- Point out the alphabet. Explain that you have written the words below it in ABC order, or alphabetical order.

- Ask a child to circle the first letter of each word and draw an arrow from that letter to the same letter in the alphabet.

- Erase *coyote, mule,* and *snake*. Repeat the process with *cricket, pig,* and *rabbit*.

- Ask children where to add *bear, elephant,* and *tiger*.

Practice/Homework Assign **Practice Book** page 65.

GRAMMAR: Naming Words for People and Animals

OBJECTIVES

- Identify naming words for people and animals.

Skill Trace	
▶ Teach	p. T67
Review	p. T83
See	*Handbook for English Language Learners*, p. 187

❶ Teach

Have children sort names for people and animals.

- Display **Chart/Transparency 6–4.** Read the title. Tell children that some naming words name people, and other naming words name animals.

- Read the word lists at the top. Point out that these words name people and animals.

- Have one child read a word that names a person. Write it in the column titled *People*.

- Have another child read a word that names an animal. Write it in the column titled *Animals*.

- Complete the chart by having children help you sort the rest of the names for people and animals.

Go over these points.

- Some naming words name people.

- Some naming words name animals.

❷ Guided Practice

Check children's understanding.

- Have children turn to Anthology page 134 of *The Sleeping Pig*. Read the sentence aloud, and ask which words name people or animals. *(Celina, pig)*

- Repeat with pages 137, 139, 141, and 142.

❸ Apply

Assign Practice Book page 67.

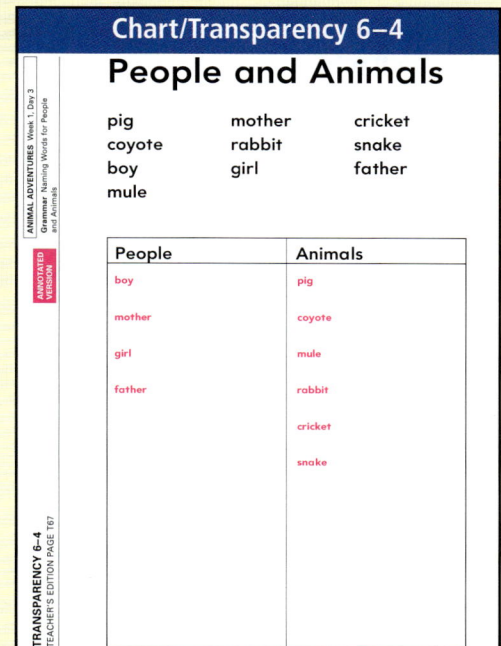

Chart/Transparency 6–4

People and Animals

pig	mother	cricket
coyote	rabbit	snake
boy	girl	father
mule		

People	Animals
boy	pig
mother	coyote
girl	mule
father	rabbit
	cricket
	snake

ANIMAL ADVENTURES Week 1, Day 3
Grammar Naming Words for People and Animals

ANNOTATED VERSION

TRANSPARENCY 6–4
TEACHER'S EDITION PAGE T67

Practice Book page 67

Week 1
Grammar Naming Words for People and Animals

Name _____

Naming Words

✏ Help the pig find the watermelon patch. Draw a line to connect the naming words. (4 points)

man   could
cat
dog   to
are   is
in   found   girl
little   cricket
have

Choose two naming words from above and write them below.

_____   _____
(1)   (1)

DAY 4
week 1

Day at a Glance
pages T68–T75

Learning to Read

Reading the Social Studies Link
What Is a Desert?

Phonics Review
Long *i* (CVC*e*)
Contractions

• • • • • • • • • • • • • • • • • • • •

Leveled Readers, T84–T87

● *The Huge Carrot*
▲ *Watermelon for Lunch*
■ *Hide-and-Seek*
◆ *The Carrot*

Word Work

Spelling: Words with Long *o*
Vocabulary: Fruits and Vegetables

Writing & Oral Language

Writing: Writing to Persuade

Daily Routines

Daily Message

Review skills. Point to each word as you read aloud the Daily Message.

Good Morning, Children!

Do you remember reading these words: <u>morning</u>, <u>found</u>, <u>shout</u>, <u>by</u>, <u>out</u>, <u>show</u>, and <u>climb</u>? They were in _____.

Have children

• respond to the question and complete the sentence; *(The Sleeping Pig)*

• circle words with *th*; *(these, They, The)*

• help put the underlined high-frequency words in alphabetical order.

Word Wall

High-Frequency Word Review Have children write sentences using this week's high-frequency words and other words from the Word Wall. Challenge children to use all of this week's words in only two or three sentences. Children can read their sentences aloud.

This <u>morning</u> I <u>found</u> <u>out</u> how to <u>climb</u>.

Come <u>by</u> and I will <u>show</u> you how to climb.

I will <u>shout</u> so you can hear me.

 Daily Phonemic Awareness

Segmenting and Counting Phonemes: Tap the Sounds

- Tell children that you will say a word and they should say the separate sounds. Have them tap once for each sound, on their desks.

  Teacher: *My word is* June. *Tap for each sound you say in* June.

  Children: /j//o͞o//n/

  Teacher: *How many sounds did you hear?* (3)

- Call on individuals to say and tap sounds for the following words as classmates count: *Luke* (3), *prune* (4), *flute* (4), *tube* (3), *drove* (4), *joke* (3).

Daily Language Practice

Grammar Skill: Which Kind of Sentence?

Spelling Skill: Words with Long o

Write the sentence, read it to children, and have them tell you how to correct it.

My noz is cold?

(My **nose** is cold.)

Daily Writing Prompt

Tell children to write in complete sentences when they respond to the prompt below or write on self-selected topics.

- **Write and draw about how you wake up in the morning.**

I use an alarm clock.

Daily Independent Reading

To increase children's reading fluency, provide a variety of theme-related books for them to read. Here are some suggestions.

- Leveled Bibliography, pages T6–T7

Choose books from this list for children to read, outside class, for at least twenty minutes a day.

- Leveled Theme Paperbacks: *Fox and Mule, The Little Red Hen, Fishing Bears*

- Leveled Readers

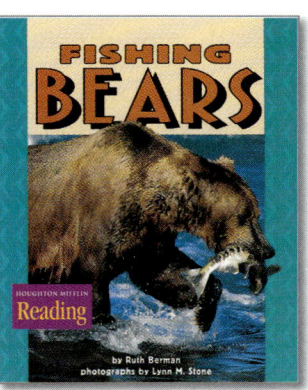

Social Studies Link

What Is a Desert?

Read Together

Skill: How to Read a Social Studies Article

- **Look** at the title and pictures.
- **Think** about what you know.
- **Predict** what you will learn.
- **Reread** if you do not understand.

A desert is a dry place that gets little or no rain. There are many deserts all over the world.

Cactus plants can grow in a desert. They can hold water for a long time. Some cactuses are as big as trees.

Arizona, USA

Namibia, Africa

Flowering Agave

Saguaro cactus

Claret Cup cactus

156

157

Social Studies Link

Skill: How to Read a Social Studies Article

Introduce the Link. Read aloud the title and explain that this is a social studies article that gives information about a place.

Discuss the Skill Lesson. Have children say what they think the article will be about (the desert) and write the topic on the board.

Model how to read the article. List on the board what children already know about the desert and what else they think they might learn.

Set a purpose for reading. Tell children that they should read to find out what a desert is like. Then read the article together, pausing to check children's understanding, and rereading if necessary.

> **The Desert**
> sandy
> dry
> cactus
> desert animals

Vocabulary

Write the Concept Vocabulary on the board and read each word. Help children to point out examples of each word in the photos on Anthology pages 156–159. Have children share what they already know about the desert and the animals that live there.

> ## Concept Vocabulary
>
> | | |
> |---|---|
> | desert | scorpions |
> | cactus | camels |

English Language Learners

Supporting Comprehension

Preview with children the names of the plants and animals before reading the article. Have them name the plant or animal in their first language and then repeat it in English.

THEME 6: Animal Adventures
(Anthology pp. 156–157)

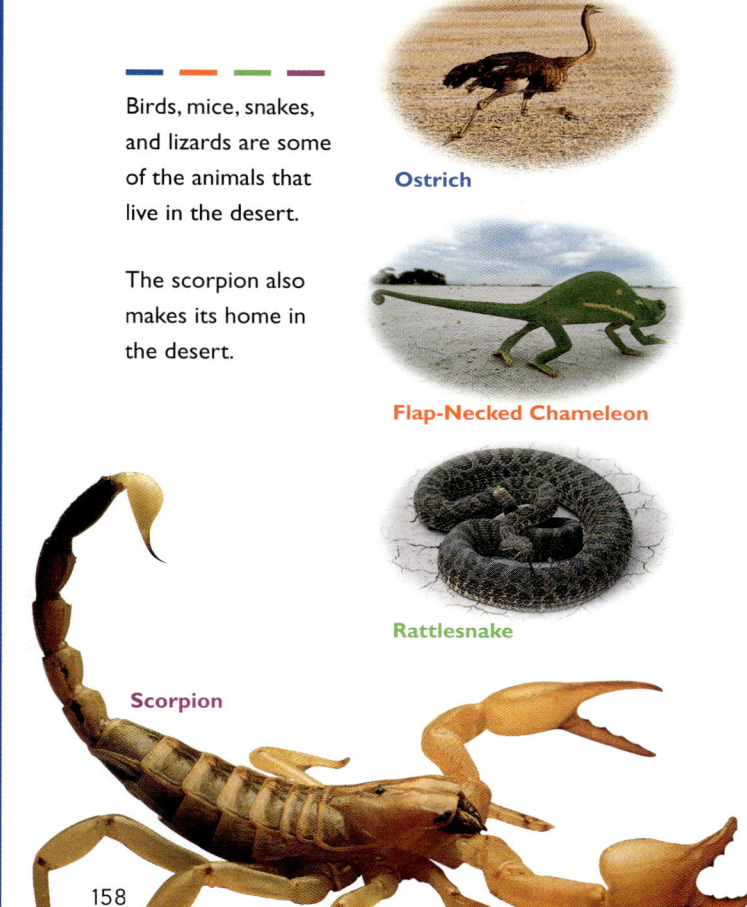

Birds, mice, snakes, and lizards are some of the animals that live in the desert.

Ostrich

The scorpion also makes its home in the desert.

Flap-Necked Chameleon

Rattlesnake

Scorpion

158

Some people move through the desert on camels. Camels can go days without food or water.

Would you like to see a desert?

159

Wrapping Up

Critical Thinking Questions

1. **NOTING DETAILS** How much rain does the desert get? (very little)

2. **CAUSE AND EFFECT** Why are cactus plants able to live in the desert? (They can store water for a long time.)

3. **DRAWING CONCLUSIONS** Why do you think people use camels to travel in the desert? (Camels can travel for days without food or water.)

4. **COMPARE AND CONTRAST** What animal appears in both *The Sleeping Pig* and "What Is a Desert?" (a snake)

REACHING ALL LEARNERS | **On Level** | **Challenge**

Extending the Topic

Allow children to draw or cut from a magazine a picture of their favorite desert plant or animal and write a sentence describing the plant or animal in their own words. Have them present their projects to the class.

Information Skills: Parts of a Book

You may want to teach children about captions, which appear in this article, as well as other parts of a book they may encounter in their curriculum area reading, such as chapters or an index. See the lesson on Parts of a Book, page R32.

Responding
(Anthology pp. 158–159)

REVIEW

OBJECTIVES

- Build words with long *i* (CVC*e*).
- Name contractions made from two words.

Target Skill Trace

Teach	Theme 5, pp. T192–T194
Reteach	Theme 5, pp. R20, R22
▶ Review	pp. T72–T73
See	*Handbook for English Language Learners*, pp. 167, 173; *Extra Support Handbook*, pp. 162, 163, 168, 169

Materials

- **Large Sound/Spelling Card** *ice cream*
- **Large Letter Cards** *b, c, d, e, f, h, i, k, l, m, n, p, q, r, s, t, u, v, w*
- **Practice Book** punchout trays and letters *b, c, d, e, f, h, i, k, l, m, n, p, q, r, s, t, u, v, w*

PHONICS: Long *i* (CVC*e*)

❶ Review

Review long *i* (CVC*e*).

- Display **Large Sound/Spelling Card** *ice cream*. Have children name the picture. Remind them that the vowel *i* stands for the long *i* sound /ī/ at the beginning of *ice cream*. Have children say /ī ī ī/ as you point to the letter.

- Display the **Large Letter Cards** on the chalkboard ledge. Model how to make words with the vowel-consonant-*e* pattern, using the word *fine*.

- Call on children to arrange the letters to make other words. (Possible answers: *bike, bite, mice, nice, price, slice, kite, rice, dine, dime, line, lime, mine, nine, pine, quite, time, vine, wide*)

❷ Guided Practice/Apply

Building Words

Guide children in building words with letter cards.

- Give pairs of children punchout trays and letters. Tell them to build as many words as possible with long *i* and the vowel-consonant-*e* pattern.

- Have partners list their words on a piece of paper.

Create a class list of long *i* (CVC*e*) words.

- After children have finished building words, combine all the lists to create a class list of long *i* (CVC*e*) words.

- Post the list in the room and have children add to it as they come across other long *i* (CVC*e*) words in their reading.

REVIEW

TARGET SKILL — PHONICS: Contractions

❶ Review

Review contractions. Remind children that sometimes two words are used to form a contraction.

- Write and read aloud *I am here.* Remind children that a short way to write *I am* is *I'm.* Below the first sentence, write and read aloud *I'm here.*

- Circle the apostrophe in *I'm.* Remind children that in a contraction, an apostrophe takes the place of one or more letters.

- Point out that in the contraction *I'm,* the apostrophe takes the place of *a* in *am.* Underline *a.*

❷ Guided Practice/Apply

Contraction Action!

Tell children they will play Contraction Action!

- Assign children partners.

- Explain that you will say two words. Child 1 should repeat the first word. Child 2 should repeat the second word. Then when you say *Action!,* both children should say the contraction.

- Demonstrate with the words *is* and *not.* Have one child say *is* and another child say *not.* You say *Action!,* and the two children should say *isn't.*

- Continue with *can not (can't), do not (don't), did not (didn't), would not (wouldn't), could not (couldn't).*

is   not

isn't

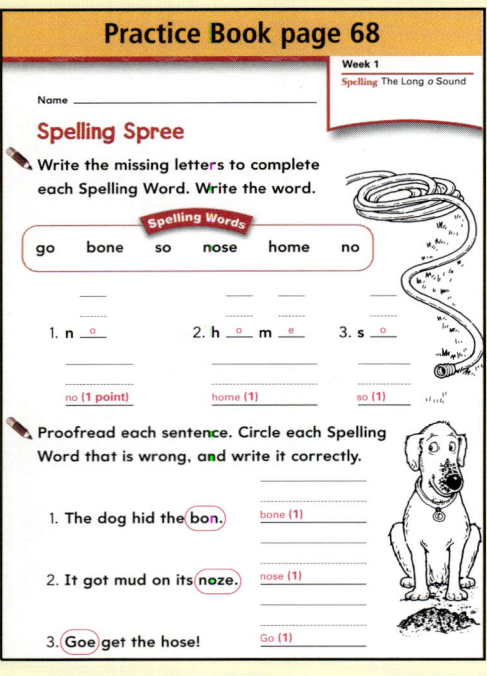

Practice Book page 68

Name _____

Week 1
Spelling The Long *o* Sound

Spelling Spree

✏ Write the missing letters to complete each Spelling Word. Write the word.

Spelling Words

| go | bone | so | nose | home | no |

1. n __o__   2. h __o__ m __e__   3. s __o__

no (1 point)   home (1)   so (1)

✏ Proofread each sentence. Circle each Spelling Word that is wrong, and write it correctly.

1. The dog hid the (bon.)   bone (1)

2. It got mud on its (noze.)   nose (1)

3. (Goe) get the hose!   Go (1)

SPELLING: Words with Long *o*

Dog Bones Tell children they will write words with the long *o* sound on their own pile of dog bones.

- Distribute paper dog bones.
- Tell children to write *bone* on a paper bone. Continue with the other Basic Words.
- Encourage children to write more long *o* words on dog bones.

Practice/Homework Assign **Practice Book** page 68.

VOCABULARY: Words That Name Fruits and Vegetables

Identify words that name fruits and vegetables. Read page 134 of *The Sleeping Pig* aloud. Ask children where the pig slept. (in the watermelon patch) Ask if watermelon is a fruit or a vegetable. (a fruit) Tell children that they will make a chart that lists the names of fruits and vegetables they know.

Practice/Apply Create a two-column chart labeled *Fruits* on one side and *Vegetables* on the other side.

- Ask children to suggest familiar fruits and vegetables. Have them tell you in which column to write each one.
- Have children check the chart to make sure each food is in the right category.

Fruits	Vegetables
apples	peas
oranges	carrots
bananas	squash
grapes	

WRITING: Writing to Persuade

OBJECTIVES

- Understand how to persuade someone.
- Contribute sentences to write a persuasive message.

❶ Teach

Discuss ideas for writing to persuade.

- Remind children that to *persuade* someone means to convince that person to do something.
- Tell children that today they will write a message to persuade others to help them improve their school.
- Have children brainstorm about things they could do to improve their school, such as planting a tree, recycling trash, or cleaning up an area.

Have children contribute to a persuasive message.

- Help children choose an idea and write a message to persuade others to help.
- Begin with a topic sentence stating the main idea.
- Model how to think of a persuasive argument.

Think Aloud *I want to persuade people to help recycle our trash. I'll tell them that if people reuse things, we won't have to burn as much trash, and our air will be cleaner.*

- Record children's sentences.
- Add a persuasive title, and read the entire message.

Go over these points.

- To persuade someone, explain what you want them to do.
- Also explain why you think it is important to do it.

❷ Practice

Check children's understanding.

- Reread the message.
- Ask *What is the main idea of our message?*
- *Would our message persuade you to help out?*
- *What could we add to make it more persuasive?*

❸ Apply

Assign Practice Book page 69. After they complete the page independently, have pairs of children read their persuasive messages to each other.

Practice Book page 69

Name _____

Week 1
Writing Writing to Persuade

List Your Reasons

Use this page to plan how to convince a friend that you should have a pet.

What kind of pet do you want?

_____
(1 point)

Write why you should get that pet.

_____
(4)
_____
_____
_____
_____

Read what you wrote to a friend. What can you add?
_____
_____
_____
_____

Day at a Glance
pages T76–T83

Learning to Read

Comprehension: Rereading for Understanding
Story Structure

Rereading for Fluency

Reading Decodable Text
The Nest

• • • • • • • • • • • • • • • •

Leveled Readers, T84–T87
- 🟢 *The Huge Carrot*
- 🔺 *Watermelon for Lunch*
- 🟦 *Hide-and-Seek*
- 🔷 *The Carrot*

Word Work

Spelling Test: Words with Long *o*
Vocabulary: High-Frequency Words

Writing & Oral Language

Grammar Review: Naming Words for People and Animals

Independent Writing

Listening and Speaking: Compare and Contrast

Daily Routines

Daily Message

Strategy Review Remind children of the Phonics/Decoding Strategy. Guide them in applying it to selected words in today's message.

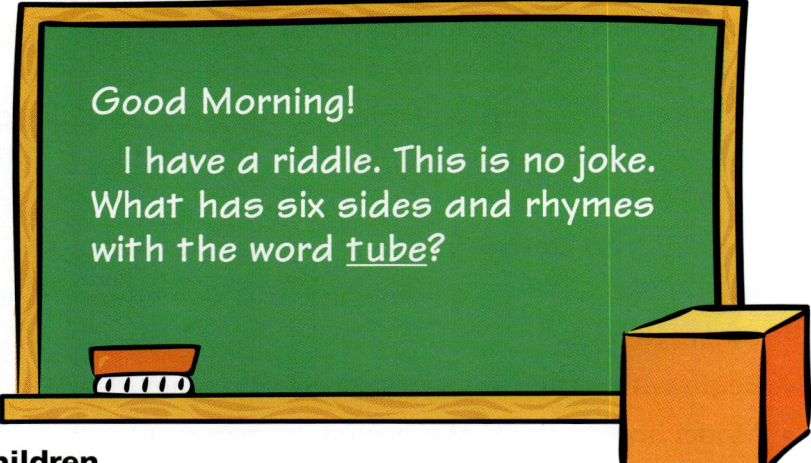

> Good Morning!
>
>   I have a riddle. This is no joke. What has six sides and rhymes with the word <u>tube</u>?

Have children

- respond to the question;
- circle the long *o* and long *u* words; *(no, joke, tube)*
- find and read the following high-frequency words: *Good, Morning, have, What,* and *the.*

Word Wall

Cumulative Review Review new and previously taught high-frequency words from the Word Wall. Have children complete **Activity Master 6–1** on Teacher's Edition page R36.

Have children

- work individually or with a partner;
- circle high-frequency words found in the word search.

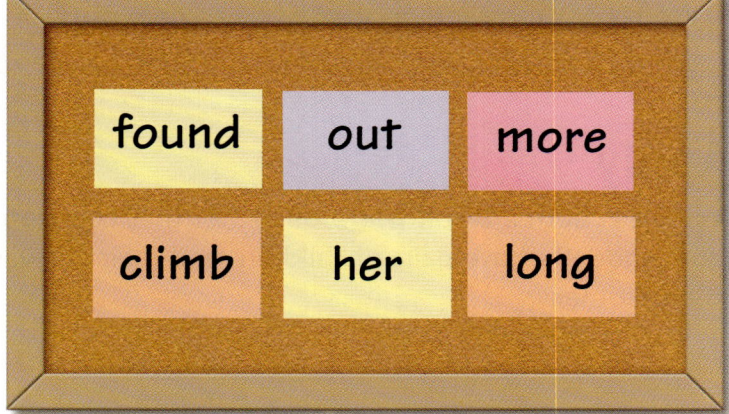

Daily Phonemic Awareness

Segmenting and Counting Phonemes: Sounds at the Board

- Call on pairs of children to come to the board.

  Have one child say the separate sounds in a word while the other child tallies the sounds on the board.

- Say to the first child: *Listen:* child. *Let's say each sound in this word:* /ch//ī//l//d/.

- Say to the second child: *As your partner says each sound again, draw a line on the board. Count the lines. How many sounds are in* child? (4)

- Continue with *rope* (3), *Sue* (2), *hose* (3), *close* (4), *cute* (3), *cube* (3).

Note For words with the /yoo/ (long *u*) sound as in *use,* some children may count two sounds for the vowel.

Daily Language Practice

Grammar Skill: Beginning Sentences with
    Capital Letters

Spelling Skill: Words with Long *o*

Write the sentence, read it to children, and have them tell you how to correct it.

can you goe with me?

(Can you **go** with me?)

Daily Writing Prompt

Remind children to write in complete sentences as they respond to the prompt below or write on self-selected topics.

- **Write and draw about your favorite dream.**

I had a dream that my cat had three kittens. They were cute, and I got to keep one.

Daily Independent Reading

To increase children's reading fluency, provide a variety of theme-related books for them to read. Here are some suggestions.

- Leveled Bibliography, pages T6–T7

Choose books from this list for children to read, outside class, for at least twenty minutes a day.

- Anthology:
  The Sleeping Pig

- Phonics Library:
  Duke's Gift, Legs Gets His Lunch, The Nest

- Book Boxes

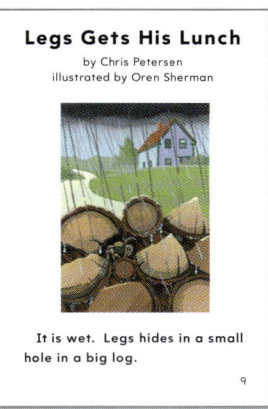

Legs Gets His Lunch
by Chris Petersen
illustrated by Oren Sherman

It is wet. Legs hides in a small hole in a big log.

9

OBJECTIVES

- Review and explain story structure in the week's selections.

Review Skill Trace	
Teach	pp. T64–T65
Reteach	p. R26
▶ Review	p. T78
See	*Extra Support Handbook,* pp. 176–177, 182–183

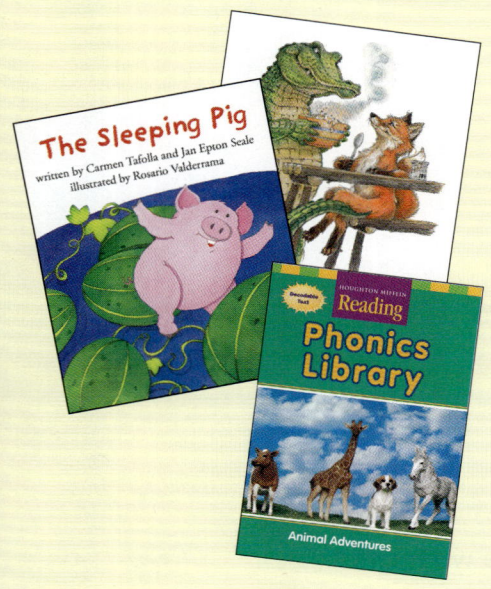

REVIEW

COMPREHENSION: Rereading for Understanding

Story Structure

Review the parts of a story. Remind children that all stories have *characters,* a *setting,* a *problem, events,* and an *ending.*

Display Chart/Transparency 6–3. Refer to it as you use the Think Aloud to review story structure in *The Sleeping Pig.*

Think Aloud — *The setting of* The Sleeping Pig *is a watermelon patch. The characters are Celina, Mrs. Pig, and the animals. The problem is that Mrs. Pig won't wake up. The characters try different things to get her up. At the end the cricket solves the problem by singing a tune.*

Review story structure in the Read Aloud. Clear the right-hand column of **Chart/Transparency 6–3** and call on children to help you fill it in for *Fox, Alligator, and Rabbit.*

- Ask children to recall the setting (the river; Alligator's house); characters (Fox, Alligator, Rabbit); problem (Rabbit must cross the river without being eaten); events (Fox tricks Alligator); ending (Rabbit crosses the river but still needs to get back).
- Ask what is similar about the story structure of these two stories. (They both have animal characters who need to solve a problem.)

Assign rereading and retelling.

- Have children think about story structure as they reread the **On My Way Practice Reader, Theme Paperbacks, Leveled Readers,** and **Phonics Library** for this week.
- Have children use a story map to retell **Phonics Library** stories *Duke's Gift* or *Legs Gets His Lunch.*

Chart/Transparency 6–3

Story Map

Story Map for _____ The Sleeping Pig

Setting (Where? When?)	a watermelon patch during the day
Characters (Who?)	Celina, Mrs. Pig, and a coyote, rabbit, snake, and cricket
Problem (What is wrong?)	Mrs. Pig is sleeping and won't get out of the watermelon patch.
Events (How does the character try to solve the problem?)	1. Celina shouts. 2. The coyote howls. 3. The rabbit hops. 4. The snake pulls.
Ending (Is the problem solved?)	A cricket sings a tune and wakes Mrs. Pig, who gets up and leaves.

ANIMAL ADVENTURES Week 1, Day 3
Comprehension Story Structure

ANNOTATED VERSION

TRANSPARENCY 6–3
TEACHER'S EDITION PAGE T64

PRACTICE

REREADING FOR FLUENCY

Rereading the Selection Have children choose part of *The Sleeping Pig* to reread orally in small groups, or suggest that they read pages 141–142. If necessary, model fluent reading. Encourage children to read with feeling and expression.

Decodable Text

HOUGHTON MIFFLIN
Reading

Phonics Library

Animal Adventures

The Nest
by Peri Jones
illustrated by Marcia Sewall

Jude found this nest in a big plant by his home. Jude left it and went to get Rose.

13

PHONICS LIBRARY

End-of-Week Skills Check

Have children preview *The Nest*. Ask them what they see happening in the nest.

Observe as children model the Phonics/Decoding Strategy.

- Have children read *The Nest*. As they read, ask individuals to tell how they use the strategy to figure out new words.

- Make note of children who have difficulty applying the strategy and take oral reading records with these children.

Prompt children in rereading the story. For children who have difficulty, use prompts such as these:

- *Look at the letters from left to right. What letters do you see?*

- *Say the sound for each letter and hold it until you say the next sound. What is the word?*

- *Is that a word you know? Does it make sense in the story?*

OBJECTIVES

- Apply the Phonics/Decoding Strategy to decode words in context.
- Recognize high-frequency words in context.
- Reread to build fluency.

Word Key

Decodable words with long *o*, long *u*, final *ft*, *lk*, *nt* ———

High-Frequency Words ———

Monitoring Student Progress

Oral Reading Records Take oral reading records of a few children each week as they read the **Phonics Library** book individually or in small groups.

Alternative Assessment Use **Teacher's Resource Blackline Master 79** to assess individual children's phonics and high-frequency word skills.

Reading Decodable Text T79

Rose <u>bent</u> down.
   "This egg will hatch in <u>no</u> time."

14

One <u>morning</u>, the egg had a <u>huge</u> crack in it.
   "It <u>broke</u>," yelled Jude.

15

Oral Language

Discuss these questions with children. Have them answer in complete sentences.

- What happens to the egg in this story? (It hatches.)
- Why do you think Jude wants to show the egg to Rose? (Answers will vary.)

Then Rose spoke, "The egg is fine. It's just hatching."
   "It's so cute," said Jude.
"It looks soft as silk."

16

![target skill icon] **Build Fluency**

Model and have children practice fluent reading.

- Point out the quotation marks that show where Jude speaks on page 15. Model reading page 15, changing your tone of voice when you come to the sentence of dialogue.

- Have children read the page aloud in unison. Encourage them to read with expression.

- Have children reread pages 15 and 16 several times until each child can read them aloud effortlessly.

![home icon] **Home Connection**

Hand out the take-home version of *The Nest*. Ask children to reread the story with their families. (See the **Phonics Library Blackline Masters**.)

TEST

SPELLING: Words with Long *o*

Test

Say each underlined word, read the sentence, and then repeat the word. Have children write only the underlined word.

Basic Words

1. Can you **go** to the shop?
2. Where did Rusty hide his **bone**?
3. I am **so** mad!
4. My dog has a wet **nose**!
5. Pedro went **home**.
6. The man has **no** hat.

REVIEW

VOCABULARY: High-Frequency Words

Review the words. Tell children you will give them clues, and they will identify some New Words.

- Say *I'm thinking of a New Word.* Give clues such as these:

  The word has five letters. It begins with c. It ends with b. (climb)
  The word has five letters. It begins with f. It ends with d. (found)
  The word has seven letters. It begins with m. It ends with g. (morning)

- Continue with the remaining high-frequency words for the week.

- Then have children clap and spell each New Word. Call on a child to move the word to the permanent Word Wall as children chant it aloud.

Practice/Apply Have vocabulary speed drills. Assemble the Word Wall Cards for this week's New Words and for several words from previous themes. Make a few other cards for decodable words that feature the week's phonics/decoding elements.

- At small group time, have children take turns holding up the cards for a partner to read.

- Then display the cards as a list on a table. Have individuals read them to you as quickly as they can.

GRAMMAR: Naming Words for People and Animals

Review Remind children that some naming words name people and animals.

List naming words for people and animals.

- Have small groups create lists of names for people and animals.

- Give each group a category, such as ocean animals, circus animals, unusual pets, family members, or community helpers.

Practice/Apply

- Have each child in the group pick a name to illustrate and label.

- Bind the drawings together to create a book.

- Give the book a title indicating the category.

Independent Writing Have children write a journal entry that includes the names of people and animals. Then have them go back and underline all the words that name people and animals.

OBJECTIVES

- Review naming words for people and animals.
- Compare and contrast information.

Review Skill Trace	
Teach	p. T67
▶ Review	p. T83
See	*Handbook for English Language Learners,* p. 187

SPEAKING AND LISTENING: Compare and Contrast

Create a chart to compare animal characters.

- Remind children that when they compare things, they think about how the things are the same and how they are different.

- Create a chart to compare the animals in the story *Fox, Alligator, and Rabbit.* Draw one big circle labeled *Shared Things* and three separate circles underneath labeled *Fox, Alligator,* and *Rabbit.*

- Point out that all three are animals. Write this under *Shared Things.* Ask children to name other shared traits or actions, and add them.

- Then have children name individual traits or actions for each animal, and write them in the appropriate circles.

- Discuss the chart to compare and contrast the animals.

 **English Language Learners**

Supporting Comprehension

Before English language learners compare and contrast the animals, review the story. Have children retell the events in order. Write *Fox, Alligator,* and *Rabbit* on the board. Have children describe each animal, and write key words on the board for reference.

● BELOW LEVEL

The Huge Carrot

Summary *In this adaptation of an old folktale, Mule tries to get a huge carrot out of the ground. When he is unsuccessful, his friend Pig gets a rope so he and Mule can try to pull the carrot out with it. But the carrot won't budge. At last, little Mole comes to help them, and the carrot finally pops out.*

Building Background and Vocabulary

Tell children that this story is about a mule that can't get a carrot out of the ground. Have them share what they know about how carrots and other root vegetables grow in the ground. Preview the illustrations, and have children point out the different ways that Mule tries to get the carrot out.

Comprehension Skill: Story Structure

Read together the Strategy Focus on the book flap. Remind children to use the strategy and to notice the important elements of the story's structure as they read the book. (See the Leveled Readers Teacher's Guide for **Vocabulary and Comprehension Practice Masters.**)

Responding

Have partners discuss how to answer the questions on the inside back cover.

Think About What You Have Read   Sample answers:

1. Mule is trying to pull up a huge carrot that is stuck in the ground.
2. Pig gets a rope. Then he and Mule tie the rope on the carrot and pull it.
3. Answers will vary.

Making Connections   Answers will vary.

Building Fluency

Model   Ask children to find question marks in the story. Then have them listen for a question as you reread pages 2–3 aloud.

Practice   Ask children to watch for another question on page 4 and to be ready to read the answer aloud together. Then have them continue to reread the remaining pages aloud together.

Story Words

Introduce the Story Words, one at a time, providing meaning with objects, pictures, gestures, and/or contex**t** sentences. Then ask children to complete the **Vocabulary Practice Master.**

Mule *p. 2*

carrot (title), *p. 2*

pulls *p. 6*

Mole *p. 7*

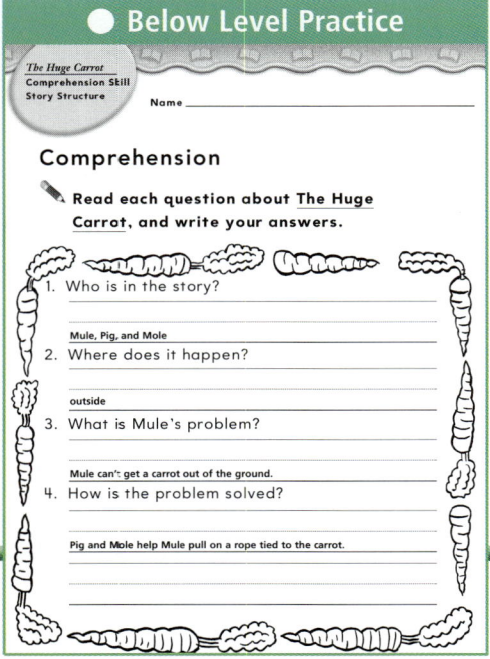

▲ ON LEVEL

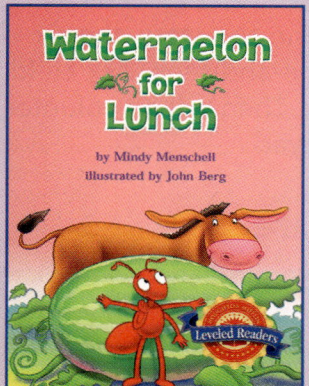

Watermelon for Lunch

by Mindy Menschell
illustrated by John Berg

Watermelon for Lunch

Summary *Ant finds a huge watermelon. She can't split it open herself, so when Mule comes along, she pretends to be the watermelon talking. She tricks Mule into kicking the melon down the hill so it cracks open. Then she can enjoy watermelon for lunch.*

Story Words

Introduce the Story Words, one at a time, providing meaning with objects, pictures, gestures, and/or context sentences. Then ask children to complete the **Vocabulary Practice Master.**

watermelon (title), *p. 2*

poke *p. 3*

shouted *p. 6*

joke *p. 8*

lunch (title), *p. 9*

huge *p. 12*

Building Background and Vocabulary

Invite discussion about children's experiences eating watermelon, nuts, oranges, bananas, or other fruits that must be opened or peeled before eating. Preview the illustrations, and have children point out where the ant is. Then ask them how they think an animal like an ant might open the watermelon in the picture in order to eat it.

Comprehension Skill: Story Structure

Read together the Strategy Focus on the book flap. Remind children to use the strategy and to notice the important elements of the story's structure as they read the book. (See the Leveled Readers Teacher's Guide for **Vocabulary and Comprehension Practice Masters.**)

Responding

Have partners discuss how to answer the questions on the inside back cover.

Think About What You Have Read Sample answers:

1. Ant wanted to poke a hole in the watermelon so she could eat it.
2. Ant tricked Mule into kicking the watermelon down the hill so it would break open.
3. Answers will vary.

Making Connections Answers will vary.

Building Fluency

Model Reread the story aloud, having children follow along in their books. Ask them to watch for the words that Ant says and the words that Mule says.

Practice After the reading, ask one of two smaller groups to point out the places where Ant speaks. Have the other group point out the places where Mule speaks. Then read the story aloud with children, pausing for the groups to read aloud the words of the characters that they found.

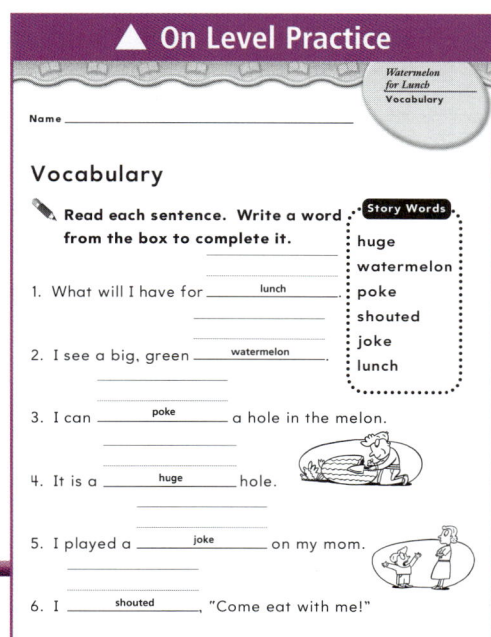

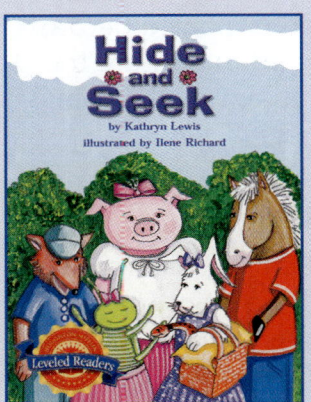

Hide-and-Seek

Summary *When some animal friends play a game of hide-and-seek in the park, Cricket is sent off to hide. But the friends seeking her soon start playing on a seesaw and forget all about their game and Cricket. Later, realizing that Cricket is missing, the friends begin to search the park for her. They finally find Cricket, who, while waiting to be found, has fallen asleep.*

Story Words

Introduce the Story Words, one at a time, providing meaning with objects, pictures, gestures, and/or context sentences. Then ask children to complete the **Vocabulary Practice Master.**

friends *p. 2*

hunt *p. 5*

seesaw *p. 5*

forgot *p. 6*

missing *p. 12*

asleep *p. 12*

■ ABOVE LEVEL

Building Background and Vocabulary

Ask children to view the cover and tell who they think the characters are. Read the title of the book together, and explain that in the story, the six animal friends go to the park and play a game of hide-and-seek. Ask children to tell about some games they like to play with friends. Then call on volunteers to tell or show how the game of hide-and-seek is played.

🔥 Comprehension Skill: Story Structure

Read together the Strategy Focus on the book flap. Remind children to use the strategy and to notice what happens at the beginning, in the middle, and at the end of the story. (See the Leveled Readers Teacher's Guide for **Vocabulary and Comprehension Practice Masters.**)

Responding

Have partners discuss how to answer the questions on the inside back cover.

Think About What You Have Read Sample answers:

1. Answers may include: play, have lunch, and then play hide-and-seek.

2. Answers should include: They are too busy doing other things and having fun.

3. Answers will vary.

Making Connections Answers will vary.

🔥 Building Fluency

Model Write the words *shouted, asked, yelled,* and *called* on the chalkboard. Read the words aloud, one at a time. Explain that these words tell how the animals in the story said some things. Ask children to follow along as you reread the story to them. Tell them to watch for words from the list.

Practice Have the group reread the story aloud together, shouting, yelling, asking, or calling the words of the animals as the text of the story indicates.

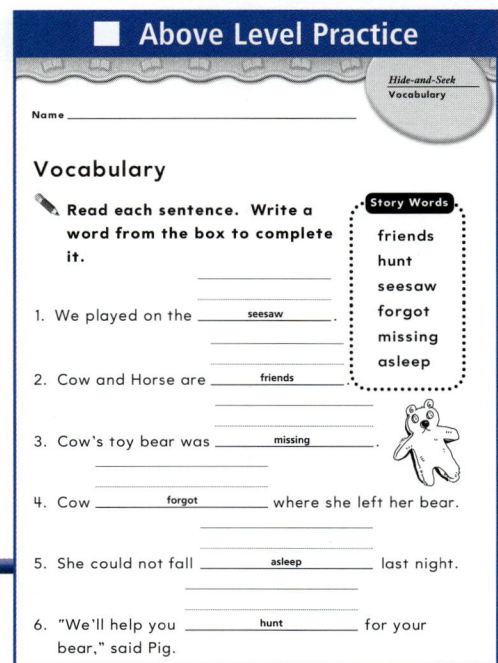

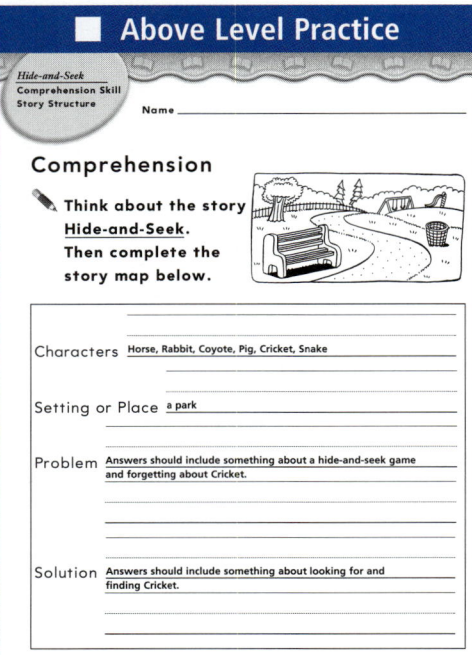

Leveled Readers

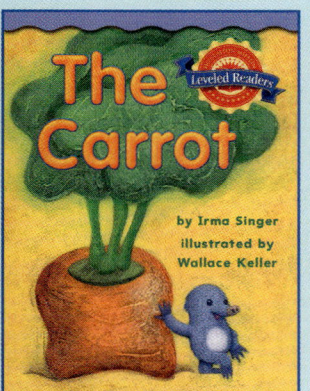

The Carrot

Summary *Mule sees a carrot and tries to pull it from the ground. His friends try to help, but they cannot get the carrot out of the ground. Finally, Mole helps them pull, and out pops the carrot!*

Story Words

Introduce the Story Words. Then ask children to complete the Story Words Practice Master.

carrot a long orange vegetable that grows underground, *p. 2*

pull to make something follow you, *p. 3*

dig to make a hole in the earth, *p. 4*

rope something made of several long pieces of string twisted together, *p. 5*

help to do something together with someone else, *p. 7*

◆ LANGUAGE SUPPORT

Building Background and Vocabulary

Model how to *pull* a chair out from the table, and *push* it back in. Ask children to pull out their chairs and then push them back in. Have children name other things they can push or pull, such as baby carriages or wagons. Then distribute the **Build Background Practice Master,** read aloud the directions, and have children complete the page. (See the Leveled Readers Teacher's Guide for **Build Background and Story Words Masters.**)

Reading Strategy: Question

Have children read the Strategy Focus on the book flap. Remind children that asking themselves questions about what they are reading can help them understand stories.

Responding

Have partners discuss how to answer the questions on the inside back cover.

Think About What You Have Read   Sample answers:

1. He wants to get the carrot out.
2. Pig and Little Mole help by getting a rope, putting it on the carrot, and pulling it out.
3. Answers will vary.

Making Connections   Answers will vary.

Building Fluency

Model   Read aloud page 8 as children follow along in their books. Point out the capital letters in POP, and explain that they mean something is loud or exciting. Model reading the words in a way that shows excitement.

Practice   Lead a choral reading of the page. Encourage children to have fun reading the word *POP!*

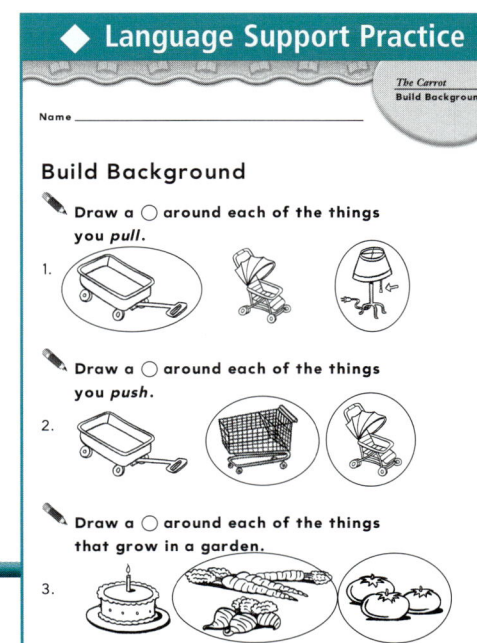

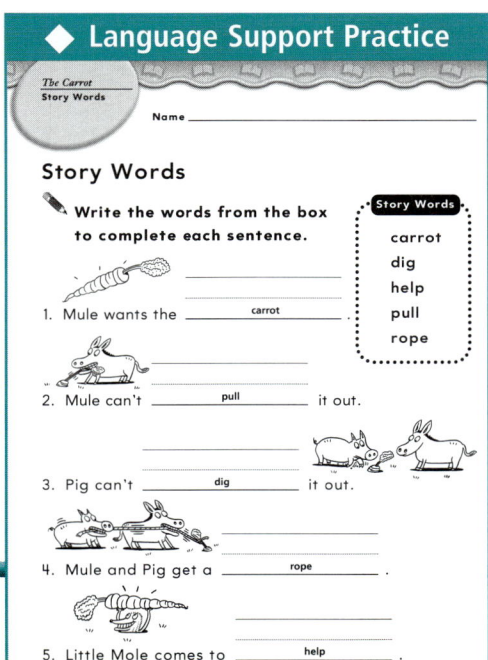

Reading-Writing Workshop

Description

In the Reading-Writing Workshop for Theme 6, *Animal Adventures*, children read Megan's description, "Fishing with My Dad," on Anthology pages 160–161. Then they follow the five steps of the writing process to write a description.

Meet the Author

Megan S.
Grade: one
State: Delaware
Hobbies: fishing, reading, and writing
What she'd like to be when she grows up: a teacher

Theme Skill Trace

Writing
- Writing to Persuade, T75
- Answering a Comprehension Question, T157
- Writing a Summary, T229

Grammar
- Naming Words for People and Animals, T83
- Naming Words for Places and Things, T165
- Naming Words for One or More, T237

Spelling
- The Long *o* Sound, T38
- Words with Long *e* (*e, ee, ea*), T120
- Words with *ay*, T190

Pacing the Workshop

Here is a suggestion for how you might pace the workshop within one week or on five separate days across the theme.

DAY 1 PREWRITING

Children
- read the student model, Anthology 160–161
- choose a topic for their description, T92
- brainstorm and organize the details for their description, T93

DAY 2 DRAFTING

Children
- use sensory language, T94
- use exact words, T95
- draft their description, T95

Focus on Writing Traits: Description

This workshop focuses on the traits of ideas and word choice. However, children should think about all of the writing traits during the writing process.

IDEAS Children need a lot of help and encouragement at the prewriting stage.

- As children brainstorm, walk around the class and ask questions about the details and events that they are planning to use in their description.

- Show excitement and interest over vivid details, particularly words that use the five senses.

- Conversations such as these will not only help children to develop details for their description but will also help them to picture their audience.

WORD CHOICE Discuss word choice throughout the writing process.

- Praise children for any exact or sensory words they use. Point out how much exact words help you picture what children are describing.

- Ask questions about any vague words. Children may think of more exact language as they explain what they mean.

Tips for Teaching the Writing Traits

- Teach one trait at a time.

- Discuss examples of the traits in the literature children are reading.

- Encourage children to talk about the traits during a writing conference.

- Encourage children to revise their writing for one trait at a time.

DAY 3 REVISING	DAY 4 PROOFREADING	DAY 5 PUBLISHING

Children

- decide how to make their description better, T96

- revise their description, T96

- have writing conferences, T96

Children

- correct spelling, punctuation, capitalization, and usage errors, T97

- improve their writing by using complete sentences, T97

Children

- publish their description, T98

- reflect on their writing experience, T98

Description

Discussing the Guidelines

Display **Chart/Transparency RWW6–1,** and discuss what makes a great description.

- Remember that children should think about all the writing traits as they write: ideas, organization, voice, word choice, sentence fluency, conventions, and presentation.

Discussing the Model

Have children read the Student Writing Model on Anthology pages 160–161.

- Discuss with children what the writer did to make her writing interesting to read.
- Use the Reading As a Writer questions on the next page.

THEME 6: Animal Adventures
(Anthology p. 160)

Student Writing Model

Read Together

A Description

A description is a picture in words that helps the reader to see, hear, taste, feel, and smell what you're writing about. Use this student writing as a model when you write your own description.

> A good **beginning** tells what the description is about.

> A good description includes **sense** words.

Fishing with My Dad

I have a big fishing rod with a small hook at the end. When I go fishing with my Dad, this is what I use. My Dad's fishing rod is tall and yellow with a big hook at the end.

160

Chart/Transparency RWW6–1

What Makes a Great Description?

When you write a **description**, remember to do these things.

- Write about one place or thing. Tell what you are writing about in the beginning.
- Use your senses to brainstorm details about your topic.
- Use sensory words that tell how something looks, sounds, feels, tastes, or smells.
- Include exact naming words to give your reader a clear picture of what you are describing.
- Write your details in an order that is easy for your readers to follow.

TRANSPARENCY RWW 6–1
TEACHER'S EDITION PAGE T90

ANIMAL ADVENTURES
Reading-Writing Workshop Description

ANNOTATED
VERSION

He usually catches huge gray catfish. I usually catch small minnows.

A good description uses **details**.

Meet the Author

Megan S.
Grade: one
State: Delaware
Hobbies: fishing, reading, and writing
What she'd like to be when she grows up: a teacher

161

Reading As a Writer

1. What is the description about? (*fishing*)

2. How does the writer describe her fishing pole? (*It is big and has a small hook at the end.*)

3. How does the writer describe her dad's fishing pole? (*It is tall and yellow and has a big hook at the end.*)

4. What words tell you how the catfish looks? (*huge* and *gray*)

5. What do you like about the writer's description? (*Responses will vary.*)

Extra Support/Intervention

Using the Workshop

Here are three options for using this workshop with children who are writing below level.

- **Emergent writers** might draw pictures to represent their description. They can dictate their description to an adult to record.

- **Early beginning writers** can draw pictures to represent the events of their description. They can then label them with single words or phrases and tell their description to an adult.

- **Late beginning and transitional writers** can write their description, adding illustrations to support their text.

Reading-Writing Workshop: Description
(Anthology p. 161)

T91

Choosing a Topic

1 **Tell children that they are going to write their own description** about one place or thing.

2 **Have children explore at least three ideas,** using the prompts below. Children can write or draw their ideas.

- When did you go on vacation? What was it like?
- What is your favorite animal?
- What can you tell about better than anyone else?

3 **Have children work with a partner** to decide which idea would be the best one to write about. Have children ask each other if they remember enough about the topic to describe it. Then review these tips with children.

Tips for Getting Started with a Topic

- Tell a partner more about your idea.
- What does your partner like best about your idea? What do you need to explain more clearly?

Organizing and Planning

Writing Traits

IDEAS Tell children that a good description paints a clear picture of what they are describing. Explain that they should include details about what they saw, felt, heard, tasted, or smelled.

1 **Display Chart/Transparency RWW6–2,** and model planning a description.

- Draw a simple sketch of a cat.
- Discuss with children the best title to tell about the picture.
- Help them list words that tell how the cat might look, sound, and feel.

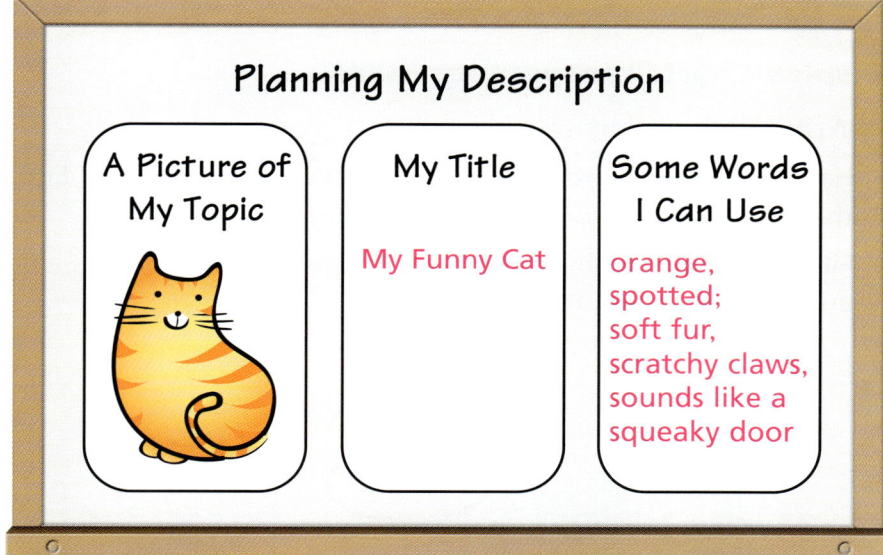

Planning My Description

A Picture of My Topic	My Title	Some Words I Can Use
	My Funny Cat	orange, spotted; soft fur, scratchy claws, sounds like a squeaky door

2 **Distribute copies of Chart/Transparency RWW6–2,** and have children plan their description. Encourage them to do the following.

- Draw what you want to describe.
- List words that tell about how it looks, feels, sounds, smells, or tastes.
- Put the words in an order that is easy to follow.
- Tell a partner about the picture, using only the list of words. Don't say what you are describing!
- Then ask your partner to guess what you drew. Tell more about your picture if your partner can't guess.

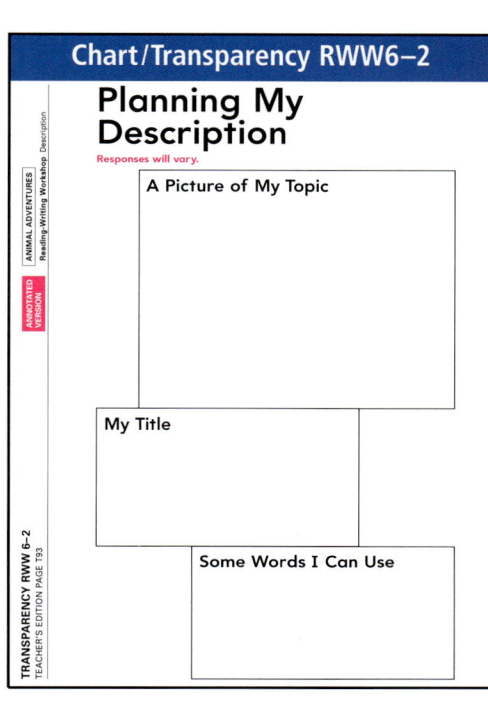

Chart/Transparency RWW6–2

Planning My Description

Responses will vary.

A Picture of My Topic

My Title

Some Words I Can Use

ANIMAL ADVENTURES   Reading-Writing Workshop: Description

ANNOTATED VERSION

TRANSPARENCY RWW 6–2
TEACHER'S EDITION PAGE T93

READING-WRITING WORKSHOP

Using Sensory Language

1 **Introduce sensory language.** Words that tell about what you heard, felt, tasted, smelled, and saw are called sensory language. These words help readers picture what you are describing.

2 **Help children recognize sensory language.** Now read the passage below, and ask children to clap when they hear a word that tells about the five senses.

> I caught the <u>cold, slippery</u> fish. It was <u>shiny and gray</u>. When I placed it on the pier, it <u>slapped</u> its tail all around. The sound it made was <u>thump-thumpity-thump</u>. As I took it home with me, I thought that <u>slimy</u> fish smelled <u>salty</u>.

3 **Display Chart/Transparency RWW6–3.**

- Write *fish* in the center circle.
- Have children brainstorm sensory words to describe fish. Encourage them to think of words for at least four senses.
- Fill in the word web as children provide sensory words. (Sample answers are shown below.)

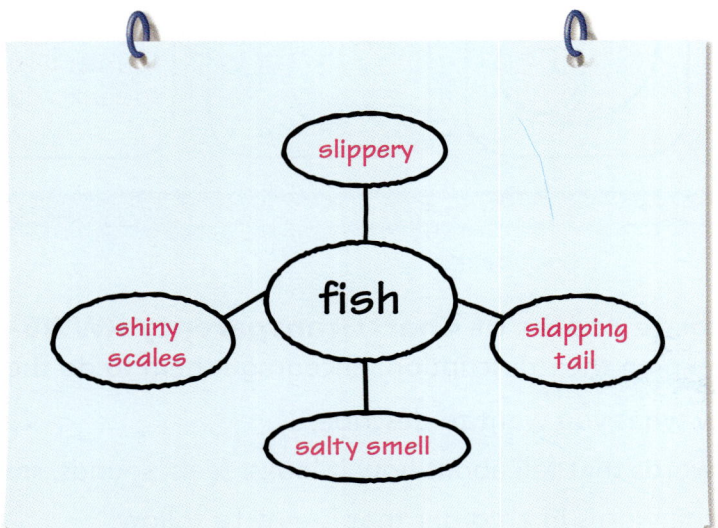

Chart/Transparency RWW6-3

Using Sensory Language

What do you want to tell about? Draw or write your ideas in the big circle. Then write describing words about it in the other circles.

Responses will vary.

TRANSPARENCY RWW 6-3
TEACHER'S EDITION PAGE T94

ANIMAL ADVENTURES
Reading-Writing Workshop Description

ANNOTATED VERSION

4 **Distribute copies of Chart/Transparency RWW6–3,** and have children fill it in for their topic. Have them use words to describe at least three senses.

Using Exact Words

Writing Traits

WORD CHOICE Explain to children that they should use exact naming words to help readers understand what they are describing.

- Write these sentences on separate lines, and read them aloud: *I got a cool gift. I got a scooter.*
- Ask, *Which sentence helps you understand exactly what the writer is describing?* (*I got a scooter.*)
- Ask them to identify the naming word in the sentence. (*scooter*)
- Explain that words such as *cool, pretty, good,* and *nice* don't help the reader understand what the writer meant to describe.

1 **Display Chart/Transparency RWW6–4.**

- Read the directions.
- Help children revise the sentences by choosing exact naming words.

2 **Explain that the words children choose** can also help them share how they feel about what they are describing.

- Write these sentences shown below on separate lines, and read them aloud.
- Ask, *Which sentence helps you understand exactly how the writer feels?* (*The ice cream is <u>the best in the world</u>.*)

The ice cream is <u>good</u>.

The ice cream is <u>the best in the world</u>.

3 **Have children draft their description.** Remind children to tell more about how things look, sound, taste, feel, or smell, using sensory words.

Chart/Transparency RWW6–4

Using Exact Words

Read each sentence. Choose an exact word from the box to replace each underlined word. Write the exact words.

hopped	soft
sour	yellow and white

1. Dan and Linn saw some <u>pretty</u> flowers.
   yellow and white
2. The dog's fur felt <u>nice</u>.
   soft
3. The pickle tasted <u>bad</u>.
   sour
4. A rabbit <u>went</u> behind the bushes.
   hopped

TRANSPARENCY RWW 6–4
TEACHER'S EDITION PAGE T95

ANIMAL ADVENTURES
Reading-Writing Workshop: Description

ANNOTATED VERSION

READING-WRITING WORKSHOP

Revising

1 **Have children evaluate and revise** their description, using **Practice Book** page 70. Remind them to write complete sentences with correct word order.

2 **Have writing conferences.**

- Group children with one or more classmates. Have each writer read their description to their partner or group.

- Encourage listeners to tell what they like about the description they heard.

- Ask listeners, *What questions do you have about this description? What else would you like to know?*

3 **Have children revise** any part of their description that they feel still needs work. Remind them to keep their listeners' comments and questions in mind.

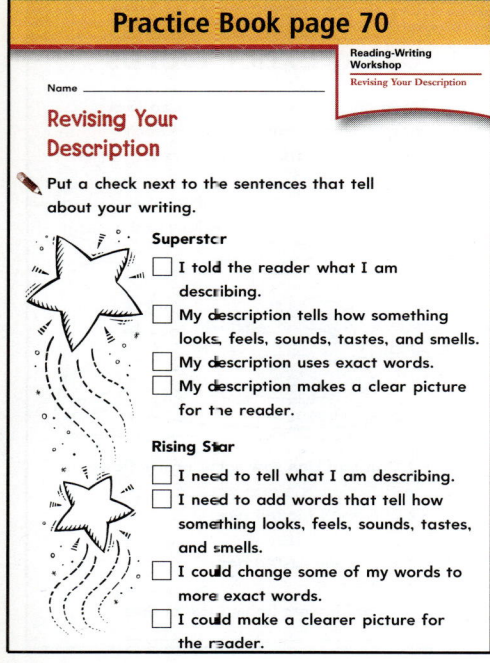

Practice Book page 70

Reading-Writing Workshop
Revising Your Description

Name _____

Revising Your Description

Put a check next to the sentences that tell about your writing.

Superstar

☐ I told the reader what I am describing.
☐ My description tells how something looks, feels, sounds, tastes, and smells.
☐ My description uses exact words.
☐ My description makes a clear picture for the reader.

Rising Star

☐ I need to tell what I am describing.
☐ I need to add words that tell how something looks, feels, sounds, tastes, and smells.
☐ I could change some of my words to more exact words.
☐ I could make a clearer picture for the reader.

Proofreading

Have children proofread their paper carefully to correct capitalization, punctuation, spelling, and usage. You might want to have children use the Word Wall or **Practice Book** pages 301–302 to help them check their spelling. Children can use the proofreading checklist and the proofreading marks on **Practice Book** page 327.

Improving Writing: Writing Sentences

Review the following with children.

- A sentence tells a complete thought.
- A sentence has two parts—the naming part and the action part.
- The naming part tells who or what the sentence is about.
- The action part tells what happens.

Emphasize to children that each sentence they write should name who or what and should tell what happens. Write the examples shown below on the board, and then discuss them.

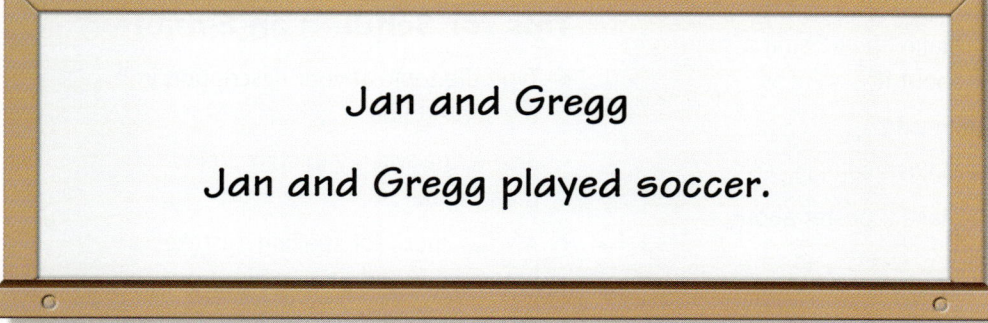

Jan and Gregg

Jan and Gregg played soccer.

- Have children identify the sentence. (*Jan and Gregg played soccer.*)
- Ask a volunteer to circle the naming part. (*Jan and Gregg*) Have another child underline the action part. (*played soccer*)
- Model crossing out the example that is not a sentence. (*Jan and Gregg*)

Assign **Practice Book** page 71. Then have children look at their description to make sure that they used complete sentences.

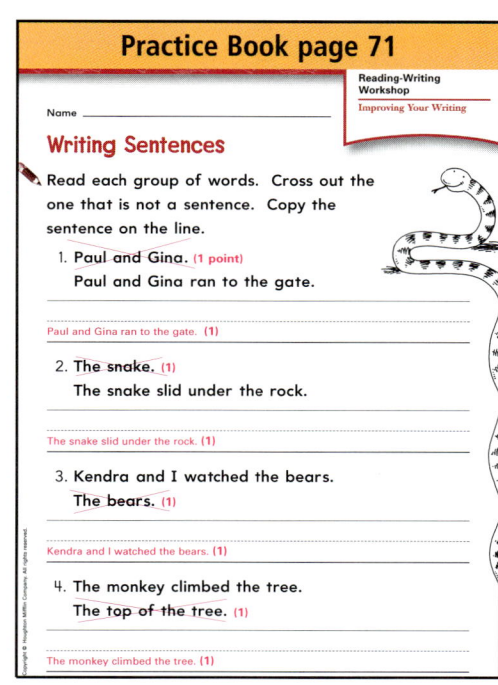

Practice Book page 71

Reading-Writing Workshop
Improving Your Writing

Name _____

Writing Sentences

Read each group of words. Cross out the one that is not a sentence. Copy the sentence on the line.

1. Paul and Gina. (1 point)
   Paul and Gina ran to the gate.

Paul and Gina ran to the gate. (1)

2. The snake. (1)
   The snake slid under the rock.

The snake slid under the rock. (1)

3. Kendra and I watched the bears.
   The bears. (1)

Kendra and I watched the bears. (1)

4. The monkey climbed the tree.
   The top of the tree. (1)

The monkey climbed the tree. (1)

Publishing

Have children publish their description.

- Discuss the Ideas for Sharing box below.
- Then ask children to decide how they want to publish their writing.
- Tell them to make a neat final copy of their description. Remind them to use good penmanship and to be sure that they have fixed all mistakes.

📁 Portfolio Opportunity

Save children's final copy of their description as an example of the development of their writing skills.

My Peppy Pal

Ideas for Sharing

Write It
- E-mail it to someone you know.
- Make a class book.

Say It
- Have classmates guess what you described.
- Make up and sing a song about it.

Show It
- Make a collage.
- Make a poster about it.

Tips for Sending an E-mail
- Type the topic of your description in the subject line.
- Skip a line when you start a new paragraph.
- Always check for spelling mistakes before you send an e-mail.

Evaluating

Have children discuss their responses to the Student Self-Assessment questions.

Evaluate children's writing, using the Writing Traits Scoring Rubric on the next page. The rubric is based on criteria in this workshop and reflects criteria children used in Revising Your Description on **Practice Book** page 70.

Monitoring Student Progress

Student Self-Assessment
- Did you use sensory words in your description?
- What exact naming words did you use?
- What parts of your description do you like best?
- What parts of your description would you change?

Description

Writing Traits Scoring Rubric

4

IDEAS The description is focused on a single, clear topic. Details tell what the writer saw, heard, tasted, smelled, or felt.

ORGANIZATION The details are presented in a clear order.

VOICE The writer clearly showed his or her feelings.

WORD CHOICE Sensory words help create a vivid picture. The words chosen say exactly what the writer means.

SENTENCE FLUENCY Sentences are complete.

CONVENTIONS There are almost no errors in spelling, punctuation, capitalization, or usage.

PRESENTATION The final copy is neat and legible with good word spacing.

3

IDEAS The description is focused on a topic. The writing needs more details that address at least three of the five senses.

ORGANIZATION The organization is generally clear.

VOICE The writer's feelings about the topic are sometimes unclear.

WORD CHOICE The writer could have used more sensory words. The words do not always tell what the writer is describing.

SENTENCE FLUENCY Some sentences are incomplete.

CONVENTIONS There are some mistakes, but they do not affect understanding.

PRESENTATION The final copy is messy in a few places but still legible.

2

IDEAS The description may not be clearly focused on a topic. Few details are included.

ORGANIZATION Many of the details are not ordered clearly.

VOICE It is often not clear how the writer felt about the topic.

WORD CHOICE Few sensory words are used. Vague words such as *nice* and *good* don't clearly say what the writer meant.

SENTENCE FLUENCY Many sentences are incomplete.

CONVENTIONS Mistakes sometimes make the paper hard to understand.

PRESENTATION The final copy is messy. It may be illegible in a few places.

1

IDEAS The description may not be focused. There are no details, or they are inappropriate.

ORGANIZATION Details are out of order. The description rambles.

VOICE It is not clear how the writer felt.

WORD CHOICE No sensory words are used. Word choice is vague or uninteresting. It may be confusing.

SENTENCE FLUENCY Most sentences are incomplete.

CONVENTIONS Many mistakes make the paper hard to understand.

PRESENTATION The final copy is messy. It may be illegible in many places.

Lesson Overview

Literature

EEK!
There's a Mouse in the House

WONG HERBERT YEE

Selection Summary

Funny animals make lots of trouble when a young girl calls them in to get rid of a mouse in the house.

---

1 ## Decodable Text

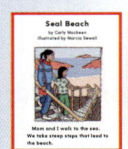  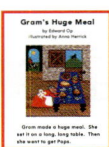

Phonics Library

- *Seal Beach*
- *Pete and Peach*
- *Gram's Huge Meal*

2 ## Background and Vocabulary

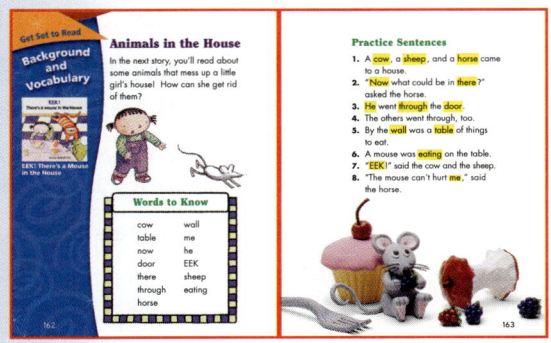

3 ## Main Selection

 *EEK! There's a Mouse in the House*
Genre: Fantasy

4 ## Math Link

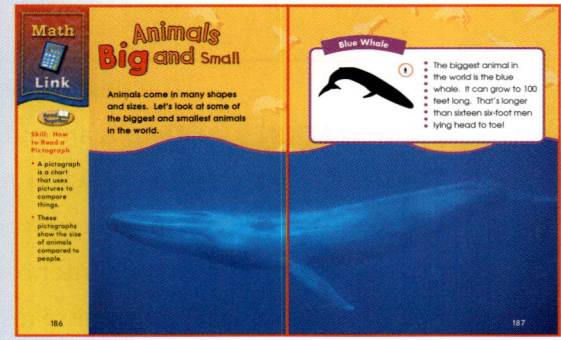

T100

Instructional Support

Planning and Practice

- Planning and classroom management
- Reading and skill instruction
- Plans and activities for reaching all learners

- Newsletters
- Observation Checklists
- Theme Activity Masters
- Alternative Weekly Tests

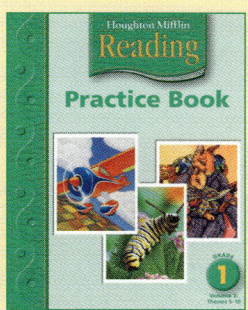

- Independent practice for skills, Level 1.3

- Decodable Text, Books 58–61, Review Books 51–61

- Charts/Transparencies
- Strategy Posters
- Blackline Masters

Reaching All Learners

 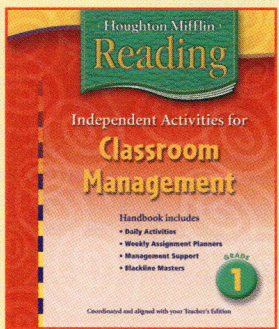

Coordinated lessons, activities, and projects for additional reading instruction

For
- Classroom Teacher
- Extended Day
- Pull Out
- Resource Teacher
- Reading Specialist

Technology

Audio Selection

EEK! There's a Mouse in the House

Get Set for Reading CD-ROM
- Background building
- Vocabulary support
- Selection Summary in English and Spanish

Accelerated Reader®

Practice quiz for the selection

www.eduplace.com

Log on to Education Place for more activities related to the selection, including vocabulary support—

e • **Glossary**
e • **WordGame**

Leveled Books for Reaching All Learners

Leveled Readers and Leveled Practice

- Independent reading for building fluency
- Topic, comprehension strategy, and vocabulary linked to main selection
- Lessons in Teacher's Edition, pages T166–T169
- Leveled practice for every book

Technology

Leveled Readers
Available on CD

Book Adventure®
Practice quizzes for the Leveled Theme Paperbacks

www.bookadventure.org

● **BELOW LEVEL**

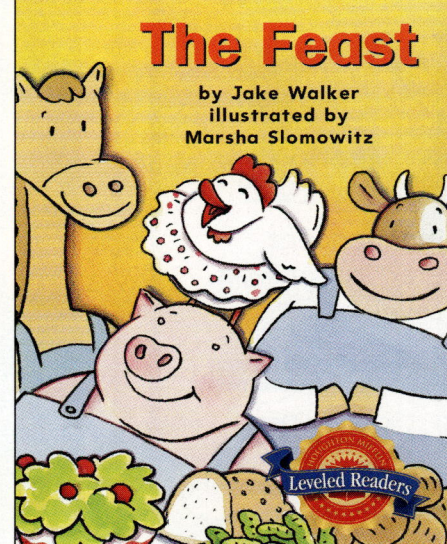

The Feast
by Jake Walker
illustrated by Marsha Slomowitz

Leveled Readers

▲ **ON LEVEL**

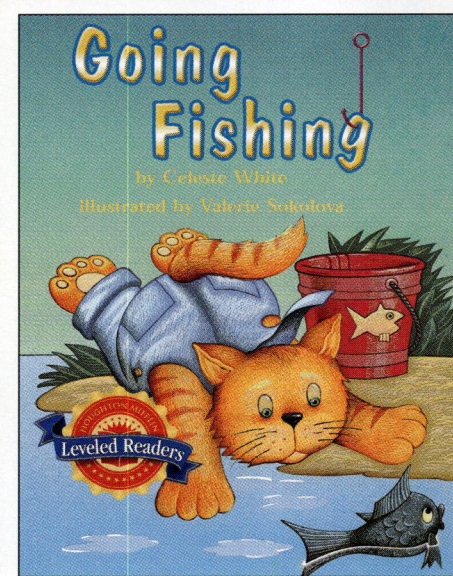

Going Fishing
by Celeste White
illustrated by Valerie Sokolova

Leveled Readers

● **Below Level Practice**

Name _____

The Feast
Vocabulary

Vocabulary

Read the story. Circle the words in it that are from the box.

The farmer gives Pig cold meat and beans for lunch. The food looks so good! Hen hops into the pig's pen. Ox and Cow jump in too. They clap and dance. They eat Pig's food. What a feast that is!

Story Words
feast
farmer
dance
cold

Draw a picture to go with the story.

Possible response: Children may draw a picture of a hen, ox, and cow clapping, dancing, or eating the pig's food inside a pigpen.

▲ **On Level Practice**

Name _____

Going Fishing
Vocabulary

Vocabulary

Read the story and circle the words in it that are from the box. Draw a picture to go with the story.

Who wants to go fishing?
We can go to the creek.
We can take my pole and some string.
Last week I walked home with five fish!

Story Words
walked
fishing
string
creek
take
pole

Children should draw something related to the story above.

● **Below Level Practice**

The Feast
Comprehension Skill
Noting Details

Name _____

Comprehension

Read each sentence. Find what the sentence tells you to and color it.

Find the dancing pig.
Children will color the dancing pig.

Find the sleeping hen.
Children will color the sleeping hen.

Find the cow eating a bean.
Children will color the cow eating a bean.

▲ **On Level Practice**

Going Fishing
Comprehension Skill
Noting Details

Name _____

Comprehension

Pick two animals from Going Fishing. Then write or draw in the chart to tell more about them. Possible answers

	Animal 1	Animal 2
What is the animal?	cat	mouse
What is its name?	Pete	Rose
What does it do?	fishes, gets wet, breaks pants strap	makes a fishing pole

■ ABOVE LEVEL

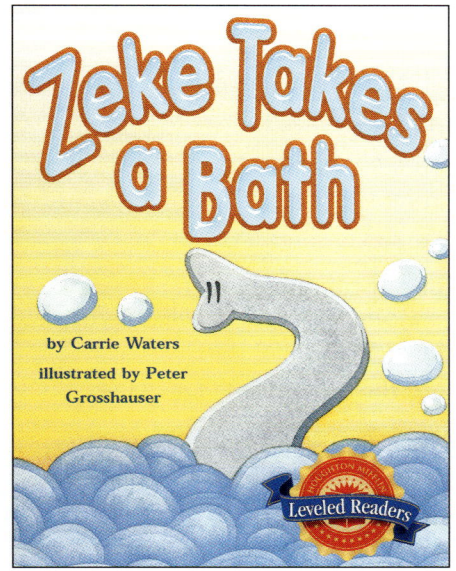

Zeke Takes a Bath

by Carrie Waters
illustrated by Peter Grosshauser

Leveled Readers

■ Above Level Practice

Name _____

Vocabulary

✏ Write words from the box to complete the sentences.

Story Words
elephant
bathtub
ducklings
stuck
free
afraid

1. Zeke is an ___elephant___
2. Baby ducks are ___ducklings___
3. Get into the ___bathtub___ to get clean.
4. I got ___stuck___ in the mud.
5. The animals tried to set Zeke ___free___
6. He was ___afraid___ of a mouse.

■ Above Level Practice

Name _____

Comprehension

✏ Look carefully at the picture. Circle two things that are wrong and write about them.

1. Probable answer: The pig has duck feet.

2. Probable answer: The horse has horns.

◆ LANGUAGE SUPPORT

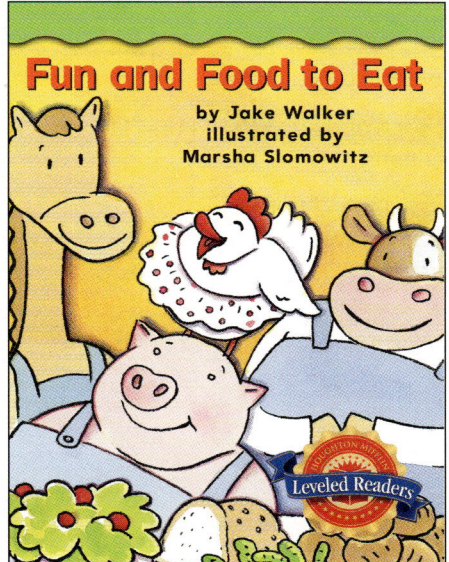

Fun and Food to Eat

by Jake Walker
illustrated by Marsha Slomowitz

Leveled Readers

◆ Language Support Practice

Name _____

Build Background

✏ Put food on the table!
Draw pictures of 4 foods you like to eat.
Drawings will vary.

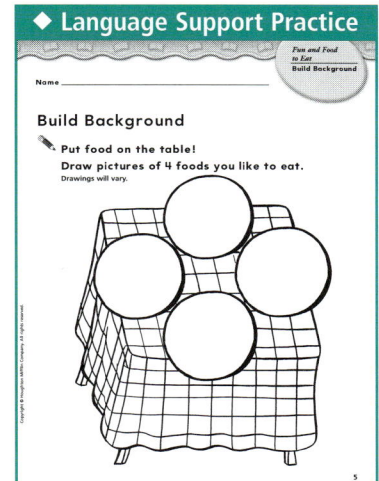

◆ Language Support Practice

Name _____

Story Words

✏ Use a word from the box to complete each sentence. There are some picture clues.

Story Words
animals
cold
food
hungry
table

1. The ___animals___ live on the farm.
2. The animals are outside. They are ___cold___
3. They want to eat. They are ___hungry___
4. The animals want to eat the ___food___
5. The food is on the ___table___

Leveled Books

- Extended independent reading in theme-related paperbacks
- Lessons in Teacher's Edition, pages R6–R8

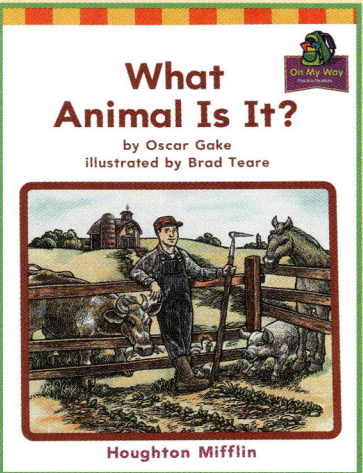

On My Way

What Animal Is It?

by Oscar Gake
illustrated by Brad Teare

Houghton Mifflin

Below Level

Suggested Books

EVERY AUTUMN COMES THE BEAR

JIM ARNOSKY

On Level

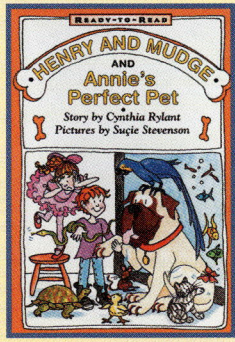

READY-TO-READ

HENRY AND MUDGE AND **Annie's Perfect Pet**

Story by Cynthia Rylant
Pictures by Suçie Stevenson

Above Level

Lesson Overview **T103**

Daily Lesson Plans

Technology
Lesson Planner CD-ROM allows you to customize the chart below to develop your own lesson plans.

T Skill tested on Integrated Theme Test and/or Theme Skills Test

 80–90 minutes

Learning to Read

Phonemic Awareness
Phonics
Comprehension

EEK!
There's a Mouse in the House
WONG HERBERT YEE

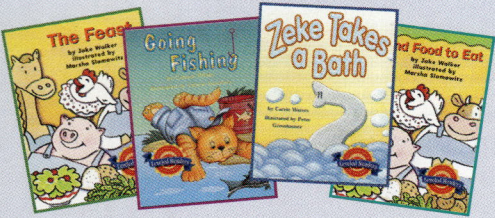

Leveled Readers
• Fluency Practice
• Independent Reading

DAY 1

Seal Beach
by Carly Mocksen
illustrated by Marcia Sewall

Mom and I walk to the sea. We take steep steps that lead to the beach. 17

Daily Routines, T110–T111
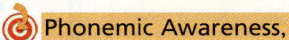
Phonics, High-Frequency Words,
🔥 Phonemic Awareness,
Independent Reading, Writing

🔥 **Listening Comprehension,** T112–T113
Tiger and Anansi

🔥 **Phonics,** T114–T116
Blending Long e Words (CV, CVCe) **T**
Vowel Pairs *ee, ea* **T**

🔥 **Reading Decodable Text,** T117–T119
Seal Beach

Leveled Readers
The Feast
Going Fishing
Zeke Takes a Bath
Fun and Food to Eat

Lessons and Leveled Practice, T166–T169

DAY 2

EEK!
There's a Mouse in the House
WONG HERBERT YEE

Daily Routines, T122–T123

Phonics, High-Frequency Words,
🔥 Phonemic Awareness,
Independent Reading, Writing

🔥 **High-Frequency Words,** T124–T125
cow, door, horse, now, table, there, through, wall **T**

Building Background, T126

🔥 **Story Vocabulary,** T127
barn, dancing, elephant, laying, marched, mercy, mouse, tangled

Reading the Selection, T128–T139

🔥 **Comprehension Strategy,** T128
Question

🔥 **Comprehension Skill,** T128
Noting Details **T**

Leveled Readers
The Feast
Going Fishing
Zeke Takes a Bath
Fun and Food to Eat

Lessons and Leveled Practice, T166–T169

 20–30 minutes

Word Work

Spelling
Vocabulary and
High-Frequency Words

DAY 1 (Word Work)

Spelling, T120
Words with Long e (e, ee, ea) **T**

🔥 **Vocabulary,** T120
Word Wall: Spelling Pattern -eat

DAY 2 (Word Work)

Spelling, T140
Practice: Words with Long e (e, ee, ea) **T**

🔥 **Vocabulary,** T140
Review: High-Frequency Words **T**

 20–30 minutes

Writing and Oral Language

Writing
Grammar
Listening/Speaking/Viewing

DAY 1 (Writing and Oral Language)

Daily Language Practice
1. Did you have fun.
   (Did you have fun?)

✏️ **Shared Writing,** T121
A Class Story

✏️ **Listening and Speaking,** T121
Compare and Contrast

DAY 2 (Writing and Oral Language)

Daily Language Practice
2. i can seee your friend
   (I can see your friend.)

✏️ **Interactive Writing,** T141
A Class Story

Target Skills of the Week

Phonemic Awarenesss	Segment Phonemes; Count Sounds in Words
Phonics	Blending Long e Words (CV, CVCe); Vowel Pairs *ee*, *ea*
Comprehension	Noting Details, Question
Vocabulary	High-Frequency Words; Rhyming Words; Expressions of Surprise
Fluency	Leveled Readers; Decodable Text: Phonics Library

DAY 3

Daily Routines, T142–T143

Phonics, High-Frequency Words,
 Phonemic Awareness,
Independent Reading, Writing

Comprehension Check, T144

Responding, T144

Comprehension Skill, T146–T147
Noting Details **T**

EEK! There's a Mouse in the House
WONG HERBERT YEE

Leveled Readers
The Feast
Going Fishing
Zeke Takes a Bath
Fun and Food to Eat

Lessons and Leveled Practice, T166–T169

Spelling, T148
Practice: Words with Long e (*e*, *ee*, *ea*) **T**

Vocabulary, T148
Rhyming Words

Daily Language Practice
3. The cat has black feat?
    (The cat has black **feet**.)

Writing: Responding, T145
Write a List

Grammar, T149
Naming Words for Places and Things **T**

DAY 4

Daily Routines, T150–T151

Phonics, High-Frequency Words,
 Phonemic Awareness,
Independent Reading, Writing

Reading the Math Link, T152–T153

Comprehension:
How to Read a Pictograph, T152
Visual Literacy: Showing with Words, T153

Phonics Review, T154–T155
Long o (CV, CVCe) and Long u (CVCe)
Final Clusters *ft, lk, nt*

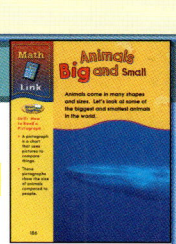

Leveled Readers
The Feast
Going Fishing
Zeke Takes a Bath
Fun and Food to Eat

Lessons and Leveled Practice, T166–T169

Spelling, T156
Practice: Words with Long e (*e*, *ee*, *ea*) **T**

Vocabulary, T156
Expressions of Surprise

Daily Language Practice
4. Hee has two cats
    (**He** has two cats.)

Independent Writing, T157
Answering a Comprehension Question **T**

DAY 5

Daily Routines, T158–T159

Phonics, High-Frequency Words,
 Phonemic Awareness,
Independent Reading, Writing

Comprehension: Rereading for Understanding
(Noting Details **T**) T160

Rereading for Fluency, T160

Reading Decodable Text,
T161–T163
Gram's Huge Meal
End-of-the-Week Skills Check

Gram's Huge Meal
by Edward Op
illustrated by Anna Herrick

Gram made a huge meal. She set it on a long, long table. Then she went to get Pops.

EEK! There's a Mouse in the House
WONG HERBERT YEE

Leveled Readers
The Feast
Going Fishing
Zeke Takes a Bath
Fun and Food to Eat

Lessons and Leveled Practice, T166–T169

Spelling, T164
Test: Words with Long e (*e*, *ee*, *ea*) **T**

Vocabulary, T164
Review: High-Frequency Words

Daily Language Practice
5. Will she et that
    (Will she **eat** that?)

Independent Writing, T165
Journal Entry

Grammar Review, T165
Naming Words for Places and Things **T**

Viewing, T165
Retelling

Managing Flexible Groups

Leveled Instruction and Leveled Practice

	DAY 1	**DAY 2**
WHOLE CLASS	• Daily Routines (TE pp. T110–T111) • Teacher Read Aloud (TE pp. T112–T113) • Phonics (TE pp. T114–T116)	• Daily Routines (TE pp. T122–T123) • High-Frequency Words (TE pp. T124–T125) • Get Set to Read, Strategy and Skill, Purpose Setting (TE pp. T126–T129) *After Reading at Small Group Time* • Wrapping Up (TE p. T139); Comprehension Preview (TE p. T136)
SMALL GROUPS		
Extra Support	**TEACHER-LED** • Phonics Library: *Seal Beach* (TE pp. T117–T119) • Selected I Love Reading Books: 58–61	**TEACHER-LED** • Anthology selection (TE pp. T128–T139) • Phonics Library: *Pete and Peach* (TE p. T125) ――――――――――― **Partner or Individual Reading** • Read with audio CD of Anthology selection. • **Fluency Practice** Reread Phonics Library: *Seal Beach* OR I Love Reading Books: 58–61.
On Level	**TEACHER-LED** • Phonics Library: *Seal Beach* (TE pp. T117–T119)	**TEACHER-LED** • Anthology selection (TE pp. T128–T139) • Phonics Library: *Pete and Peach* (TE p. T125) • **Fluency Practice** Reread Phonics Library: *Seal Beach* (TE pp. T117–T119) ✔ OR begin Leveled Reader: On Level (TE p. T167).
Challenge	**Partner or Individual Reading** • Phonics Library: *Seal Beach* • **Fluency Practice** Reread Little Big Book *Two's Company* OR book from Leveled Bibliography.	**Partner or Individual Reading** • Anthology selection • Phonics Library: *Pete and Peach* • **Fluency Practice** Reread Phonics Library: *Seal Beach*
English Language Learners	**TEACHER-LED** • Phonics Library: *Seal Beach* (TE pp. T117–T119) • Selected I Love Reading Books: 58–61	**TEACHER-LED** • Phonics Library: *Pete and Peach* (TE p. T125) • **Fluency Practice** Reread Phonics Library: *Seal Beach* (TE pp. T117–T119) ✔ ――――――――――― **Partner or Individual Reading** • Read with audio CD of Anthology selection.

Independent Activities

• Get Set for Reading CD-ROM or audio CD of Anthology selection
• Journals: selection notes, questions
• Complete, review **Practice Book** (pp. 72–78, 79–80) and **Leveled Reader Practice Blackline Masters** (TE pp. T166–T169).

✔ Opportunity to informally assess oral reading rate.

- Daily Routines (TE pp. T142–T143)

After Reading at Small Group Time
- Responding (TE p. T144)
- Comprehension lesson (TE pp. T146–T147)

- Daily Routines (TE pp. T150–T151)
- Math Link (TE pp. T152–T153)
- Phonics Review (TE pp. T154–T155)

- Daily Routines (TE pp. T158–T159)
- Rereading for Understanding (TE p. T160)
- Responding: Select from activities (TE p. T145)

TEACHER-LED
- Read Anthology selection aloud to answer Guiding Comprehension. (TE pp. T128–T139)
- **Fluency Practice** Reread Phonics Library: *Pete and Peach* OR selected I Love Reading Books: 58–61. ✔

TEACHER-LED
- Read On My Way Practice Reader. (TE p. R6)
- Begin Leveled Reader: Below Level (TE p. T166) OR book from Leveled Bibliography.
- **Fluency Practice** Reread Phonics Library: *Seal Beach, Pete and Peach,* ✔ OR selected I Love Reading Review Books: 58–61.

TEACHER-LED
- Phonics Library: *Gram's Huge Meal* (TE pp. T161–T163)
- Complete Leveled Reader: Below Level (TE p. T166)
- **Fluency Practice** Reread On My Way Practice Reader (TE p. R6), Phonics Library books, OR selected I Love Reading Review Books: 58–61. ✔

Individual Reading
- Reread with audio CD of Anthology selection.
- **Fluency Practice** Reread Phonics Library: *Pete and Peach* OR complete Leveled Reader: On Level.

Partner Reading
- Reread Anthology selection, partners alternating pages.
- **Fluency Practice** Reread Phonics Library: *Seal Beach, Pete and Peach,* OR Leveled Reader: On Level (TE p. T167).

TEACHER-LED
- Phonics Library: *Gram's Huge Meal* (T161–T163) AND reread Link. (T152–T153)
- **Fluency Practice** Reread Phonics Library, Anthology, OR Leveled Reader. ✔

Partner or Individual Reading
- Suggested Trade Book (TE p. R7) or another book from Leveled Bibliography.

TEACHER-LED
- Read aloud from Anthology to answer Guiding Comprehension. (T128–T139) ✔

Partner or Individual Reading
- Leveled Reader (TE p. T168) OR book from Bibliography

TEACHER-LED
- **Fluency Practice** Reread Anthology selection, Link, OR Phonics Library books. ✔

Partner or Individual Reading
- Begin book from Leveled Bibliography (TE p. R8).
- Reread Little Big Book *Two's Company.*

Individual Reading
- Phonics Library: *Gram's Huge Meal*
- Complete Suggested Trade Book (R8) or another book from Bibliography.
- **Fluency Practice** Reread Anthology selection and Link, Little Big Book, Above Level Theme Paperback, OR Leveled Reader.

TEACHER-LED
- Reread Anthology selection, first half. (TE pp. T128–T133)

Partner or Individual Reading
- Reread Phonics Library: *Pete and Peach.*
- Selected I Love Reading Books: 58–61

TEACHER-LED
- Reread Anthology sel., last half. (T134–T139)
- Begin Leveled Reader: Language Support (T169) OR On My Way Practice Reader (R6).

Individual Reading
- **Fluency Practice** Phonics Library: *Seal Beach, Pete and Peach*

TEACHER-LED
- Phonics Library: *Gram's Huge Meal* (TE pp. T161–T163)
- Complete Leveled Reader: Language Support (T169) OR On My Way Practice Reader (R6).
- **Fluency Practice** Reread week's Phonics Library books, Anthology selection, OR selected I Love Reading Books: 58–61. ✔

- Reread familiar selections.
- Read trade book from Leveled Bibliography (TE pp. T6–T7).
- Responding activities (TE pp. T144–T145)
- Activities related to *EEK! There's a Mouse in the House* at Education Place: www.eduplace.com

Turn the page for more independent activities. ➡

Independent Activities

Assign these activities while you work with small groups.

Differentiated Instruction for Small Groups

- **Handbook for English Language Learners,** pp. 188–197

- **Extra Support Handbook,** pp. 184–193

Independent Activities

- Daily Routines, pp. T111, T123, T143, T151, T159

- Challenge/Extension Activities, pp. R17, R23, R29

- **Classroom Management Handbook,** pp. 130–137

- **Challenge Handbook,** pp. 68–69

Look for more independent activities in the Classroom Management Kit.

Phonics Center

Find a Rhyme

👥 Pairs	🕐 20 minutes
Objective	Match rhyming words.
Materials	Teacher's Resource Blackline Master 80, scissors

Have children play a matching game with rhyming words.

- Tell children to cut out word cards from **Blackline Master 80.**

- Partners match word cards that rhyme.

- If children finish early, they can make more of their own rhyming word cards.

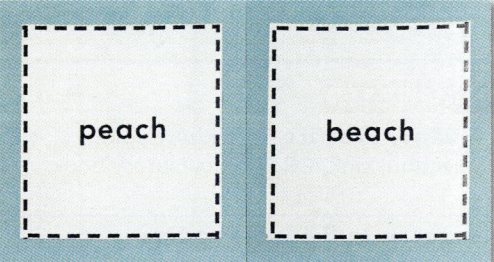

Art Center

EEK! Drawings

👤 Singles	🕐 25 minutes
Objective	Create and label a drawing.
Materials	paper, crayons

Remind children of the story *EEK! There's a Mouse in the House.*

- Have children think of other things that would surprise someone and make them say, "EEK!"

- Tell children to choose one of these things to draw.

- Children can label their drawings *EEK!*

Consider copying and laminating these activities for use in centers.

Writing Center

Mouse's Letter

👤 Singles	🕐 30 minutes
Objective	Write a letter.
Materials	writing paper, pencil

Children can write a letter from Mouse, telling Elephant why it should not be afraid of a mouse. You might provide a letter model for children to follow.

- Letters should begin, "Dear Elephant."
- Children write a few sentences from Mouse, telling Elephant why it should not be afraid.
- Letters should end, "Sincerely, Mouse."

Dear Elephant,
I am a nice mouse. I am small and you are big. You should not be afraid of me.
                    Sincerely,
                    Mouse

Science Center

Elephant Study Center

👥 Groups	🕐 45 minutes
Objective	Find information about elephants.
Materials	books and magazines about elephants

Put books, magazines, or encyclopedias with information about elephants in the Science Center. Have three or four children work together to use the books to answer the following questions:

- How big are elephants?
- Where do elephants live?
- What do elephants eat?
- Are elephants really afraid of mice?

Social Studies Center

Animals at Home

👤 Pairs	🕐 20 minutes
Objective	Categorize animals according to where they usually live.
Materials	animal word cards, large paper folded into thirds

Create a set of word cards for the animals from *EEK! There's a Mouse in the House*. The word cards should say: *mouse, cat, dog, pig, cow, sheep, hen, horse, elephant*.

- Partners divide a large sheet of paper into thirds and label the sections *house*, *farm*, and *wild*.
- Children sort the animal word cards by placing them in the category where that animal usually lives.

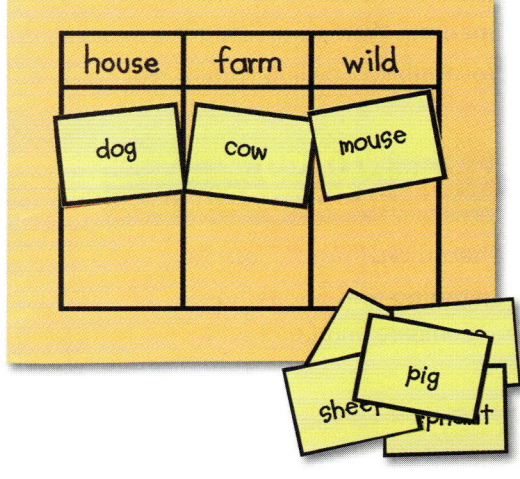

Day at a Glance
pages T110–T121

Learning to Read

Teacher Read Aloud
Tiger and Anansi

Phonics Instruction
Blending Long *e* Words
(CV, CVC*e*)
Vowel Pairs *ee, ea*

Reading Decodable Text
Seal Beach

....

Leveled Readers, *T166–T169*
- ● *The Feast*
- ▲ *Going Fishing*
- ■ *Zeke Takes a Bath*
- ◆ *Fun and Food to Eat*

Word Work

Spelling: Words with Long *e*
Vocabulary: Spelling Pattern *-eat*

Writing & Oral Language

Shared Writing: A Class Story
Listening and Speaking:
Compare and Contrast

Daily Routines

Daily Message

Review phonics and language skills. Point to each word as you read aloud the Daily Message.

> Good Morning, Children!
>
> My friends Maria, Bill, Deb, and Tim went to the zoo. They saw elephants, birds, seals, and other animals. Have you ever been to the zoo?

Have children

- respond to the question;
- circle words that mean more than one; (*friends, elephants, birds, seals, animals*)
- list four naming words;
- find the following high-frequency words: *Good, Morning, Children, My, friends, birds, other,* and *animals.*

Word Wall

High-Frequency Word Review Briefly review these and other high-frequency words daily. Have children practice reading, chanting, spelling, and writing them.

morning	by	show
found	out	climb
shout		

Blackline Master for these Word Wall Cards appears on page R33.

Daily Phonemic Awareness

Blending and Segmenting Phonemes: Clap the Sounds

- One at a time, say the words *cheese, please, eat, so, treat,* and *beach.*

- Ask children to say the separate sounds. Examples: /ch/ /ē/ /z/ for *cheese*; /s/ /ō/ for *so.*

- Have children clap once for each sound they say and tell you how many times they clapped. Example: After clapping three times for *cheese,* children should say "Three!"

Daily Language Practice

Grammar Skill: Which Kind of Sentence?
Write the sentence, read it to children, and have them tell you how to correct it.

Did you have fun.

(Did you have fun?)

Daily Writing Prompt

Have children respond to the prompt below or write on self-selected topics. Remind children to write complete sentences, beginning with a capital letter and ending with a punctuation mark.

- **Draw and write about a desert animal.**

A snake lives in the desert. It crawls through sand. It looks for food. It hides from any enemies.

Daily Independent Reading

To increase children's reading fluency, provide a variety of theme-related books for them to read. Here are some suggestions.

- Leveled Bibliography, pages T6–T7

Choose books from this list for children to read, outside class, for at least twenty minutes a day.

- Anthology: *The Sleeping Pig*

- Phonics Library: *Duke's Gift, Legs Gets His Lunch,* and *The Nest*

- Book Boxes

The Nest
by Peri Jones
illustrated by Marcia Sewall

Jude found this nest in a big plant by his home. Jude left it and went to get Rose.

13

Daily Routines T111

Listening Comprehension

Tiger and Anansi

OBJECTIVES
- Listen to note important story details.

Building Background

Tell children that many stories about Anansi the spider are told in different parts of the world. This version comes from Jamaica. Explain that in the stories, clever Anansi often outsmarts others.

Fluency Modeling

Explain that as you read the story, you will model how to read with expression and feeling.

Noting Details

Explain that listening carefully to important details will help children remember the story.

Guiding Comprehension

1. **NOTING DETAILS** Who do the animals think is the weakest in the forest at the beginning of the story? (Anansi)

2. **NOTING DETAILS** What does Anansi do to trick Snake? (He gets Snake to lie along a tree and then ties Snake to the tree.)

Once upon a time, Tiger was king of the forest because he was the strongest. When Tiger whispered, even the trees listened. When Tiger yelled, the trees shook with fear. Anansi the spider was the weakest. When he whispered, no one listened. When he yelled, everyone laughed.

One day Anansi said to Tiger, "The animals know that you are the strongest. That is why so many things are named after you. There are Tiger lilies, Tiger moths, and Tiger stories. I am the weakest, so nothing is named after me. Tiger, can the stories be named after me?"

Tiger especially liked these stories and did not want them to be named after Anansi. So he decided to play a trick on Anansi. "If you catch Snake and bring him to me alive, then the stories will be named after you."

"I will try my best," said Anansi, and Tiger laughed to himself because he knew that Anansi was too weak to capture Snake.

Anansi walked to the river and greeted Snake. "You know, Snake, every night the animals gather to discuss who is the strongest, the weakest, and the longest."

"Certainly, I'm the longest," Snake said proudly.

"Even longer than that bamboo tree?" asked Anansi doubtfully, as Snake stretched himself out so that Anansi could see just how long he was.

"Go bring the tree here," snapped Snake, "and you will see who is longer."

Anansi fetched the tree and snake slithered onto it, stretching himself from the bottom of the tree to its tip. "Really, Snake, you must stop moving your tail. I cannot measure properly," said Anansi.

"Then tie me to the bamboo! You will see that I am longer!" said Snake as he stretched to make sure his head reached beyond the tip of the bamboo. As Snake stretched, Anansi tied him securely to the tree.

Anansi then brought Snake, tree and all, to Tiger. When Tiger saw how clever Anansi had been, he agreed that the stories would be called Anansi stories.

OBJECTIVES

- Segment phonemes and count sounds.
- Associate the long *e* sound, /ē/, with the CV and CVC*e* patterns.
- Blend and read words with long *e* (CV, CVC*e*).

Target Skill Trace

Teach	pp. T114–T115
Reteach	p. R16
Review	p. T226
See	*Handbook for English Language Learners,* p. 189; *Extra Support Handbook,* p. 184

Materials

- Large Sound/Spelling Card *eagle*
- Blending Routines Card 1
- Large Letter Cards *b, e, h, m, s, w*

INSTRUCTION

PHONICS: Blending Long *e* Words (CV, CVC*e*)

❶ Phonemic Awareness Warm-Up

Model how to segment phonemes and count sounds.

- Segment *she:* /sh//ē/. Then clap and count the sounds in *she.* (2)
- Have children repeat each of the following words, say its sounds, and clap and count the sounds: *we* (/w//ē/, 2), *these* (/th//ē//z/, 3), *me* (/m//ē/, 2), *steep* (/s/ /t//ē//p/, 4), *clean* (/k//l//ē//n/, 4), *Steve* (/s//t//ē//v/, 4), *peach* (/p//ē//ch/, 3), *teeth* (/t//ē//th/, 3), *meet* (/m//ē//t/, 3), *wheat* (/hw//ē//t/, 3).

❷ Teach Phonics

Connect sounds to letters: *e*, /ē/.

- Display **Large Sound/Spelling Card** *eagle.* Have children name the picture. Point to the letter *e*. Explain that the /ē/ sound at the beginning of *eagle* is called the long *e* sound. Have children say /ēēē/ as you point to the letter.
- Write *he* and read it aloud, elongating the long *e* sound. Explain that the letter *e* stands for the long *e* sound at the end of some words. Point to the *e* pattern on the back of **Large Sound/ Spelling Card** *eagle.*
- Write *these* and read it aloud. Ask children what pattern they recognize. (vowel-consonant-*e*) Underline *ese*. Remind children that with this pattern, the first vowel usually has a long sound, and the final *e* is silent.

Model how to blend long *e* words with the CV pattern.

- Place **Large Letter Cards** *b* and *e* together. Using **Blending Routine 1,** model how to blend *be*. Repeat with *she, we, he, me.*

Model how to blend long e words with the CVCe pattern.

- Write *pet* and have children blend it. Have them say the sound for *e* in *pet*. Remind them that /ĕ/ is called the short *e* sound.

- Change the lowercase *p* to a capital *P* and add *e* to make *Pete*, and read the word. Point out the *e*-consonant-*e* pattern. Explain that in words with this pattern, the first *e* stands for the long *e* sound, and the final *e* is silent. Point to the e_e pattern on the back of **Large Sound/Spelling Card** *eagle*.

- Model how to blend *these, Steve*.

❸ Guided Practice

Check understanding. Write *me, we, theme, these, Eve, she, he, be, Pete, Steve*. Have children blend and read each word as you point to the letters.

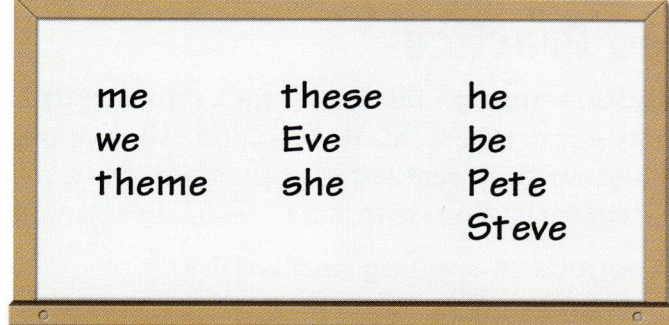

Connect sounds to spelling and writing.

- Say *me*. Ask children to think about the sounds and then write the word.

- Have a child build *me* with **Large Letter Cards** along the board ledge so children can check their work.

- Repeat with *be, he, we, she*.

- Tell children that you will say a word with the *e*-consonant-*e* pattern, and they are to write the word. Say *these*. Have children repeat *these* and then write it.

- Write *these* on the board, and have children check their work.

- Repeat with *Steve, theme,* and the sentence *Pete and Eve are here*.

❹ Apply

Assign Practice Book pages 72–73.

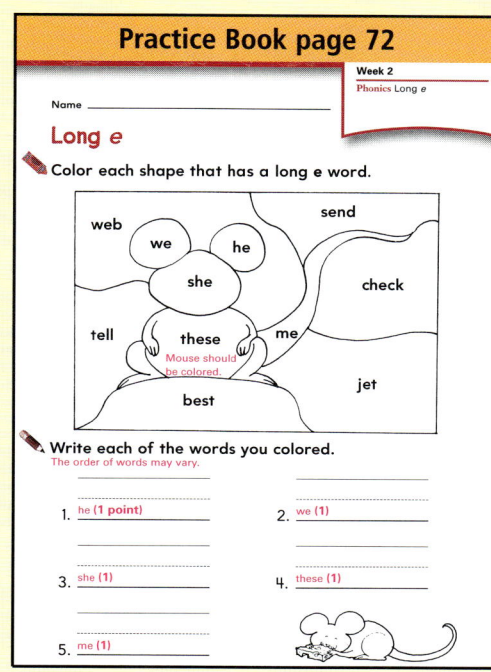

Practice Book page 72

Week 2
Phonics Long *e*

Name _____

Long *e*

Color each shape that has a long e word.

Write each of the words you colored.
The order of words may vary.

1. he **(1 point)**   2. we **(1)**

3. she **(1)**   4. these **(1)**

5. me **(1)**

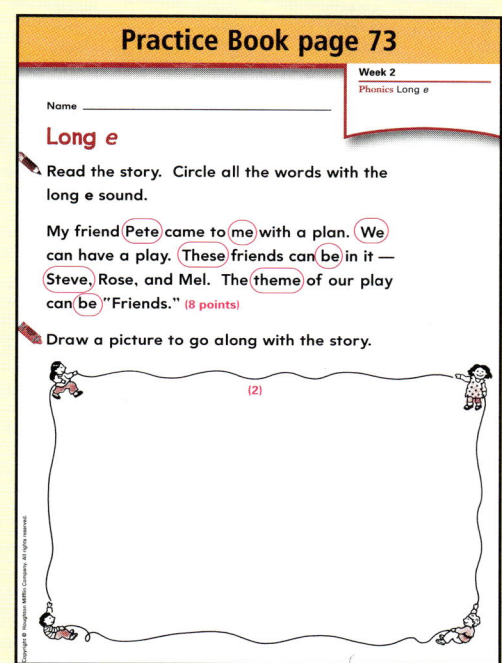

Practice Book page 73

Week 2
Phonics Long *e*

Name _____

Long *e*

Read the story. Circle all the words with the long e sound.

My friend Pete came to me with a plan. We can have a play. These friends can be in it — Steve, Rose, and Mel. The theme of our play can be "Friends." **(8 points)**

Draw a picture to go along with the story.
(2)

Monitoring Student Progress

If . . .	Then . . .
children score 11 or below on **Practice Book** pages 72–73,	use the Reteaching lesson on Teacher's Edition page R16.
children have met the lesson objectives,	use the Challenge/ Extension activities on Teacher's Edition page R17.

OBJECTIVES

- Associate the long *e* sound, /ē/, with vowel pairs *ee, ea.*
- Blend and read words with vowel pairs *ee, ea.*

Target Skill Trace

Teach	p. T116
Reteach	p. R16
Review	p. T227
See	*Handbook for English Language Learners,* p. 195; *Extra Support Handbook,* pp. 185, 190–191

Materials

- **Large Sound/Spelling Card** *eagle*
- **Blending Routines Card 1**
- **Picture Cards** *feet, jeep, queen, sheep, wheel; jeans, leaf, leash, peach*
- **Large Letter Cards** *a, b, c, e(2), h, k, l, m, n, p, r, s, t(2), w*

Practice Book page 74

Name _____

Week 2
Phonics Vowel Pairs *ee, ea*

Words with *ee, ea*

Read each word. If the word has long *e* spelled **ea,** write it under **peach.** If the word has long *e* spelled **ee,** write it under **jeep.**

Word Bank

bean	sheep	seat	beep
keep	eat	teeth	beach

The order of words in each column may vary.

peach

jeep

1. bean **(1 point)**   2. keep **(1)**

3. eat **(1)**   4. sheep **(1)**

5. seat **(1)**   6. teeth **(1)**

7. beach **(1)**   8. beep **(1)**

Monitoring Student Progress

If . . .	Then . . .
children score 12 or below on **Practice Book** pages 74–75,	use the Reteaching lesson on Teacher's Edition page R16.
children have met the lesson objectives,	use the Challenge/Extension activities on Teacher's Edition page R17.

INSTRUCTION

PHONICS: Vowel Pairs *ee, ea*

TARGET SKILL

❶ Teach Phonics

Connect sounds to letters: *ee, ea,* /ē/.

- Display **Large Sound/Spelling Card** *eagle* and remind children that the /ē/ sound at the beginning of *eagle* is called the long *e* sound. Point out the spellings *ee* and *ea,* and explain that the first vowel, *e,* usually has the long *e* sound, and the second vowel, *e* or *a,* is silent.

- Display **Picture Cards** *queen* and *peach.* Have children name the pictures and say the sound they hear in the middle of each name, /ē/. Write *queen* and *peach.* Underline *ee* and *ea* and read the words with children.

Model how to blend words with *ee* and *ea.* Write *seed.* Underline *ee.* Using **Blending Routine 1,** model how to blend *seed.* Continue with *seat, feet, tree, green, sea, knee, dream, peep, sweet, speak, cheek.*

❷ Guided Practice

Check understanding. Display **Large Letter Cards** *a, b, c, e(2), h, k, l, m, n, p, r, s, t(2), w.* Make *keep* and call on a child to blend and read the word. Repeat with *sleep, beach, bean, meal, bee, meat, seal, street, sweep, seat, team, teeth, tree, wheat, cream.*

Connect sounds to spelling and writing.

Display and name **Picture Cards** *feet, jeep, queen, sheep, wheel.* Ask children to help you write the picture names using *ee* to spell the /ē/ sound. Call on children to write each word. Repeat for **Picture Cards** *jeans, leaf, leash, peach,* using *ea.*

Note: Tell children that for words such as *geese* and *leave,* a silent *e* at the end signals that the vowel pair spells a long vowel sound.

❸ Apply

Assign Practice Book pages 74–75.

Practice Book page 75

Name _____

Week 2
Phonics Vowel Pairs *ee, ea*

Words with *ee, ea*

Read each sentence. Write each word in dark print below the picture it names.

A **bee** stung a dog.
The dog broke its **leash.**
The dog ran to a **tree.**
The dog ate a **peach.**

1. peach **(2 points)**   2. tree **(2)**

3. leash **(2)**   4. bee **(2)**

Animal Adventures

Seal Beach

by Carly Mackeen
illustrated by Marcia Sewall

Mom and I walk to the sea. We take steep steps that lead to the beach.

17

PHONICS LIBRARY

Reading Decodable Text

Have children preview *Seal Beach*. Have them describe what they see in the pictures.

Model the Phonics/Decoding Strategy. Read the steps of the strategy on **Poster B** and use the strategy to read the story title.

Think Aloud *I see two words. The letters in the first word are S, e, a, l. I know that the letters* ea *stand for the /ē/ sound. I blend the sounds, /s//ē//l/,* Seal. Seal *is a word I know. I see the letters* ea *in the second word, too. I think about the sounds for the letters and blend them, /b//ē//ch/,* Beach. *I put the two words together.* Seal Beach *is the title of the story!*

Apply the Phonics/Decoding Strategy. Have children read *Seal Beach*. If necessary, coach them in applying the strategy to words such as *steep*.

- *Look at the letters from left to right. What are they?* (s, t, e, e, p)
- *Blend the sounds. What is the word?* (steep)
- *Is* steep *a word you know? If you don't know what* steep *means, what else can you try? Does it make sense in the sentence?*

OBJECTIVES

- Apply the Phonics/Decoding Strategy to decode words in context.
- Reread to build fluency.

Word Key

Decodable words with long e and vowel pairs *ee, ea* ————

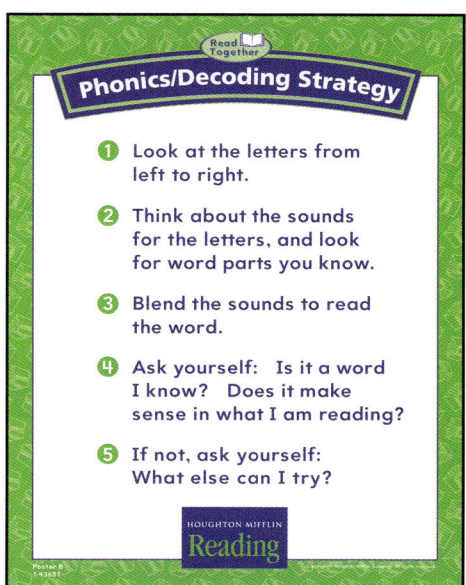

Reading Decodable Text   T117

We see seals. These seals swim and dive. We see them eat fish and squid.

18

This seal pup wakes up from its nap. It can't see its mother.

19

Oral Language

Discuss these questions with children. Have them answer in complete sentences.

- What do the girl and her mom watch the seals do? (They watch the seals swim, dive, and eat.)

- What is a baby seal called? (It is called a pup.)

- Describe what the mother seal and her pup look like. How are they alike? How are they different? (They are both the same shape; both have fins and whiskers; the mother is bigger and darker; the pup is smaller, lighter, and has spots.)

The seal pup <u>keeps</u> looking.
At last it <u>sees</u> its mother. She is
back to <u>feed</u> her pup!

20

Build Fluency

Model fluent reading.

- Read aloud pages 17 and 18. Then have children read the pages aloud.

- Repeat for the remaining pages.

Have children practice fluent reading. Have children reread the pages several times until each child can read them aloud effortlessly.

Home Connection

Hand out the take-home version of *Seal Beach*. Ask children to reread the story with their families. (See the **Phonics Library Blackline Masters.**)

OBJECTIVES

- Write the Basic Words.
- Learn to associate the long *e* sound with the letter *e* and vowel pairs *ee, ea.*
- Make words with spelling pattern *-eat.*

Materials

- teacher-made word card *eat*

SPELLING WORDS

Basic

eat*	me*
feet	mean
he*	see

Challenge

maybe	sheep*

Forms of these words appear in the literature.

Practice Book page 307

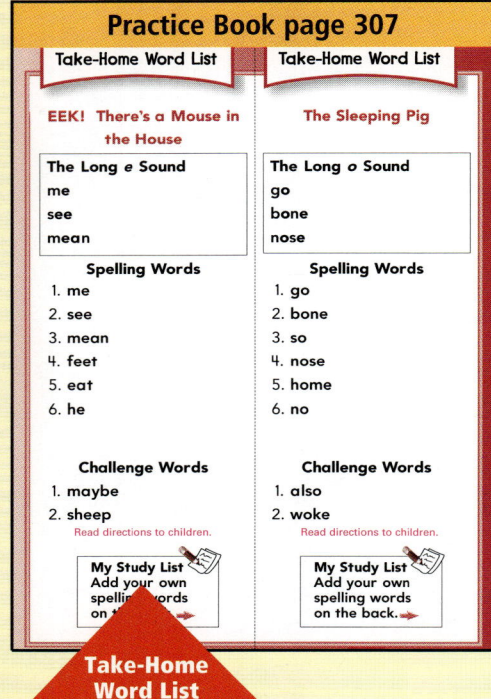

Take-Home Word List	Take-Home Word List
EEK! There's a Mouse in the House	**The Sleeping Pig**
The Long *e* Sound	The Long *o* Sound
me	go
see	bone
mean	nose
Spelling Words	**Spelling Words**
1. me	1. go
2. see	2. bone
3. mean	3. so
4. feet	4. nose
5. eat	5. home
6. he	6. no
Challenge Words	**Challenge Words**
1. maybe	1. also
2. sheep	2. woke
Read directions to children.	Read directions to children.
My Study List Add your own spelling words on the back.	**My Study List** Add your own spelling words on the back.

Take-Home Word List

INSTRUCTION

SPELLING: Words with Long *e* (*e, ee, ea*)

❶ Teach the Principle

Pretest Say each underlined word, read the sentence, and repeat the word. Have children write only the underlined word.

Basic Words

1. Is this for **me**?
2. Did you **see** the big bug?
3. I know what you **mean**.
4. An ant has six **feet**.
5. What do you like to **eat** for dinner?
6. Ted can see that **he** will win.

Teach Write the Basic Words, and read them with children.

- Ask children what vowel sound they hear in all the Spelling Words. (/ē/) Point out that /ē/ is the long *e* sound, and it is spelled three different ways: *e, ee, ea.*

- Underline the long *e* spelling in *me.* Tell children that the long *e* sound can be spelled with one *e,* as in *me.* Repeat with *feet* and *eat* and the long *e* spellings *ee* and *ea.*

❷ Practice/Apply

- Make three columns on the board. Label them *e, ee,* and *ea.*

- Have children write each spelling word in the correct column and underline each long *e* spelling.

Practice/Homework Assign **Practice Book** page 307, the Take-Home Word List.

INSTRUCTION

VOCABULARY: Spelling Pattern *-eat*

Teach Post *eat* on the Word Wall and write it on the board.

- Ask children *What word would I make if I added the letter s at the beginning of eat?* (*seat*) Have children tell you how to spell *seat* as you write it.

- Continue with *beat, heat, neat, meat, treat,* and *wheat.*

Practice/Apply Have partners write a rhyme using words that end in the letters *eat.*

SHARED WRITING: A Class Story

OBJECTIVES
- Contribute sentences to a class story.
- Compare and contrast story characters.

Materials
- *Tiger and Anansi*, page T112, or another Read Aloud selection from the Leveled Bibliography, pages T6–T7.

Discuss the topic for a class story. Tell children that today they will write a class story about a trick played by Anansi. Explain that Anansi the spider is famous for being clever. Remind children that a story has characters, a setting, a problem, a solution, and an ending.

Prompt children to contribute to the story.

- Tell children that first they must plan their story. Ask *Who are the characters? Where does the story take place? What is the problem? How could Anansi solve the problem in a clever way?*
- Record children's ideas as they plan the story.
- Say *Let's begin by writing* Once upon a time. Record children's sentences until the story is completed. Reread the finished story.

Act out the story. Have children make simple masks for the characters and act out the story for the class.

LISTENING AND SPEAKING: Compare and Contrast

Review how to compare and contrast. Tell children that comparing Tiger and Anansi can help them understand the characters better. Reread the story if necessary.

Draw a Venn diagram. Ask children to think of things that are the same or different about Tiger and Anansi. Add their ideas to the diagram.

Check children's understanding. After the diagram is completed, ask children to compare and contrast details. Use the following prompts:

- *How are Tiger and Anansi the same? How are they different?*
- *How would the story have been different if Snake did not let Anansi tie him to the bamboo?*

Tiger   Both   Anansi

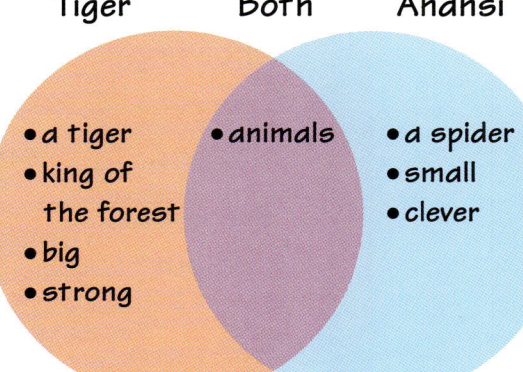

- a tiger
- king of the forest
- big
- strong

- animals

- a spider
- small
- clever

English Language Learners

Supporting Comprehension

Prompt children to describe the characters by asking *Who is the king of the forest? Who is the weakest animal? What does Anansi the spider want named after him? Who wants to play a trick on the spider?* Write children's responses on the board as a reference.

DAY 2
week 2

Day at a Glance
pages T122–T141

Learning to Read

High-Frequency Words

Reading Decodable Text
Pete and Peach

Reading the Anthology
EEK! There's a Mouse in the House

• • • • • • • • • • • • • • •

Leveled Readers, *T166–T169*

● *The Feast*
▲ *Going Fishing*
■ *Zeke Takes a Bath*
◆ *Fun and Food to Eat*

Word Work

Spelling: Words with Long *e*
Vocabulary: High-Frequency Words

Writing & Oral Language

Interactive Writing: A Class Story

Daily Routines

Daily Message

Review phonics and language skills. Point to each word as you read aloud the Daily Message.

Good Morning, Children!
Today we will read a book about a mouse. Do you think he lives in a house or a tree?

Have children

• respond to the question;
• circle words with the long e sound; *(we, read, he, tree)*
• find two words that rhyme; *(mouse, house; we, he, tree)*
• find and read the following high-frequency words: *Good, Morning, Children, Today, you, lives,* and *house.*

Word Wall

High-Frequency Word Review Briefly review these and other high-frequency words daily. Have children practice reading, chanting, spelling, and writing words from the Word Wall. Have individuals point to words on the Word Wall while the class reads them aloud.

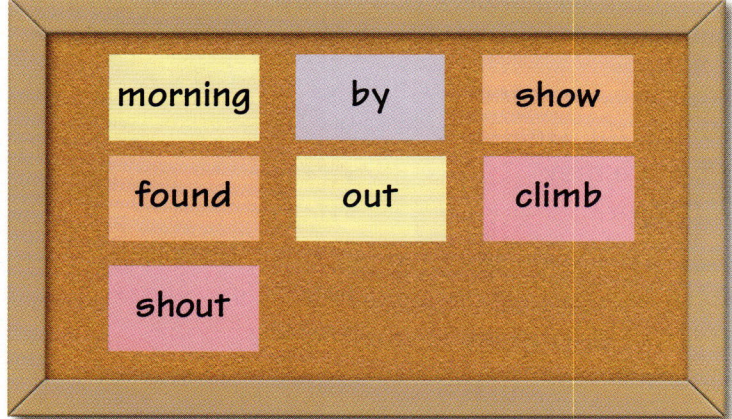

Blackline Master for these Word Wall Cards appears on page R33.

Daily Phonemic Awareness

Segmenting and Counting Phonemes: Complete the Poem

- Read aloud the poem shown, replacing the blank with *fan*.

- Now reread, stopping after *meet* and *treat*. Have partners whisper the separate sounds in each word and hold up fingers to signal the number of sounds.

- For *fan* have children say the sounds with you and count them: /f//ă//n/. (3)

- Pause after the fourth line and point to two children. Ask partners to think of words to replace *A fan* on subsequent readings. They complete the poem, saying the separate sounds in the noun they have chosen.

- Call on children to guess the new word and tell how many sounds are in it. Examples: A /h//ō//z/ (A *hose*, 3); Some /ī//s/ (Some *ice*, 2)

> I skipped along with my dog Zeat,
> We saw someone you'd like to meet.
> Our neighbor Pete
> Gave us a treat:
> A _____ we'll use
> To beat the heat.

Daily Language Practice

Grammar Skill: Beginning Sentences with Capital Letters

Spelling Skill: Words with Long *e*

Write the sentence, read it to children, and have them tell you how to correct it.

i can seee your friend.

(I can **see** your friend.)

Daily Writing Prompt

Remind children to begin sentences with a capital letter and end them with a punctuation mark when responding to the prompt below, or writing about self-selected topics.

- **Draw and write about an animal you think is interesting.**

Daily Independent Reading

To increase children's reading fluency, provide a variety of theme-related books for them to read. Here are some suggestions.

- Leveled Bibliography, pages T6–T7

Choose books from this list for children to read, outside class, for at least twenty minutes a day.

- Phonics Library: *Seal Beach*
- Leveled Readers

OBJECTIVES

- Recognize new high-frequency words:

cow	*door*	*horse*
table	*there*	*wall*
now	*through*	

- Read and write high-frequency words.

Target Skill Trace

Teach	pp. T124–T125
Reteach	p. R22
Review	pp. T140, T164, T194
See	*Handbook for English Language Learners*, pp. 191, 193; *Extra Support Handbook*, pp. 188–189

Materials

- Word Wall Cards for Week 2, Teacher's Edition, p. R34
- **Practice Book** punch-out high-frequency word cards for Theme 6, Week 2

Chart/Transparency 6–5

Animals in the House!

Once <u>there</u> was a little brown <u>cow</u>. She lived with a <u>horse</u> and some hens. One morning, they all walked right <u>through</u> the <u>door</u> of the house. They went to the <u>table</u> by the <u>wall</u>. They wanted to see what they could find to eat. <u>Now</u> what do you think of that?

TRANSPARENCY 6–5
TEACHER'S EDITION PAGE T124

ANIMAL ADVENTURES Week 2, Day 2
High-Frequency Words

ANNOTATED
VERSION

TARGET SKILL HIGH-FREQUENCY WORDS

❶ Teach

Review last week's high-frequency words.

- Point to the words *morning, found, shout, by, show, out,* and *climb* on the Word Wall.

- Have children read these words aloud, repeating any words that give them difficulty.

Introduce the new high-frequency words.

- Hold up the Word Wall Card *door* and read the word aloud.

- Have the class clap and spell *door* several times: *d-o-o-r, door!*

- Choose a child to post *door* on the New Words section of the Word Wall.

- Repeat the procedure for the other new high-frequency words, *cow, table, now, there, through, horse,* and *wall*.

Display Chart/Transparency 6–5.

- Have children read the story with you.

- Call on individuals to read one of the underlined words and use it in a sentence of their own.

❷ Guided Practice

Have children put the words in alphabetical order.

- Have children help you to decide which word to write first *(cow)* and last *(wall)*.

- Have partners work together to write the words *now, door,* and *horse* in alphabetical order between *cow* and *wall*. They can compare their lists with the rest of the class.

- Write *table, there,* and *through*. Explain how to list words in alphabetical order when they all start with the same letter.

- Have children practice writing *table, there,* and *through* in alphabetical order.

❸ Apply

Assign one or more of the following activities.

- Have children complete **Practice Book** pages 76 and 77 independently, in pairs, or in small groups.

- Have partners practice reading their punch-out word cards to one another.

- Have children read the **Phonics Library** story *Pete and Peach* independently, with partners, or in small groups.

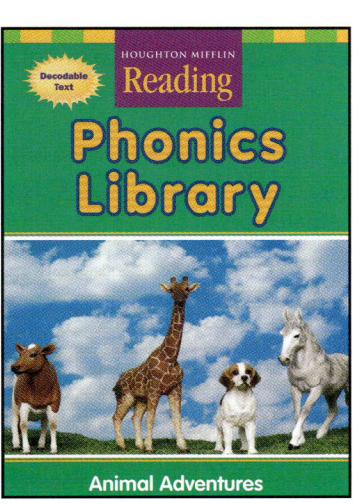

Pete and Peach

by Mack Duffy
illustrated by Anne-Marie Arcand

"Let's run and leap," yells Pete the horse.
But Peach the cow just sits in the green, green grass.

21

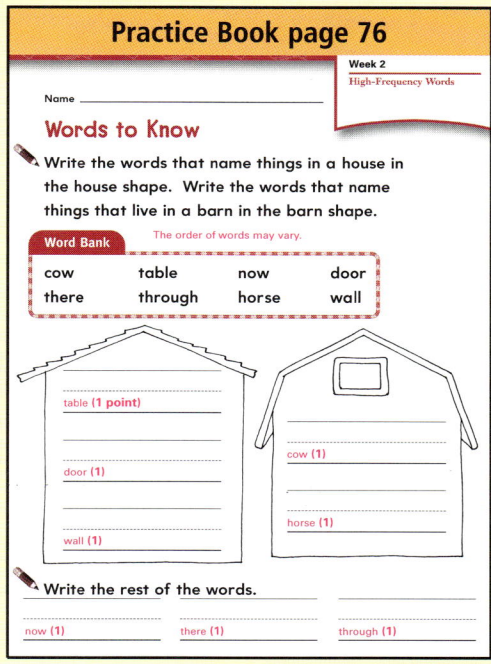

Practice Book page 76

Week 2
High-Frequency Words

Name _____

Words to Know

Write the words that name things in a house in the house shape. Write the words that name things that live in a barn in the barn shape.

Word Bank   The order of words may vary.

| cow | table | now | door |
| there | through | horse | wall |

table **(1 point)**

door **(1)**

wall **(1)**

cow **(1)**

horse **(1)**

Write the rest of the words.

now **(1)**   there **(1)**   through **(1)**

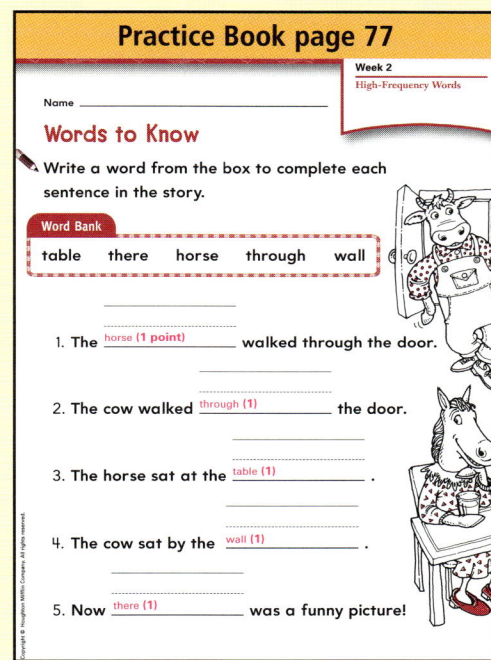

Practice Book page 77

Week 2
High-Frequency Words

Name _____

Words to Know

Write a word from the box to complete each sentence in the story.

Word Bank

| table | there | horse | through | wall |

1. The ___horse **(1 point)**___ walked through the door.

2. The cow walked ___through **(1)**___ the door.

3. The horse sat at the ___table **(1)**___ .

4. The cow sat by the ___wall **(1)**___ .

5. Now ___there **(1)**___ was a funny picture!

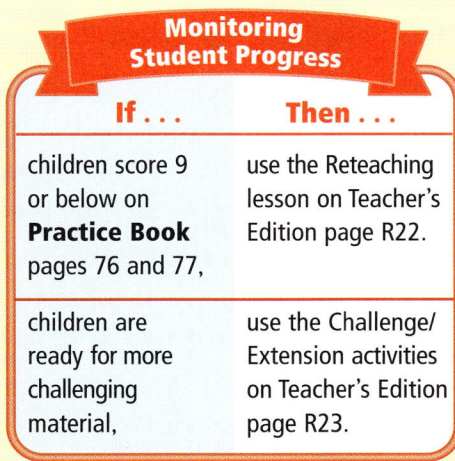

Monitoring Student Progress

If . . .	Then . . .
children score 9 or below on **Practice Book** pages 76 and 77,	use the Reteaching lesson on Teacher's Edition page R22.
children are ready for more challenging material,	use the Challenge/ Extension activities on Teacher's Edition page R23.

Building Background

Key Concept: Animal Behaviors

Ask children who have pets to describe the kinds of things their pets do. Turn to Anthology page 164. Ask:

- What are the animals in the picture doing?

- Do real animals do these things?

- Do you think the animals in this story are real or make-believe?

Reviewing Vocabulary

Words to Know

High-Frequency Words

cow	door	horse
now	table	there
through	wall	

Words with long e and vowel pairs ee, ea

EEK!	eating	he
me	sheep	squeezed

Use "Get Set to Read."

- Read Anthology page 162 together. Remind children that the Words to Know are either words they already know or words that contain sounds they know.

- Read the Practice Sentences together. Ask children what helped them to read each word. Review words or skills as necessary.

- Remind children that these words will appear in the story.

THEME 6: Animal Adventures
(Anthology p. 162)

Background and Vocabulary

EEK! There's a Mouse in the House

Animals in the House

In the next story, you'll read about some animals that mess up a little girl's house! How can she get rid of them?

Words to Know	
cow	wall
table	me
now	he
door	EEK
there	sheep
through	eating
horse	

162

English Language Learners

Language Development

Beginning/Preproduction Have children repeat each Story Vocabulary word as you help them point to its picture in the illustrations. Demonstrate that *EEK!* is something a person might say if they are surprised or frightened.

Early Production and Speech Emergence Ask children questions using each of the Story Vocabulary words. Have them answer individually in complete sentences, repeating the word. Example: *Who is* dancing *on page 170? A* cow *is* dancing.

Intermediate and Advanced Fluency Have children look at the story illustrations and discuss how the animal characters are different from real animals. Encourage them to ask questions about anything they don't understand.

Practice Sentences

1. A <mark>cow</mark>, a <mark>sheep</mark>, and a <mark>horse</mark> came to a house.
2. "<mark>Now</mark> what could be in <mark>there</mark>?" asked the horse.
3. <mark>He</mark> went <mark>through</mark> the <mark>door</mark>.
4. The others went through, too.
5. By the <mark>wall</mark> was a <mark>table</mark> of things to eat.
6. A mouse was <mark>eating</mark> on the table.
7. "<mark>EEK</mark>!" said the cow and the sheep.
8. "The mouse can't hurt <mark>me</mark>," said the horse.

163

Introducing Story Vocabulary

Story Vocabulary

These words support the Key Concept and are important to children's understanding of the selection.

<mark>barn</mark> a large farm building used as a home for farm animals

<mark>dancing</mark> moving to music

<mark>elephant</mark> a very big animal with thick skin, big ears, sharp tusks, and a long trunk

<mark>laying</mark> making eggs

<mark>marched</mark> walked together, in rhythm, with the same size steps

<mark>mercy</mark> a word used to show surprise

<mark>mouse</mark> a small animal with short hair, sharp teeth, and a thin, almost hairless tail

<mark>tangled</mark> became twisted together

 e • Glossary
e • WordGame

Use Chart/Transparency 6–6.

- Point out the first picture and read the sentence together.
- Point to the words *mouse* and *marched*.
- Read the remaining sentences, pointing to the underlined words.
- Ask children to look for these words as they read, and to use them as they discuss the selection.

Practice Assign **Practice Book** page 78.

Chart/Transparency 6–6
Look at That!

Mouse <u>marched</u>.
What did Mouse see?
A hen was <u>laying</u> an egg in the <u>barn</u>.
An <u>elephant</u> was <u>dancing</u>!
Look out, Elephant!
<u>Mercy</u>! The elephant is <u>tangled</u>. No more dancing now!

Practice Book page 78

Week 2
Story Vocabulary EEK!
There's a Mouse in the House

Name _____

EEK! Look at These Words!

Write a word from the box that goes with each picture.

Word Bank

marched	elephant	tangled
dancing	barn	mouse

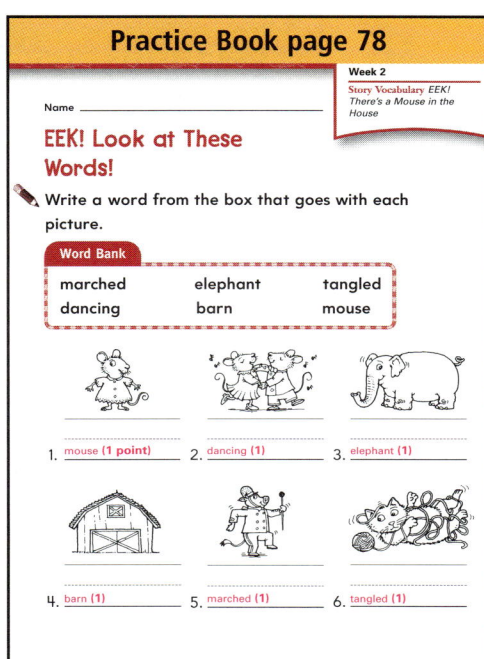

1. mouse (1 point)   2. dancing (1)   3. elephant (1)

4. barn (1)   5. marched (1)   6. tangled (1)

Introducing Vocabulary
(Anthology p. 163)   **T127**

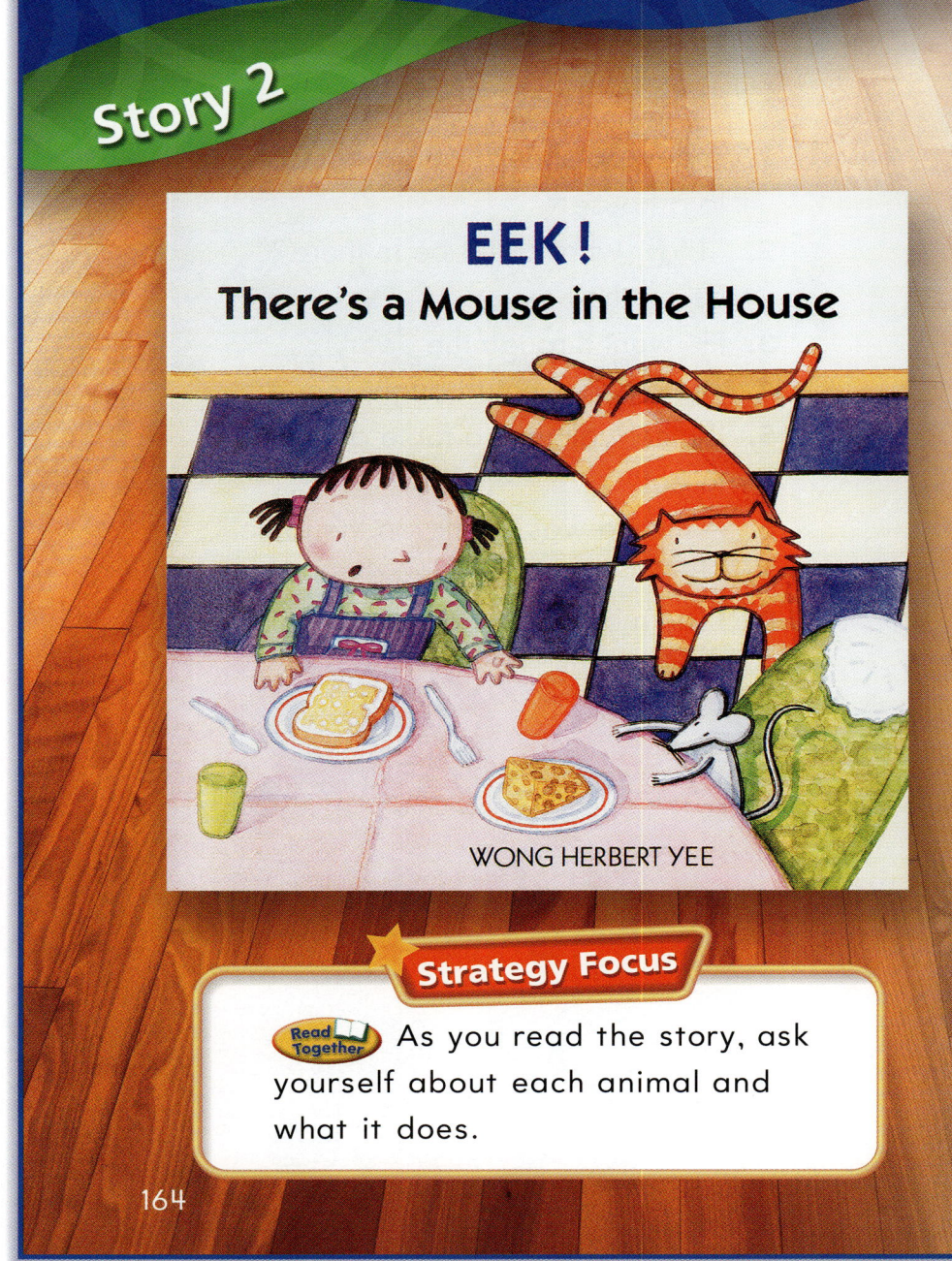

Story 2

EEK!
There's a Mouse in the House

WONG HERBERT YEE

Strategy Focus

 As you read the story, ask yourself about each animal and what it does.

164

TARGET SKILL

COMPREHENSION STRATEGY

Question

Teacher Modeling Read the title, the author and illustrator's name, and the Strategy Focus on Anthology page 164. Then read aloud page 165 and model the Question strategy.

Think Aloud *I want to ask a question using what I understand about this story. So far, I know that there is a mouse in a little girl's house, and she wants a cat to chase it. I could ask,* What will the cat do?

✓ **Test Prep** Some children can get distracted when taking a test. Tell them to use the Question strategy to check their understanding and to help them stay focused on what they are reading.

TARGET SKILL

COMPREHENSION SKILL

Noting Details

Remind children that noticing details about a story can help them remember it.

- Ask what characters they noticed when you read page 165.
- Ask what is happening on page 165.

English Language Learners

Supporting Comprehension

Ask children to tell you which animals usually stay in a house and which animals usually stay outside or in a barn. Write children's responses on the board. Ask what they would do if they found an animal like a horse or an elephant in the house.

THEME 6: Animal Adventures
(Anthology p. 164)

EEK!

There's a <mark>mouse</mark> in the house.

Send in the cat
to chase that rat!

Purpose Setting

- Preview the illustrations on Anthology pages 166–167. Have children ask themselves questions about what the animals are doing and read to find the answers. Tell children to continue this pattern as they read the whole story.

- Remind children to pay attention to different animals and what they do in the story.

- Ask children to turn to Responding on Anthology page 184. Read the questions aloud. Encourage children to think about the answers to these questions as they read *EEK! There's a Mouse in the House.*

Journal ▶ You may want children to record their questions and important story details by writing in their journals.

Extra Support/Intervention

Preview pages 165–173.

pages 165–167 What comes to chase the mouse? What chases the cat?

pages 168–169 What animals are in this picture? How are they behaving?

pages 170–171 What animal is in the picture on the wall?

pages 172–173 What is the new animal on this page? Is it the same animal as in the picture on page 171?

Preview pages 174–183.

pages 174–177 What kinds of trouble are the animals making? What do you think will make them stop?

pages 178–179 What animal arrives at the door? How does this change how the other animals are acting?

pages 180–181 Why do you think the animals go outside?

pages 182–183 How does the mouse make the elephant feel? How can you tell?

Story Vocabulary

<mark>mouse</mark> a small animal with short fur, sharp teeth, and a thin, almost hairless tail

Word Key

Words with long e *(e, ee, ea)* ——————

High-Frequency Words ——————

Story Vocabulary ——————

Reading the Selection
(Anthology p. 165)   **T129**

Uh-oh!

The cat knocked over a lamp.

Send in the dog
to catch that scamp!

166

Dear me!

The dog has broken a dish.

And now the cat is after the fish.

Send in the hog
to shoo that dog!

167

CRITICAL THINKING
Guiding Comprehension

1 **PROBLEM SOLVING** Do you think it was a good idea to call in the cat and dog to chase the mouse away? Why or why not? (No, the cat and dog are only making more trouble.)

READING STRATEGY
Phonics/Decoding

Teacher/Student Modeling Some children may need help decoding the following words: *uh-oh* (page 166); *dear, broken, shoo* (page 167); *mistake* (page 168). Coach them in applying what they already know about letter sounds to read the words. For *uh-oh, broken,* and *mistake,* help children break each word into two parts, sound out each part, and blend the word.

THEME 6: Animal Adventures
(Anthology pp. 166–167)

Extra Support/Intervention

Strategy Modeling: Question

Use this example to model the strategy.

A question I could ask about the animals so far is, Why did the girl send for the dog? *I know from the story that the answer to my question is,* The girl sent for the dog to catch the cat.

Oh my!

The hog is <u>eating</u> the cake.

Sending the hog
was a big mistake.

Send in the <u>cow</u>.

Send that cow NOW!

168

169

CRITICAL THINKING
Guiding Comprehension

2 **NOTING DETAILS** What do you notice about the pictures of the animals on the wall on each page? Why do you think the illustrator did this? (Each picture shows the animal that will appear on the next page. The illustrator is probably trying to give the reader a clue about what will happen next.)

COMPREHENSION STRATEGY
Question

Teacher/Student Modeling Point out the pig, dog, cat, and mouse on this page. Ask children to think of questions they could ask about these animals. Then discuss the answers to their questions.

Extra Support/Intervention

Concepts of Print

Capital Letters Have children look at the word *NOW* on Anthology page 168. Point out that the author has used all capital letters. Explain that this tells readers that the word is important and they should read the word to show this.

Model reading the sentence, "Send that cow NOW!" with emphasis on *NOW*. Then have children practice reading other sentences in the selection that have a word in all capital letters. Examples: *EEK* (pages 165, 182), *ALL* (page 176), *BIG* (page 179).

Reading the Selection
(Anthology pp. 168–169)   **T131**

Oh no!

The cow is **dancing** with a mop.

Send in the sheep to make her stop!

170

171

CRITICAL THINKING
Guiding Comprehension

3 DRAWING CONCLUSIONS Why do you think the illustrator drew musical notes above the radio and the cow's head? *(to show that the radio is playing music and the cow is whistling along)*

4 MAKING PREDICTIONS Do you think the sheep will be able to make the cow stop dancing? What makes you think as you do? *(probably not; none of the animals have been able to stop the other animals so far.)*

Story Vocabulary

dancing moving to music

 **Extra Support/Intervention**

Review pages 165–173.

Before children join in Stop and Think, have them

- take turns modeling **Question** and other strategies they used;
- **summarize** the important parts of the story up to this point.

On Level | **Challenge**

Literature Discussion

Have small groups discuss the story, using their own questions or prompts from Guiding Comprehension.

THEME 6: Animal Adventures
(Anthology pp. 170–171)

T132

Goodness!

The sheep is <mark>tangled</mark> in yarn.

Send in the hen from the <mark>barn</mark>!

172

173

Stop and Think

Critical Thinking Questions

1. **CAUSE AND EFFECT** What happens each time a new animal comes into the house? (The animal doesn't help and it makes more trouble.)

2. **NOTING DETAILS** What is the little girl's expression on each page? What does this tell you about how she feels? (She looks surprised and worried. She probably hopes the animals will stop before they ruin the whole house.)

Strategies in Action

Have individuals model **Question** and other strategies they used. Make sure children summarize the story so far.

Discussion Options

Review Predictions/Purpose Ask children if they found answers to all their questions. Have them continue reading to find out what will happen to all of the animals.

Share Group Discussions If children discussed the story in groups, have them share their questions and answers.

Story Vocabulary

<mark>barn</mark> a large farm building used as a home for farm animals

<mark>tangled</mark> twisted together; mixed up

Monitoring Student Progress

If . . .	Then . . .
children have successfully completed the Extra Support activities on page T132,	have them read the rest of the story cooperatively.

Reading the Selection
(Anthology pp. 172–173) **T133**

Mercy!

The hen is laying eggs
on the table.

Send in the horse
from the stable!

174   175

CRITICAL THINKING
Guiding Comprehension

5 DRAWING CONCLUSIONS Why do you think the little girl
is outside? (Maybe she wants to get away from the animals
in the house, or she could be going out to get the horse.)

READING STRATEGY
Phonics/Decoding

Teacher/Student Modeling If children need help decoding
goodness and *yarn* (page 172) or *stable* (page 174), coach them
in applying what they already know about letter sounds and
word parts to help them read the words. Help them to break
goodness and *stable* into two parts. Then have them decode
each of the parts and blend the word.

THEME 6: Animal Adventures
(Anthology pp. 174–175)

Story Vocabulary

mercy a word used to show surprise

laying making eggs

Heavens!

The horse kicked a hole in the <u>wall</u>.

Send in the <mark>elephant</mark> to get rid of them ALL!

176

177

CRITICAL THINKING
Guiding Comprehension

6 MAKING GENERALIZATIONS What size are most elephants? What would happen if an elephant tried to go inside a house? (Elephants are big; it probably would have trouble fitting into a house.)

READING STRATEGY
Phonics/Decoding

Teacher/Student Modeling If children need help decoding the words *heavens* (page 176) and *room* (page 179) coach them in applying what they already know about letter sounds to help them read the words. If children have trouble reading *squeezed* (page 179) or other long *e* words underlined in the story, review the phonics lesson on Day 1. Then have children practice reading the long *e* words in the selection.

Story Vocabulary

<mark>elephant</mark> a very big animal with thick skin, big ears, sharp tusks, and a long trunk

REACHING ALL LEARNERS
English Language Learners

Language Development

Pause at the end of Anthology page 176 to point out that *wall* and *all* end with the same sounds. Say that they are rhyming words. Model the words and have children repeat several times. After reading, go back through the story and help children find other rhyming pairs, such as *cat/rat, lamp/scamp, dish/fish, hog/dog, cake/mistake, cow/now, mop/stop, yarn/barn, table/stable.*

Reading the Selection
(Anthology pp. 176–177)   **T135**

178

The elephant was BIG,
but he squeezed through the door.

Once he was in,
there was room for no more.

179

Comprehension Preview

Noting Details

Teach

Explain that noting details in pictures and text can help children understand a story better. Remind children that the picture on the wall of each illustration in this story can help them predict what animal will enter next.

Practice/Apply

Have children page through the story, noting the animal's picture on the wall and its name in the text. Ask how the picture of the horse on page 175 is different from the other animal pictures. (It is a picture in a book instead of on the wall.) Then have children tell what each animal does when it comes into the house.

Target Skill Trace	
Preview; Teach	pp. T112, T128, T136; T146–T147
Reteach	p. R28
Review	p. T160

Out of the house <mark>marched</mark> the cat and the cow.

Out came the horse and the hen and the hog.

Out walked the sheep.

Out ran the dog.

180

181

CRITICAL THINKING
Guiding Comprehension

 **CAUSE AND EFFECT** Why do all the animals go outside?
(The elephant is too big and no one else can fit in the house anymore.)

COMPREHENSION STRATEGY
Question

Student Modeling Have children model asking questions based on what they have read so far. If children need help, remind them that they can ask about the characters and what they do, or use the prompt in the Extra Support box on this page.

Story Vocabulary

<mark>marched</mark> walked together, in rhythm, with the same size steps

REACHING ALL LEARNERS **Extra Support/Intervention**

Strategy Modeling: Question

Use this example to model the strategy.

Based on what I've read so far I could ask, What animals left the house? What animals are still inside the house? Why didn't all the animals leave the house?

Reading the Selection
(Anthology pp. 180–181)

T137

But then from within,
there came a shout:

EEK! There's a mouse in the house!

182

Meet the Author and Illustrator

This is **Wong Herbert Yee**'s first children's book. While he was writing it, he read it to his young daughter, Ellen. If she laughed at a sentence, he kept it in the story.

Internet

Find out more about Wong Herbert Yee at Education Place.
www.eduplace.com/kids

183

CRITICAL THINKING
Guiding Comprehension

8 **DRAWING CONCLUSIONS** Why do you think the elephant doesn't make the mouse leave the house? (The elephant is frightened of the mouse.)

TARGET SKILL

READING STRATEGY
Phonics/Decoding

Teacher/Student Modeling Write *within* on the board. Tell children that this word is made of two smaller words they already know. Help children identify *with* and *in*, and then blend them together to read the whole word. Then discuss the meaning of *within* with children.

REACHING ALL LEARNERS

Extra Support/Intervention

Selection Review

Before children join in Wrapping Up, have them

- take turns modeling **Question** and other strategies they used;
- **summarize** the important parts of the story.

On Level	Challenge

Literature Discussion

Have small groups discuss the story, using their own questions and questions from Think About the Story on Anthology page 184.

THEME 6: Animal Adventures
(Anthology pp. 182–183)

Wrapping Up

Critical Thinking Questions

1. **STORY STRUCTURE** Do the animals help the little girl solve her problem? (No, the mouse is still in the house.)

2. **NOTING DETAILS** What does the elephant shout at the end of the story? Why? ("EEK! There's a mouse in the house." It's afraid of the mouse.)

Strategies in Action

Have children take turns modeling **Question** and other strategies they used. Also ask them to summarize the entire story.

Discussion Options

Review Predictions/Purpose Ask children to discuss what finally happened to all the animals and why.

Share Group Discussions Have children share the results of their literature discussions.

Monitoring Student Progress

If . . .	Then . . .
children have difficulty summarizing important details and events in the story,	guide them in rereading and summarizing the story in two or three parts.

OBJECTIVES
- Spell the Basic Words.
- Review spelling of high-frequency words.

Challenge

Writing Sentences

Have children write two sentences that include the words *maybe* and *sheep*.

PRACTICE

SPELLING:
Words with Long *e* (*e, ee, ea*)

Review the principle. Remind children that the long *e* sound can be spelled three different ways: *e, ee, ea.*

Practice/Apply Tell children they can clap, chant, and write their Spelling Words.

- Have children number a sheet of paper from 1 to 6.
- Tell them to clap and chant the Spelling Word *me: m-e, me!* Then have children write the word *me* next to number 1.
- Repeat with *see, mean, feet, eat,* and *he.*

REVIEW

VOCABULARY:
High-Frequency Words

Review the words. Read the New Words section of the Word Wall with children. Tell them they will use some of these words to finish rhymes.

Practice/Apply Read each rhyme below. Have children clap and spell their answers.

- *A dog said, "Bow-wow!"*
  "Moo," answered the ___. (cow)
- *A girl named Mabel*
  was sitting at the ___. (table)
- *The cat walked across the floor*
  and right out the ___. (door)
- *Bob shouted, "Wow!*
  I'm having lots of fun right ___." (now)
- *My teacher said, "Whatever you do,*
  turn your paper in when you are ___." (through)
- *This word is not ball or fall.*
  I saw a spider crawl up the ___! (wall)

INTERACTIVE WRITING: A Class Story

OBJECTIVES
- Contribute sentences to write a class story.
- Participate by writing letters, words, and punctuation.

Introduce the topic for a class story.

- Remind children that Anansi tricks Snake so that Tiger will name the forest stories after him.
- Tell children that they will write another Anansi adventure.
- Remind them that a story has characters, a setting, a problem, a solution, and an ending.

Prompt children to contribute to the class story.

- Help children plan the story. Ask *Who will be the characters? What will be the problem?*
- Model how to begin the story.

Think Aloud *First we need to decide on the problem. Suppose the animals have an argument. Anansi will do something clever to help them solve the problem. I will write,* One day, Anansi met Rabbit and Ant. They were arguing about who was the fastest animal.

- Help children figure out Anansi's clever solution to the problem and a good ending for the story. Ask *What will Anansi do to solve the problem? What lesson will the animals learn?*
- Record children's sentences. Invite them to write familiar letters, words, and punctuation.
- Reread the completed story.

Make the class story into an Anansi Big Book.

- Type the story on the computer, dividing the text into two- or three-sentence blocks.
- Paste each text block on a sheet of paper.
- Have children illustrate the text on each page.
- Staple the pages together to create an Anansi Big Book.
- Reread the Anansi adventure together.

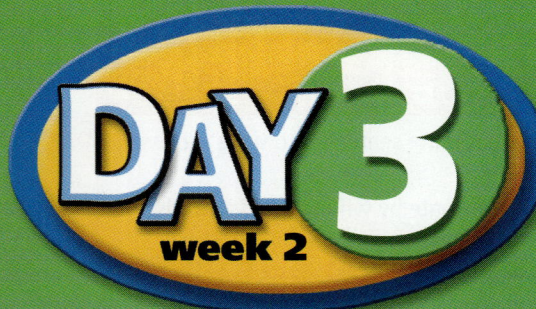

DAY 3 week 2

Day at a Glance
pages T142–T149

Learning to Read

Responding
Comprehension Instruction
Noting Details

Leveled Readers, *T166–T169*
- ● *The Feast*
- ▲ *Going Fishing*
- ■ *Zeke Takes a Bath*
- ◆ *Fun and Food to Eat*

Word Work

Spelling: Words with Long *e*
Vocabulary: Rhyming Words

Writing & Oral Language

Writing: Responding
Grammar: Naming Words for Things and Places

Daily Routines

Daily Message

Review skills. Point to each word as you read aloud the Daily Message.

> Dear Class,
>
> Saturday I went to a farm. I walked through the barn door and saw a big brown cow. Then I rode a horse. I had so much fun. Did you ever ride a horse?

Have children

- answer the question in a class poll (*yes* or *no*);
- circle the long *o* words; (rode, so)
- find and read the following high-frequency words: *through, door, brown, cow, horse,* and *you.*

Word Wall

High-Frequency Word Review Review these and other high-frequency words by holding up the Word Wall Cards and having children read the word and find it on the Word Wall. Then have children use each word in a sentence.

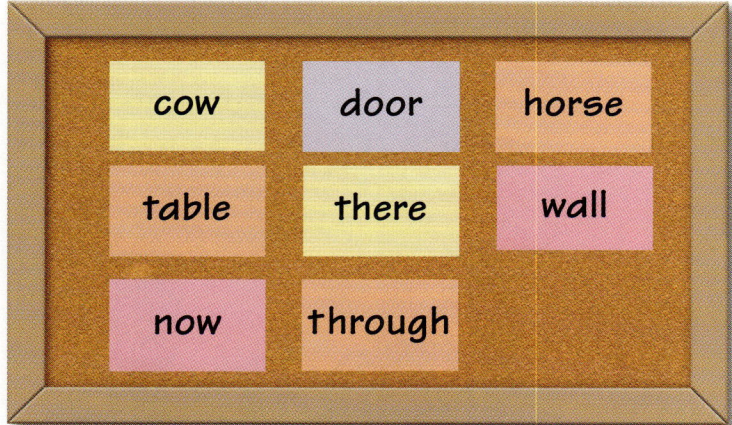

cow	door	horse
table	there	wall
now	through	

Blackline Master for this week's Word Wall Cards appears on page R34.

Daily Phonemic Awareness

Segmenting and Counting Phonemes: Cheer the Sounds

- Have children form groups and choose leaders.

- Say one of the following words to each group: *seem, bleach, mean, sleep, wheel, peach, weak.*

- Have the group leader begin a cheer with "Give me a _____!" and say the first sound in the word. The group then repeats the sound. After children cheer the remaining sounds of the word in the same way, they end with "What's the word? It's _____!"

- Suggest that children make up a movement for each sound in the word. Ask how many motions they will need to match the number of sounds.

- Continue with new words, giving everyone a chance to be the leader.

Daily Language Practice

Grammar Skill: Which Kind of Sentence?

Spelling Skill: Words with Long *e*

Write the sentence, read it to children, and have them tell you how to correct it.

The cat has black feat?

(The cat has black **feet.**)

Daily Writing Prompt

Have children write in response to the prompt below or write on a self-selected topic. Remind children to write complete sentences, beginning with a capital letter and ending with punctuation.

- **Write and draw about a farm animal.**

Cows live on farms.
Cows eat grass.

Daily Independent Reading

To increase children's reading fluency, provide a variety of theme-related books for them to read. Here are some suggestions.

- Leveled Bibliography, pages T6–T7

Choose books from this list for children to read, outside class, for at least twenty minutes a day.

- Anthology: *EEK! There's a Mouse in the House*

- Phonics Library: *Seal Beach, Pete and Peach*

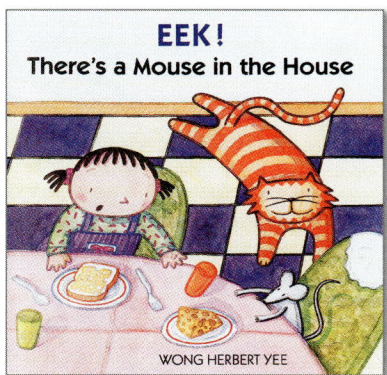

EEK!
There's a Mouse in the House

WONG HERBERT YEE

Responding

Comprehension Check

Have children reread or finish reading the selection. Then assign **Practice Book** page 79 to assess children's comprehension of the selection.

Think About the Story

Have children discuss or write their answers. Sample answers are provided; accept reasonable responses.

1. **DRAWING CONCLUSIONS** Sample answer: she didn't like the mouse; it frightened her.

2. **DRAWING CONCLUSIONS** No, the animals didn't help get the mouse out of the house; they just caused trouble.

3. **PROBLEM SOLVING** Answers will vary.

 4. **Connecting/Comparing** Is this a good story for a theme about animal adventures? Why or why not? (Answers will vary, but should be supported by examples from the story and the theme.)

THEME 6: Animal Adventures
(Anthology p. 184)

Responding

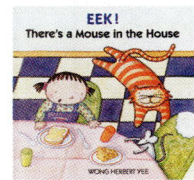

Read Together

EEK!
There's a Mouse in the House

Think About the Story

1. How did the girl feel about the mouse?

2. Was it a good idea for the girl to call in the animals? Why?

3. What would you do if you were the girl in this story?

Internet

Take an Online Poll

What animal from *EEK! There's a Mouse in the House* would you want for a pet? Visit Education Place to place your vote.

www.eduplace.com/kids

184

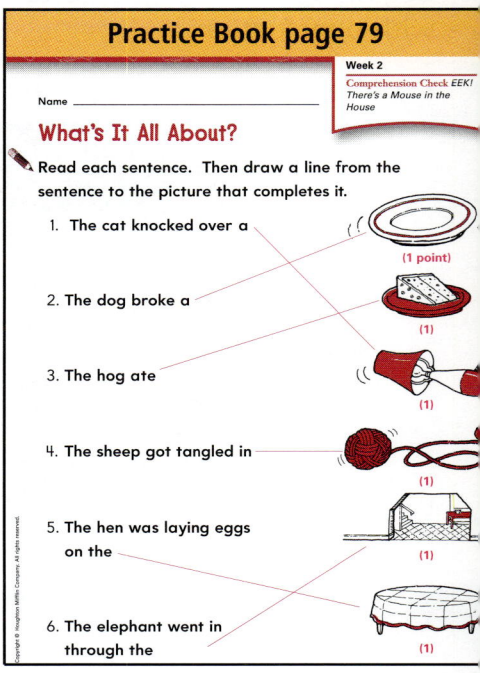

Practice Book page 79

Week 2
Comprehension Check *EEK! There's a Mouse in the House*

Name _____

What's It All About?

Read each sentence. Then draw a line from the sentence to the picture that completes it.

1. The cat knocked over a

(1 point)

2. The dog broke a

(1)

3. The hog ate

(1)

4. The sheep got tangled in

(1)

5. The hen was laying eggs on the

(1)

6. The elephant went in through the

(1)

Additional Responses

Listening/Speaking

Act Out the Story

Act out the story with some partners. Each of you can be a different character. Make sure to use each character's actions.

 Informing

Write a List

Pick an animal from the story. Make a list of clean-up chores for the animal.

Cat
1. Pick up the lamp.

Tips

- Think about what the animal needs to clean up.
- Number each thing on your list.

185

Additional Responses

Personal Response Have children share their personal responses to *EEK! There's a Mouse in the House* orally or in small groups.

Journal ▶ Ask children to write or draw what they think a better solution to the girl's problem would have been.

Sing a Song Children may enjoy singing a song with many animal names. Music and lyrics for "Animal Song" are on page R39.

REACHING ALL LEARNERS

Extra Support/ Intervention	English Language Learners

Writing Support

Help children choose an animal from the story and think of the mess that it made. Then have children write two things the animal can do to clean up this mess.

Supporting Comprehension

Beginning/Preproduction Have children draw pictures of themselves seeing a mouse. Help them label their pictures.

Early Production and Speech Emergence Have children finish this sentence: *When I see a mouse I _____.*

Intermediate and Advanced Fluency Have children find different ways to complete this sentence: *If there were a mouse in my house, I would _____.*

Monitoring Student Progress

Monitoring Student Progress

Student Self-Assessment Have children assess their reading with questions such as

- What questions did I ask during reading that helped me understand the story better?

- How did I keep track of the different things the animals did in the house?

Responding
(Anthology p. 185)

OBJECTIVES

- Use pictures and words to identify details in a story.
- Use details to retell a story.

Target Skill Trace

Preview; Teach	pp. T112, T128, T136; T146–T147; Theme 2; Theme 9
Reteach	p. R28
Review	p. T160
See	*Extra Support Handbook,* pp. 186–187, 192–193

INSTRUCTION

COMPREHENSION: Noting Details

❶ Teach

Discuss noting details. Explain that readers use details from words and pictures to help them understand and remember a story.

- Say that details can be about characters or events.
- Ask individuals, *Who is a character in* EEK! There's a Mouse in the House? *What is something this character did?*
- Explain that children use details when they answer questions about a story.

Modeling Reread Anthology pages 165–166 aloud. Then demonstrate how to remember important details.

Think Aloud *I want to remember details about the characters and what they did. The first animal called into the house is the cat, so I'll write* cat *on the board. The cat knocked over the lamp, so I'll draw a picture of a lamp next to the word* cat. *This will help me to remember what the cat did.*

❷ Guided Practice

Create a details chart.

- Have children page through the story and name the animals as they appear.
- Write the animals' names on the board.
- Have children copy the animals' names and draw a picture to help them remember what each animal did, as in the Think Aloud.

❸ Apply

Choose one or more of these activities.

- Have partners make a list of the animals in *The Sleeping Pig*, note one detail about each animal to help them remember what the animal did, and use the list to retell the story.
- Assign **Practice Book** page 80.
- Have children apply this skill as they read the **Leveled Readers.** You may also select books from the Leveled Bibliography for this theme (pages T6–T7).

Test Prep Tell children that questions on reading tests usually focus on important details only. Explain that noting important details as they read can help children do better on reading tests.

Leveled Readers and Leveled Practice

Children at all levels apply the comprehension skill as they read their Leveled Readers. See lessons on pages T166–T169.

- ● **BELOW LEVEL** — *The Feast* by Jake Walker illustrated by Marsha Slomowitz
- ▲ **ON LEVEL** — *Going Fishing*
- ■ **ABOVE LEVEL** — *Zeke Takes a Bath* by Carrie Waters illustrated by Peter Grosshauser
- ◆ **LANGUAGE SUPPORT** — *Fun and Food to Eat* by Jake Walker illustrated by Marsha Slomowitz

Reading Traits

Teaching children how to note details is one way of encouraging them to "read the lines" of a selection. This comprehension skill supports the reading trait **Establishing Comprehension.**

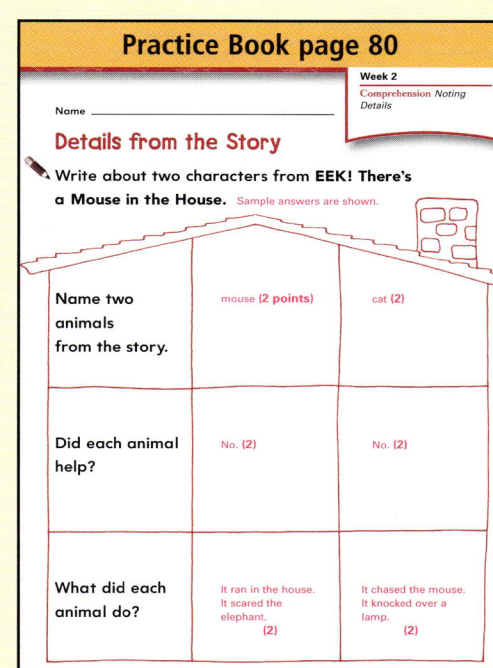

Practice Book page 80

Name _____

Week 2
Comprehension *Noting Details*

Details from the Story

Write about two characters from **EEK! There's a Mouse in the House.** Sample answers are shown.

Name two animals from the story.	mouse (**2 points**)	cat (2)
Did each animal help?	No. (2)	No. (2)
What did each animal do?	It ran in the house. It scared the elephant. (2)	It chased the mouse. It knocked over a lamp. (2)

Monitoring Student Progress

If . . .	Then . . .
children score 8 or below on **Practice Book** page 80,	use the Reteaching lesson on Teacher's Edition page R28.
children have met the lesson objectives,	use the Challenge/ Extension activities on Teacher's Edition page R29.

Practice Book page 81

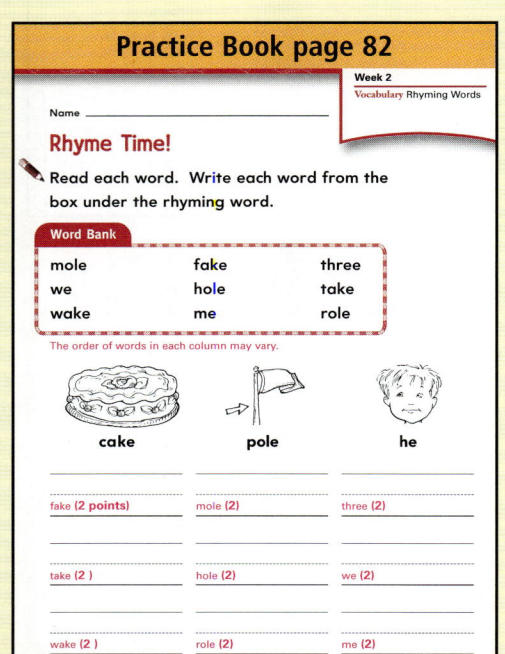

Name _____

Week 2
Spelling The Long *e* Sound

The Long *e* Sound

Write each word from the box under the word with the same long e spelling.

Spelling Words

| me | see | mean | feet | eat | he |

The order of words in each column may vary.

we	meet	treat
1. me (1 point)	2. see (1)	3. mean (1)
4. he (1)	5. feet (1)	6. eat (1)

Draw a silly picture to match the silly sentence.

(2)

He sees mean beans that eat feet.

SPELLING:
Words with Long *e* (*e, ee, ea*)

Which Word? Give partners word cards for the Basic Words and the following directions.

- *Put the stack of cards face-down.*
- *Take turns with your partner. Pick up a word card, read it silently, and give your partner clues about the word.*

Tell children they can use clues such as these:

- the meaning of the word
- the number of letters in the word
- a sentence clue, saying "blank" where the word should be, for example, *I'm hungry. I want to _____!* (*eat*)

Practice/Homework Assign **Practice Book** page 81.

Practice Book page 82

Name _____

Week 2
Vocabulary Rhyming Words

Rhyme Time!

Read each word. Write each word from the box under the rhyming word.

Word Bank

mole	fake	three
we	hole	take
wake	me	role

The order of words in each column may vary.

cake	pole	he
fake (2 points)	mole (2)	three (2)
take (2)	hole (2)	we (2)
wake (2)	role (2)	me (2)

VOCABULARY:
Rhyming Words

Rhyming Pairs Tell children they will listen for rhyming words in *EEK! There's a Mouse in the House*.

- Read Anthology page 165 aloud.
- Ask children if they hear any words that rhyme. Write *mouse/house, cat/rat*.
- Reread the story aloud as children listen for rhyming words.
- Write all the rhyming pairs, and read the list with the class.
- Ask children if they notice any patterns in how the words are spelled. (Rhyming words often end with the same letters.)

Practice/Homework Assign **Practice Book** page 82.

GRAMMAR: Naming Words for Places and Things

OBJECTIVES

• Identify naming words for places and things.

Skill Trace	
Teach	p. T149
Review	p. T165
See	*Handbook for English Language Learners*, p. 197

❶ Teach

Explain that naming words can name places and things.

• Remind children that some naming words name people and animals. Tell them that some naming words name places and things.

• Write *We went to the farm.* Point out that the word *farm* names a place.

• Write *There is a book on the table.* Point out that the words *book* and *table* name things.

• Write these sentences, and have children identify the words for places and things.

> Which room is yours?
>
> Please pick up your plate.
>
> That is my bike.
>
> Close the door.
>
> Do not pick those flowers.
>
> Let's go to the zoo.

Go over these points.

• Some naming words name places.

• Some naming words name things.

❷ Guided Practice

Check children's understanding. Have children look through *EEK! There's a Mouse in the House* to find words that name places and things. Tell them to list the words on paper and then compare lists with a partner.

❸ Apply

Assign Practice Book page 83.

Practice Book page 83

Week 2
Grammar Naming Words for Things and Places

Name _____

Naming Words

Read each sentence. Circle the naming word and draw a picture of it.

1. Here is a green (vase.)
   (1 point)

2. That (house) is small. (1)

3. Where is my (sled?) (1)

Use one of the circled words in a sentence.

_____
(2)
_____

Day at a Glance
pages T150–T157

Learning to Read

Reading the Math Link
Animals Big and Small

Phonics Review
Long *o* (CV, CVC*e*) and Long *u* (CVC*e*)

• • • • • • • • • • • • • • • • • • •

Leveled Readers, *T166–T169*

● *The Feast*
▲ *Going Fishing*
■ *Zeke Takes a Bath*
◆ *Fun and Food to Eat*

Word Work

Spelling: Words with Long *e*
Vocabulary: Expressions of Surprise

Writing & Oral Language

Writing: Answering a Comprehension Question

Daily Routines

Daily Message

Review skills. Point to each word as you read aloud the Daily Message.

> Good Morning, Children!
>
> What would you do if you found a mouse in your house? Would you shout for a cow? Would you call for a horse to chase it out the door? I would _____.

Have children

- suggest ways to complete the unfinished sentence;
- circle the long *a* word; (chase)
- find and read the following high-frequency words: *Good, Morning, Children, would, found, house, shout, cow, call,* and *horse*.

Word Wall

High-Frequency Word Review Write the following sentences on the board. Read the sentences with children and have them complete the sentences, using this week's words from the Word Wall.

> Will you walk _____ the _____? (through; door)
>
> _____ is a picture on the _____. (There; wall)
>
> The _____ and the _____ are in the barn _____. (cow; horse; now)
>
> I left the book on the _____. (table)

Daily Phonemic Awareness

Segmenting and Counting Phonemes: Pennies for Sounds

- Distribute pennies or counters to children.

- One at a time, say the words *beep, leash, creep, sweet, peak,* and *fleece.* Ask children to say the separate sounds in each word. Examples: /b//ē//p/ for *beep*; /k//r//ē//p/ for *creep.*

- Have children put down a penny for each sound they say, forming a horizontal line. Have them count the pennies and tell how many sounds are in the word.

Daily Language Practice

Grammar Skill: Punctuation

Spelling Skill: Words with Long *e*

Write the sentence, read it to children, and have them tell you how to correct it.

Hee has two cats

(**He** has two cats.)

Daily Writing Prompt

Remind children to write in complete sentences when responding to the prompt below or writing on self-selected topics.

- **Write and draw about what you would do if you found a mouse in your house.**

Daily Independent Reading

To increase children's reading fluency, provide a variety of theme-related books for them to read. Here are some suggestions.

- Leveled Bibliography, pages T6–T7

Choose books from this list for children to read, outside class, for at least twenty minutes a day.

- Anthology: *EEK! There's a Mouse in the House*

- Theme Paperbacks: *Fox and Mule, The Little Red Hen, Fishing Bears*

- Leveled Readers

- Book Boxes

Math Link

Animals Big and Small

Animals come in many shapes and sizes. Let's look at some of the biggest and smallest animals in the world.

Skill: How to Read a Pictograph

- A pictograph is a chart that uses pictures to compare things.
- These pictographs show the size of animals compared to people.

186

Blue Whale

The biggest animal in the world is the blue whale. It can grow to 100 feet long. That's longer than sixteen six-foot men lying head to toe!

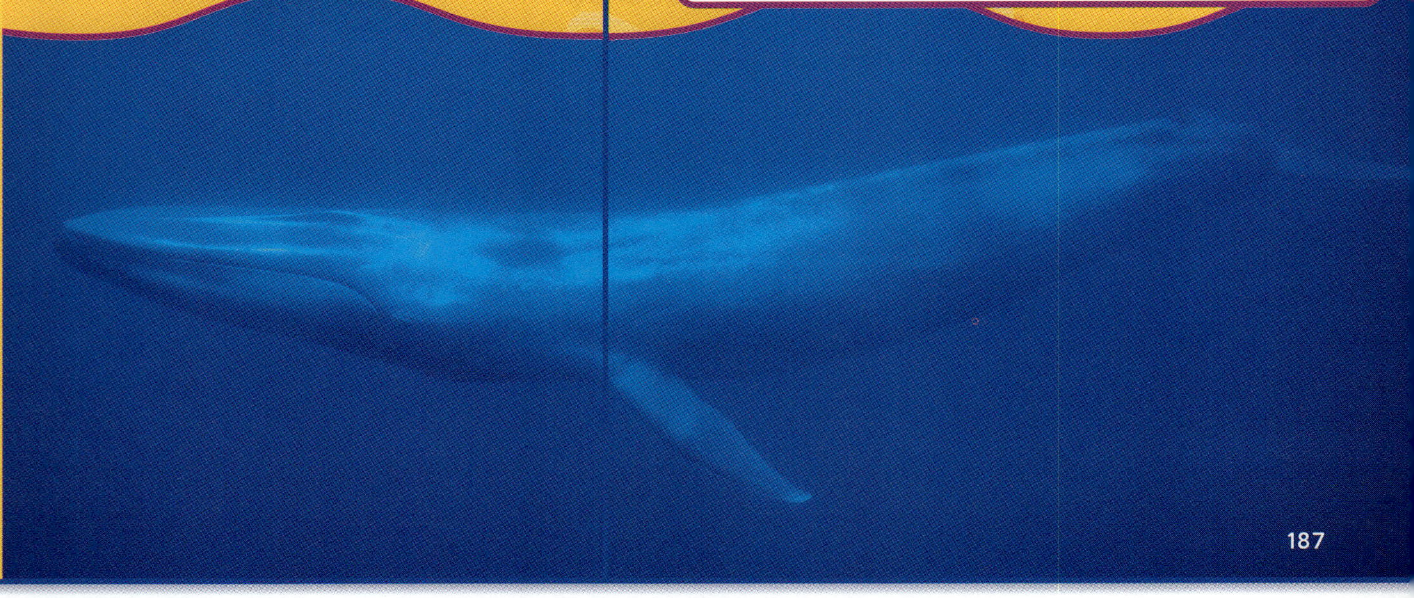

187

Math Link

Skill: How to Read a Pictograph

Introduce the Link. Read aloud the title and explain that this article tells about some of the biggest and smallest animals on Earth.

Discuss the Skill Lesson. Point out that the pictographs in this article help readers to understand more about the animals.

Model how to read a pictograph. Read aloud the paragraph about the blue whale. Explain that the pictograph shows how small a person would look standing next to a blue whale.

Set a purpose for reading. Tell children to look for animals that are larger than people and those that are smaller than people. Then read the article together.

Vocabulary

Write the Concept Vocabulary on the board and read each word. Point to *Cuba* on a map. Explain *harvest* and ask how children think the harvest mouse got its name. Point out the pictographs and have children find inches and feet on a yardstick. If possible, have children measure out the length or height of each animal shown in the pictograph.

Concept Vocabulary

pictograph	harvest
feet	Cuba
inches	

REACHING ALL LEARNERS

Extra Support/Intervention

Language Development

Review the adjectives *big, bigger, biggest; long, longer, longest; small, smaller, smallest; tall, taller, tallest.* Make sure children understand that *big* and *small* refer to over-all size, *tall* refers to height, and *long* refers to length.

THEME 6: Animal Adventures
(Anthology pp. 186–187)

Giraffe

- Giraffes are the tallest animals in the world.
- Some giraffes grow as tall as nineteen feet.
- That's taller than three men standing on top of each other's shoulders!

Harvest Mouse

Some harvest mice are no more than three inches long. That's about as long as a grown-up's finger!

Bee Hummingbird

The bee hummingbird from Cuba is just two inches long. That's shorter than a grown-up's thumb!

188   189

Wrapping Up

Critical Thinking Questions

1. **NOTING DETAILS** How long can a whale grow to be? (100 feet long)

2. **NOTING DETAILS** What is the tallest animal in the world? (a giraffe)

3. **COMPARE AND CONTRAST** Which animals are bigger than a person? (whale, giraffe) Which are smaller? (harvest mouse, bee hummingbird)

4. **COMPARE AND CONTRAST** Which animal from *EEK! There's a Mouse in the House* would be closest in size to a blue whale? (the elephant) Which animal would be closest in size to a bee hummingbird? (the mouse)

Visual Literacy

Showing with Words

Teach

Have children look at the words *Big* and *Small* in the article's title. Explain that sometimes words in the title of a story or article are written in a way that shows what they mean. Point out that *Big* is written in big letters and *Small* is written in little letters.

Practice/Apply

Have children think of words to describe their favorite animals such as *furry, feathery, huge, spotted,* and *striped.* Write the words on the board. Then ask children to choose a word and write it in a way that shows what it means.

Math Link
(Anthology pp. 188–189)   **T153**

OBJECTIVES

- Make words with long *o* (CV, CVC*e*) and long *u* (CVC*e*).
- Review final clusters *ft, lk, nt*.

Target Skill Trace

Teach	pp. T32–T34
Reteach	pp. R12, R14
Review	pp. T154–T155
See	*Handbook for English Language Learners*, pp. 179, 185; *Extra Support Handbook*, pp. 174, 175, 180, 181

Materials

- **Large Sound/Spelling Cards** *ocean, unicorn*
- **Large Letter Cards** *d, e, l, n, o, r, s, u*
- **Practice Book** punchout trays and letters *d, e, l, n, o, r, s, u*
- teacher-made word cards *rose, nose, tune, rude, under, understood*
- **Picture Cards** *raft, milk, ant*
- **Teacher's Resource Blackline Master 81**

REVIEW

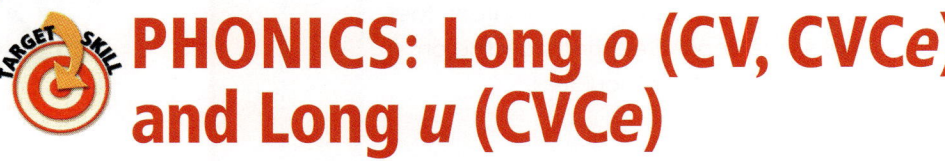

PHONICS: Long *o* (CV, CVC*e*) and Long *u* (CVC*e*)

❶ Review

Review long *o* (CV, CVC*e*) and long *u* (CVC*e*).

- Display **Large Sound/Spelling Card** *ocean*. Have children name the picture. Point to the letter *o*. Remind children that the /ō/ sound at the beginning of *ocean* is called the long *o* sound. Remind them that *o* also stands for the /ō/ sound at the end of *so* and in the middle of *hose*. Have children say /ōōō/ as you point to the letter.

- Repeat for **Large Sound/Spelling Card** *unicorn*. Remind children that the /yoo/ sound at the beginning of *unicorn* is called the long *u* sound. Say that *u* stands for the /yoo/ sound in *cube* and the /oo/ sound in *flute*. Have children say /yoo/ and /oo/ as you point to the letter.

❷ Guided Practice/Apply

Making Words

Get ready. Place the **Large Letter Cards** in a pocket chart. Distribute punchout letters to children. Name the letters as children hold up their matching punchout letters.

Have children make words. Say the directions and sentences below. After children make each word, ask a child to display the word with **Large Letter Cards.** Have children check their work.

Take four letters and make the word nose. *(My nose itches.)*

Change the first letter to make rose. *(The rose is red.)*

Change one letter to make rode. *(I rode my bike.)*

Change one letter to make rude. *(Don't be rude.)*

Change one letter to make rule. *(Obey the rule.)*

Extension/Challenge *Add one letter to* rude *and rearrange the letters to make* under. *(I looked under the bed.)*

Big Word Make a big word using all the letters. (*understood*)

Word Sort Have children sort the word cards into piles of words with long *o*, long *u*, and short *u*.

PHONICS:
Final Clusters *ft, lk, nt*

❶ Review

Review final clusters *ft, lk, nt*. Write *ft, lk, nt*. Display **Picture Cards** *raft, milk, ant* under the consonant clusters. Have children name the pictures.

- Remind children that sometimes two consonants come together at the end of a word.

- Ask children what letters stand for the sounds at the end of *raft*. (*ft*) Repeat for *milk* and *ant*. (*lk, nt*)

❷ Guided Practice/Apply

Game Show

Get ready to play Game Show.
- Cut apart the clue cards from **Blackline Master 81.**

- Label three columns on the board *ft, lk, nt*.

- Tape the cards under the appropriate cluster with the clues facing the board, hidden from view. On the other side of the cards, write 100, 200, 300, and 400 as shown.

Play the game.
- Have children take turns choosing a category and an amount. For example, a child may say, "I want a word that ends with *ft* for 400."

Game Show		
ft	lk	nt
100	100	100
200	200	200
300	300	300
400	400	400

- Turn over the 400 card in the *ft* column, and read the clue aloud. Have the child answer the clue with a word.

- If the child's answer is correct, write the word on the clue card, and tape it back on the board so that both the clue and the answer show. If the child's answer is incorrect, turn the card over and go on to the next child. Help children keep track of their scores as they play.

Practice Book page 84

Name

Spelling Spree

Week 2
Spelling The Long e Sound

Write the Spelling Word for each clue.

same as I

1. me **(1 point)**

not nice   him

2. mean **(1)**   3. he **(1)**

Spelling Words

me
see
mean
feet
eat
he

Proofread each sentence. Circle each Spelling Word that is wrong, and write it correctly.

4. Do you (sea) the cow?   see **(1)**

5. It has big (fete).   feet **(1)**

6. It likes to (eet) grass.   eat **(1)**

PRACTICE

SPELLING:
Words with Long *e* (*e, ee, ea*)

"Could It Be?" Asked the Flea Tell children they will play a game called "Could It Be?" Asked the Flea.

- Ask children what vowel sound they hear in the words *be* and *flea*. (long e)
- Tell children that you will say a word. If the word has the long *e* sound, children should say *"Could it be?" asked the flea.*
- If children are correct, you will say *Yes indeed, Mr. Flea.* If they are incorrect, you will say *Sorry, Mr. Flea. Listen more carefully!*
- Have children write each word with the long *e* sound.
- Repeat with *me, get, set, he, feet, met, mean, men, ten, eat, ship, see.*

Practice/Homework Assign **Practice Book** page 84.

INSTRUCTION

VOCABULARY:
Expressions of Surprise

Identify words of surprise.

- Display Anthology page 164. Point out the word *EEK!* in the story title.
- Tell children that *EEK!* is an expression of surprise. Remind them that each time an animal comes into the house and does something funny, the girl uses a new expression of surprise.
- Have children look at Anthology pages 165–166, reading the expressions *EEK!* and *Uh-oh!*

Practice/Apply

- Have small groups list all the expressions of surprise in the story.
- Have groups compare lists and practice saying the expressions in surprised voices.

WRITING: Answering a Comprehension Question

❶ Teach

Discuss answering questions about a story. Remind children that after they read *EEK! There's a Mouse in the House,* they answered questions about the story. Say that answering questions is a way to make sure they understand the story. Point out that sometimes children are asked to write the answer to a question.

Demonstrate how to write the answer to a question.

- Say *Let's think about how to answer a question.*
- Write and read aloud *What two animals are sent into the house first in the story?*
- Model the process of answering the question.

Think Aloud *I know that the cat is sent in to chase the mouse, and the dog is sent in to chase the cat. I'll write* A cat and a dog are sent into the house first.

Go over these points.

- To answer a question, think about what happens in the story.
- Write your answer in a complete sentence.

❷ Practice

Check children's understanding. Ask *What animal shouts "EEK!" when it sees the mouse?* Have children agree on the answer and write it in a sentence. (The elephant shouts, "EEK!")

❸ Apply

Assign Practice Book page 85. After they have finished independently, have pairs of children read their sentences to each other to make sure they answer the questions.

Practice Book page 85

Week 2
Writing Answering a Question

Name _____

What Happened?

Read each question about **EEK! There's a Mouse in the House.** Write your answer in a complete sentence.
Sample answers are provided.

1. What was the first animal that came in the house?

The mouse was the first animal that came in the house. (2 points)

2. How do you think it got in the house?

It came through a hole in the wall. (2)

3. Why did the girl think the elephant could get rid of all the other animals?

He was big. (2)

Writing **T157**

Day at a Glance
pages T158–T165

Learning to Read

Comprehension: Rereading for Understanding
Noting Details
Rereading for Fluency
Reading Decodable Text
Gram's Huge Meal

• • • • • • • • • • • • • • • • •

Leveled Readers, T166–T169

- ● *The Feast*
- ▲ *Going Fishing*
- ■ *Zeke Takes a Bath*
- ◆ *Fun and Food to Eat*

Word Work

Spelling Test: Words with Long *e*
Vocabulary: High-Frequency Words

Writing & Oral Language

Grammar Review: Naming Words for Places and Things
Independent Writing
Viewing: Retelling

Daily Routines

Daily Message

Strategy Review Remind children of the Phonics/Decoding Strategy. Guide them in applying it to selected words in today's message.

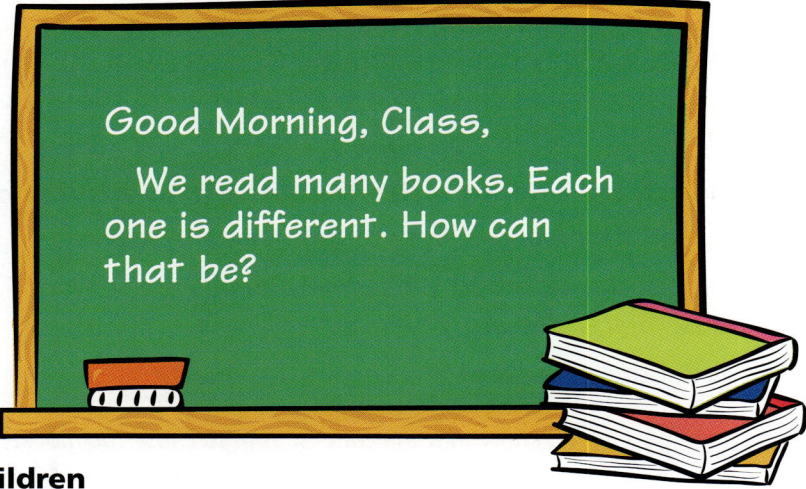

> Good Morning, Class,
>
> We read many books. Each one is different. How can that be?

Have children

- respond to the question;
- circle the long e words; *(We, read, each, be)*
- find and read the following high-frequency words: *many, one,* and *How.*

Word Wall

Cumulative Review Review new and previously taught high-frequency words from the Word Wall. Have children use **Activity Master 6–2** on Teacher's Edition page R37 to play a matching game.

Have children

- cut out the word cards;
- work with a partner;
- place cards face-down and take turns turning over two cards at a time, trying to match rhyming words.

grow

show

Daily Phonemic Awareness

Segmenting and Counting Phonemes: Foot-Stomping Sounds

- One at a time, say the words *bead, treat, cheap, cheek, feast, deep,* and *green*.

- Ask children to say the separate sounds. Examples: /b/ /ē/ /d/ for *bead*; /t/ /r/ /ē/ /t/ for *treat*.

- Have children stomp one foot for each sound they say and tell you how many times they stomped. Example: After stomping three times for *bead*, children should say "Three!"

Daily Language Practice

Grammar Skill: Punctuation
Spelling Skill: Words with Long *e*
Write the sentence, read it to children, and have them tell you how to correct it.

Will she et that

(Will she **eat** that?)

Daily Writing Prompt

Have children write on self-selected topics or in response to the prompt below. Remind them to write in complete sentences.

- **Write and draw about something you like to do on weekends.**

On Saturday I go to the park with my dad. We jog together. Then we get a snack.

Daily Independent Reading

To increase children's reading fluency, provide a variety of theme-related books for them to read. Here are some suggestions.

- Leveled Bibliography, pages T6–T7

Choose books from this list for children to read, outside class, for at least twenty minutes a day.

- Anthology: *EEK! There's a Mouse in the House*

- Phonics Library: *Seal Beach, Pete and Peach, Gram's Huge Meal*

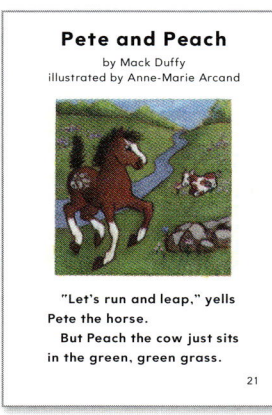

Pete and Peach
by Mack Duffy
illustrated by Anne-Marie Arcand

"Let's run and leap," yells
Pete the horse.
But Peach the cow just sits
in the green, green grass.

21

REREADING

WEEK 2

OBJECTIVES

- Review noting details in the week's selections.

Review Skill Trace

Teach	pp. T146–T147
Reteach	p. R28
► Review	p. T160
See	*Extra Support Handbook,* pp. 186–187, 192–193

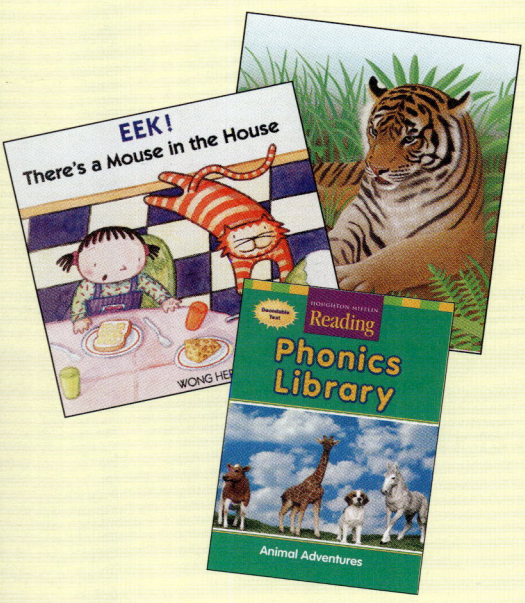

TARGET SKILL COMPREHENSION: Rereading for Understanding

Noting Details

Review reasons for noting details. Remind children that noting details about characters and what they do can help readers to better understand and enjoy a story.

Display Chart/Transparency 6–7. Refer to it as you use the Think Aloud to review noting details in the Read Aloud story, *Tiger and Anansi.*

Think Aloud *The characters in* Tiger and Anansi *are Tiger, Anansi, and Snake. Now I'll think about the important things the characters do: Tiger asks Anansi to get Snake; Anansi tricks snake; Anansi brings Snake to Tiger.*

Review noting details in *EEK! There's a Mouse in the House.* Call on children to help you fill in the right-hand column of the chart/transparency.

- Ask who the characters are and what they did.
- Ask what details are similar in the two stories. (Both stories have animal characters; both stories have a very small animal and a very large animal.)

Assign rereading and retelling.

- Have children reread these other selections for this week, thinking about story structure: **On My Way Practice Reader, Theme Paperbacks, Phonics Library, Leveled Readers.**
- Have children reread *Pete and Peach* or *Seal Beach,* and make a list of story details to retell the story to a partner.

Chart/Transparency 6–7

Noting Details

Responses will vary.

	Tiger and Anansi	EEK! There's a Mouse in the House
Characters	Tiger Anansi Snake	the girl mouse cat rat hog cow dog sheep
What they did	Tiger asked Anansi to get Snake. Anansi tricked Snake. Anansi brought Snake to Tiger.	The cat knocked over the lamp. The dog broke a dish. The hog ate the cake.

TARGET SKILL REREADING FOR FLUENCY

Rereading the Selection Have children choose part of *EEK! There's a Mouse in the House* to reread orally in small groups, or suggest that they read pages 179–180. If necessary, model fluent reading. Encourage children to read with feeling and expression.

Phonics Library

Animal Adventures

Gram's Huge <u>Meal</u>

by Edward Op
illustrated by Anna Herrick

Gram made a huge <u>meal</u>. She set it on a long, long <u>table</u>. Then she went to get Pops.

25

PHONICS LIBRARY

End-of-Week Skills Check

Have children preview *Gram's Huge Meal*. Ask them what kinds of food they see in the pictures.

Observe as children model the Phonics/Decoding Strategy.

- Have children read *Gram's Huge Meal*. As they read, ask individuals to tell how they use the strategy to figure out new words.

- Make note of children who have difficulty applying the strategy and take oral reading records with these children.

Prompt children in rereading the story. For children who have difficulty, use prompts such as these:

- *Look at the letters from left to right. What letters do you see?*

- *Say the sound for each letter and hold it until you say the next sound. What is the word?*

- *Is that a word you know? Does it make sense in the story?*

OBJECTIVES

- Apply the Phonics/Decoding Strategy to decode words in context.
- Recognize high-frequency words in context.
- Reread to build fluency.

Word Key

Decodable words with long *e* and vowel pairs *ee, ea* ———

High-Frequency Words ———

Monitoring Student Progress

Oral Reading Records Take oral reading records of a few children each week as they read the **Phonics Library** book individually or in small groups.

Alternative Assessment Use **Teacher's Resource Blackline Master 82** to assess individual children's phonics and high-frequency word skills.

A white <u>cow</u> with black spots <u>leaned</u> in.

"Pops will not <u>eat</u> <u>these</u> <u>beans</u> and <u>peas</u>," she said. "This is a <u>fine</u> <u>feast</u>."

26

A big black <u>horse</u> stuck his neck in.

"Pops will not eat these <u>green</u> <u>grapes</u>," he said. "This is a <u>real</u> <u>treat</u>."

27

Oral Language

Discuss these questions with children. Have them answer in complete sentences.

• What part of the meal won't Pops eat? (He won't eat beans, peas, and green grapes.)

• Why do you think Pops says the meal is just right? (He is probably happy because the animals took away the food he doesn't like.)

Pops and Gram came in.
"Yum!" said Pops. "Now this
meal is just right!"

28

Build Fluency

Model and have children practice fluent reading.

- Read aloud page 27. Then have children read it with you.

- Call attention to the exclamation points on page 28. Explain that this mark means to read with excitement.

- Read the page aloud. Have children read it in unison.

- Have children reread pages 27 and 28 several times until each child can read them aloud effortlessly.

Home Connection

Hand out the take-home version of *Gram's Huge Meal*. Ask children to reread the story with their families. (See the **Phonics Library Blackline Masters**.)

OBJECTIVES
- Take a test on the Basic Words.
- Review the week's high-frequency words.

OBJECTIVES
- Take a test on the Basic Words.
- Review the week's high-frequency words.

Materials
- Word Wall Cards, p. R34
- Word Wall Cards from previous weeks
- teacher-made word cards for vocabulary speed drills

TEST

SPELLING:
Words with Long *e* (*e, ee, ea*)

Test

Say each underlined word, read the sentence, and then repeat the word. Have children write only the underlined word.

Basic Words

1. Is this for **me**?
2. Did you **see** the big bug?
3. I know what you **mean**.
4. An ant has six **feet**.
5. What do you like to **eat** for dinner?
6. Ted can see that **he** will win.

REVIEW

VOCABULARY:
High-Frequency Words

Review the words. Tell children they will play "I Spy" with New Words from the Word Wall. Explain that you will pick a word, and they will ask yes-or-no questions to figure out the word.

- Say *I spy a word. What is it?* If necessary, prompt children to ask questions such as these:

  Does it begin with *m*?

  Does it have more than two letters?

  Does it rhyme with another word on the Word Wall?

- Allow children to ask questions until they identify the word.
- Then have children clap and spell each New Word. Call on a child to move the word to the permanent Word Wall as children chant it aloud.

Practice/Apply Have vocabulary speed drills. Assemble the Word Wall Cards for this week's New Words and several other words from previous weeks. Make a few other cards for decodable words that feature the week's phonics/decoding elements.

- At small group time, have children take turns holding up the cards for a partner to read.
- Then display the cards as a list on a table. Have individuals read them to you as quickly as they can.

GRAMMAR: Naming Words for Places and Things

Review Remind children that some naming words name places and things.

List naming words for places and things.

- Have small groups create lists of names for places and things.
- Give each group a category, such as places in the school, places people work, places to have fun, toys, vehicles, fruits, or plants.

Practice/Apply

- Have each child in the group pick a name to illustrate and label.
- Bind the list and the drawings together to create a book.
- Give the book a title indicating the category.

Independent Writing Have children write a journal entry that includes the names of places and things. Then have them go back and underline all the words that name places and things.

OBJECTIVES

- Review naming words for places and things.
- Retell a story using illustrations as a guide.

Review Skill Trace	
Teach	p. T149
▶ Review	p. T165
See	*Handbook for English Language Learners,* p. 197

VIEWING: Retelling

Have children retell a story.

- Tell children that retelling a story is a good way to help them understand and remember the story.
- Have pairs of children retell *EEK! There's a Mouse in the House* to each other, using the words and the illustrations to guide them.
- Remind them that the picture on the wall in each illustration gives a clue about what will happen next.

English Language Learners

Supporting Comprehension

Review the story with English language learners before they retell it, asking questions such as these for Anthology page 165: *What animal is running away from the girl? What do you see on the table? What animal is in the picture on the wall? Does the girl look happy?* Write key words on the board for reference.

Leveled Readers

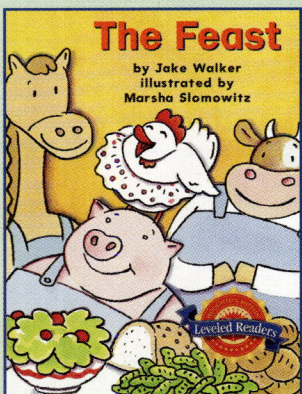

The Feast

Summary *On a cold, snowy night a farmer lets a shivering group of animals into his house. As the farmer and his wife sit down at their table to eat a wonderful feast, the animals start to have fun. Soon, the animals are dancing and clapping to music on the radio. And after an excited horse jumps on the dinner table, the animals end up with a feast of their own.*

Story Words

Introduce the Story Words, one at a time, providing meaning with objects, pictures, gestures, and/or context sentences. Then ask children to complete the Vocabulary Practice Master.

cold p. 2

farmer p. 2

feast (title), p. 3

dance p. 5

Building Background and Vocabulary

Explain that this book is about what happens when some farm animals are invited into the farmhouse during dinner. Encourage children to share what they know about real farm animals and stories they've read or heard about farm animals that act like people. Be sure children know that a *feast* is a special, big meal.

Comprehension Skill: Noting Details

Read together the Strategy Focus on the book flap. Remind children to use the strategy and to note details as they read the book. (See the Leveled Readers Teacher's Guide for **Vocabulary and Comprehension Practice Masters**.)

Responding

Have partners discuss how to answer the questions on the inside back cover.

Think About What You Have Read Sample answers:

1. It's snowing outside and the animals are cold.
2. The animals sit and watch the farmer and his wife. But they can't sit still, and they soon begin to dance and leap about.
3. Answers will vary.

Making Connections Answers will vary.

Building Fluency

Model Help children locate some of the words in the story that describe actions, such as *sit, dance, clap, jumps up,* and *fall down.* Then invite them to follow along and watch for the words that describe actions as you reread the story aloud.

Practice Have partners take turns reading the pages. As one child reads, the partner can pantomime the action described on that page.

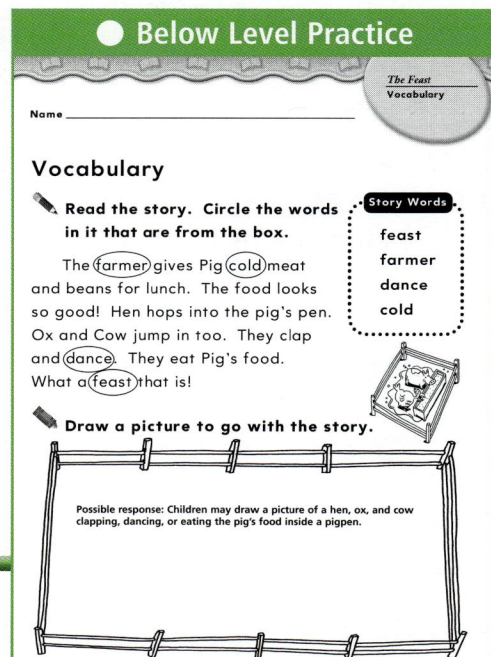

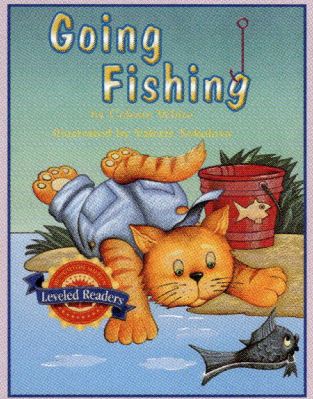

Going Fishing

Summary *After falling in the creek, Pete, a cat that likes to fish, tries to repair his torn strap. But he finds that something he needs is missing. Pete's friend Ben has lost something, too. Pete watches outside the barn to find out what might have happened to their things. Soon the friends discover that Rose, the mouse, borrowed their things to make a fishing pole for Pete so he wouldn't have to get wet.*

Story Words

Introduce the Story Words, one at a time, providing meaning with objects, pictures, gestures, and/or context sentences. Then ask children to complete the **Vocabulary Practice Master.**

fishing (title), *p. 2*

creek *p. 2*

walked *p. 3*

string *p. 3*

take *p. 5*

pole *p. 11*

Building Background and Vocabulary

Tell children that this story is about three friends, Pete, Ben, and Rose. Have children preview the illustrations to determine what kind of animals Pete, Ben, and Rose are. Then invite them to share what they know about fishing and fishing equipment.

Comprehension Skill: Noting Details

Read together the Strategy Focus on the book flap. Remind children to use the strategy and to note details as they read the book. (See the Leveled Readers Teacher's Guide for **Vocabulary and Comprehension Practice Masters.**)

Responding

Have partners discuss how to answer the questions on the inside back cover.

Think About What You Have Read   Sample answers:

1. Pete ripped the strap on his pants while he was fishing.

2. a mouse named Rose

3. Yes. She made a fishing pole for Ben and went fishing with them.

Making Connections   Answers will vary.

Building Fluency

Model   Write a set of quotation marks on the chalkboard, and remind children that they can find the words that the characters say by looking for sets of quotation marks like these. Reread the story aloud, asking children to follow along and to watch for the words spoken by the characters.

Practice   Invite children to work with partners to reread the story. Have one child read any narrative parts, and the other read the quotes. Have partners switch roles on subsequent pages. Suggest that they read page 12 aloud together.

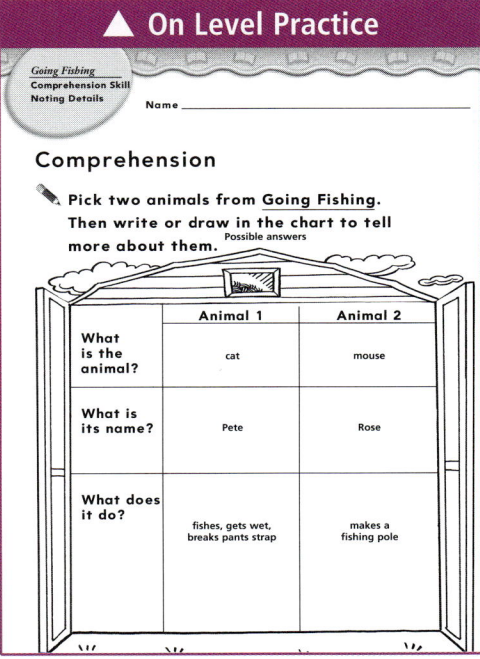

Leveled Readers

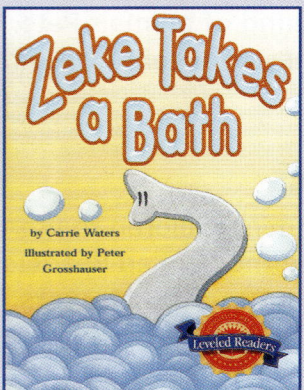

Zeke Takes a Bath

Zeke Takes a Bath
by Carrie Waters
Illustrated by Peter Grosshauser

Summary *Some farm animals are surprised to find Zeke, an elephant, taking a bath behind their barn. When they ask him to get out of the tub so that the ducklings can swim there, he says he is stuck. The animals then try to pull, push, and tip Zeke out of the tub, but without success. Zeke seems content to stay in the tub. But when he sees a mouse, he leaps up out of the tub and runs away.*

Story Words

Introduce the Story Words, one at a time, providing meaning with objects, pictures, gestures, and/or context sentences. Then ask children to complete the **Vocabulary Practice Master.**

elephant *p. 2*

bathtub *p. 3*

ducklings *p. 6*

stuck *p. 6*

free *p. 7*

afraid *p. 11*

■ ABOVE LEVEL

Building Background and Vocabulary

Have children share what they know about where horses, cows, sheep, ducks, and elephants usually live. Explain that this story is about a group of farm animals that discover an elephant taking a bath in a tub behind their barn.

⏺ Comprehension Skill: Noting Details

Read together the Strategy Focus on the book flap. Remind children to use the strategy and to note details as they read the book. (See the Leveled Readers Teacher's Guide for **Vocabulary and Comprehension Practice Masters.**)

Responding

Have partners discuss how to answer the questions on the inside back cover.

Think About What You Have Read Sample answers:

1. The animals had never seen an elephant on their farm.
2. Mother duck needed the tub for her ducklings, but there was no room for them.
3. Answers will vary.

Making Connections Answers will vary.

⏺ Building Fluency

Model Point out the set of quotation marks in the first sentence on page 2 that show the words that the sheep said. Read the line aloud. Ask children to find the other words on the same page that the sheep said, and to read those words aloud with you.

Practice Have children reread the story in small groups in which one child reads the narrative parts, and the others take turns reading the words spoken by each of the animals.

■ Above Level Practice

Zeke Takes a Bath
Vocabulary

Name _____

Vocabulary

✎ Write words from the box to complete the sentences.

Story Words
elephant
bathtub
ducklings
stuck
free
afraid

1. Zeke is an _____ elephant _____.

2. Baby ducks are _____ ducklings _____.

3. Get into the _____ bathtub _____ to get clean.

4. I got _____ stuck _____ in the mud.

5. The animals tried to set Zeke _____ free _____.

6. He was _____ afraid _____ of a mouse.

■ Above Level Practice

Zeke Takes a Bath
Comprehension Skill
Noting Details

Name _____

Comprehension

✎ Look carefully at the picture. Circle two things that are wrong and write about them.

1. Probable answer: The pig has duck feet.

2. Probable answer: The horse has horns.

Leveled Readers

Fun and Food to Eat

Summary *One cold night the farmer and his wife invite their animals inside, where it is warm. When the farmer and his wife sit down to eat, the animals entertain themselves. When the animals dance on the table, the food falls on the floor. Now they have a warm fire AND a hot meal!*

Story Words

Introduce the Story Words. Then ask children to complete the **Story Words Practice Master.**

animals living things that are not plants, *p. 2*

cold feeling a lack of warmth, chilly, *p. 2*

hungry wanting to eat food, *p. 4*

table a piece of furniture with a flat top and legs, *p. 6*

food things to eat, (title), *p. 8*

◆ LANGUAGE SUPPORT

Building Background and Vocabulary

Have children brainstorm a list of their favorite foods to eat. Record their responses on the board or on chart paper. Then have children complete the **Build Background Practice Master.** Invite them to compare the foods they drew with a partner's drawings. (See the Leveled Readers Teacher's Guide for **Build Background and Story Words Masters.**)

Reading Strategy: Question

Have children read the Strategy Focus on the book flap. Remind children to ask themselves questions as they read: *What do the people do? What do the animals do?*

Responding

Have partners discuss how to answer the questions on the inside back cover.

Think About What You Have Read Sample answers:

1. He lets the animals come inside the house.
2. Possible answer: Yes, because they are hungry and want to eat.
3. Answers will vary.

Making Connections Answers will vary.

Building Fluency

Model Have children point to each word on pages 2–3 as they follow along with the recording of *Fun and Food to Eat* on audio CD.

Practice Have children read aloud with the recording until they are able to read the text on their own, accurately and with expression.

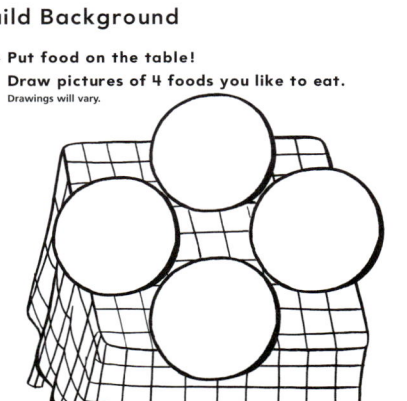

◆ **Language Support Practice**

Name _____

Build Background

✎ Put food on the table!
Draw pictures of 4 foods you like to eat.
Drawings will vary.

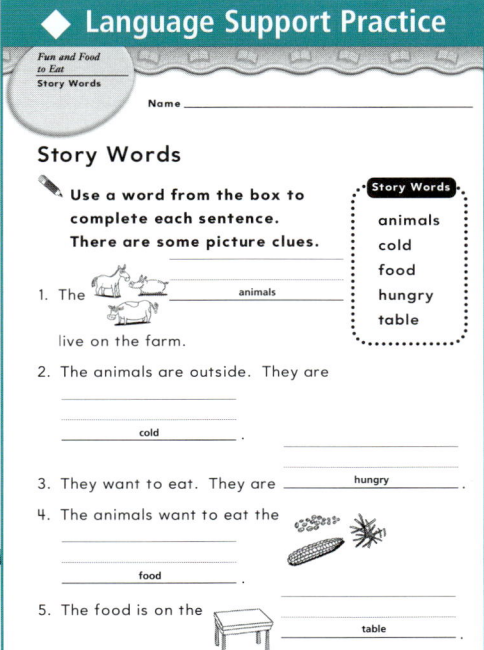

◆ **Language Support Practice**

Fun and Food to Eat
Story Words

Name _____

Story Words

✎ Use a word from the box to complete each sentence. There are some picture clues.

Story Words
animals
cold
food
hungry
table

1. The ___animals___ live on the farm.

2. The animals are outside. They are ___cold___.

3. They want to eat. They are ___hungry___.

4. The animals want to eat the ___food___.

5. The food is on the ___table___.

Lesson Overview

Literature

RED-EYED TREE FROG

BY JOY COWLEY • PHOTOGRAPHS BY NIC BISHOP

Selection Summary

Experience a day in the life of a red-eyed tree frog dwelling in a rain forest.

1 Decodable Text

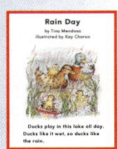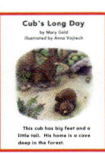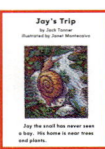

Phonics Library

- *Rain Day*
- *Cub's Long Day*
- *Jay's Trip*

2 Background and Vocabulary

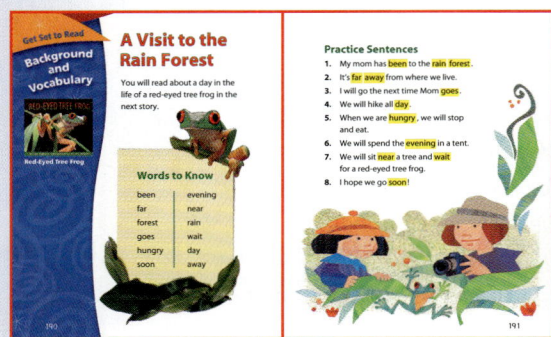

3 Main Selection

Red-Eyed Tree Frog
Genre: Nonfiction

4 Poetry Link

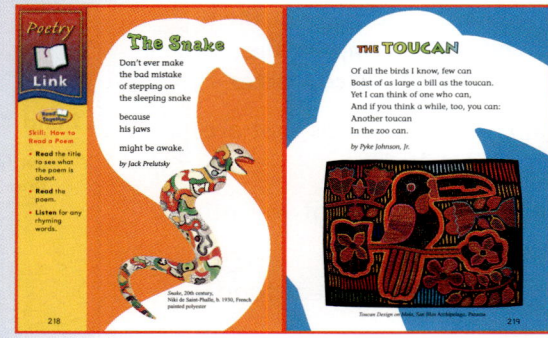

Instructional Support

Planning and Practice

- Planning and classroom management
- Reading and skill instruction
- Plans and activities for reaching all learners

- Newsletters
- Observation Checklists
- Theme Activity Masters
- Alternative Weekly Tests

- Independent practice for skills, Level 1.3

- Decodable Text, Books 62–63, Review Books 58–63

- Charts/ Transparencies
- Strategy Posters
- Blackline Masters

Reaching All Learners

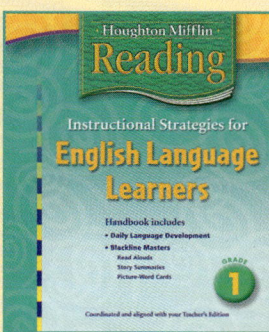

Coordinated lessons, activities, and projects for additional reading instruction

For
- Classroom Teacher
- Extended Day
- Pull Out
- Resource Teacher
- Reading Specialist

Technology

Audio Selection
Red-Eyed Tree Frog

Get Set for Reading CD-ROM
- Background building
- Vocabulary support
- Selection Summary in English and Spanish

Accelerated Reader®
Practice quiz for the selection

www.eduplace.com
Log on to Education Place for more activities related to the selection, including vocabulary support—

- e • Glossary
- e • WordGame

Lesson Overview **T171**

Leveled Books for Reaching All Learners

Leveled Readers and Leveled Practice

- Independent reading for building fluency
- Topic, comprehension strategy, and vocabulary linked to main selection
- Lessons in Teacher's Edition, pages T238–T241
- Leveled practice for every book

Technology

Leveled Readers
Available on CD

Book Adventure®
Practice quizzes for the Leveled Theme Paperbacks

www.bookadventure.org

● BELOW LEVEL

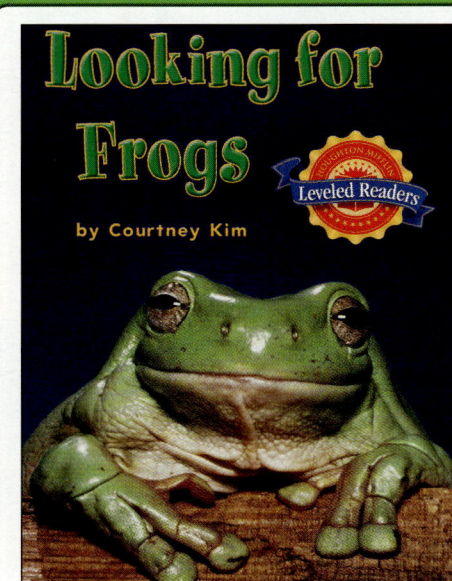

Looking for Frogs
by Courtney Kim
Leveled Readers

▲ ON LEVEL

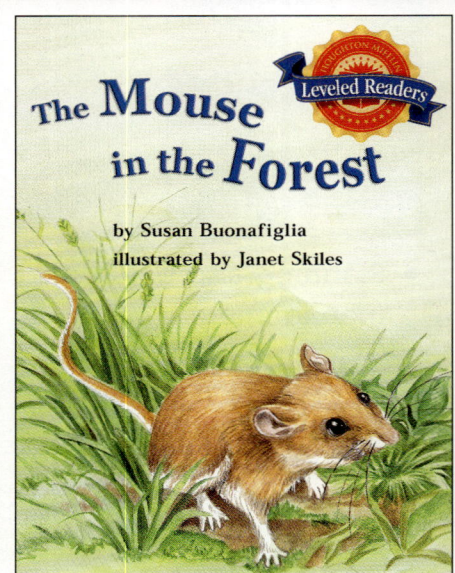

The Mouse in the Forest
by Susan Buonafiglia
illustrated by Janet Skiles
Leveled Readers

● Below Level Practice

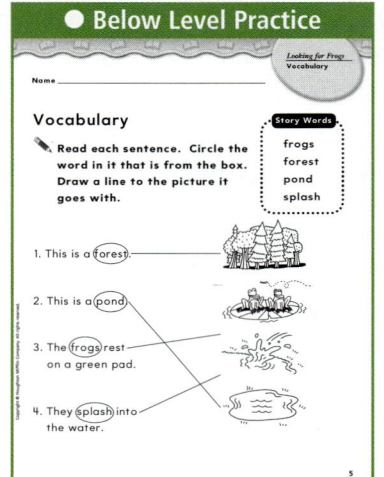

● Below Level Practice

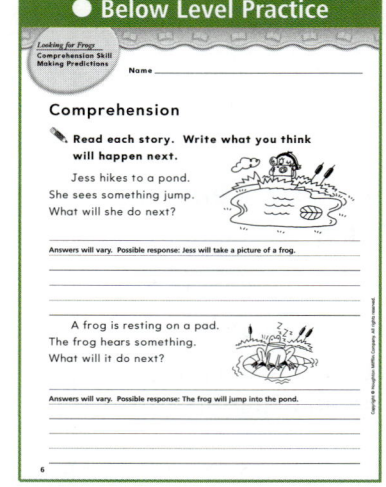

▲ On Level Practice

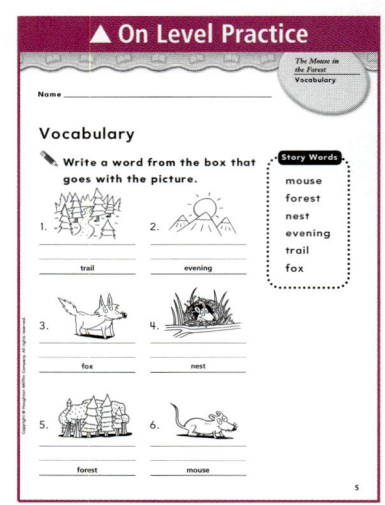

▲ On Level Practice

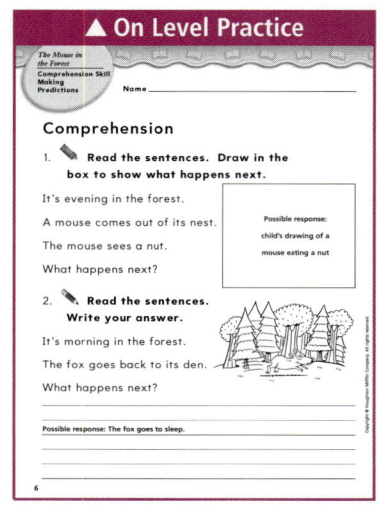

■ ABOVE LEVEL

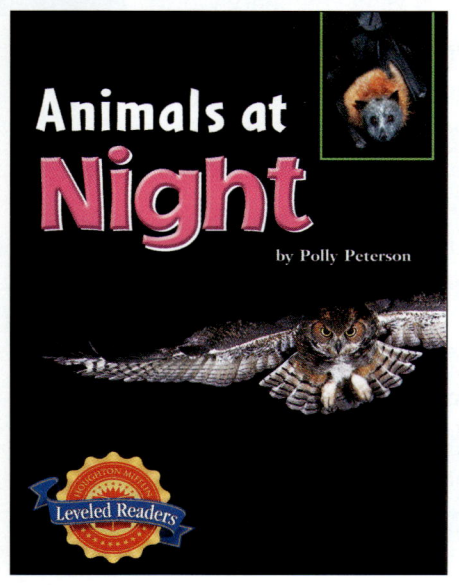

Animals at Night by Polly Peterson

■ Above Level Practice

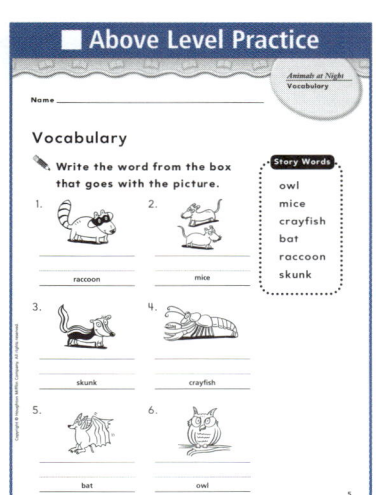

Vocabulary

✎ Write the word from the box that goes with the picture.

Story Words
owl
mice
crayfish
bat
raccoon
skunk

■ Above Level Practice

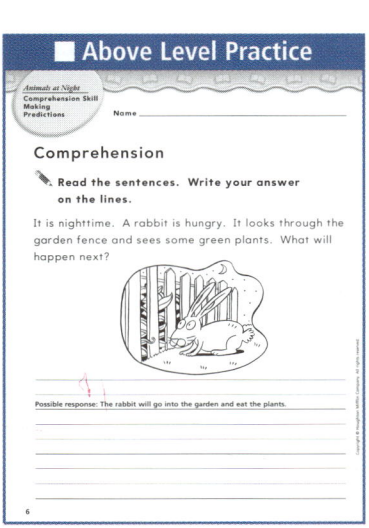

Comprehension

✎ Read the sentences. Write your answer on the lines.

It is nighttime. A rabbit is hungry. It looks through the garden fence and sees some green plants. What will happen next?

◆ LANGUAGE SUPPORT

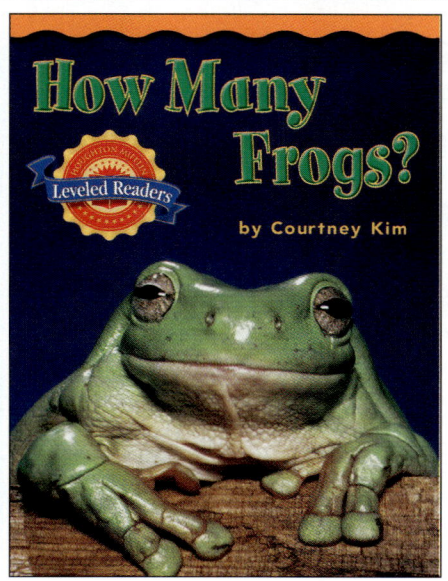

How Many Frogs? by Courtney Kim

◆ Language Support Practice

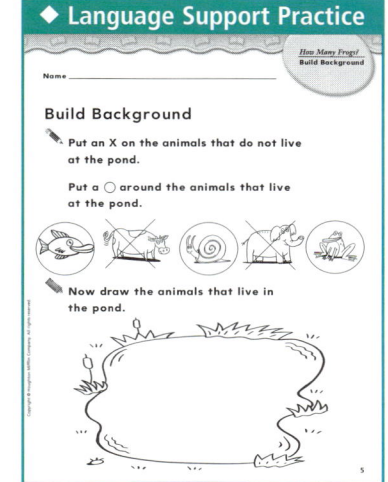

Build Background

✎ Put an X on the animals that do not live at the pond.

Put a ○ around the animals that live at the pond.

✎ Now draw the animals that live in the pond.

◆ Language Support Practice

Story Words

✎ Write the words from the box to label the picture.

Story Words
fish
frog
pond
snails
splash

Leveled Books

- Extended independent reading in theme-related paperbacks
- Lessons in Teacher's Edition, pages R9–R11

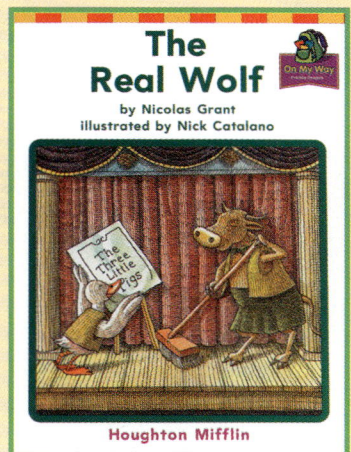

The Real Wolf by Nicolas Grant illustrated by Nick Catalano

Houghton Mifflin

Below Level

Suggested Books

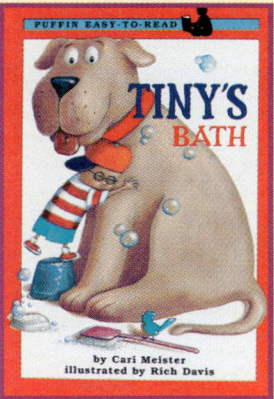

TINY'S BATH by Cari Meister illustrated by Rich Davis

On Level

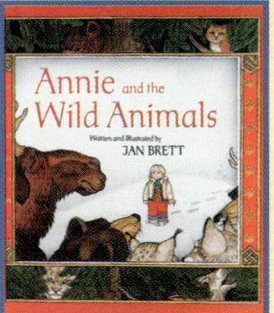

Annie and the Wild Animals Written and Illustrated by JAN BRETT

Above Level

Daily Lesson Plans

Technology
Lesson Planner CD-ROM allows you to customize the chart below to develop your own lesson plans.

T Skill tested on Integrated Theme Test and/or Theme Skills Test

---

 80–90 minutes

Learning to Read

Phonemic Awareness
Phonics
Comprehension

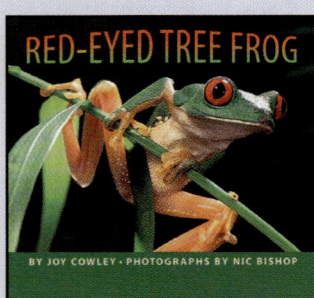

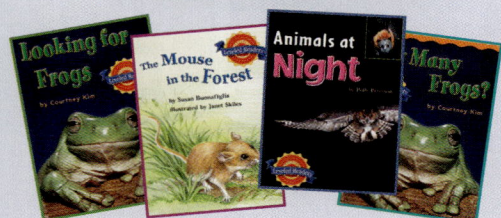

Leveled Readers
- Fluency Practice
- Independent Reading

 20–30 minutes

Word Work

Spelling
Vocabulary and High-Frequency Words

 20–30 minutes

Writing and Oral Language

Writing
Grammar
Listening/Speaking/Viewing

WEEK 3 / **DAILY LESSON PLANS**

DAY 1

Daily Routines, T180–T181
Phonics, High-Frequency Words,
Phonemic Awareness,
Independent Reading, Writing

Listening Comprehension, T182–T183
Life in a Rain Forest

Phonics, T184–T186
Vowel Pairs *ai, ay* **T**

Reading Decodable Text, T187–T189
Rain Day

Rain Day
by Tina Mendoza
illustrated by Kay Chorao
Ducks play in this lake all day. Ducks like it wet, so ducks like the rain.
29

Leveled Readers
Looking for Frogs
The Mouse in the Forest
Animals at Night
How Many Frogs?

Lessons and Leveled Practice, T238–T241

Spelling, T190
Words with *ay* **T**

Vocabulary, T190
Word Wall: Spelling Pattern *-ay*

Daily Language Practice
1. I and Jan walk home.
   (**Jan** and **I** walk home.)

✏ **Shared Writing,** T191
A Class Summary

Listening, T191
To Retell

DAY 2

Daily Routines, T192–T193
Phonics, High-Frequency Words,
Phonemic Awareness,
Independent Reading, Writing

High-Frequency Words, T194–T195
been, evening, far, forest, goes, hungry, near, soon **T**

Building Background, T196

Story Vocabulary, T197
boa, caterpillar, eyed, eyes, iguana/s, katydid, macaw, moves, poisonous, tongue, toucan

Reading the Selection, T198–T211

Comprehension Strategy, T198
Predict/Infer

Comprehension Skill, T198
Making Predictions **T**

Leveled Readers
Looking for Frogs
The Mouse in the Forest
Animals at Night
How Many Frogs?

Lessons and Leveled Practice, T238–T241

Spelling, T212
Practice: Words with *ay* **T**

Vocabulary, T212
Review: High-Frequency Words **T**

Daily Language Practice
2. Will you play with me.
   (Will you **play** with me?)

✏ **Interactive Writing,** T213
A Class Summary

Target Skills of the Week

Phonemic Awarenesss	Segment Phonemes; Count Sounds in Words
Phonics	Vowel Pairs *ai, ay*
Comprehension	Making Predictions, Predict / Infer
Vocabulary	High-Frequency Words; Parts of the Body; Animal Action Words
Fluency	Leveled Readers; Decodable Text: Phonics Library

DAY 3

Daily Routines, T214–T215

Phonics, High-Frequency Words,

🎯 **Phonemic Awareness,**

Independent Reading, Writing

Comprehension Check, T216

Responding, T216

🎯 **Comprehension Skill,** T218–T219
Making Predictions **T**

Leveled Readers

Looking for Frogs
The Mouse in the Forest
Animals at Night
How Many Frogs?

Lessons and Leveled Practice, T238–T241

Spelling, T220
Practice: Words with *ay* **T**

🎯 **Vocabulary,** T220
Parts of the Body

Daily Language Practice
3. I can saay it four time.
    (I can **say** it four times.)

✏️ **Writing: Responding,** T217
Write a Riddle

Grammar, T221
Naming Words for One or More **T**

DAY 4

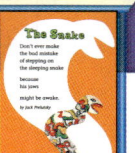

Daily Routines, T222–T223

Phonics, High-Frequency Words,

🎯 **Phonemic Awareness,**

Independent Reading, Writing

Reading the Poetry Link, T224–T225

Comprehension:
How to Read a Poem, T224

🎯 **Phonics Review,** T226–T227
Long e (CV, CVCe)
Vowel Pairs *ee, ea*

Leveled Readers
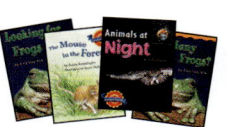
Looking for Frogs
The Mouse in the Forest
Animals at Night
How Many Frogs?

Lessons and Leveled Practice, T238–T241

Spelling, T228
Practice: Words with *ay* **T**

🎯 **Vocabulary,** T228
Animal Action Words

Daily Language Practice
4. Maye Don come over!
    (**May** Don come over?)

✏️ **Independent Writing,** T229
Writing a Summary

DAY 5

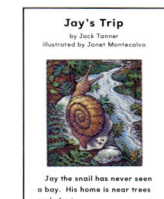

Daily Routines, T230–T231

Phonics, High-Frequency Words,

🎯 **Phonemic Awareness,**

Independent Reading, Writing

🎯 **Comprehension: Rereading for Understanding**
(Making Predictions **T**) T232

🎯 **Rereading for Fluency,** T232

🎯 **Reading Decodable Text,** T233–T235
Jay's Trip
End-of-the-Week Skills Check

> **Jay's Trip**
> by Jack Tanner
> Illustrated by Janet Montecalvo
>
> Jay the snail has never seen a bay. His home is near trees and plants.
>
> 37

Leveled Readers
Looking for Frogs
The Mouse in the Forest
Animals at Night
How Many Frogs?

Lessons and Leveled Practice, T238–T241

Spelling, T236
Test: Words with *ay* **T**

🎯 **Vocabulary,** T236
Review: High-Frequency Words

Daily Language Practice
5. what dayy can you be here?
    (**What day** can you be here?)

✏️ **Independent Writing,** T237
Journal Entry

Grammar Review, T237
Naming Words for One or More **T**

Listening and Speaking, T237
Listening for Information

Managing Flexible Groups

Leveled Instruction and Leveled Practice

	DAY 1	DAY 2
WHOLE CLASS	• Daily Routines (TE pp. T180–T181) • Teacher Read Aloud (TE pp. T182–T183) • Phonics (TE pp. T184–T186)	• Daily Routines (TE pp. T192–T193) • High-Frequency Words (TE pp. T194–T195) • Get Set to Read, Strategy and Skill, Purpose Setting (TE pp. T196–T199) *After Reading at Small Group Time* • Wrapping Up (TE p. T211); Comprehension Preview (TE p. T207)
SMALL GROUPS		
Extra Support	**TEACHER-LED** • Phonics Library: *Rain Day* (TE pp. T187–T189) • Selected I Love Reading Books: 62–63	**TEACHER-LED** • Anthology selection (TE pp. T198–T211) • Phonics Library: *Cub's Long Day* (TE p. T195) **Partner or Individual Reading** • Read with audio CD of Anthology selection. • **Fluency Practice** Reread Phonics Library: *Rain Day* OR selected I Love Reading Books: 62–63.
On Level	**TEACHER-LED** • Phonics Library: *Rain Day* (TE pp. T187–T189)	**TEACHER-LED** • Anthology selection (TE pp. T198–T211) • Phonics Library: *Cub's Long Day* (TE p. T195) • **Fluency Practice** Reread Phonics Library: *Rain Day* (TE pp. T187–T189) ✔ OR begin Leveled Reader: On Level (TE p. T239).
Challenge	**Partner or Individual Reading** • Phonics Library: *Rain Day* • **Fluency Practice** Reread Little Big Book *Two's Company* OR book from Leveled Bibliography.	**Partner or Individual Reading** • Anthology selection • Phonics Library: *Cub's Long Day* • **Fluency Practice** Reread Phonics Library: *Rain Day*.
English Language Learners	**TEACHER-LED** • Phonics Library: *Rain Day* (TE pp. T187–T189) • Selected I Love Reading Books: 62–63	**TEACHER-LED** • Phonics Library: *Cub's Long Day* (TE p. T195) • **Fluency Practice** Reread Phonics Library: *Rain Day*. (TE pp. T187–T189) ✔ **Partner or Individual Reading** • Read with audio CD of Anthology selection.

Independent Activities

- Get Set for Reading CD-ROM or audio CD of Anthology selection
- Journals: selection notes, questions
- Complete, review **Practice Book** (pp. 86–90, 91–92) and **Leveled Reader Practice Blackline Masters** (TE pp. T238–T241).

✔ Opportunity to informally assess oral reading rate.

DAY 3	DAY 4	DAY 5
• Daily Routines (TE pp. T214–T215)	• Daily Routines (TE pp. T222–T223)	• Daily Routines (TE pp. T230–T231)
After Reading at Small Group Time • Responding (TE p. T216) • Comprehension lesson (TE pp. T218–T219)	• Poetry Link (TE pp. T224–T225) • Phonics Review (TE pp. T226–T227)	• Rereading for Understanding (TE p. T232) • Responding: Select from activities (TE p. T217)

DAY 3

TEACHER-LED
- Read Anthology selection aloud to answer Guiding Comprehension. (TE pp. T198–T211)
- **Fluency Practice** Reread Phonics Library: *Cub's Long Day* OR selected I Love Reading Books: 62–63. ✔

Individual Reading
- Reread with audio CD of Anthology selection.
- **Fluency Practice** Reread Phonics Library: *Cub's Long Day* OR complete Leveled Reader: On Level.

TEACHER-LED
- Read aloud from Anthology to answer Guiding Comprehension. (T198–T211) ✔

Partner or Individual Reading
- Leveled Reader (TE p. T240) OR book from Bibliography

TEACHER-LED
- Reread Anthology selection, first half. (TE pp. T198–T206)

Partner or Individual Reading
- Reread Phonics Library: *Cub's Long Day*.
- Selected I Love Reading Books: 62–63

DAY 4

TEACHER-LED
- Read On My Way Practice Reader. (TE p. R9)
- Begin Leveled Reader: Below Level (TE p. T238) OR book from Leveled Bibliography.
- **Fluency Practice** Reread Phonics Library: *Rain Day, Cub's Long Day,* ✔ OR selected I Love Reading Review Books: 62–63.

Partner Reading
- Reread Anthology selection, partners alternating pages.
- **Fluency Practice** Reread Phonics Library: *Rain Day, Cub's Long Day,* OR Leveled Reader: On Level (TE p. T239).

TEACHER-LED
- **Fluency Practice** Reread Anthology selection, Link, OR Phonics Library. ✔

Partner or Individual Reading
- Begin book from Leveled Bibliography (TE p. R11).
- Reread Little Big Book *Two's Company.*

TEACHER-LED
- Reread Anthology sel., last half. (T207–T211)
- Begin Leveled Reader: Language Support (T241) OR On My Way Practice Reader (R9).

Individual Reading
- **Fluency Practice** Phonics Library: *Rain Day, Cub's Long Day*

DAY 5

TEACHER-LED
- Phonics Library: *Jay's Trip* (TE pp. T233–T235)
- Complete Leveled Reader: Below Level (TE p. T238)
- **Fluency Practice** Reread On My Way Practice Reader (TE p. R9), Phonics Library books, OR selected I Love Reading Review Books: 62–63. ✔

TEACHER-LED
- Phonics Library: *Jay's Trip* (T233–T235) AND reread Link. (T224–T225)
- **Fluency Practice** Reread Phonics Library, Anthology, OR Leveled Reader. ✔

Partner or Individual Reading
- Suggested Trade Book (TE p. R10) or another book from Leveled Bibliography.

Individual Reading
- Phonics Library: *Jay's Trip*
- Complete Suggested Trade Book (R11) or another book from Bibliography.
- **Fluency Practice** Reread Anthology selection and Link, Little Big Book, Above Level Theme Paperback, OR Leveled Reader.

TEACHER-LED
- Phonics Library: *Jay's Trip* (TE pp. T233–T235)
- Complete Leveled Reader: Language Support (T241) OR On My Way Practice Reader (R9).
- **Fluency Practice** Reread week's Phonics Library books, Anthology selection, OR selected I Love Reading Books: 62–63. ✔

- Reread familiar selections.
- Read trade book from Leveled Bibliography (TE pp. T6–T7).
- Responding activities (TE pp. T216–T217)
- Activities related to *Red-Eyed Tree Frog* at Education Place: www.eduplace.com

Turn the page for more independent activities.

Classroom Management

Independent Activities

Assign these activities while you work with small groups.

Differentiated Instruction for Small Groups

- **Handbook for English Language Learners,** pp. 198–207
- **Extra Support Handbook,** pp. 194–203

Independent Activities

- Daily Routines, pp. T181, T193, T215, T223, T231
- Challenge/Extension Activities, pp. R19, R25, R31
- **Classroom Management Handbook,** pp. 138–145
- **Challenge Handbook,** pp. 70–71

Look for more independent activities in the Classroom Management Kit.

Phonics Center

Word Booklets

👤 Singles	⏱ 45 minutes
Objective	Create a picture dictionary of *ai* and *ay* words.
Materials	Teacher's Resource Blackline Masters 199–200, pencil, crayons

- Have children look through classroom books, games, and labels for words with *ai* and *ay*.
- Children can write the words on **Blackline Masters 199–200** and illustrate them.

Social Studies Center

Survival Kit

👥 Groups	⏱ 30 minutes
Objective	Create a frog's survival kit.
Materials	*Red-Eyed Tree Frog,* paper, crayons, bucket or box

- Have groups of three look through *Red-Eyed Tree Frog* to help them think about what the frog would need for food, drink, and shelter.
- Each group member should draw a different item the frog would need.
- Children place their drawings in a box or bucket to create a frog's survival kit.
- Different groups can compare the items they put in their kits.

Consider copying and laminating these activities for use in centers.

Writing Center
Animal Mysteries

👥 Pairs	🕐 25 minutes
Objective	Write an animal description.
Materials	writing paper, pencil

- Have individuals write a description of an animal they read about, without naming the animal.
- Pairs of children can exchange descriptions and try to guess their partner's animal.

> My feathers are red, blue, and yellow.

Science Center
Camouflaged Frogs

👤 Singles	🕐 25 minutes
Objective	Color frogs and test their camouflage.
Materials	paper, crayons, scissors

- Have children color a picture of a frog to match a colorful surface in the room.
- Children can cut out their frogs and place them on the surface to test how well the camouflage works.
- Have children test the frog's camouflage on other surfaces as well.

Technology Center
Create a Book Cover

👤 Singles	🕐 30 minutes
Objective	Create a book cover.
Materials	computer, crayons, paper

Ask children to design a new book cover for *Red-Eyed Tree Frog*.

- Have them use a computer to type the title, *Red-Eyed Tree Frog*, using the shift key to make capital letters.
- Children can use the toolbar to change the font and size of the type.
- Have children print out their cover and use crayons to draw a picture beneath the title.

Red-Eyed Tree Frog

DAY 1
week 3

Day at a Glance
pages T180–T191

Learning to Read

Teacher Read Aloud
Life in a Rain Forest

Phonics Instruction
Vowel Pairs *ai*, *ay*

Reading Decodable Text
Rain Day

• •

Leveled Readers, *T238–T241*

● *Looking for Frogs*
▲ *The Mouse in the Forest*
■ *Animals at Night*
◆ *How Many Frogs?*

Word Work

Spelling: Words with *ay*
Vocabulary: Spelling Pattern *-ay*

Writing & Oral Language

Shared Writing: A Class Summary
Listening: To Retell

Daily Routines

Daily Message

Review skills. Point to each word as you read aloud the Daily Message.

> Hello Children!
>
> How did you get to school this morning?
>
> How many people walked?____
> How many people came by bus?____
> How many people came by car? ____
> How many people rode bikes? ____

Have children

• respond to the questions (you write the total by each question);

• create four towers with math cubes, using a different color cube for each mode of transportation and compare the towers;

• circle words with long *a*, long *i*, and long *o*; (came (2), rode, bikes)

• find these high-frequency words: *How, many, people, walked,* and *car.*

Word Wall

High-Frequency Word Review Briefly review these and other high-frequency words daily. Have children practice reading, chanting, spelling, and writing them.

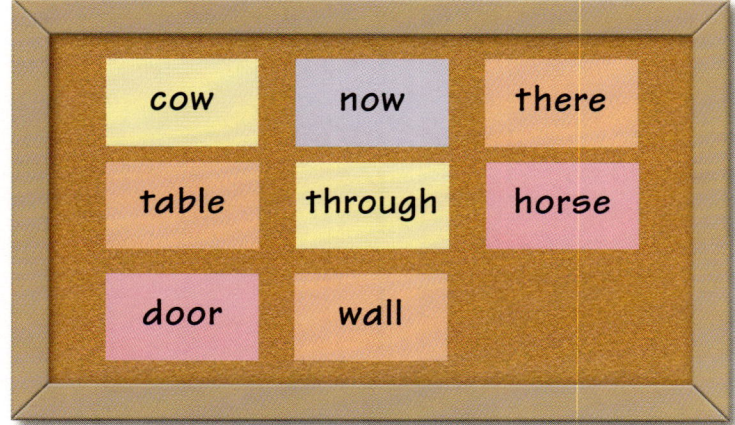

Blackline Master for these Word Wall Cards appears on page R34.

Daily Phonemic Awareness

Segmenting and Counting Phonemes: Tap the Sounds

- Tell children that you will say a word and they should say the separate sounds. Have them tap once for each sound on their desk.

  Teacher: *My word is* chain. *Tap for each sound you say in* chain.

  Children: */ch//ā//n/*

  Teacher: *How many sounds did you hear?* (3)

- Call on individuals to say and tap sounds for the following words as classmates count: *plain* (4), *day* (2), *grain* (4), *tray* (3), *paid* (3), *main* (3), and *hay* (2).

Daily Language Practice

Grammar Skill: Using *I* or *me* in Sentences
Write the sentence, read it to children, and have them tell you how to correct it.

I and Jan walk home.

(**Jan** and **I** walk home.)

Daily Writing Prompt

Have children write on self-selected topics or in response to the prompt below. Remind children to write in complete sentences.

- **Draw and write about a place you would like to visit.**

I would like to visit a zoo.

Daily Independent Reading

To increase children's reading fluency, provide a variety of theme-related books for them to read. Here are some suggestions.

- Leveled Bibliography, pages T6–T7

Choose books from this list for children to read, outside class, for at least twenty minutes a day.

- Anthology: *EEK! There's a Mouse in the House*
- Phonics Library: *Seal Beach, Pete and Peach, Gram's Huge Meal*
- Leveled Readers

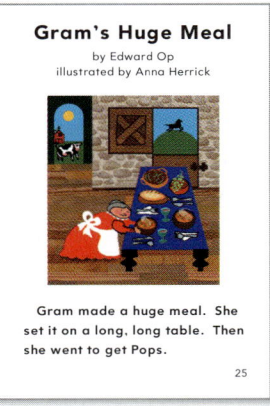

Gram's Huge Meal
by Edward Op
illustrated by Anna Herrick

Gram made a huge meal. She set it on a long, long table. Then she went to get Pops.

25

Listening Comprehension

* Listen to determine accuracy of predictions.

Building Background

Tell children that many different plants and animals live in the rain forest. Have children discuss what they know about the rain forest.

Fluency Modeling

Explain that you will model how to read facts and opinions clearly and with expression.

Making Predictions

Explain these concepts: Readers often make predictions as they are reading; to do this, readers use what they know and clues from the story or article.

Before reading the selection aloud, show children the picture on page T183 and read the title. Then ask children to predict what they will learn from the selection.

Guiding Comprehension

1. **MAKING PREDICTIONS** Did you predict that *Life in a Rain Forest* would be a story or an informational article? (Answers will vary.)

2. **MAKING PREDICTIONS** What did you predict you would learn? Did you learn any of those things? (Answers will vary.)

3. **NOTING DETAILS** Where do the animals in the rain forest get their food? (in the trees and on the ground)

Teacher Read Aloud

Life in a Rain Forest

Do you know what a rain forest is like? Picture a forest where it rains every day and it is always very hot. Add so many huge trees that the ground is dark and shadowy all day long. Big leaves and vines hang on everything. Now think of all kinds of animals everywhere you look—up in the trees, down on the ground, hiding in the bushes. Now you can visualize what a rain forest looks like!

It is very hard to move around in a rain forest. There are no cars. The ground is always wet, and there are bushes and trees everywhere. Hundreds of plants can live in a patch of rain forest shorter than a school bus!

Some animals in the rain forest spend their whole lives in trees and never need to come down to the ground for anything at all! Animals like monkeys, squirrels, bats, and parrots all eat fruits and nuts up there.

Some creatures are even built to live high above the ground. Flying squirrels can glide from tree to tree, and monkeys can swing from branch to branch. Sloths and porcupines hang by their tails.

Trees in the rain forest can grow to be 200 feet tall—that's taller than a ten-story building.

Where do animals that don't live in the trees get their food? Some get food from the ground. Deer, buffalo, and wild pigs snack on seeds, roots, and fallen fruit. Elephants munch on low plants. Panthers and tigers quietly prowl for their next meal.

Rain forests have survived for millions of years because plants and animals help each other in some way. They work together every day. Trees feed the animals, who in turn spread the seeds so more trees can grow. Each animal and plant has its own special job to do in the life of the rain forest.

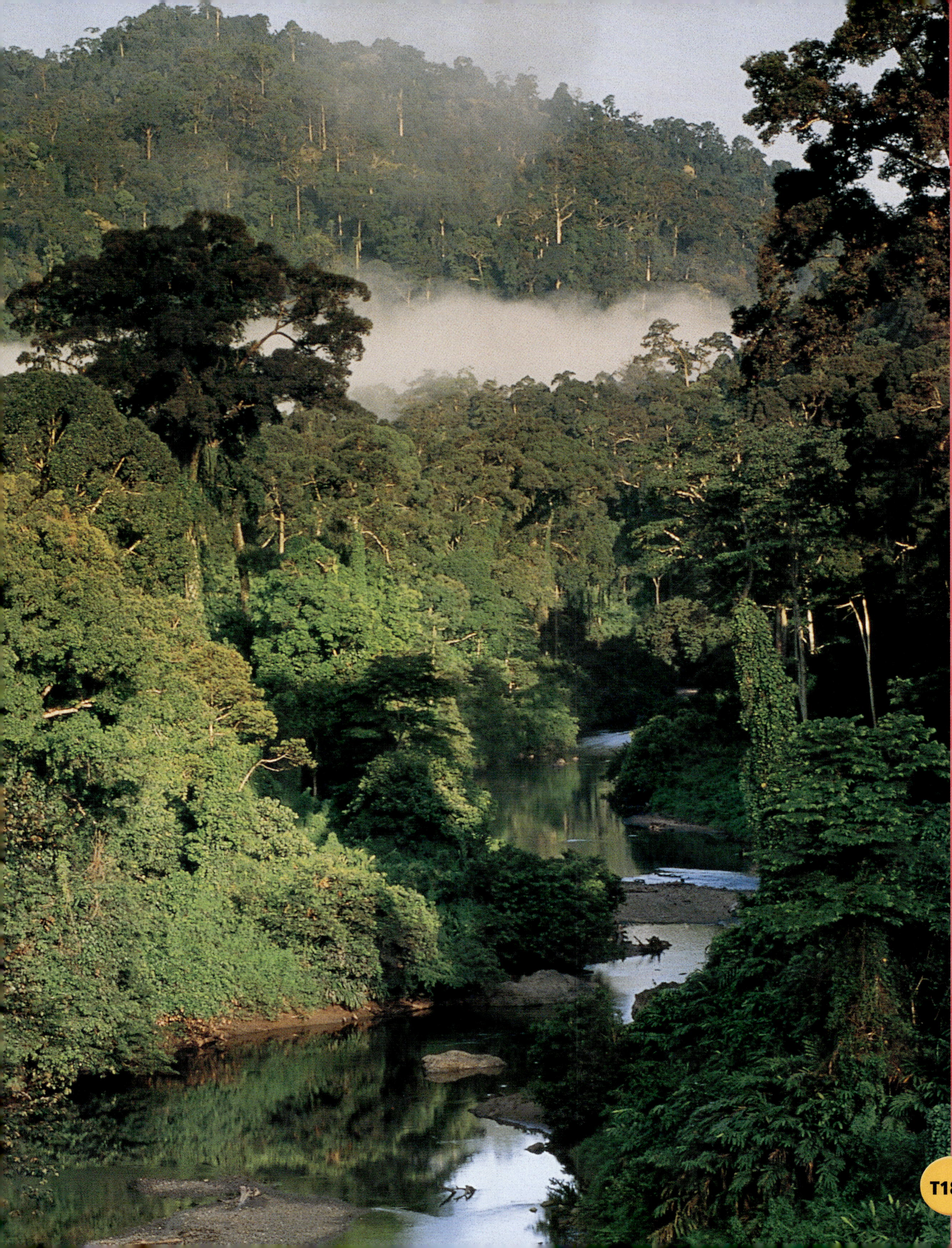

DAY
1

OBJECTIVES

- Segment phonemes and count sounds.
- Associate the sound /ā/ with vowel pairs *ai, ay.*
- Blend and read words with *ai, ay.*

Target Skill Trace

Teach	pp. T184–T186
Reteach	p. R18
Review	Theme 7, pp. T72–T73
See	*Handbook for English Language Learners,* pp. 199, 205; *Extra Support Handbook,* pp. 194–195, 200–201

Materials

- Large Sound/Spelling Card *acorn*
- Picture Cards *braid, chain, train; gray, hay, tray*
- Blending Routines Card 1
- Large Letter Cards *a, c, d, f, i, l, m, n, p, r, s, t, w, y*

INSTRUCTION

TARGET SKILL PHONICS: Vowel Pairs *ai, ay*

❶ Phonemic Awareness Warm-Up

Model how to segment phonemes and count sounds.

- Segment *say:* /s//ā/. Then clap and count the sounds in *say.* (2)
- Have children repeat each of the following words, say its sounds, and clap and count the sounds: *play* (/p//l//ā/, 3), *rain* (/r//ā//n/, 3), *train* (/t//r//ā//n/, 4), *stay* (/s//t//ā/, 3), *pay* (/p//ā/, 2), *wait* (/w//ā//t/, 3), *stray* (/s//t//r//ā/, 4), *main* (/m//ā//n/, 3), *spray* (/s//p//r//ā/, 4).

❷ Teach Phonics

Connect sounds to letters: *ai, ay,* /ā/.

- Display **Large Sound/Spelling Card** *acorn* and have children name the picture. Remind them that the /ā/ sound at the beginning of *acorn* is called the long *a* sound.

- Point out the vowel pairs *ai* and *ay* on the back of the card. Explain that when one of these letter pairs appears in a word, the first vowel, *a,* usually has the long *a* sound, and the second vowel, *i* or *y,* is silent.

- Display **Picture Card** *braid,* and have children name the picture. Write *braid,* and underline the vowel pair *ai.* Have children read *braid* with you. Repeat with *chain, train, gray, hay, tray.*

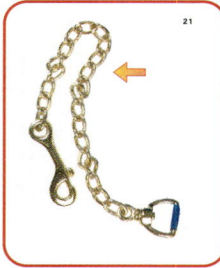

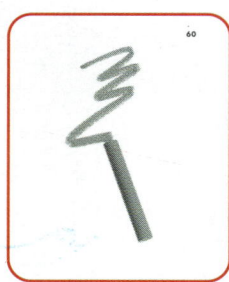

Model how to blend words with *ai* and *ay*.

- Write *say*. Underline *ay* and tell children you will use the long *a* sound for these letters.

- Using **Blending Routine 1,** model how to blend *say*.

- Continue with *nail, day, mail, main, stray, spray, snail, aim, bait*.

❸ Guided Practice

Check understanding.

- Display **Large Letter Cards** *r, a, i, n*. Have children blend *rain* and tell what letters spell the long *a* sound. (*ai*)

- Repeat with *stay, wait, may, pay, claim, drain, faint, maid, pain, paid, plain*.

I see r-a-i-n.
The word is rain.
The letters ai
spell the long
a sound.

Practice Book page 86

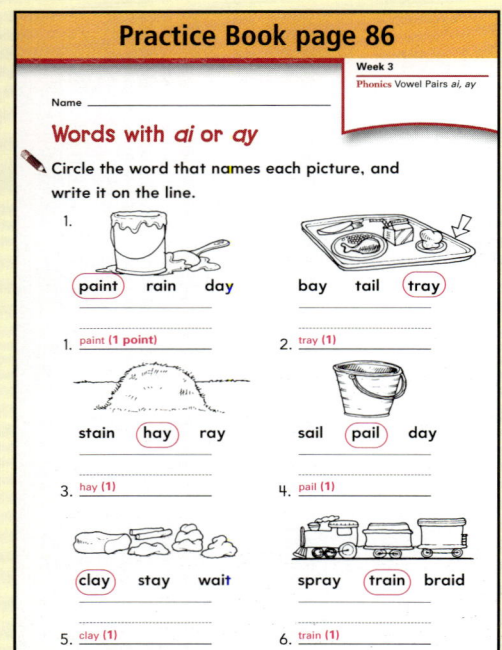

Practice Book page 87

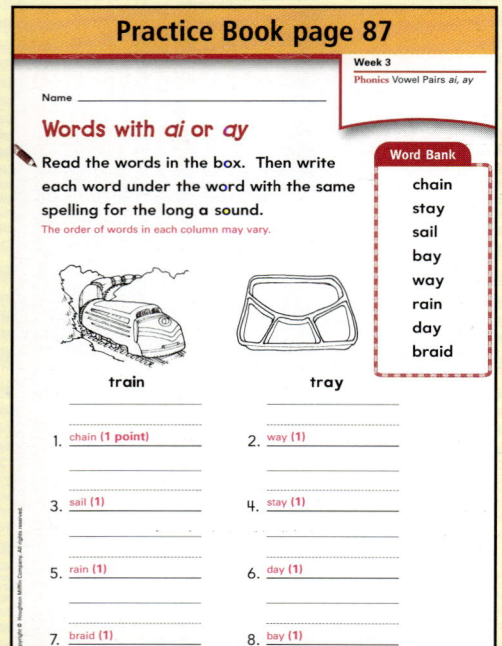

Monitoring Student Progress

If . . .	Then . . .
children score 10 or below on **Practice Book** pages 86–87,	use the Reteaching lesson on Teacher's Edition page R18.
children have met the lesson objectives,	use the Challenge/ Extension activities on Teacher's Edition page R19.

INSTRUCTION

PHONICS:
Vowel Pairs *ai*, *ay* continued

Connect sounds to spelling and writing.

- Tell children that you will say a word with the letters *ai*, and they are to write the word.
- Say *sail*. Have children repeat *sail* and then write it. Write *sail* on the board, and have children check their work.
- Repeat with *main, pail, brain, chain, gain, stain, strain, waist,* and the sentence *I sent the note by snail mail.*
- Now tell children you will say a word with the letters *ay*, and they are to write the word. Continue with *day, clay, hay, lay, ray, sway, may, gray, way, stay, Ray,* and the sentence *May will play by the bay.*

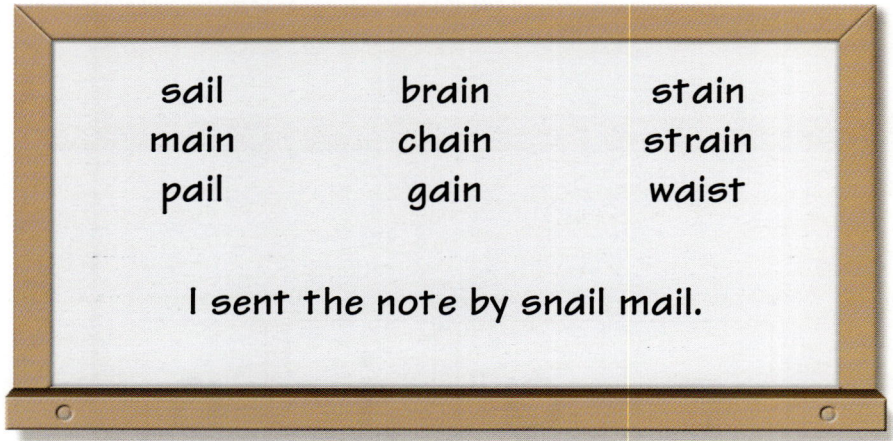

❹ Apply
Assign Practice Book pages 86–87.

HOUGHTON MIFFLIN

Reading

Decodable Text

Phonics Library

Animal Adventures

Rain Day

by Tina Mendosa
illustrated by Kay Chorao

Ducks play in this lake all <u>day</u>.
Ducks like it wet, so ducks like
the <u>rain</u>.

29

PHONICS LIBRARY

Reading Decodable Text

Have children preview _Rain Day_. Have them describe what happens in the pictures.

Model the Phonics/Decoding Strategy. Read the steps of the strategy on **Poster B** and use the strategy to read the story title.

Think Aloud _I see the first word has the vowel pair_ ai, _which stands for the long_ a _sound, /ā/. I'll blend the sounds /r//ā//n/,_ Rain. _The next word has_ ay, _which also stands for the /ā/ sound. I'll blend, /d//ā/,_ Day. _The title is_ Rain Day.

Apply the Phonics/Decoding Strategy. Have children read _Rain Day_. If necessary, coach them in applying the strategy to words such as _tail_.

- _Look at the letters from left to right. What sound does_ t _stand for?_ (/t/)
- _What sound does_ ai _stand for?_ (/ā/)
- _What sound does_ l _stand for?_ (/l/)
- _Blend the sounds. What is the word?_ (tail)
- _Does this word make sense in the story?_ (yes)

Word Key

Decodable words with vowel pairs
_ai, ay_ ————

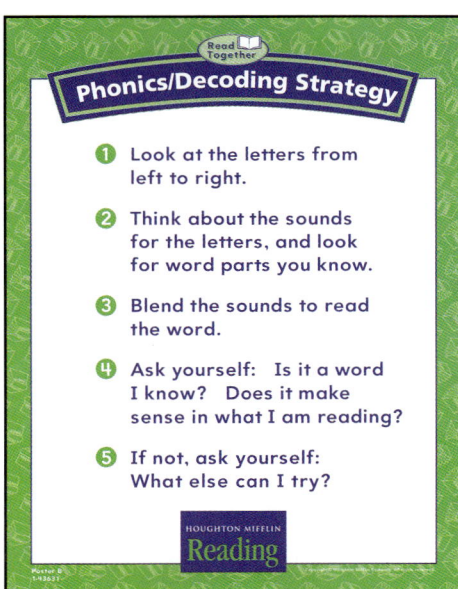

Read Together

Phonics/Decoding Strategy

❶ Look at the letters from left to right.

❷ Think about the sounds for the letters, and look for word parts you know.

❸ Blend the sounds to read the word.

❹ Ask yourself: Is it a word I know? Does it make sense in what I am reading?

❺ If not, ask yourself: What else can I try?

HOUGHTON MIFFLIN
Reading

Reading Decodable Text **T187**

Frogs play in this pond all day.
Frogs like it wet, so frogs like
the rain.

30

This dog wags her <u>tail</u> and
jumps. Will she like it wet, too?
She <u>may</u> play in the rain.

31

Oral Language

Discuss the story. Have children answer in complete
sentences.

- What kind of weather is it? (It is a rainy day.)

- What do the girl and the dog do outside? (They stamp
  their feet, splash, and play in the rain.)

- How can you tell that the animals and the girl like wet
  weather? (The story says they like it wet and they like
  playing in the rain; they look happy in the illustrations.)

We stamp our feet and splash.
We like it wet. We like playing
in the rain.

32

Build Fluency

Model fluent reading.

- Read aloud page 29. Then have children read the same page aloud.
- Repeat the process for the remaining pages.

Have children practice fluent reading. Have partners reread the pages several times until each child can read them aloud effortlessly.

Home Connection

Hand out the take-home version of *Rain Day*. Ask children to reread the story with their families. (See the **Phonics Library Blackline Masters.**)

OBJECTIVES

- Associate /ā/ with the vowel pair *ay*.
- Make words with spelling pattern *-ay*.

Materials

- teacher-made word card *day*

SPELLING WORDS

Basic

day*	say
may	stay
play	way

Challenge

away*	holiday

Forms of these words appear in the literature.

Practice Book page 309

Take-Home Word List	Take-Home Word List
Animal Adventures **Spelling Review**	**Red-Eyed Tree Frog**
Spelling Words	**The Long *a* Sound** **Spelled *ay***
1. go	day say
2. me	play
3. day	**Spelling Words**
4. feet	1. day
5. nose	2. say
6. eat	3. play
7. play	4. may
8. mean	5. way
9. home	6. stay
10. stay	
Read directions to children.	**Challenge Words**
See the back for Challenge Words.	1. away
	2. holiday
	Read directions to children.
My Study List Add your own spelling words on the back. →	**My Study List** Add your own spelling words on the back. →

Take-Home Word List

INSTRUCTION

SPELLING: Words with *ay*

❶ Teach the Principle

Pretest Say each underlined word, read the sentence, and repeat the word. Have children write only the underlined word.

Basic Words

1. We went to the lake that <u>day</u>.
2. What did you <u>say</u> to Mom?
3. His cat likes to <u>play</u> with yarn.
4. Ask Dad if we <u>may</u> go with you.
5. Liz can find the <u>way</u>.
6. Would you <u>stay</u> with me?

Teach Write the Basic Words on the board.

- Have children read the words with you.
- Ask children what vowel sound they hear in all the Spelling Words. (/ā/)
- Tell children that in each Spelling Word, the letters *ay* stand for the long *a* sound.

❷ Practice/Apply

Cheer of Rhymes

- Have children underline the letters *ay* in each word.
- Cheer the Basic Words with children, emphasizing the rhyming pattern, and ending with the refrain /āāā/.

Practice/Homework Assign **Practice Book** page 309, the Take-Home Word List.

INSTRUCTION

VOCABULARY: Spelling Pattern *-ay*

Teach Post the word *day* on the Word Wall. Ask children *What word would I make if I changed the letter* d *to* s? (say) Have children tell you how to spell *say* as you write it on the board. Continue with *bay, clay, gray, hay, lay, pay, ray, sway, tray,* and *spray*.

Practice/Apply Have partners write a rhyme using words that end in the letters *ay*.

SHARED WRITING: A Class Summary

OBJECTIVES

- Contribute sentences to a class summary.
- Listen to retell a story.

Materials

Life in a Rain Forest, page T182, or another Read Aloud selection from the Leveled Bibliography, pages T6–T7.

Discuss the idea for a class summary. Tell children that today they will write a class summary of *Life in a Rain Forest*. Explain that a summary is a short description of what the selection is about. Reread the selection if necessary.

Prompt children to contribute to the summary.

- Say *Let's begin by writing a topic sentence telling the main idea. I'll write* Many kinds of plants and animals live in a rain forest.
- Tell children that now you need to add sentences that tell more about the main idea. Ask *What kinds of plants live in a rain forest? What kinds of animals live there?*
- Prompt children to retell the main points. Record their sentences.
- Reread the finished summary.

Illustrate and display the summary. Have children illustrate the rain forest, and display the summary with illustrations.

LISTENING: To Retell

Explain how to listen and prepare for retelling a story. Tell children you will tell them a short story. After you finish, they will retell the story with a small group. Tell children to listen for what happens at the beginning, middle, and end of the story.

Tell a short story. Say *Ben lived in Texas in the United States. He really wanted to visit a rain forest, so he planned a trip to Brazil. Ben flew to South America on an airplane. When he got to Brazil, he joined a group of tourists. The rain forest was hot, wet, and very beautiful! Ben took pictures of frogs, birds, lizards, insects, and many other animals. After two weeks, Ben flew back to Texas. All his friends enjoyed hearing about his trip and seeing his wonderful pictures.*

Have children retell the story. Have small groups retell the story one sentence at a time as they sit together in a circle.

Check children's understanding. Read the story aloud again. Ask groups if they forgot any part of it. If so, which part?

English Language Learners

Supporting Comprehension

English language learners will benefit from hearing the story several times. First, have them listen for the character's name and the animals he saw. Second, have them listen for place names and the character's actions. Third, have them listen for the sequence of events.

DAY 2
week 3

Day at a Glance
pages T192–T213

Learning to Read

High-Frequency Words
Reading Decodable Text
Cub's Long Day
Reading the Anthology
Red-Eyed Tree Frog

Leveled Readers, *T238–T241*
- ● *Looking for Frogs*
- ▲ *The Mouse in the Forest*
- ■ *Animals at Night*
- ◆ *How Many Frogs?*

Word Work

Spelling: Words with *ay*
Vocabulary: High-Frequency Words

Writing & Oral Language

Interactive Writing: A Class Summary

Daily Routines

Daily Message

Review phonics and language skills. Point to each word as you read aloud the Daily Message.

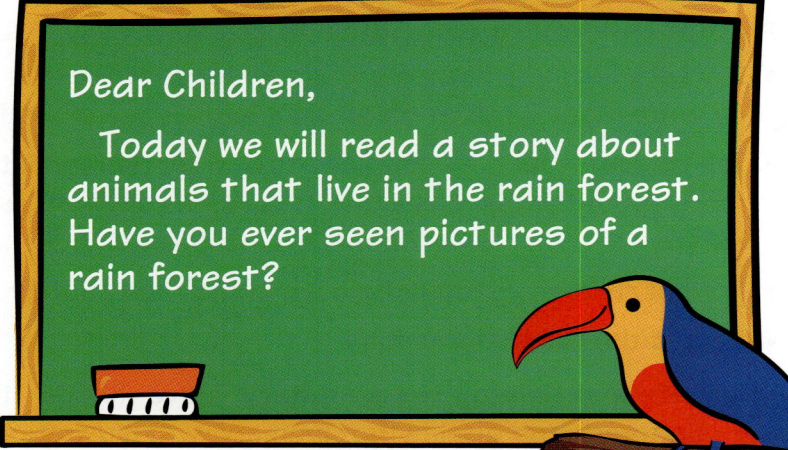

Dear Children,
Today we will read a story about animals that live in the rain forest. Have you ever seen pictures of a rain forest?

Have children

- respond to the question;
- circle words with *ai, ay, ea,* and *ee*; *(rain, Today, read, seen)*
- tell whether each sentence is an asking sentence or a telling sentence;
- find and read the following high-frequency words: *Today, what, live, Have, pictures,* and *you.*

Word Wall

High-Frequency Word Review Briefly review these and other high-frequency words daily. Have children practice reading, chanting, spelling, and writing words from the Word Wall. Then have children choose one word from the Word Wall. Taking turns, have them say the word aloud, spell it, and then use it in a sentence.

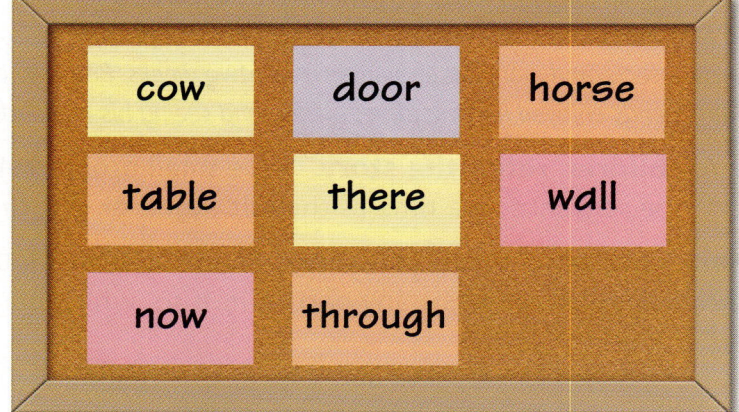

Blackline Master for these Word Wall Cards appears on page R34.

Daily Phonemic Awareness

Segmenting and Counting Phonemes: Sounds at the Board

- Call on pairs of children to come to the board.

 Have one child say the separate sounds in a word while the other child tallies the sounds on the board.

 Say to the first child: *Listen:* gain. *Let's say each sound in this word: /g//ā//n/.*

 Say to the second child: *As your partner says each sound again, draw a line on the board. Count the lines. How many sounds are in* gain? (3)

 Continue with *train* (4), *stay* (3), *Spain* (4), *day* (2), *play* (3), *may* (2), and *chain* (3).

Daily Language Practice

Grammar Skill: Punctuating an Asking Sentence
Spelling Skill: Words with *ay*
Write the sentence, read it to children, and have them tell you how to correct it.

Will you playe with me.

(Will you **play** with me?)

Daily Writing Prompt

Remind children to write complete sentences, beginning with a capital letter and ending with punctuation when responding to the prompt below or when writing on self-selected topics.

- **Draw and write about what the weather is like today.**

The hot sun is out today.

Daily Independent Reading

To increase children's reading fluency, provide a variety of theme-related books for them to read. Here are some suggestions.

- Leveled Bibliography, pages T6–T7

Choose books from this list for children to read, outside class, for at least twenty minutes a day.

- Phonics Library: *Rain Day*
- Leveled Readers

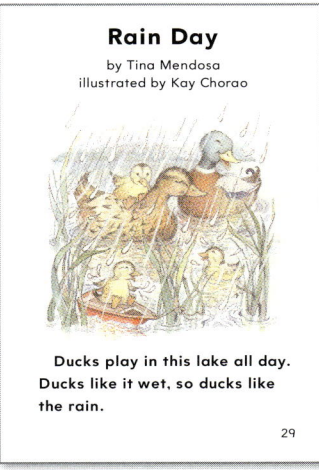

Rain Day
by Tina Mendosa
illustrated by Kay Chorao

Ducks play in this lake all day. Ducks like it wet, so ducks like the rain.

29

Daily Routines T193

OBJECTIVES

- Recognize new high-frequency words:

been	goes	evening
far	hungry	near
forest	soon	

- Read and write high-frequency words.

Target Skill Trace

Teach	pp. T194–T195
Reteach	p. R24
Review	pp. T212, T236; Theme 7, p. T42
See	*Handbook for English Language Learners*, pp. 201, 203; *Extra Support Handbook*, pp. 198–199

Materials

- Word Wall Cards for Week 3, Teacher's Edition, p. R35
- **Practice Book** punch-out high-frequency word cards for Theme 6, Week 3

INSTRUCTION

TARGET SKILL HIGH-FREQUENCY WORDS

1 Teach

Review last week's high-frequency words.

- Point to the words *cow, table, now, door, there, through, horse,* and *wall* on the Word Wall.
- Have children read these words, repeating any words that give them difficulty.

Introduce new high-frequency words.

- Hold up the Word Wall Card *been* and read the word aloud.
- Have the class clap and spell *been* several times: *b-e-e-n, been!*
- Choose a child to post *been* on the New Words section of the Word Wall.
- Repeat the procedure for the other new high-frequency words, *far, forest, goes, hungry, soon, evening,* and *near.*

Display Chart/Transparency 6–8.

- Have children read the story with you.
- Call on individuals to read one of the underlined words and use it in a sentence of their own.

Chart/Transparency 6–8

Evening in the Forest

It is <u>evening</u> in the <u>forest</u>. Many animals will wake up now. A skunk wakes up. It is <u>hungry</u>. It <u>goes</u> here and there looking for a good meal. It does not have to walk <u>far</u>! There are bugs <u>near</u> that tree. It has <u>been</u> a good evening. <u>Soon</u> it will be morning. The skunk will go back to sleep.

ANIMAL ADVENTURES Week 3, Day 2
High-Frequency Words

ANNOTATED VERSION

TRANSPARENCY 6–8
TEACHER'S EDITION PAGE T194

❷ Guided Practice

Draw a chart as shown and have children copy it.

- Tell children to write each new high-frequency word under the chart column that tells how many letters are in the word.
- Have individuals fill in their answers in the chart you drew.

3	4	6	7
far	goes near been soon	forest hungry	evening

❸ Apply

Assign one or more of the following activities.

- Have children complete **Practice Book** pages 88 and 89 independently, in pairs, or in small groups.
- Have partners practice reading their punch-out word cards.
- Have children read the **Phonics Library** story *Cub's Long Day* independently, with partners, or in small groups.

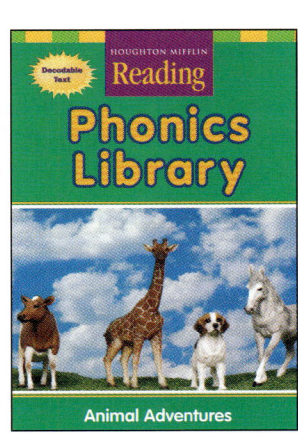

Cub's Long Day
by Mary Gold
illustrated by Anna Vojtech

This cub has big feet and a little tail. His home is a cave deep in the forest.

33

Practice Book page 88

Week 3
High-Frequency Words

Name _____

Words to Know

Read each pair of sentences. Circle the sentence that tells about the picture.

1. (Evening is here when the sun goes down.) (2 points)
   The horse climbs the hill.

2. The bird goes in its nest.
   (The forest has been a home to many animals.) (2)

3. It is not far to the lake.
   (The animal is hungry.) (2)

4. (The house is near the forest.) (2)
   Soon a horse will come by.

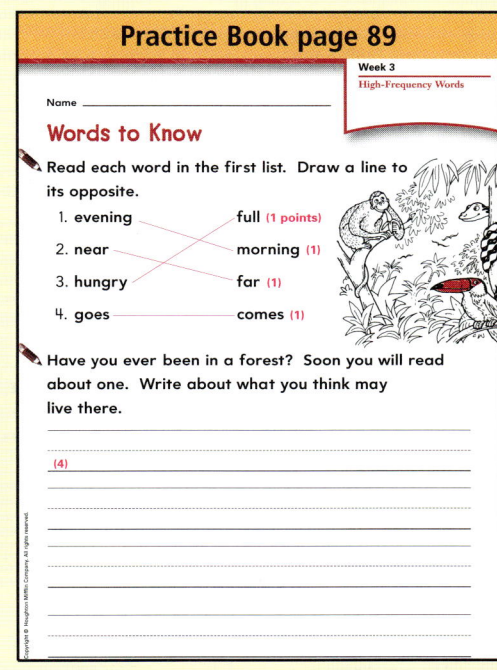

Practice Book page 89

Week 3
High-Frequency Words

Name _____

Words to Know

Read each word in the first list. Draw a line to its opposite.

1. evening — full (1 points)
2. near — morning (1)
3. hungry — far (1)
4. goes — comes (1)

Have you ever been in a forest? Soon you will read about one. Write about what you think may live there.

(4)

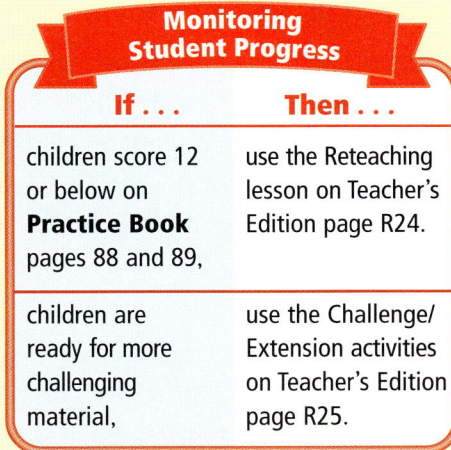

Monitoring Student Progress

If . . .	Then . . .
children score 12 or below on **Practice Book** pages 88 and 89,	use the Reteaching lesson on Teacher's Edition page R24.
children are ready for more challenging material,	use the Challenge/ Extension activities on Teacher's Edition page R25.

Building Background

Key Concept: Rain Forests

Ask children what animals they see on Anthology pages 194–195 and where they think these animals live.

- Explain that the frog children will read about lives in the rain forest.

- Have children recall what they learned about the rain forest in the Read Aloud story, *Life in a Rain Forest.*

Reviewing Vocabulary

Words to Know

High-Frequency Words

been	evening	far	forest
goes	hungry	near	soon

Words with *ai, ay*

rain	day	wait	away

Use "Get Set to Read."

- Read Anthology page 190 together. Remind children that the Words to Know are either words they already know or words that contain sounds they know.

- Read the Practice Sentences together. Ask children what helped them to read each word. Review words or skills as necessary.

- Remind children that these words will appear in the story.

Get Set to Read

Background and Vocabulary

RED-EYED TREE FROG
BY JOY COWLEY • PHOTOGRAPHS BY NIC BISHOP
Red-Eyed Tree Frog

A Visit to the Rain Forest

You will read about a day in the life of a red-eyed tree frog in the next story.

Words to Know

been	evening
far	near
forest	rain
goes	wait
hungry	day
soon	away

190

English Language Learners

Language Development

Beginning/Preproduction Have children repeat each Story Vocabulary word as you help them point to its example in the illustration. Then pantomime *near* and *far.* Use pictures to demonstrate *evening* and *day.*

Early Production and Speech Emergence Use each Story Vocabulary word in a question and have individuals repeat the word in their answer. Example: *What has red* eyes? *The tree frog has red* eyes.

Intermediate and Advanced Fluency Review Story Vocabulary with children. Then have them page through the story. Encourage them to discuss what they know about the pictures and to ask questions about anything that is unfamiliar.

Practice Sentences

1. My mom has **been** to the **rain** **forest**.
2. It's **far** **away** from where we live.
3. I will go the next time Mom **goes**.
4. We will hike all **day**.
5. When we are **hungry**, we will stop and eat.
6. We will spend the **evening** in a tent.
7. We will sit **near** a tree and **wait** for a red-eyed tree frog.
8. I hope we go **soon**!

191

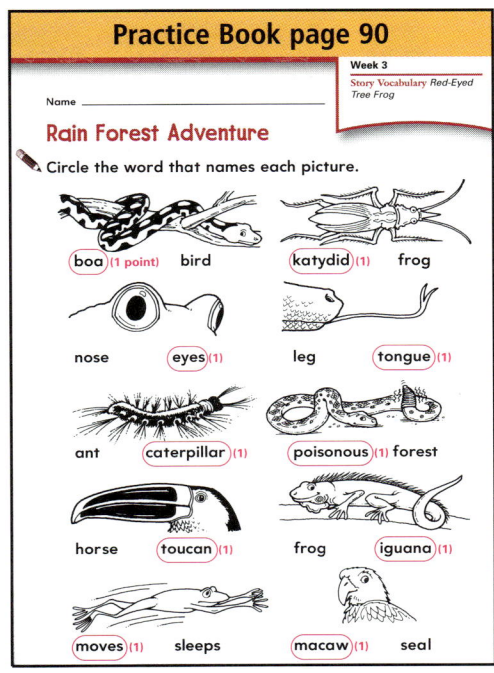

Chart/Transparency 6–9

In the Rain Forest

macaw

toucan

boa

red-eyed tree frog

iguana

caterpillar

katydid

Which animal is <u>poisonous</u>?
Which animal <u>moves</u> its long <u>tongue</u>?
Which animal has red <u>eyes</u>?

Practice Book page 90

Week 3
Story Vocabulary Red-Eyed Tree Frog

Name _____

Rain Forest Adventure

Circle the word that names each picture.

boa (1 point)   bird   katydid (1)   frog

nose   eyes (1)   leg   tongue (1)

ant   caterpillar (1)   poisonous (1) forest

horse   toucan (1)   frog   iguana (1)

moves (1)   sleeps   macaw (1)   seal

Introducing Story Vocabulary

Story Vocabulary

These words support the Key Concept and are important to children's understanding of the selection.

boa a large, nonpoisonous snake

caterpillar a creature that looks like a worm and turns into a moth or butterfly

eyed having eyes of a certain kind

eyes parts of the body used for seeing

iguana/s large lizards that often have spines along their backs

katydid a large green insect, related to the grasshopper

macaw a large parrot with colorful feathers and a curved bill

moves changes place; does not stay still

poisonous causing injury, sickness, or death if taken into the body

tongue part of the mouth; used for tasting and speaking

toucan a colorful bird that has a large, long, brightly colored bill

e • Glossary
e • WordGame

Use Chart/Transparency 6–9.

- Point to each rain forest animal and read the captions with the class.
- Have children predict answers to the questions at the bottom.
- Ask children to look for these words as they read, and to use them as they discuss the selection.

Practice Assign **Practice Book** page 90.

Introducing Vocabulary
(Anthology p. 191)

T197

COMPREHENSION STRATEGY
Predict/Infer

Teacher Modeling   Read the title, the author's and photographer's names, and the Strategy Focus on Anthology page 192. Then have children look at the photograph on page 195 and model the Predict/Infer strategy.

Think Aloud   *I see from the picture on page 195 that the red-eyed tree frog has its eyes closed. I think it is sleeping. I predict that it will wake up.*

Test Prep   Children can use the Predict/Infer strategy before reading a test passage. First, they should use the title and any illustrations to predict whether the passage is fiction or nonfiction. Then they should predict what will happen or what they will learn.

COMPREHENSION SKILL
Making Predictions

Remind children that clues in a story can help them make a prediction about what will happen next. Remind children of the prediction you made in the Think Aloud above. Ask:

- Why do you think I predicted that the red-eyed tree frog would wake up?

- Does anyone have any other predictions about the frog?

As children read, have them make predictions about what the tree frog will do.

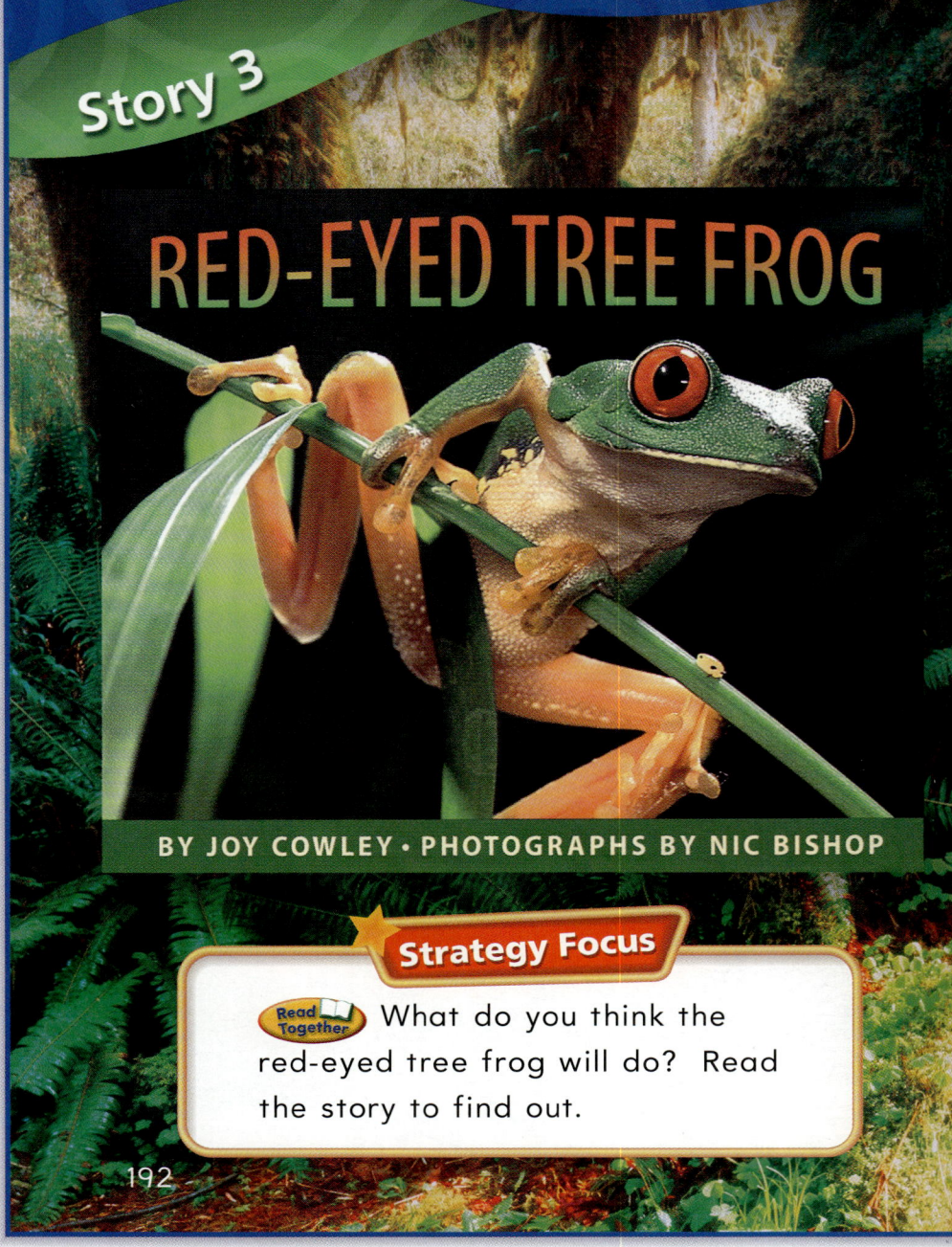

Story 3

RED-EYED TREE FROG

BY JOY COWLEY · PHOTOGRAPHS BY NIC BISHOP

Strategy Focus

 What do you think the red-eyed tree frog will do? Read the story to find out.

192

English Language Learners

Language Development

Make a chart with a list of animals that appear in the story. Say each animal name on the chart and have children repeat it. Check pronunciation and correct as necessary. As children go through the story, have them check off each animal as they encounter it. Then help children write an adjective to describe each animal.

THEME 6: Animal Adventures
(Anthology p. 192)

Evening comes to the rain forest.

193

Purpose Setting

- Tell children to think about what the red-eyed tree frog will do next and check their predictions as they read.

- Remind children to pay attention to clues in the text to make predictions and to use their reading strategies as they read.

- Ask children to turn to Anthology page 216. Read the questions aloud. Encourage children to think about the answers to these questions as they read *Red-Eyed Tree Frog*.

Journal ▶ You may want children to use their journals to record their predictions and revise them as they read.

Extra Support/Intervention

Preview pages 193–207.

pages 193–195 What time of day is it? What is the frog doing?

pages 196–199 What kinds of creatures does the frog meet?

pages 200–201 The frog is hungry. Do these bugs look good to eat?

pages 202–207 What happens when the frog meets a boa snake?

Preview pages 208–214.

pages 208–209 What does the frog see on the leaf?

pages 210–211 What does the frog do with the moth?

pages 212–213 What is the frog doing here?

page 214 It was evening at the beginning of the story. What time is it now?

Word Key

Words with *ai, ay* —————

High-Frequency Words —————

Story Vocabulary

Reading the Selection
(Anthology p. 193)
T199

The **macaw** and the **toucan** will soon go to sleep.

194

But the red-**eyed** tree frog has been asleep all day.

195

CRITICAL THINKING
Guiding Comprehension

1 NOTING DETAILS Which animals on these pages sleep at night? Which one sleeps in the day? (The macaw and toucan sleep at night; the red-eyed tree frog sleeps in the day.)

TARGET SKILL

READING STRATEGY
Phonics/Decoding

Teacher/Student Modeling Write *asleep* on the board. Divide it into two parts, *a* and *sleep*. Coach children in applying what they already know about words and letter sounds to blend the parts and read the word. If necessary, review that the initial *a* in *asleep* has the schwa sound. Other words to review with the initial schwa sound are *another* (page 198) and *along* (page 203).

Story Vocabulary

macaw a large parrot with colorful feathers and a curved bill

toucan a colorful bird that has a large, long, brightly colored bill

eyed having eyes of a certain kind

THEME 6: Animal Adventures

It wakes up hungry.
What will it eat?

Here is an <mark>iguana</mark>.
Frogs do not eat <mark>iguanas.</mark>

196

197

CRITICAL THINKING

Guiding Comprehension

2 **NOTING DETAILS** How does the frog feel when it wakes up? (hungry)

3 **DRAWING CONCLUSIONS** Why do you think frogs don't eat iguanas? (Possible responses: An iguana is too big for a frog to eat; iguanas have spines.)

Story Vocabulary

iguana/s large lizards that often have spines along their backs

Do iguanas eat frogs?
The red-eyed tree frog does
not <u>wait</u> to find out.
It hops onto another branch.

198

The frog is hungry but it will
not eat the ant.

199

 **TARGET SKILL**

COMPREHENSION STRATEGY

Predict/Infer

Teacher/Student Modeling Ask children to make a prediction about something the frog might do, based on what they have read so far. If they need help, remind them that the frog is hungry, or use the Extra Support/Intervention box on this page.

REACHING ALL LEARNERS

Extra Support/Intervention

Strategy Modeling: Predict/Infer

Use this example to model the strategy.

I know that the frog is hungry. I don't think the frog will eat the ant because ants are not good food for a red-eyed tree frog. I predict that the frog will keep looking for food until it finds just the right meal.

THEME 6: Animal Adventures
(Anthology pp. 198–199)

It will not eat the katydid.

200

Will it eat the caterpillar?
No!

The caterpillar is poisonous.

201

CRITICAL THINKING
Guiding Comprehension

4 **CAUSE AND EFFECT** What might happen if the frog ate the poisonous caterpillar? (It might get sick or die.)

5 **MAKING GENERALIZATIONS** What do you think frogs usually eat? (Sample response: flies and other kinds of insects.)

Story Vocabulary

katydid a large green insect, related to the grasshopper

caterpillar a creature that looks like a worm and turns into a moth or butterfly

poisonous causing injury, sickness, or death if taken into the body

REACHING ALL LEARNERS

English Language Learners

Supporting Comprehension

Pause at the end of page 201. Point to the word *poisonous*. Explain that if the red-eyed tree frog eats the caterpillar, the frog will get sick and maybe even die.

Something **moves** near the frog.
Something slips and slithers along a branch.
It is a hungry **boa** snake.

202   203

CRITICAL THINKING
Guiding Comprehension

❻ MAKING PREDICTIONS What do you think will happen to the frog? (Sample response: It will get away from the snake.)

READING STRATEGY
Phonics/Decoding

Teacher/Student Modeling Have children use what they know about final endings to decode *slips* and *slithers*. Point out that the final -*s* in *slips* has the /s/ sound, while in *slithers* it has the /z/ sound. Have children find other words with the -*s* ending in the selection and tell whether they hear a final /s/ or /z/. Examples: *flicks, tastes* (page 204); *lands* (page 208); *climbs* (page 211); *shuts, eyes* (page 212).

THEME 6: Animal Adventures
(Anthology pp. 202–203)

T204

Story Vocabulary

moves changes place; does not stay still

boa a large nonpoisonous snake

REACHING ALL LEARNERS **Extra Support/Intervention**

Strategy Modeling: Predict/Infer

Use this example to model the strategy.

The snake is hungry. I think it wants to eat the red-eyed tree frog. I predict that the frog will try to hop away from the snake.

English Language Learners

Language Development

Review the following descriptive verbs with children: *slips* (p. 203), *slithers* (p. 203), *flicks* (p. 204). Use examples or mime to clarify meaning. Encourage children to look for more descriptive verbs in the selection. Explain any words that children have trouble with.

The snake flicks its tongue. It tastes frog in the air. Look out, frog!

204   205

GET SKILL

READING STRATEGY

Phonics/Decoding

Teacher/Student Modeling Point out that in the word *air*, the letters *a*, *i*, and *r* are pronounced /âr/. Write *chair* and *fair*. Ask children to use what they know about the word *air* to decode these words.

GET SKILL

COMPREHENSION STRATEGY

Predict/Infer

Student Modeling Have children make a prediction about what will happen to the frog. Have them confirm or revise their prediction as they read.

Story Vocabulary

tongue part of the mouth; used for tasting and speaking

REACHING ALL LEARNERS

Extra Support/Intervention

Review pages 193–207.

Before children join in Stop and Think, have them

- take turns modeling **Predict/Infer** and other strategies they used;
- **summarize** the important parts of the story up to this point.

On Level	Challenge

Literature Discussion

Have small groups discuss the story, using their own questions or prompts from Guiding Comprehension.

Reading the Selection
(Anthology pp. 204–205)   **T205**

JUMP!

JUMP!

206

207

Stop and Think

Critical Thinking Questions

1. **DRAWING CONCLUSIONS** Why do you think the author shows all the different creatures the frog sees? (Sample response: to show readers what other kinds of animals live in the rain forest with the frog)

2. **MAKING PREDICTIONS** What do you think will happen to the frog after it lands? (Sample response: It will get away from the snake and find something to eat.)

Strategies in Action

Have individuals model **Predict/Infer** and other strategies they used. Make sure children summarize the story so far.

Discussion Options

Review Predictions/Purpose Ask children if their predictions about the frog were correct and have them make new predictions for the second part of the story.

Share Group Discussions If children discussed the story in groups, have them share their questions and answers.

Monitoring Student Progress

If . . .	Then . . .
children have successfully completed the Extra Support activities on page T205,	have them read the rest of the story cooperatively.

THEME 6: Animal Adventures
(Anthology pp. 206–207)

The frog lands on a leaf, far away from the boa. What does the frog see on the leaf?

208

A moth!

209

Comprehension Preview

Making Predictions

TARGET SKILL

Teach

Tell children that an important part of making predictions is looking for clues in words and pictures. On pages 204–205, point out the picture of the snake near the frog and the words "Look out, frog!" Explain that both the words and the picture tell readers the frog is in danger, and that it will probably try to hop away from the snake.

Practice/Apply

Have children look at pages 208–213 to find clues in the words and pictures that tell them

- the frog will not be hungry anymore.
- the frog will go to sleep again.

Target Skill Trace	
▶ Preview; Teach	pp. T182, T198, T207; T218–T219
Reteach	p. R30
Review	p. T232

<u>Clues</u>
- frog eats a moth
- frog shuts its eyes

Reading the Selection
(Anthology pp. 208–209)   **T207**

Crunch, crunch, crunch!

210

The tree frog is no longer hungry.
It climbs onto a leaf.

211

CRITICAL THINKING

Guiding Comprehension

7 **CAUSE AND EFFECT** Why is the frog no longer hungry?
(It's eating a moth.)

READING STRATEGY

Phonics/Decoding

Teacher/Student Modeling Write *longer*. Cover the *-er* ending and have children use what they know about letter sounds to blend *long*. Then uncover the *-er* and have them blend the whole word.

English Language Learners

Language Development

The phrase "no longer" may confuse some children. Explain that it's a way of saying "not anymore." On page 211, the first sentence means that the frog is not hungry anymore.

The red-eyed tree frog shuts its <mark>eyes</mark> . . .

and goes to sleep . . .

212

213

CRITICAL THINKING
Guiding Comprehension

8 **DRAWING CONCLUSIONS** What time of day do you think it is? How do you know? (It must be morning because the frog is going to sleep; the frog stays awake at night and sleeps during the day.)

REACHING ALL LEARNERS

Extra Support/Intervention

Concepts of Print

Italics Point out the words *Crunch, crunch, crunch* on page 210. Explain that writers often put words for sounds in italics.

Points of Ellipsis Point out the points of ellipsis on Anthology page 212. Explain that these marks tell the reader the sentence will continue on the next page.

Ask children to find the ellipsis on page 213. Then have children practice rereading the whole sentence beginning on page 212 and ending on page 214.

Reading the Selection
(Anthology pp. 212–213)   **T209**

as morning comes to the rain forest.

214

Meet the Author and the Photographer

Joy Cowley loves animals, especially frogs. When she saw these pictures, she liked them very much. She decided to write a children's book to go with them.

Nic Bishop went to the rain forest to take photographs of the red-eyed tree frogs. One frog became a family pet.

Internet

Visit Education Place to learn more about Joy Cowley and Nic Bishop.
www.eduplace.com/kids

215

CRITICAL THINKING

Guiding Comprehension

9 **COMPARE AND CONTRAST** How is the last page in the story similar to the first page? How is it different? (Both pages show the rain forest at a certain time of day; the first page shows evening and the last page shows morning.)

REACHING ALL LEARNERS

Extra Support/Intervention

Selection Review

Before children join in Wrapping Up, have them
- take turns modeling **Predict/Infer** and other strategies they used;
- **summarize** the important parts of the story.

On Level | **Challenge**

Literature Discussion

Have small groups discuss the story, using their own questions and questions from Think About the Story on Anthology page 216.

Wrapping Up

Critical Thinking Questions

1. DRAWING CONCLUSIONS Do you think life is easy or difficult for the red-eyed tree frog? Explain. (Sample response: difficult; there are many dangers in the rain forest and it's hard for the frog to find food.)

2. TOPIC, MAIN IDEA, DETAILS What do you think is the main idea of this selection? (Sample response: what one night is like for a red-eyed tree frog in the rain forest)

Strategies in Action

Have children take turns modeling **Predict/Infer** and other strategies they used. Also ask them to summarize the selection.

Discussion Options

Review Predictions/Purpose Discuss why children's predictions were or were not accurate.

Share Group Discussions Have children share the results of their literature discussions.

Monitoring Student Progress

If . . .	Then . . .
children have difficulty answering the Guiding Comprehension questions on pages T208–T210,	guide them in rereading portions of the text and discussing their answers.

Challenge

Writing Riddles

Have children think of riddles for the following Challenge Words: *away, holiday.*

PRACTICE

SPELLING: Words with *ay*

Review the principle. Remind children that in each Spelling Word, the letters *ay* stand for the long *a* sound.

Practice/Apply Tell children you will give them clues for writing the Spelling Words.

- Have children number a sheet of paper from 1 to 6.
- Read the following clues, and have children write the words.

  1. *When you tell someone something, you _____ it.* (say)

  2. *When you build with blocks or sail a toy boat, you _____ .* (play)

  3. *Saturday is a _____.* (day)

  4. *When you don't leave, you _____.* (stay)

  5. *When you are allowed to do something, you _____.* (may)

  6. *When a car is coming, you get out of the _____.* (way)

REVIEW

VOCABULARY: High-Frequency Words

Review the words. Read the New Words section of the Word Wall with children. Tell them you will give them clues to identify some of these words.

Practice/Apply Read the following clues. Have children find the matching New Word, and then clap and spell the word.

- *This word means "a long distance."* (far)
- *This is a place where there are often many trees.* (forest)
- *This is a how you feel when you want something to eat.* (hungry)
- *This word is the opposite of* far. (near)
- *This is another word for the beginning part of the night.* (evening)
- *This word means "in a short time."* (soon)

INTERACTIVE WRITING: A Class Summary

OBJECTIVES
- Contribute sentences to write a class summary.
- Participate by writing letters, words, and punctuation.

Present the idea for a class summary.

- Tell children that today they will write a class summary of *EEK! There's a Mouse in the House.*

- Explain that the summary will be a short description of what happens in the story.

- Reread the selection if necessary.

Prompt children to contribute to the class summary.

- Tell children that first they need to think about what happened in the story.

- Ask *What happens at the beginning of the story? What happens next? How does the story end?*

- Record children's ideas on the board. Tell children you will use these ideas to write the summary.

- Model how to begin the summary.

Think Aloud *I know that a girl finds a mouse in her house. I will begin the summary by writing* A girl finds a mouse in her house.

- Ask *What does the girl do to get the mouse out of the house? Does her idea work?*

- Record children's sentences. Invite them to write familiar letters, words, and punctuation.

- Ask *What happens next?* Continue with the sequence of animals in the story.

- Ask *What happens at the end of the story?*

- Read the finished summary aloud to the class. Ask *If you had not read* EEK! There's a Mouse in the House, *does this summary tell you what happens in the story?*

Illustrate and display the class summary. Have children illustrate the class summary, and display it on a bulletin board.

> A girl finds a mouse in her house. She sends in other animals to help, but they all make a mess. Then most of the animals leave, but the elephant is still in the house. The mouse scares the elephant. The elephant shouts, "EEK!"

Day at a Glance
pages T214–T221

Learning to Read

Responding
Comprehension Instruction
Making Predictions

•••••••••••••••••••••

Leveled Readers, *T238–T241*
- ● *Looking for Frogs*
- ▲ *The Mouse in the Forest*
- ■ *Animals at Night*
- ◆ *How Many Frogs?*

Word Work

Spelling: Words with *ay*
Vocabulary: Parts of the Body

Writing & Oral Language

Writing: Responding
Grammar: Naming Words for One or More

Daily Routines

Daily Message

Review skills. Point to each word as you read aloud the Daily Message.

Dear Class,

When I go for a walk in the woods, I bring snacks in case I get hungry. Is there a forest near your home or is it far away?

Have children

- respond to the question;
- circle words with long *a* and long *o*; (*case, go, home*)
- find the following high-frequency words: *walk, hungry, there, forest, near, your, far,* and *away*.

Word Wall

High-Frequency Word Review Review these and other high-frequency words by holding up the Word Cards and having children read the word and find it on the Word Wall. Then have children chant the spelling of each word: f-a-r *spells* far! Place the Word Cards face-down on a table. Call on individuals to pick a card, read it aloud, spell the word, and then use it in a sentence.

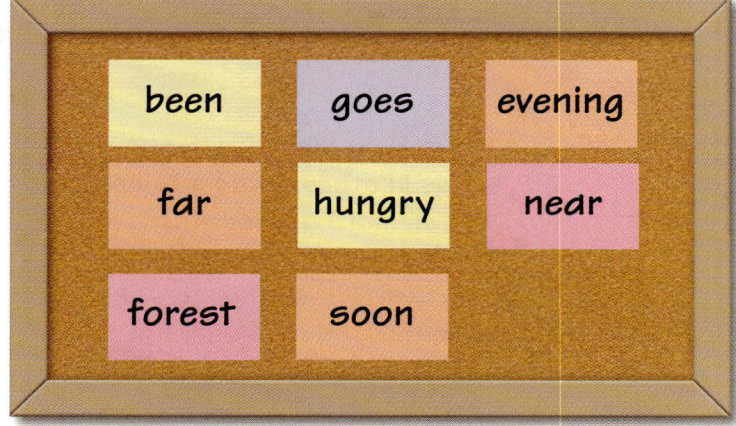

been   goes   evening
far   hungry near
forest soon

Blackline Master for this week's Word Wall Cards appears on page R35.

Daily Phonemic Awareness

Segmenting and Counting Phonemes: Clap the Sounds

- One at a time, say the words *maid, bait, braid, drain, plain,* and *claim.*

- Ask children to say the separate sounds. Examples: /m//ā//d/ for *maid;* /b//r//ā//d/ for *braid.*

- Have children clap once for each sound they say and tell you how many times they clapped. Example: After clapping four times for *braid,* children should say "Four!"

Daily Language Practice

Grammar Skill: Naming Words for One or More
Spelling Skill: Words with *ay*
Write the sentence, read it to children, and have them tell you how to correct it.

> I can saay it four time.

(I can **say** it four **times**.)

 # Daily Writing Prompt

Have children write on self-selected topics or respond to the prompt below. Remind children to write complete sentences.

- **Write about a frog in a pond.**

> Once upon a time a frog lived in a pond.

Daily Independent Reading

To increase children's reading fluency, provide a variety of theme-related books for them to read. Here are some suggestions.

- Leveled Bibliography, pages T6–T7

Choose books from this list for children to read, outside class, for at least twenty minutes a day.

- Anthology: *Red-Eyed Tree Frog*

- Leveled Readers

- Phonics Library: *Cub's Long Day*

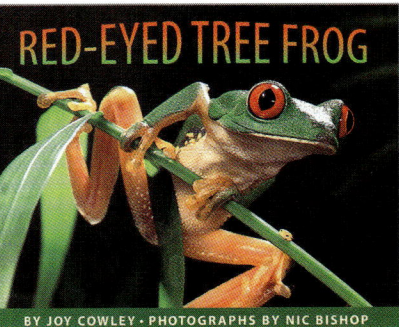

RED-EYED TREE FROG

BY JOY COWLEY · PHOTOGRAPHS BY NIC BISHOP

Responding

Comprehension Check

Have children reread or finish reading the selection. Then assign **Practice Book** page 91 to assess children's comprehension of the selection.

Think About the Story

Have children discuss or write their answers. Sample answers are provided; accept reasonable responses.

1. **DRAWING CONCLUSIONS** Answers will vary.

2. **DRAWING CONCLUSIONS** Sample answer: he can find moths to eat; he must look out for snakes.

3. **MAKING GENERALIZATIONS** Answers will vary.

 4. **Connecting/Comparing** How are the animals in *EEK! There's a Mouse in the House* different from those in *Red-Eyed Tree Frog?* (The animals in *EEK! There's a Mouse in the House* are made-up characters; the animals in *Red-Eyed Tree Frog* are real.)

Responding

RED-EYED TREE FROG
BY JOY COWLEY · PHOTOGRAPHS BY NIC BISHOP

Read Together

Think About the Story

1. Do you think this rain forest is quiet or noisy? Why?

2. What do you think the red-eyed tree frog has learned about living in the rain forest?

3. Would you like to visit the rain forest? Why?

Internet

Go on a Web Field Trip

Visit a rain forest at Education Place.

www.eduplace.com/kids

216

THEME 6: Animal Adventures
(Anthology p. 216)

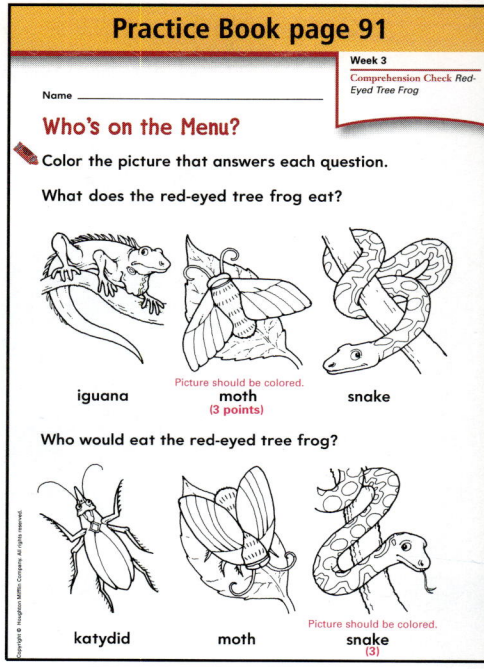

Practice Book page 91

Week 3
Comprehension Check Red-Eyed Tree Frog

Name _____

Who's on the Menu?

Color the picture that answers each question.

What does the red-eyed tree frog eat?

iguana   moth (Picture should be colored. 3 points)   snake

Who would eat the red-eyed tree frog?

katydid   moth   snake (Picture should be colored. 3)

Math
Comparing Sizes

A red-eyed tree frog is nearly as long as this ruler. Find things in your classroom that are about the same size.

Creating

Write a Riddle

Write a riddle about one of the animals in the story. Have a partner read your riddle and guess the animal.

Tips
- Study a picture of the animal.
- Use describing words.

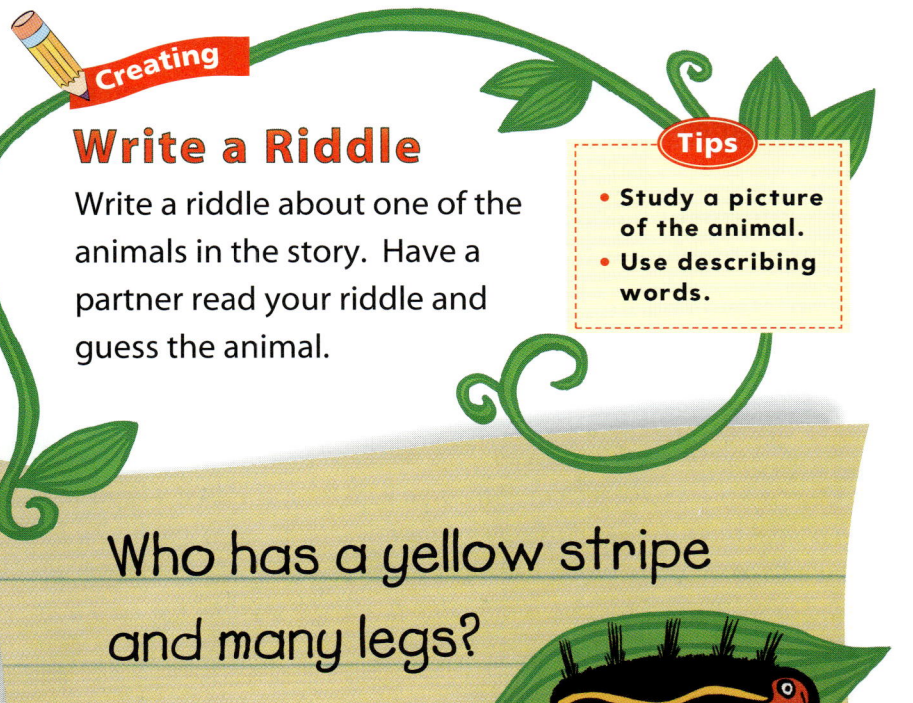

Who has a yellow stripe and many legs?

217

Additional Responses

Personal Response Have children share their personal responses to *Red-Eyed Tree Frog* orally or in small groups.

Journal ▶ Ask children to write or draw in their journals about other frogs they have seen in real life or in books.

REACHING ALL LEARNERS

Extra Support/Intervention	English Language Learners
Writing Support Ask children to name and describe anything they know about the animals they saw in the selection. Then have each child choose an animal and pick two things that help to describe the animal. Have them use these as clues for their riddles.	**Supporting Comprehension** **Beginning/Preproduction** Draw an outline of a tree on chart paper. Have children draw pictures of the animals from the story in the tree. Help them to label the pictures. **Early Production and Speech Emergence** Have children work in small groups to talk about the sounds the animals in the story might make. **Intermediate and Advanced Fluency** Help children to complete the following sentence in different ways: *I want to visit the rain forest because _____.*

Monitoring Student Progress

Monitoring Student Progress

Student Self-Assessment Have children assess their reading with questions such as

- What was the hardest word I read on my own?
- How did I keep track of my predictions?

Responding
(Anthology p. 217)

Target Skill Trace

Preview; Teach	pp. T182, T198, T207; T218–T219; Theme 3; Theme 10
Reteach	p. R30
Review	p. T232
See	*Extra Support Handbook,* pp. 196–197, 202–203

INSTRUCTION

COMPREHENSION: Making Predictions

❶ Teach

Discuss making predictions. Explain that readers make predictions about what might happen in a story by using clues in the pictures and words, as well as what they already know.

- Have children revisit *Red-Eyed Tree Frog* and review some of the predictions they made earlier as they read. (The frog will hop away from the snake; the frog will not be hungry anymore.)

- Discuss information children used from the pictures, words, and their own knowledge to make their predictions.

Modeling Have children turn to Anthology pages 212–213 and look at the photographs. Demonstrate how to make and check a prediction.

Think Aloud   *On page 212 I read, "The red-eyed tree frog shuts its eyes." I see the picture of the frog with its eyes closed. I know that when an animal shuts its eyes it usually means it will go to sleep. I think the frog must be tired from looking for food all night. I predict that it will go to sleep. I'll read ahead to see if my prediction is right. The next page says the red-eyed tree frog "goes to sleep." My prediction was correct.*

❷ Guided Practice

Guide children in making predictions. Ask them what they think the red-eyed tree frog will do when it wakes up again.

- List what children know about the rain forest, the animals that live there, and the red-eyed tree frog.

- List children's predictions about what the frog will do.

- Have children discuss what predictions are the best, based on what they know about the tree frog and where it lives.

THE FROG WILL

- look for food
- meet other rain forest animals
- stay away from boa snakes

❸ Apply

Choose one or more of these activities.

- Have partners choose a book from the Houghton Mifflin Classroom Bookshelf or the library. Have children look at the pictures, read the title and first few pages of the book, and then make a prediction about what will happen. Ask them to provide reasons for their predictions.

- Assign **Practice Book** page 92.

- Have children apply this skill as they read the **Leveled Readers.** You may also select books from the Leveled Bibliography for this theme (pages T6–T7).

✔️ **Test Prep** Tell children that when they make predictions, they use details from a story to predict what might happen later in the story. Explain that some test questions ask children to identify the details that helped them predict an event that happened in a story.

Leveled Readers and Leveled Practice

Children at all levels apply the comprehension skill as they read their Leveled Readers. See lessons on pages T238–T241.

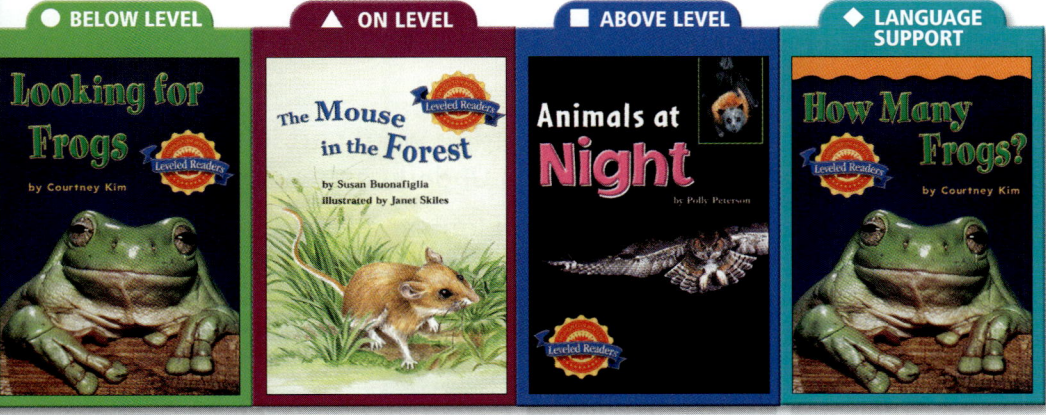

● BELOW LEVEL — Looking for Frogs by Courtney Kim

▲ ON LEVEL — The Mouse in the Forest by Susan Buonafiglia illustrated by Janet Skiles

■ ABOVE LEVEL — Animals at Night by Polly Peterson

◆ LANGUAGE SUPPORT — How Many Frogs? by Courtney Kim

Reading Traits

As children develop the ability to make predictions, they are learning to "read between the lines" of a selection. This comprehension skill supports the reading trait **Realizing Context.**

Practice Book page 92

Week 3
Comprehension Making Predictions

Name _____

What Happens Next?

🖉 Read each story. Write what you think will happen next. Sample answers are shown.

The red-eyed tree frog wakes up. It is hungry. It sees a moth on a leaf. What will the frog do?

_____
The frog will eat the moth. **(5 points)**
_____
_____

The red-eyed tree frog is waiting on a leaf. It hears an animal move. It's a snake! What will the frog do?

_____
The frog will jump. **(5)**
_____
_____

Monitoring Student Progress

If . . .	Then . . .
children score 7 or below on **Practice Book** page 92,	use the Reteaching lesson on Teacher's Edition page R30.
children have met the lesson objectives,	use the Challenge/Extension activities on Teacher's Edition page R31.

Practice Book page 93

Name _____

Week 3
Spelling The Long *a* Sound
Spelled *ay*

The Long *a* Sound Spelled *ay*

Read the story. Use the box to help you find and circle words with long a.

What a nice (day) to go out and (play). (May) we go out? We can (stay) here or go (way) over there by the trees. What do you (say)? **(6 points)**

Spelling Words

day
say
play
May
way
stay

SPELLING:
Words with *ay*

Stump the Teacher Tell children they will try to stump you today.

- Have children give you multiple clues about a Spelling Word, and guess the word.
- When you guess a word correctly, have children tell you how to spell the word as you write it on the board.
- Repeat with the remaining Spelling Words.

Practice/Homework Assign **Practice Book** page 93.

VOCABULARY:
Parts of the Body

List Body Parts Write the title of the selection *Red-Eyed Tree Frog,* and read it aloud.

- Ask children if they see any word or word part in the title that names a part of the body. *(eye)* Underline the word.
- Reread the selection as children look and listen for body parts.
- Ask them to list the body parts named or shown in the book.
- Point out that both people and frogs have eyes. Ask *Does the frog have body parts that people do not have? Which ones?*
- Finally, ask children to name other body parts.

Practice/Homework Assign **Practice Book** page 94.

Practice Book page 94

Name _____

Week 3
Vocabulary Parts of the Body

Parts of the Body

Read each word. Label the girl with the words.

nose **(1 point)**

teeth **(1)**

neck **(1)**

leg **(1)**

hand **(1)**

feet **(1)**

Word Bank

nose
neck
leg
feet
hand
teeth

GRAMMAR: Naming Words for One or More

OBJECTIVES

- Identify naming words for one or more than one.
- Write naming words for one or more than one.

❶ Teach

Demonstrate examples of one and more than one.

- Tell children that naming words can name one or more than one person, animal, place, or thing.
- Show children one pencil and ask them to name the object. (pencil) Write *pencil* on the board.
- Show them a group of pencils and ask them to name the objects. (pencils) Write *pencils* underneath *pencil*.
- Ask children how the two naming words are different. (*Pencils has an s at the end.*) Tell children that many naming words end in *s* to name more than one.

Have children identify words that name more than one.

- Display **Chart/Transparency 6–10.** Ask children to find a naming word that names more than one. Circle the word.
- Repeat with the other plural words.

Go over these points.

- Naming words can name one or more than one person, animal, place, or thing.
- Many naming words end in *s* to name more than one.

Skill Trace

Teach	p. T221
Review	p. T237
See	*Handbook for English Language Learners,* p. 207

Chart/Transparency 6–10

❷ Guided Practice

Check children's understanding.

- Label two columns on the board *One* and *More Than One*.
- Have children look through *Red-Eyed Tree Frog* to find naming words for one or more than one.
- Write each naming word in the appropriate column on the board.

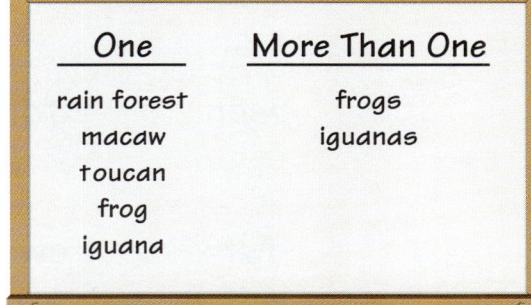

One	More Than One
rain forest	frogs
macaw	iguanas
toucan	
frog	
iguana	

❸ Apply

Assign Practice Book page 95.

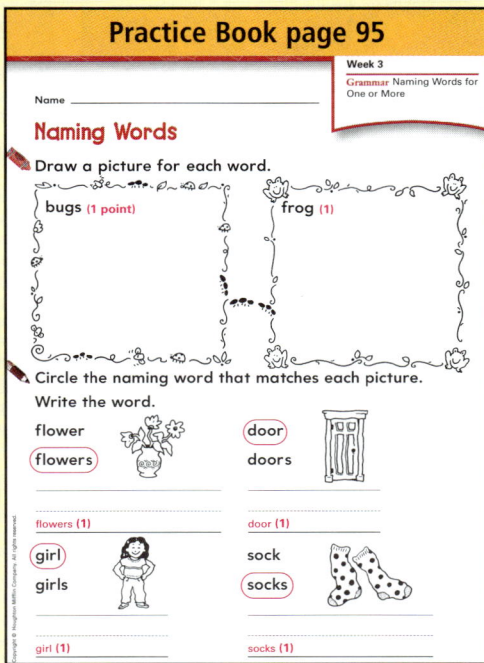

Practice Book page 95

Grammar **T221**

DAY 4
week 3

Day at a Glance
pages T222–T229

Learning to Read

Reading the Poetry Link
The Snake
The Toucan

Phonics Review
Long *e* (*e*, CV, CV*Ce*)
Vowel Pairs *ee*, *ea*

. . . .

Leveled Readers, *T238–T241*
- ● *Looking for Frogs*
- ▲ *The Mouse in the Forest*
- ■ *Animals at Night*
- ◆ *How Many Frogs?*

Word Work

Spelling: Words with *ay*
Vocabulary: Animal Action Words

Writing & Oral Language

Writing: Writing a Summary

Daily Routines

Daily Message

Review skills. Point to each word as you read aloud the Daily Message.

Dear Children,

What is your favorite time of day? Is it morning, afternoon, or evening? I like this time of day because _____.

Have children

- respond to the questions and complete the unfinished sentence;
- circle words with long *i* and long *a*; (*time, like, favorite, day*)
- find and read the following high-frequency words: *Children, What, your, morning,* and *evening*.

Word Wall

Speed Drill Using the **Practice Book** punchout word cards, have children practice reading the words by doing a speed drill. Working in pairs, have children take turns holding up the cards for their partner to read. After children have practiced reading the words, display the cards and ask individuals to read them to you as quickly as they can.

Blackline Masters for this theme's Word Wall Cards appear on pages R33–R35.

Daily Phonemic Awareness

Segmenting and Counting Phonemes: Sounds in Riddles

- Read aloud the following riddles. Have children answer with words containing the long *a* sound.

- After children say each answer, have them say the separate sounds in the word and hold up a finger for each sound they say. Have them tell you how many sounds are in the word.

- Say:
  There are seven of me in one week. I am a _____. (*day, /d//ā/, 2*)
  Some people ride on me. I run on tracks. I am a _____. (*train, /t//r//ā//n/, 4*)
  I can make people wet if they forget an umbrella. I am _____. (*rain, /r//ā//n/, 3*)
  You play me with your friends. I am a _____. (*game, /g//ā//m/, 3*)

Daily Language Practice

Grammar Skill: Which Kind of Sentence?
Spelling Skill: The Long *a* Sound Spelled *ay*
Write the sentence, read it to children, and have them tell you how to correct it.

Maye Don come over!

(**May** Don come over?)

Daily Writing Prompt

Have children draw and write on self-selected topics or respond to the prompt below. Remind them to write in complete sentences.

- **Write and draw about what you would like to see if you visited the rain forest.**

I would like to see a parrot in the rain forest.

Daily Independent Reading

To increase children's reading fluency, provide a variety of theme-related books for them to read. Here are some suggestions.

- Leveled Bibliography, pages T6–T7

Choose books from this list for children to read, outside class, for at least twenty minutes a day.

- Anthology: *Red-Eyed Tree Frog*

- Leveled Theme Paperbacks: *Fox and Mule, The Little Red Hen, Fishing Bears*

- Leveled Readers

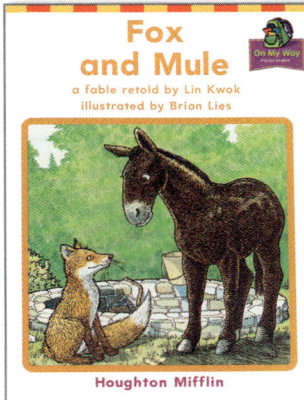

Fox and Mule
a fable retold by Lin Kwok
illustrated by Brian Lies

On My Way

Houghton Mifflin

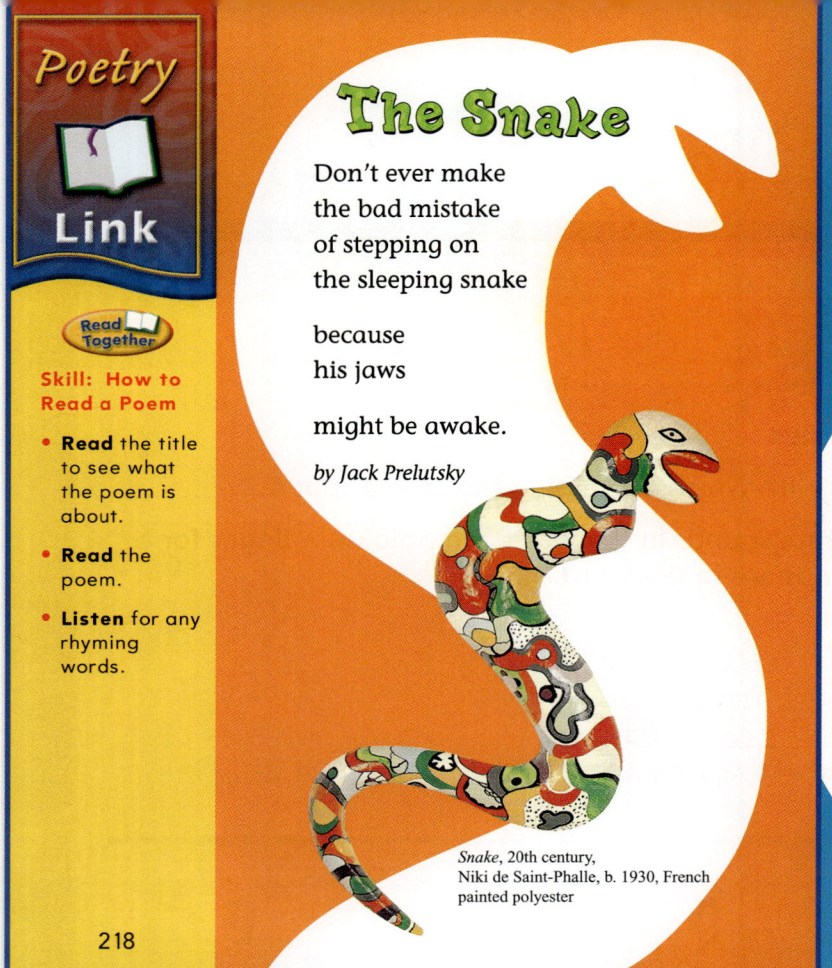

Poetry Link

Skill: How to Read a Poem

- **Read** the title to see what the poem is about.
- **Read** the poem.
- **Listen** for any rhyming words.

The Snake

Don't ever make
the bad mistake
of stepping on
the sleeping snake

because
his jaws

might be awake.

by Jack Prelutsky

Snake, 20th century,
Niki de Saint-Phalle, b. 1930, French
painted polyester

218

THE TOUCAN

Of all the birds I know, few can
Boast of as large a bill as the toucan.
Yet I can think of one who can,
And if you think a while, too, you can:
Another toucan
In the zoo can.

by Pyke Johnson, Jr.

Toucan Design on Mola, San Blas Archipelago, Panama

219

Poetry Link

Skill: How to Read a Poem

Introduce the Link. Read aloud the poem titles and the poets' names.

Discuss the Skill Lesson. Explain that poems can tell stories, give information, share feelings, or just be silly. Sometimes poems have rhyme or rhythm.

Model how to read the first poem. Read the title and have children predict what it will be about. Then read the poem. Point out the rhyming words and clarify any parts of the poem that children found confusing.

Set a purpose for reading. Have children predict what the second poem will be about. Also tell them to listen for rhyming words. Then read the poem together.

Vocabulary

Write the Concept Vocabulary on the board and read each word. Explain the meanings. Point out the snake's *jaws* and the toucan's *bill* in the pictures on Anthology pages 218–219. Explain that *few* can mean "not many." Ask children how long they think a *while* is. Then help children think of examples of things that people *boast* about.

Concept Vocabulary

jaws	bill
few	while
boast	

THEME 6: Animal Adventures
(Anthology pp. 218–219)

Wrapping Up

Critical Thinking Questions

1. **MAKING PREDICTIONS** What is the poet saying might happen to you if you step on a sleeping snake? (The snake may bite.)

2. **NOTING DETAILS** What part of the toucan is very large? (its bill)

3. **DRAWING CONCLUSIONS** What is the only other bird the poet can think of that has a bill as large as a toucan? (another toucan in the zoo)

4. **COMPARE AND CONTRAST** How are the pictures of the toucan and the snake different from the photographs of the real animals in *Red-Eyed Tree Frog*? How are they similar? (Sample answer: The colors are different but the shapes of the animals are similar.)

REACHING ALL LEARNERS

Extra Support/Intervention

Strategy Support

Help children to read the lines one at a time and then ask a question about what they just read to check understanding. For example, ask, *Why do you need to be careful not to step on a sleeping snake?* If children need to clarify something, help them to reread and discuss what they found confusing.

On Level	Challenge

Extending the Topic

If children enjoy reading these poems, provide them with other animal poems to read. Allow small groups to read their favorite poems to one another and discuss what they like about the poems.

OBJECTIVES

- Build words with long *e* (CV, CVC*e*).
- Read words with vowel pairs *ee, ea.*

Target Skill Trace

Teach	pp. T114–T116
Reteach	p. R16
▶ Review	pp. T226–227
See	*Handbook for English Language Learners,* pp. 189, 195; *Extra Support Handbook,* pp. 184, 185, 190–191

Materials

- **Large Sound/Spelling Card** *eagle*
- **Large Letter Cards** *b, E, e*(2), *h, m, P, S, s, t, v, w*
- **Practice Book** punchout trays and letters *b, E, e*(2), *h, m, P, S, s, t, v, w*

REVIEW

PHONICS: Long *e* (CV, CVC*e*)

❶ Review

Review long *e* (CV, CVC*e*). Display **Large Sound/Spelling Card** *eagle.* Have children name the picture. Point to the letter *e.* Remind children that the /ē/ sound at the beginning of *eagle* is called the long *e* sound. Remind them that *e* also stands for the /ē/ sound at the end of *be* and in the middle of *Pete.* Display the spellings *e* and *e_e* shown on the card. Have children say /ē ē ē/ as you point to the letter.

❷ Guided Practice/Apply

Making Words

Get ready. Place the **Large Letter Cards** in a pocket chart. Distribute punchout letters to children. Name the letters as children hold up their matching punchout letters.

Have children make words. Say the directions and sentences below. After children make each word, ask a child to display the word with **Large Letter Cards.** Have children check their work.

Take two letters and make the word me. (*Come with me.*)

Change the first letter to make be. (*Don't be late!*)

Change the first letter to make we. (*Where are we going?*)

Change the first letter to make he. (*Is he coming with us?*)

Add one letter to make she. (*Will she come too?*)

Take three letters and make the name Eve. (*Eve is my friend.*)

Add two letters to make the name Steve. (*I like Steve, too.*)

Change two letters to make the word these. (*Look at these pictures.*)

PHONICS: Vowel Pairs *ee*, *ea*

❶ Review

Review vowel pairs *ee*, *ea*. Display the spellings *ee* and *ea* shown on **Large Sound/Spelling Card** *eagle*. Remind children that the long e sound at the beginning of *eagle* can also be spelled with the letters *ee* and *ea*. Have children say /ē ē ē/ as you point to the letter pairs.

❷ Guided Practice/Apply

Comic Pairs

Write comic pairs of words on the board.

flea beach	neat geese
feet treat	cheap jeep
weak sheep	seal wheel
green teeth	mean queen

- Read the comic pairs of words with children.
- Ask children what they notice about these pairs of words. (They are silly. Each word has a long e sound. Each word contains the vowel pair ee or ea. Some comic pairs rhyme.)

Have each child illustrate a comic pair.

- Have each child choose one pair of words to illustrate.
- Have children take turns sharing their work.

OBJECTIVES

- Spell the Basic Words.
- List words that show animal actions.

Practice Book page 96

Name _____

Week 3
Spelling The Long *a* Sound
Spelled *ay*

Spelling Spree

✏ Write the missing letters to complete each Spelling Word. Write the word.

Spelling Words

day
say
play
may
way
stay

1. st a y   1. stay (1 point)

2. w a y   2. way (1)

3. d a y   3. day (1)

✏ Proofread each sentence. Circle each Spelling Word that is wrong, and write it correctly.

1. What did you (saye?)   say (1)

2. (Mae) I go out to play?   May (1)

3. Let's (palay) a game.   play (1)

SPELLING:
Words with *ay*

Word Clues Tell children you will read clues, and they will write words that end with the letters *ay*.

- Read each clue, and have children write the word.
- Ask a child to write the word on the board, and have children check and correct their spelling.

1. *This is a kind of bird. It is often blue.* (*jay*)

2. *This is a cat that is lost.* (*stray*)

3. *This is a color. You can make it if you mix black and white paint.* (*gray*)

4. *This is something a horse eats.* (*hay*)

Practice/Homework Assign **Practice Book** page 96.

TARGET SKILL
VOCABULARY:
Animal Action Words

Identify words that name animal actions. Read the last sentence on Anthology page 198 from *Red-Eyed Tree Frog*.

- Ask *What does the frog do when it sees the iguana?* (It hops.)
- Say *The author could have chosen other words to describe the same thing. What other action words mean about the same thing as* hops? (*jumps, bounds, leaps*)
- Explain that action words are words that tell what someone or something is doing.

Practice/Apply Choose one or both activities.

- Have pairs of children search through the book for other animal action words.
- Have each child write and illustrate a sentence about an animal action from the story.

The snake slithers by the frog.

WRITING: Writing a Summary

OBJECTIVES
- Contribute sentences to write a class summary.
- Write a summary.

❶ Teach

Explain what a summary is. Tell children that when they read a selection and stop in the middle to tell what has happened so far, they are summarizing, or giving a summary of the selection.

- Explain that a summary is a short description of the important events in a selection.
- Say that today children will summarize *Red-Eyed Tree Frog*. Reread the selection if necessary.

Model summarizing a story. Ask children to summarize the selection in a few sentences. Model how to begin the summary.

Think Aloud *I know that the red-eyed tree frog lives in the rain forest and wakes up hungry. I'll write* In the rain forest, the red-eyed tree frog wakes up hungry.

- Ask *What happens next?* Record children's sentences.
- Ask *What happens at the end of the selection?* Prompt children to complete the summary.
- Reread the summary. Ask children if the summary explains what the whole selection is about in a few sentences.

Go over these points.
- A **summary** is a short description of a selection.
- A summary includes the important events in the selection.

❷ Practice

Check children's understanding.
- Have children help you write a summary of *Tiger and Anansi*. Reread the selection if necessary.
- Reread the finished summary, and ask children if it tells the important events of the story.
- Revise the summary as necessary.

❸ Apply

Assign Practice Book page 97. After they finish independently, have pairs of children read their summaries to each other to make sure they have told the important events in the story.

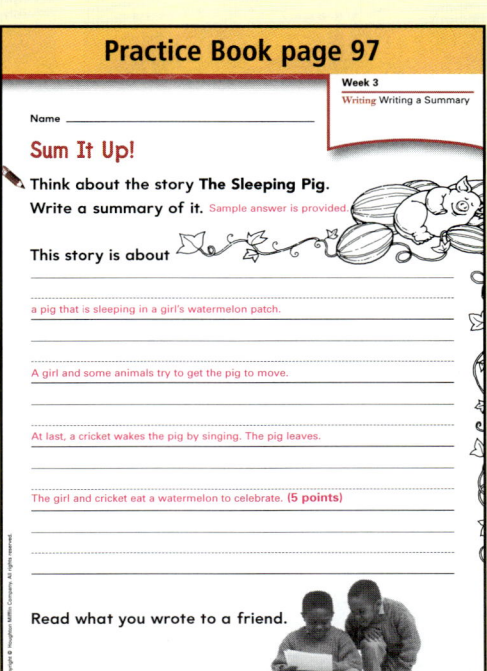

Practice Book page 97

Week 3
Writing Writing a Summary

Name _____

Sum It Up!

Think about the story **The Sleeping Pig**.
Write a summary of it. Sample answer is provided.

This story is about

a pig that is sleeping in a girl's watermelon patch.

A girl and some animals try to get the pig to move.

At last, a cricket wakes the pig by singing. The pig leaves.

The girl and cricket eat a watermelon to celebrate. **(5 points)**

Read what you wrote to a friend.

Day at a Glance
pages T230–T237

Learning to Read

Comprehension: Rereading for Understanding
Making Predictions

Rereading for Fluency

Reading Decodable Text
Jay's Trip

- - - - - - - - - - - - - - - -

Leveled Readers, T238–T241

- ● *Looking for Frogs*
- ▲ *The Mouse in the Forest*
- ■ *Animals at Night*
- ◆ *How Many Frogs?*

Word Work

Spelling Test: Words with *ay*
Vocabulary: High-Frequency Words

Writing & Oral Language

Grammar Review: Naming Words for One or More

Independent Writing

Listening and Speaking: Listening for Information

Daily Routines

Daily Message

Strategy Review Remind children of the Phonics/Decoding Strategy. Guide them in applying it to selected words in today's message.

> Good Morning, Class,
>
> What do you think when you are hungry? Do you hope it is time to eat soon? Do you get a snack, or... do you wait until the next meal?

Have children

- respond to the questions;
- circle words with *ai* and *ea*; (*wait, eat, meal*)
- find and read the following high-frequency words: *What, you, are, hungry,* and *soon.*

Word Wall

Cumulative Review Review new and previously taught high-frequency words from the Word Wall. Have children complete **Activity Master 6–3** on Teacher's Edition page R38.

Have children

- cut out the word cards;
- read and spell the words on the word cards;
- glue each word card next to the word with the opposite meaning.

evening	morning
far	near

Daily Phonemic Awareness

Segmenting and Counting Phonemes: Animal Names

- Tell children that you will say some animal names and that they should say the separate sounds in each word. Example: /f/ /r/ /ŏ/ /g/.

- Have children clap once for each sound they say and tell you how many times they clapped. Example: After clapping four times for *frog,* children say "Four!"

- Continue with *snake* (4), *cat* (3), *whale* (3), *dog* (3), *fox* (3), *cow* (2), *bee* (2), and *ant* (3).

Daily Language Practice

Grammar Skill: Beginning Sentences with Capital Letters

Spelling Skill: Words with *ay*

Write the sentence, read it to children, and have them tell you how to correct it.

> what dayy can you be here?

(What **day** can you be here?)

Daily Writing Prompt

Remind children to write in complete sentences when they respond to the prompt below or write on self-selected topics.

- **Write and draw about what the rain forest is like during the day.**

In the daytime the red-eyed frog sleeps.

Daily Independent Reading

To increase children's reading fluency, provide a variety of theme-related books for them to read. Here are some suggestions.

- Leveled Bibliography, pages T6–T7

Choose books from this list for children to read, outside class, for at least twenty minutes a day.

- Anthology: *Red-Eyed Tree Frog*

- Phonics Library: *Rain Day, Cub's Long Day, Jay's Trip*

- Leveled Readers

Cub's Long Day
by Mary Gold
illustrated by Anna Vojtech

This cub has big feet and a little tail. His home is a cave deep in the forest.

33

OBJECTIVES

- Review making predictions in the week's selections.

Review Skill Trace

Teach	pp. T218–T219
Reteach	p. R30
▶ Review	p. T232
See	*Extra Support Handbook,* pp. 196–197, 202–203

Materials

- Teacher's Resource Blackline Master 83

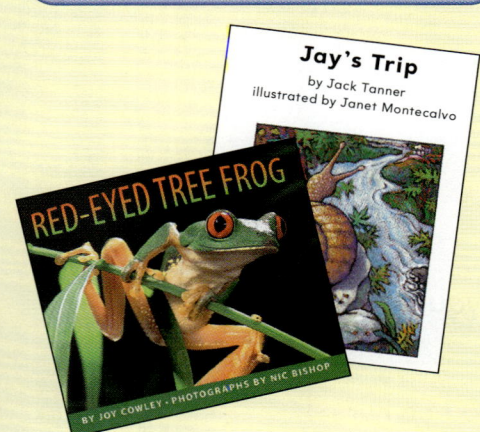

Jay's Trip
by Jack Tanner
illustrated by Janet Montecalvo

RED-EYED TREE FROG
BY JOY COWLEY • PHOTOGRAPHS BY NIC BISHOP

COMPREHENSION: Rereading for Understanding

Making Predictions

Review how to make predictions. Remind children that they can use text and picture clues and their own knowledge to make predictions about stories and to understand what they read.

Distribute Teacher's Resource Blackline Master 83. Record in the first column the predictions children made about *Red-Eyed Tree Frog*. Then model how to check a prediction.

Think Aloud *In* Red-Eyed Tree Frog *I predicted that the frog would eat a fly, because I know that some frogs eat flies. When I read, I found out that the frog ate a moth. My prediction wasn't correct, but it was close because moths and flies are both flying insects.*

Have children predict what will happen in *Jay's Trip*.

- Read the title and look at the pictures with children.

- Have children write on **Blackline Master 83** who they think Jay is and what he will do.

- Follow the lesson for *Jay's Trip* on pages T233–T235. Then review with children whether or not their predictions were correct.

Assign rereading and retelling.

- Have children reread these other selections for this week and then retell the story to a partner, explaining why their predictions were correct or incorrect: **On My Way Practice Reader, Theme Paperbacks, Phonics Library, Leveled Readers.**

- Have partners make predictions about a book from the Leveled Bibliography and then read to check their predictions.

REREADING FOR FLUENCY

Rereading the Selection Have children choose part of *Red-Eyed Tree Frog* to reread orally in small groups, or suggest that they read pages 203–204. If necessary, model fluent reading. Encourage children to read with feeling and expression.

Phonics Library

Animal Adventures

Jay's Trip

by Jack Tanner
illustrated by Janet Montecalvo

<u>Jay</u> the <u>snail</u> has never seen
a <u>bay</u>. His home is <u>near</u> trees
and plants.

37

PHONICS LIBRARY

End-of-Week Skills Check

Have children preview *Jay's Trip*. Ask them what happens to the snail in the pictures.

Observe as children model the Phonics/Decoding Strategy.

- Have children read *Jay's Trip*. As they read, ask individuals to tell how they use the strategy to figure out new words.

- Make note of children who have difficulty applying the strategy, and take oral reading records with these children.

Prompt children in rereading the story. For children who have difficulty, use prompts such as these:

- *Look at the letters from left to right. What letters do you see?*

- *Say the sound for each letter and hold it until you say the next sound. What is the word?*

- *Is that a word you know? Does it make sense in the story?*

OBJECTIVES

- Apply the Phonics/Decoding Strategy to decode words in context.
- Recognize high-frequency words in context.
- Reread to build fluency.

Word Key

Decodable words with vowel pairs
ai, ay ———

High-Frequency Words ———

Monitoring Student Progress

Oral Reading Records Take oral reading records of a few children each week as they read the **Phonics Library** book individually or in small groups.

Alternative Assessment Use **Teacher's Resource Blackline Master 84** to assess individual children's phonics and high-frequency word skills.

One fine <u>day</u>, Jay takes a nap on this big red leaf. While Jay sleeps, he <u>sails</u> a long <u>way</u>.

38

When Jay wakes up, he is at a beach on a <u>bay</u>! <u>Kay</u> gets Jay and sets him in her <u>gray</u> <u>pail</u>. "This snail is <u>far</u> from his home," she thinks.

39

Oral Language

Discuss these questions with children. Have them answer in complete sentences.

- Where does Jay sail to? (He sails to a bay.)
- Where does Jay finally make his new home? (He makes his new home in Kay's garden.)

That evening, Kay goes home.
Soon Jay is right at home, too!

40

Build Fluency

Model and have children practice fluent reading.

- Call attention to the commas on page 38. Explain that commas show where a reader should make a short pause in a longer sentence.

- Read the page aloud. Have children read it in unison.

- Read aloud page 39.

- Have children reread pages 38 and 39 several times until each child can read them aloud effortlessly.

Home Connection

Hand out the take-home version of *Jay's Trip*. Ask children to reread the story with their families. (See the **Phonics Library Blackline Masters**.)

TEST

SPELLING: Words with *ay*

Test

Say each underlined word, read the sentence, and then repeat the word. Have children write only the underlined word.

Basic Words

1. We went to the lake that **day**.
2. What did you **say** to Mom?
3. His cat likes to **play** with yarn.
4. Ask Dad if we **may** go with you.
5. Liz can find the **way**.
6. Would you **stay** with me?

REVIEW

TARGET SKILL VOCABULARY: High-Frequency Words

Review the words. Tell children they will count the number of letters in this week's New Words on the Word Wall.

- Ask children to find a two-letter word on the Word Wall. Then have children find the other two-letter words.
- Repeat with three-letter words.
- Finally, have children clap and spell each New Word. Call on a child to move the word to the permanent Word Wall as children chant it aloud.

Practice/Apply Have vocabulary speed drills. Assemble the word cards for this week's New Words and several others from previous weeks. Make a few other cards for decodable words that feature the week's phonics/decoding elements.

- At small group time, have children take turns holding up the cards for a partner to read.
- Then display the cards as a list on a table. Have individuals read them to you as quickly as they can.

forest   evening   goes   near   hungry   been

GRAMMAR: Naming Words for One or More

OBJECTIVES
- Review naming words for one or more than one.
- Listen for information.

Review Skill Trace	
Teach	p. T221
▶ Review	p. T237
See	*Handbook for English Language Learners*, p.207

Review Remind children that naming words name one or more than one person, animal, place, or thing.

Have children write a postcard to a friend. Tell children to imagine they have traveled to a rain forest. Say they will send a postcard to a partner.

- Give each child heavy paper shaped like a postcard.
- Tell children to draw the rain forest on one side of the postcard.
- Have them write a message about the rain forest on the back.
- Tell them to include at least two words that name one and two words that name more than one person, animal, place, or thing.

Practice/Apply
- Have pairs of children exchange postcards and read the messages.
- Tell them to check the words in the postcard message that name one and more than one person, animal, place, or thing.

Independent Writing Have children write a journal entry about their trip to the rain forest. Remind them to use naming words for one and more than one correctly.

LISTENING AND SPEAKING: Listening for Information

Have children listen for information in a selection. Tell children that listening for information will help them learn new things.

- Reread *Life in a Rain Forest* as children listen for information about which animals live in trees and which live on the ground.
- After reading the selection, ask
  Which animals live in trees?
  Which animals live on the ground?
  When you heard a fact you were listening for, what did you do?

English Language Learners

Supporting Comprehension
Pause after each paragraph, and ask children what they heard about where animals live. Prompt children if necessary. Write their answers on the board as a reference.

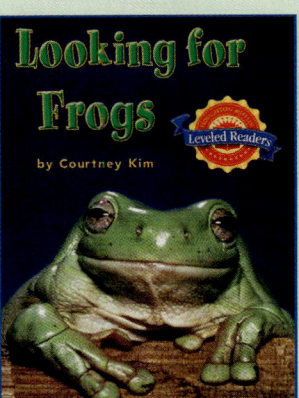

Looking for Frogs

Summary *This photo essay shows and tells about the places we can go to look for frogs and the things we might see while we are looking for them.*

Story Words

Introduce the Story Words, one at a time, providing meaning with objects, pictures, gestures, and/or context sentences. Then ask children to complete the **Vocabulary Practice Master.**

frogs (title), *p. 2*

forest *p. 3*

pond *p. 4*

splash *p. 8*

● BELOW LEVEL

Building Background and Vocabulary

Invite children to look through the book at the pictures of frogs and other animals. Tell them that the pictures are photos, taken with a camera, of real frogs. Explain that the photos and words show and tell what the frogs are like and where they live. Invite children to share what they already know about real frogs and where they have seen them.

● Comprehension Skill: Making Predictions

Read together the Strategy Focus on the book flap. Remind children to use the strategy and to make predictions about what will happen next as they read the book. (See the Leveled Readers Teacher's Guide for **Vocabulary and Comprehension Practice Masters.**)

Responding

Have partners discuss how to answer the questions on the inside back cover.

Think About What You Have Read Sample answers:

1. Answers may include: in a pond on green (lily) pads.
2. Answers should include that they'll hop or splash into the pond.
3. Answers will vary.

Making Connections Answers will vary.

● Building Fluency

Model Explain that in this book, the author writes sentences that go with the pictures as if she was speaking to the reader. Point out the words *you* on page 2 and *We* on page 3. Ask children to read these pages with you.

Practice Have children reread the book aloud with partners, pointing to their partners as they read the word *you* and to themselves on the word *we*.

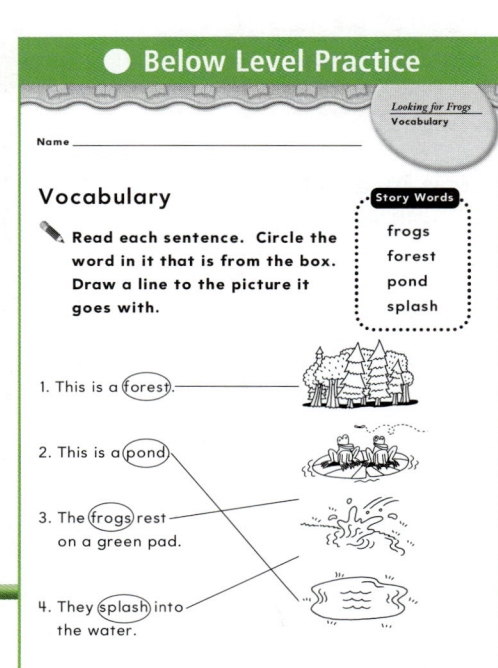

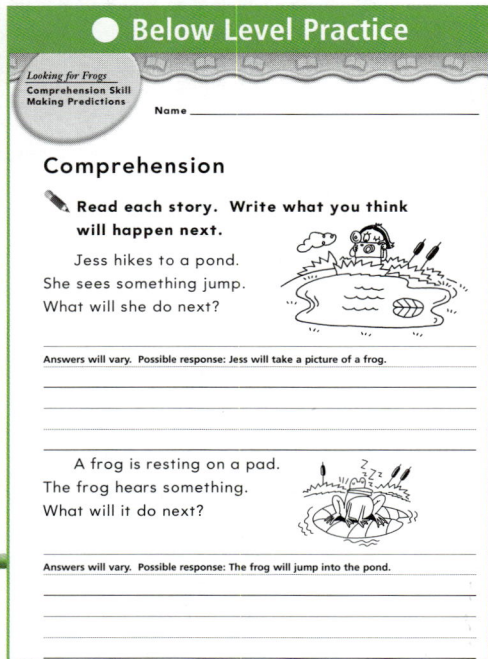

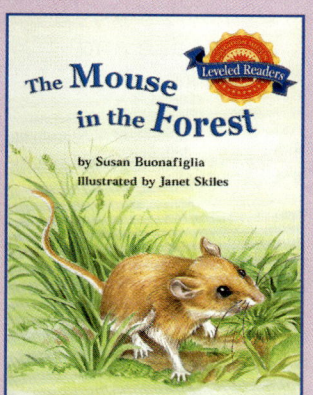

The Mouse in the Forest

Summary *In this nonfiction book, readers learn about the life of a forest mouse. All night long, as it searches for food, the mouse tries to avoid being caught by larger animals, such as hungry foxes. When the sun rises again, the mouse goes back into its nest, ready to sleep all day.*

Story Words

Introduce the Story Words, one at a time, providing meaning with objects, pictures, gestures, and/or context sentences. Then ask children to complete the **Vocabulary Practice Master.**

forest (title), p. 2

mouse (title), p. 3

nest p. 3

evening p. 4

trail p. 7

fox p. 10

▲ ON LEVEL

Building Background and Vocabulary

Discuss the cover picture and tell children that this book gives information about what a mouse that lives in a forest does. Encourage them to share what they know about mice or other animals that live in forests.

Comprehension Skill: Making Predictions

Read together the Strategy Focus on the book flap. Remind children to use the strategy and to make predictions about what will happen next to the mouse as they read the book. (See the Leveled Readers Teacher's Guide for **Vocabulary and Comprehension Practice Masters.**)

Responding

Have partners discuss how to answer the questions on the inside back cover.

Think About What You Have Read Sample answers:

1. The mouse looks for food, washes, and escapes from a fox.
2. It's harder to see at night, so it can get away from other animals.
3. Answers will vary but should include that they could find out more by looking in books and magazines and by asking people at a pet shop.

Making Connections Answers will vary.

Building Fluency

Model Invite children to follow along as you reread pages 2 through 4 aloud. Then ask them to find the questions on page 4 and to read them aloud together. Have children reread pages 5 and 6 to find the answers.

Practice Have children reread the rest of the book with partners. Children can alternate reading the questions and answers. Before they begin reading, have them locate the questions.

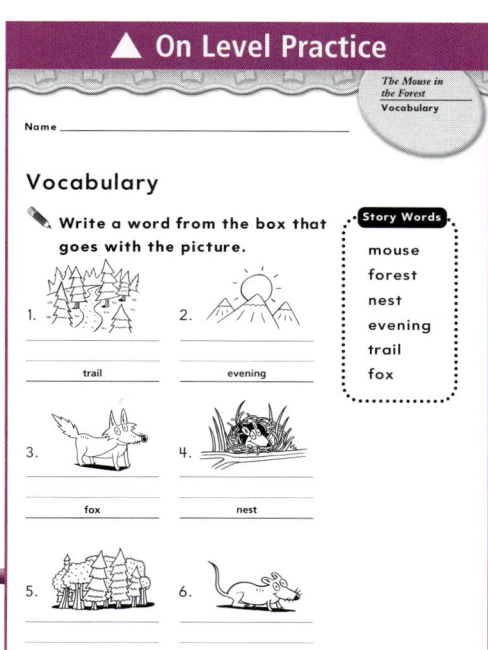

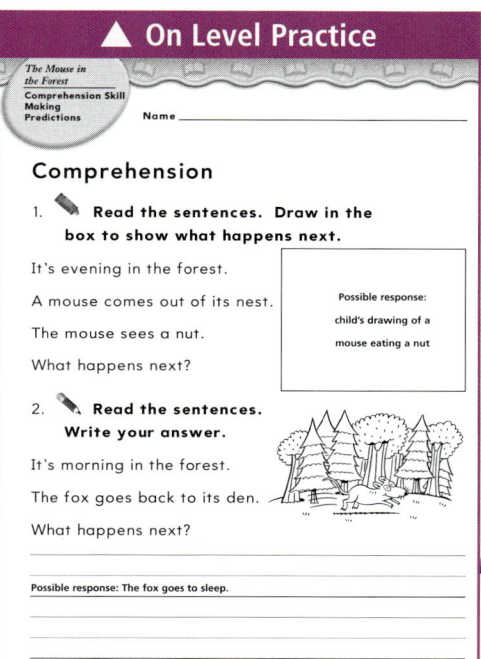

■ ABOVE LEVEL

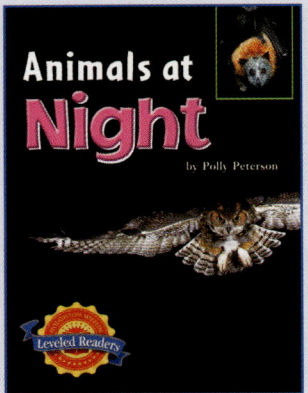

Animals at Night

Summary *This photo essay describes some nocturnal animals and tells where they live and what they do at night. Some animals described are owls, mice, frogs, raccoons, bats, skunks, fireflies, and slugs.*

Story Words

Introduce the Story Words, one at a time, providing meaning with objects, pictures, gestures, and/or context sentences. Then ask children to complete the **Vocabulary Practice Master.**

owl *p. 3*

mice *p. 4*

crayfish *p. 7*

raccoon *p. 7*

bats *p. 8*

skunk *p. 9*

Building Background and Vocabulary

Discuss the title and preview the photos with children, pointing out that most of the animals shown and described in this book are awake and looking for food at night.

Comprehension Skill: Making Predictions

Read together the Strategy Focus on the book flap. Remind children to use the strategy and to make predictions about what is happening as they read the book. (See the Leveled Readers Teacher's Guide for **Vocabulary and Comprehension Practice Masters.**)

Responding

Have partners discuss how to answer the questions on the inside back cover.

Think About What You Have Read Sample answers:

1. Answers should include: They sleep at night, but all the other animals in this book are awake at night.

2. The slug and the rabbit eat the tender leaves of the plants. The people see the holes these animals have eaten in their garden plants.

3. Answers will vary.

Making Connections Answers will vary.

Building Fluency

Model Reread pages 2 and 3 aloud to the children, asking them to notice the simple and direct way in which you read the information.

Practice Beginning on page 4, have children continue to reread the book aloud as a group, imitating your tone as they read.

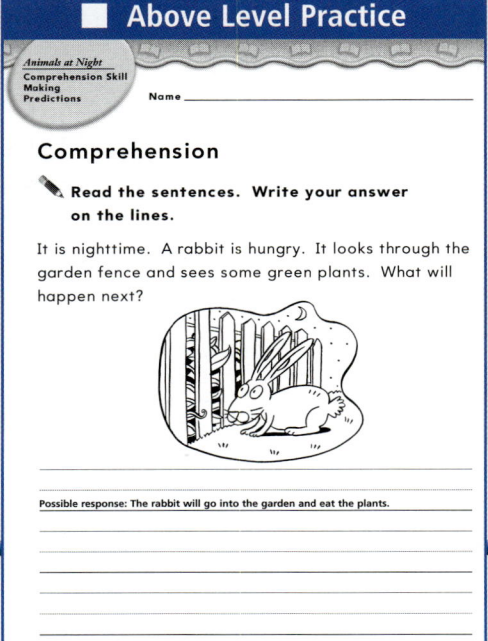

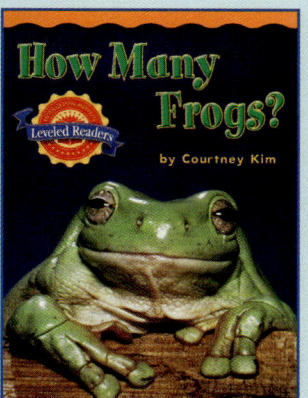

How Many Frogs?

Summary *A family looks for frogs in a forest and in a pond. They find fish and snails in the pond. They look on the green lily pads for frogs. When they find frogs, one splashes into the water.*

Story Words

Introduce the Story Words. Then ask children to complete the Story Words Practice Master.

frog a small, smooth-skinned animal that lives in or near water, *p. 2*

pond a body of water that is smaller than a lake, *p. 4*

fish a large group of water animals with backbones, fins, and gills for breathing underwater, *p. 5*

snails slow-moving animals that have spiral shells, *p. 5*

splash to scatter water all around, *p. 8*

Building Background and Vocabulary

Show children photographs or pictures of woodland animals and pond life. Have children describe what they see, along with other creatures they might see in similar habitats. Write the children's ideas on the board. Then distribute the **Build Background Practice Master** and have children complete the page. (See the Leveled Readers Teacher's Guide for **Build Background** and **Story Words Masters.**)

Reading Strategy: Question

Have children read the Strategy Focus on the book flap. Remind children to think about the answer to the question as they read.

Responding

Have partners discuss how to answer the questions on the inside back cover.

Think About What You Have Read Sample answers:

1. They look in a forest and a pond.
2. They live in the water.
3. Answers will vary.

Making Connections Answers will vary.

Building Fluency

Model Read aloud pages 4–7 as children follow along in their books.

Practice Lead an echo reading of the same text: read each page and have children repeat after you. Reread several times until children can read the text on their own.

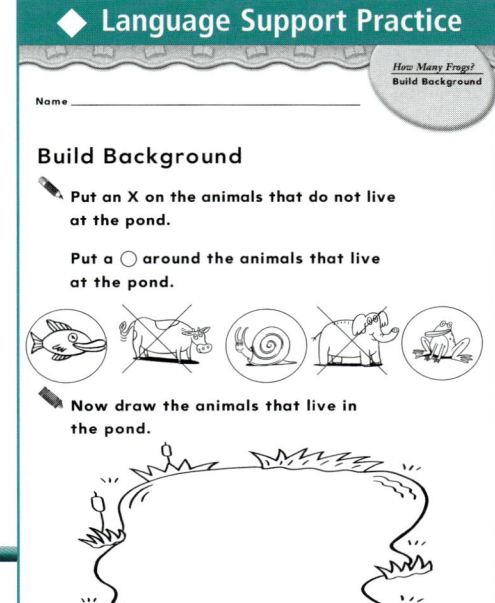

Preparing for Tests

Taking Tests

Filling in the Blank

Some tests have sentences with a blank in them. You must decide which answer choice best fills in the blank. Look at this sample test for *Red-Eyed Tree Frog.* The correct answer is shown.

> Read the sentence. Fill in the circle next to the best answer.
>
> 1   The red-eyed tree frog _____ all day.
>   ● sleeps   ○ climbs   ○ eats

Tips

- Put your finger on the number next to the sentence.
- Find the circle that goes with the correct answer.
- Fill in the whole circle.

220

Now see how one student figured out the best answer.

First, I read the directions. Then I read the test sentence. I need to find out what the frog does all day.

I look back in the story. The beginning tells what the frog does. I will look there.

I read the test sentence to myself, using each answer choice. The last two choices do not tell about the frog in the daytime. The first choice is best.

221

THEME	STRATEGY
5	Phonics
▶ 6	Filling in the Blank
7	Writing a Personal Response
8	Choosing the Best Answer
9	Writing an Answer to a Question
10	Writing a Personal Narrative

TAKING TESTS: Filling in the Blank

Taking Tests provides instruction and practice in different test formats. It will help you prepare children for the **Integrated Theme Test** and the **Theme Skills Test,** as well as state and national standardized tests.

Introducing the Strategy

Discuss filling in the blank.

- Have children turn to Anthology pages 220–221.
- Read aloud the test directions, the question, and the answer choices.
- Read aloud and discuss each step in the Tips box.
- Read aloud each thought balloon.
- Talk about each step as you read and review the sample answer with children.

Test Practice

Assign Practice Book pages 99–100. Encourage children to think about the tips and the thought balloons on Anthology pages 220–221.

- Distribute **Practice Book** pages 99–100 and have children fill in the blanks.
- Remind children that they can go back to the story if they need to refresh their memory.
- Tell children to make their best choice if they are still unsure of the answer.

REVIEW

SPELLING: Review/Assessment

Spelling Review

Review the Spelling Lessons on pages T38, T120, and T190.
Assign Practice Book pages 101–102. Children can also use the Take-Home Word List for the theme on **Practice Book** page 309.

Spelling Pretest/Test

Basic Words

1. The truck can **go** fast.
2. He has a red **nose**.
3. Lee went **home** at five.
4. Kate and Dale like **me**.
5. The cow will **eat** the hay.
6. The **mean** duck bit him.
7. Jack has socks on his **feet**.
8. The **day** is hot.
9. The cat will **play**.
10. Max will **stay** home.

Challenge Words

11. The chick **woke** up.
12. The **sheep** eat grass.
13. The fox ran **away**.

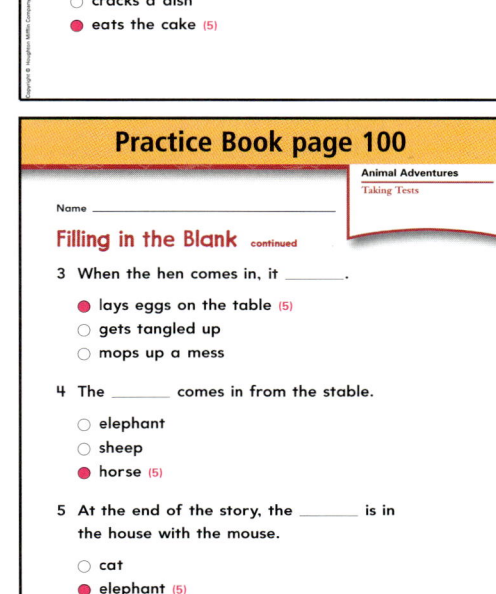

Practice Book page 99

Animal Adventures
Taking Tests

Name _____

Filling in the Blank

Now use what you have learned about taking tests. Answer these fill-in-the-blank questions about **Eek! There's a Mouse in the House.** Look back at the story if you need to. This practice will help you when you take this kind of test.

Read each sentence. Fill in the circle next to the best answer.

1 The girl would like the _____ to chase the rat.
- ○ dog
- ● cat (5 points)
- ○ cow

2 The hog _____ but does not chase the dog.
- ○ hops with a mop
- ○ cracks a dish
- ● eats the cake (5)

Practice Book page 100

Animal Adventures
Taking Tests

Name _____

Filling in the Blank continued

3 When the hen comes in, it _____.
- ● lays eggs on the table (5)
- ○ gets tangled up
- ○ mops up a mess

4 The _____ comes in from the stable.
- ○ elephant
- ○ sheep
- ● horse (5)

5 At the end of the story, the _____ is in the house with the mouse.
- ○ cat
- ● elephant (5)
- ○ cow

Practice Book page 309

Take-Home Word List	Take-Home Word List
Animal Adventures Spelling Review	**Red-Eyed Tree Frog**
Spelling Words	**The Long *a* Sound Spelled *ay***
1. go	day say
2. me	play
3. day	**Spelling Words**
4. feet	1. day
5. nose	2. say
6. eat	3. play
7. play	4. may
8. mean	5. way
9. home	6. stay
10. stay	

Read directions to children.
See the back for Challenge Words.

Challenge Words
1. away
2. holiday
Read directions to children.

My Study List Add your own spelling words on the back.

My Study List Add your own spelling words on the back.

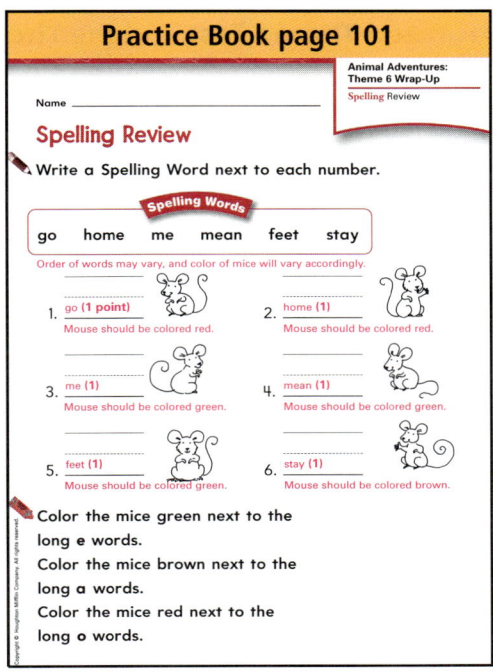

Practice Book page 101

Animal Adventures:
Theme 6 Wrap-Up
Spelling Review

Name _____

Spelling Review

Write a Spelling Word next to each number.

Spelling Words
go   home   me   mean   feet   stay

Order of words may vary, and color of mice will vary accordingly.

1. go (1 point)
Mouse should be colored red.

2. home (1)
Mouse should be colored red.

3. me (1)
Mouse should be colored green.

4. mean (1)
Mouse should be colored green.

5. feet (1)
Mouse should be colored green.

6. stay (1)
Mouse should be colored brown.

Color the mice green next to the long e words.
Color the mice brown next to the long a words.
Color the mice red next to the long o words.

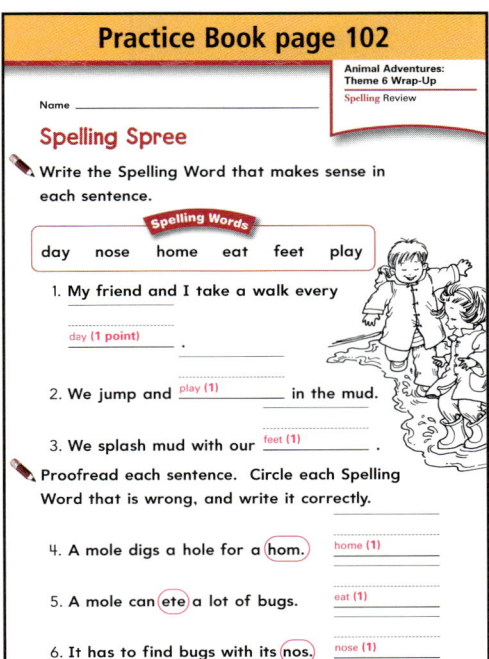

Practice Book page 102

Animal Adventures:
Theme 6 Wrap-Up
Spelling Review

Name _____

Spelling Spree

Write the Spelling Word that makes sense in each sentence.

Spelling Words
day   nose   home   eat   feet   play

1. My friend and I take a walk every _____.
day (1 point)

2. We jump and _____ in the mud.
play (1)

3. We splash mud with our _____.
feet (1)

Proofread each sentence. Circle each Spelling Word that is wrong, and write it correctly.

4. A mole digs a hole for a (hom.)
home (1)

5. A mole can (ete) a lot of bugs.
eat (1)

6. It has to find bugs with its (nos.)
nose (1)

Take-Home Word list

Assessing Student Progress

Monitoring Student Progress

Test Preparation

Throughout the theme, children have had opportunities to read and think critically. They have practiced, applied, and reviewed reading skills and strategies. They have also learned and practiced test-taking strategies. These strategies will help them understand different test formats and do well on tests.

Monitoring Student Progress

Throughout Theme 6, you monitored your children's progress by using the following program features:

- Guiding Comprehension questions
- Literature discussion circle
- Skill lesson applications
- Oral reading records
- Monitoring Student Progress boxes

Your children are now ready for the theme assessments, which allow you to assess each child's progress formally.

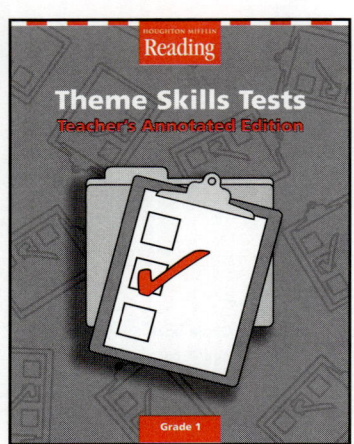

Testing Options

The **Integrated Theme Test** and the **Theme Skills Test** are formal group assessments used to evaluate children's performance on theme objectives.

Integrated Theme Test
- Assesses children's progress as readers and writers in a format that reflects instruction
- Integrates reading and writing skills: phonics, comprehension strategies and skills, high-frequency words, and writing
- Uses decodable passages to test children's reading skills in context

Theme Skills Test
- May be used as a pretest or administered following the theme
- Assesses children's mastery of discrete reading and language arts skills taught in the theme: phonics, comprehension skills, high-frequency words, spelling, and grammar
- Consists of individual skill subtests, which can be administered separately

Fluency Assessment

Oral reading fluency is a useful measure of a child's development of rapid automatic word recognition. In the early stages of reading development, oral fluency should be observed informally.

- Consider decoding and comprehension, as well as reading rate, when evaluating children's reading development.

- You can use the **Leveled Reading Passages Assessment Kit** to assess fluency or a **Leveled Reader** from this theme at the appropriate level for each child.

- Check children's oral fluency rate three times during the year. If children are having difficulty learning to read, you might want to check their fluency rate more often.

- For information on how to select appropriate text, administer fluency checks, and interpret results, see the **Teacher's Assessment Handbook,** pp. 25–28.

Using Multiple Measures

In addition to the tests mentioned on page T244, multiple measures might include the following:

- **Emerging Literacy Survey** results

- Oral reading records

- Observation Checklist from this theme

- Children's writing from lessons or activities in this theme

- Description from the Reading-Writing Workshop

- Other writing, projects, or artwork

- One or more items selected by the child

Children's progress is best evaluated through multiple measures. Multiple measures of assessment can be collected in a portfolio. The portfolio provides a record of children's progress over time and can be useful when conferencing with the child, parents, or other educators.

Technology

Managing Assessment

The **Learner Profile®** **CD-ROM** lets you record, manage, and report your assessment of children's progress electronically.

You can

- record children's progress on objectives in Theme 6.

- add or import additional objectives, including your state standards, and track your children's progress against these.

- record and manage results from the **Integrated Theme Test** and the **Theme Skills Test** for Theme 6, as well as results from other reading assessments.

- organize information about children's progress and generate a variety of assessment reports.

- use **Learner Profile To Go** to record children's progress throughout the day on a hand-held computer device and then upload the information to a desktop computer.

Turn the page to continue.

Using Assessment to Plan Instruction

You can use the results of theme assessments to determine an individual child's needs for additional skill instruction and to modify instruction during the next theme. For more detail, see the test manuals or the **Teacher's Assessment Handbook.**

This chart shows Theme 6 resources for differentiating additional instruction. As you look ahead to Theme 7, you can plan to use the corresponding Theme 7 resources.

Differentiating Instruction

Assessment Shows	Use These Resources	
Difficulty with Decoding or Oral Fluency **Emphasize** Phonemic awareness and phonics; rereading for fluency	• **Get Set for Reading CD-ROM** • Reteaching: Phonics, **Teacher's Edition,** pp. R12, R14; R16; R18 • Reteaching: High-Frequency Words, **Teacher's Edition,** pp. R20; R22; R24 • **Extra Support Handbook,** pp. 174–175, 178–179, 180–181; 184–185, 188–189, 190–191; 194–195, 198–199, 200–201 • **Handbook for English Language Learners,** pp.178–179, 180–181, 182–183, 184–185, 186; 188–189, 190–191; 192–193, 194–195, 196; 198–199, 200–201, 202–203, 204–205, 206	• **Lexia Phonics CD-ROM Primary Intervention** • Leveled Bibliography, **Teacher's Edition,** pp. T6–T7 • **Phonics Library,** Theme 6 • **I Love Reading Books** • **On My Way Practice Readers** • Below Level **Leveled Readers** • Below Level lessons for **Leveled Readers, Teacher's Edition,** pp. T84; T166; T238
Difficulty with Comprehension **Emphasize** Oral comprehension; strategy development; story comprehension; vocabulary development; Teacher-Supported Reading	• **Get Set for Reading CD-ROM** • Reteaching: Comprehension, **Teacher's Edition,** pp. R26; R28; R30 • **Phonics Library,** Theme 6	• **Extra Support Handbook,** pp. 176–177, 182–183; 186–187, 192–193; 196–197, 202–203 • Below Level **Leveled Readers** • Below Level lessons for **Leveled Readers, Teacher's Edition,** pp. T84; T166; T238
Overall High Performance **Emphasize** Independent reading and writing; vocabulary development; critical thinking	• Challenge/Extension Activities: Phonics, **Teacher's Edition,** pp. R13, R15; R17; R19 • Challenge/Extension Activities: High-Frequency Words, **Teacher's Edition,** pp. R21; R23; R25 • Challenge/Extension Activities: Comprehension, **Teacher's Edition,** pp. R27; R29; R31	• Above Level **Theme Paperback** • Above Level **Leveled Readers** • Above Level lessons for **Leveled Readers, Teacher's Edition,** pp. T86; T168; T240 • Challenge Activity Masters, **Challenge Handbook,** CH6–1 to CH6–6

Resources for Theme 6

Contents

Two's Company

by Shirley Greenway

Some animals live alone, some live in families, and some in groups, each with its own special name. Two is company, but three can be a flock or a herd, a school or a pod . . .

One sheep alone, **two** sheep together—

a **flock** of sheep grazing in the snow.

One small fish, **two** shimmering fish—

a **shoal** of silvery fish swimming.

One fox sniffing, **two** foxes digging—

a **skulk** of foxes hunting in the night.

One honeybee working, **two** honeybees around a flower—

a **swarm** of honeybees buzzing.

One zebra on the savanna, **two** friendly zebras in the bush—

a **herd** of zebras gathered at the watering hole.

One goose floating, **two** geese flying—

a **gaggle** of geese rising into the sky.

One dolphin somersaulting in the sea, **two** dolphins swimming together—

a **school** of dolphins gliding through blue water.

One macaw all alone, **two** macaws meeting—

a **family** of macaws sitting on a wall.

One kangaroo hopping, **two** kangaroos boxing—

a **troop** of kangaroos resting in the shade.

HOUGHTON MIFFLIN
Reading
TWO'S Company
by Shirley Greenway
Photographs by Oxford Scientific Films

One mouse nibbling, **two** mice kissing—

a **nest** of mice hidden in the grass.

One stately camel, **two** comical camels—

a **train** of camels traveling across the sand.

One walrus showing his fine tusks, **two** walruses enjoying a swim—

a **pod** of walruses sunbathing on the rocks.

One lazy lion yawning, **two** contented lions resting—

a **pride** of lions drinking in the afternoon.

So, whether you belong to a family or a pair, a group or a gathering, a class or a crowd—it's nice to be one, and fun to be two, but sometimes it's good to be many.

On My Way
Practice Readers

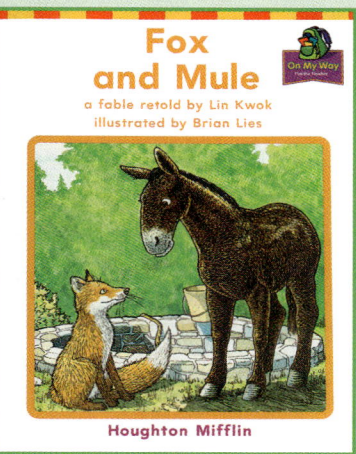

Fox and Mule
a fable retold by Lin Kwok
illustrated by Brian Lies

Houghton Mifflin

Fox and Mule

Summary *This fable tells how Fox, who gets trapped in a well, tricks Mule into helping him get out.*

Building Background

Read the title and author's name aloud. Tell children they will be reading a fable about a trick Fox plays on Mule. Have them predict how Fox might trick Mule.

Supporting the Reading

Introducing the Book Page through the book with children. You may want to point out the following words: *deep, footsteps, loudly, thirsty, leap.* Use the suggestions below to prepare children for reading on their own.

page 2: *Which two words rhyme?* (fell, well)

page 3: *The word* deep *begins like* den. *Can you point to the word* deep?

page 5: Footsteps *is made up of two smaller words. Can you find the word* footsteps?

page 6: *Which words have the long* u *sound?* (Mule, cute)

page 8: *The word* thirsty *begins with /th/. Point to* thirsty.

Prompting Strategies Listen to and observe children as they read, and use prompts such as the following to help them apply strategies:

• *Look at the letters in this word and blend the sounds for the letters.*

• *Why did you hesitate? What else could you try?*

• *Is there something you don't understand here?*

Responding

Discuss with children the trick that Fox played on Mule and what lesson they think Mule might have learned. Did any part of the story surprise them?

Activity Have groups of three reread the story, each taking the part of a character and the narrator.

▲ ON LEVEL

The Little Red Hen

Summary *None of the animals will help the little red hen bake bread, but they are all very eager to eat the finished product.*

Building Background

Read the title and author's and illustrator's names out loud. If children are familiar with the story, ask them to share what they know about the little red hen.

Supporting the Reading

Introducing the Book Page through the book with children. The suggestions below can help prepare children to read the story independently.

page 4: *The little red hen finds some grains of wheat. Wheat begins like* when. *Can you find the word* wheat?

page 8: *There are four different words that begin with* w. *What are they?* (watered, weeded, watched, wheat)

page 20: *The word* flour *rhymes with* hour. *Can you find the word* flour?

page 24: *The word* oven *begins with* o *and ends with* n. *Point to the word* oven.

Prompting Strategies Listen to and observe children as they read, and use prompts such as the following to help them apply strategies:

- *What is the sound for that letter?*
- *What would make sense here?*
- *Try rereading this part.*

Responding

Discuss with children whether they think the hen did the right thing at the end of the story.

Activity Children can do a dramatic rereading of the story.

Fishing Bears

Summary *This book describes the characteristics, behavior, and habitat of Alaskan brown bears.*

Building Background

Read aloud the title and the names of the author and photographer. Take a picture walk through the book, pointing out the map, diagram, and glossary. Ask children to share what they know about bears in the wild.

Supporting the Reading

Introducing the Book Page through the book with children. The suggestions below can help prepare children to read the story on their own.

page 4: *This is an Alaskan brown bear. Can you point to the words* Alaskan brown bear?

page 10: *The word in italics is* omnivores. *It tells that brown bears eat both plants and animals.*

page 15: *This bear is fishing for food that begins with /s/. What is the name of the food?* (salmon)

page 24: *Can you find the word that means "sleeping a deep winter sleep"?* (hibernating)

Prompting Strategies Listen to and observe children as they read, and use prompts such as the following to help them apply strategies:

- *Do you see any word parts you know?*
- *Can you read this page quickly?*
- *Can you explain this section in your own words?*

Responding

Allow children an opportunity to share their thoughts on what they learned from the book. Ask volunteers to read aloud the information they found most interesting.

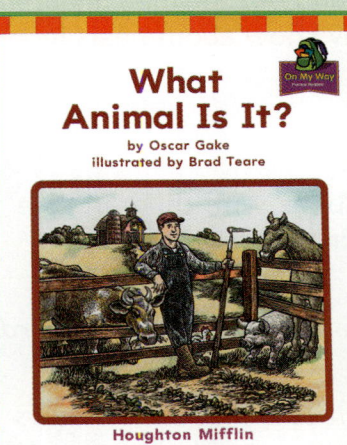

What Animal Is It?

Summary *A busy farmer finds time to take care of his animals, grow vegetables, and prepare a feast for his neighbors.*

● BELOW LEVEL

Building Background

Read aloud the title and the author's name. Ask children to share what they know about what happens on farms.

Supporting the Reading

Introducing the Book Page through the book with children. You may want to point out the following words: *Farmer, farm, barn, corn.* Use the suggestions below to prepare children for reading on their own.

page 1: *The name of the farm begins with two capital letters. Can you read the name and point to it?* (Green Hills)

page 2: *The word* barn *rhymes with* yarn. *Point to the word* barn.

page 8: *Which word has the long* e *sound spelled* ee? (seeds)

page 12: *The word* feast *begins like* fun. *Can you point to the word* feast?

Prompting Strategies Listen to and observe children as they read, and use prompts such as the following to help them apply strategies:

- *Do you see any word parts you already know?*
- *Look at the letters in this word and blend the sounds for the letters.*
- *If something doesn't make sense, try reading it.*

Responding

Ask children to discuss their reactions to the book. Were they able to answer the animal riddles?

Activity Children can work in pairs to write clues about other animals and share them with the group.

Suggested Trade Book

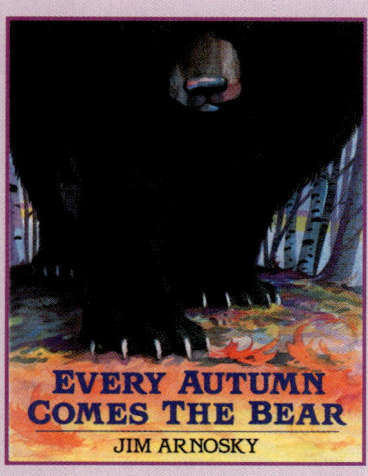

Every Autumn Comes the Bear

This book is listed on the Leveled Bibliography for this theme, pages T6–T7. You can use this lesson with Every Autumn Comes the Bear or another favorite book from your classroom library.

Building Background

Display the cover of the book and read aloud the title and the author and illustrator. Ask children what they think this story will be about. Discuss anything they know about the main topic of the book.

Supporting the Reading

Introducing the Book Take a picture walk through the book, incorporating story vocabulary or difficult names as you do so. Make note of any special features in the book that children should be aware of. Prompt children to discuss what they think is happening with questions such as the following:

- *What do you think this character is doing?*
- *What do you think will happen next?*

Prompting Strategies Listen to and observe children as they read, and use prompts such as the following to help them apply strategies:

- *Look at the letters in this word. Can you sound it out?*
- *Does that make sense in the sentence?*
- *Do you see any word parts you know?*
- *What else could you try?*
- *What made you stop?*
- *Try rereading to see if that word is right.*

Responding

Ask children a question or two specific to the story to determine their overall understanding of what they have read. Find out what their favorite part of the story was.

Suggested Trade Book

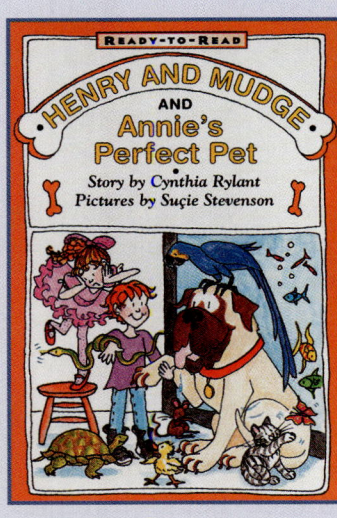

Henry and Mudge and Annie's Perfect Pet

This book is listed on the Leveled Bibliography for this theme, pages T6–T7. You can use this lesson with Henry and Mudge and Annie's Perfect Pet *or another favorite book from your classroom library.*

Building Background

Display the book cover and read aloud the title and the names of the author and illustrator. Ask children to predict what they think this book will be about. Give them a chance to share what they already know about the main topic of the book.

Supporting the Reading

Introducing the Book Take a picture walk through the book, incorporating story vocabulary or difficult names as you do so. Make note of any special features in the book that children should be aware of. Prompt children to discuss what they think is happening with questions such as the following:

- *What can you tell me about the setting of this story?*
- *What problem do you think this person might have?*
- *What do you think this character learns?*

Prompting Strategies Listen to and observe children as they read, and use prompts such as the following to help them apply strategies:

- *Look at the letters in this word. Can you sound it out?*
- *Do you see any word parts you know?*
- *What else could you try?*
- *Is there something you don't understand here?*
- *What do you think this section means? Can you say it in your own words?*

Responding

Have children discuss how they felt about the book. In order to get a sense of how well they read, ask them to reread a page or passage. Ask them to explain any strategies they used as they read.

On My Way
Practice Readers

The Real Wolf
by Nicolas Grant
illustrated by Nick Catalano

Houghton Mifflin

The Real Wolf

Summary *Hen saves the day when a real wolf interrupts the animals' performance of* The Three Little Pigs.

Building Background

Read aloud the title and author's name. Explain that this story tells about a surprising performance of *The Three Little Pigs*. Have children share what they know about *The Three Little Pigs*.

Supporting the Reading

Introducing the Book Page through the book with children. You may want to point out the following words: *wolf, curtain, goat, lazy, blow*. Use the suggestions below to prepare children for reading on their own.

page 2: *The word* curtain *begins with* c. *Can you find the word* curtain?

page 4: Wolf *begins like* wild. *Point to the word* wolf.

page 7: *Can you find the word* lazy? *It begins with* l.

page 11: *What word rhymes with* main? (brain)

Prompting Strategies Listen to and observe children as they read, and use prompts such as the following to help them apply strategies:

- *Look at the letters in this word. Can you sound it out?*
- *What else could you try?*
- *What did this part mean? Can you tell it in your own words?*

Responding

Ask children what they thought of this story. Did they think it was funny? Why? Have children reread the story alone or in pairs. Observe individual strengths and weaknesses as you have children read a page or two aloud.

Suggested Trade Book

WEEK 3

LEVELED BOOKS

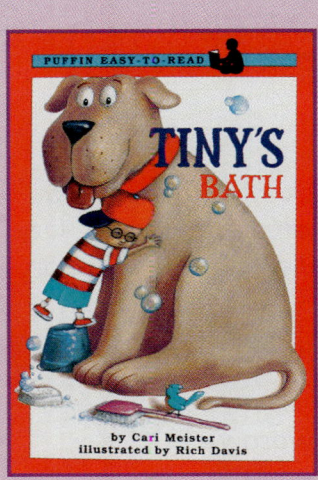

Tiny's Bath

This book is listed on the Leveled Bibliography for this theme, pages T6–T7. You can use this lesson with Tiny's Bath or another favorite book from your classroom library.

Building Background

Display the cover of the book and read aloud the title and the names of the author and illustrator. Ask children what they think this story will be about. Discuss anything they know about the main topic of the book.

Supporting the Reading

Introducing the Book Take a picture walk through the book, incorporating story vocabulary or difficult names as you do so. Make note of any special features in the book that children should be aware of. Prompt children to discuss what they think is happening with questions such as the following:

- *What do you think this character is doing?*
- *What do you think will happen next?*

Prompting Strategies Listen to and observe children as they read, and use prompts such as the following to help them apply strategies:

- *Look at the letters in this word. Can you sound it out?*
- *Does that make sense in the sentence?*
- *Do you see any word parts you know?*
- *What else could you try?*
- *What made you stop?*
- *Try rereading to see if that word is right.*

Responding

Ask children a question or two specific to the story to determine their overall understanding of what they have read. Find out what their favorite part of the story was.

Suggested Trade Book

■ ABOVE LEVEL

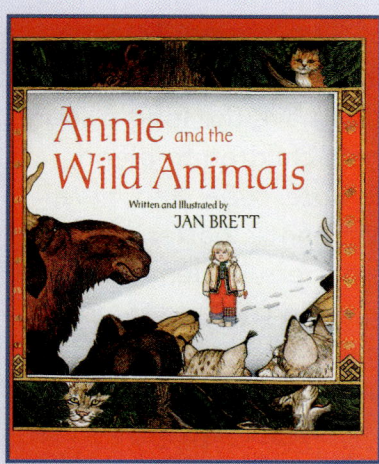

**Annie and the
Wild Animals**

This book is listed on the Leveled
Bibliography for this theme, pages T6–T7.
You can use this lesson with Annie and the
Wild Animals or another favorite book from
your classroom library.

Building Background

Display the book cover and read aloud the title and the names of the author and illustrator. Ask children to predict what they think this book will be about. Give them a chance to share what they already know about the main topic of the book.

Supporting the Reading

Introducing the Book Take a picture walk through the book, incorporating story vocabulary or difficult names as you do so. Make note of any special features in the book that children should be aware of. Prompt children to discuss what they think is happening with questions such as the following:

- *What can you tell me about the setting of this story?*
- *What problem do you think this person might have?*
- *What do you think this character learns?*

Prompting Strategies Listen to and observe children as they read, and use prompts such as the following to help them apply strategies:

- *Look at the letters in this word. Can you sound it out?*
- *Do you see any word parts you know?*
- *Do you know a word that sounds like that?*
- *What else could you try?*
- *Is there something you don't understand here?*
- *What do you think this section means? Can you say it in your own words?*

Responding

Have children discuss how they felt about the book. In order to get a sense of how well they read, ask them to reread a page or passage. Ask them to explain any strategies they used as they read.

Long *o* (CV, CVC*e*) and Long *u* (CVC*e*)

OBJECTIVES

- Associate the long *o* sound with the letter *o* and the long *u* sound with the letter *u*.
- Blend phonemes.
- Blend and read words with long *o* and long *u*.

Target Skill Trace

- Long *o* (CV, CVC*e*) and Long *u* (CVC*e*), pp. T32–T33

Materials

- **Large Sound/Spelling Cards** *ocean, unicorn;* **Large Letter Cards** *g, r, s, t;* **Picture Cards** *bus, cube, fox, hose, hug, lock, mule, note;* **Blending Routines Card 2; Phonics Library** story *Duke's Gift;* **I Love Reading Books**, Books 51–54

Teach

Display **Large Sound/Spelling Card** *ocean* and have children name the picture. Then say *no* and ask children to repeat it after you. Tell children that the sound at the end of *no* is the long sound for *o*, /ō/ as in *ocean*. Have them say /ō/–/ō/–/ō/ with you. Be sure that children's mouths are in the correct position as they say the sound.

Display **Picture Card** *note* and have children identify the picture. Ask them which *o* sound they hear in *note*, the long *o* sound, /ō/, or the short *o* sound, /ŏ/. Follow the same procedure with **Picture Cards** *fox, hose,* and *lock*.

Next, display **Large Sound/Spelling Card** *unicorn* and have children name the picture. Say *cute* and ask children to repeat it. Remind them that the /yōo/ sound in *cute* is the long sound for *u*. Have them say /yōo/ after you, /yōo/–/yōo/–/yōo/. Tell children that long *u* can also sound like /ōo/. Have them chant /ōo/–/ōo/–/ōo/. Be sure that their mouths are in the correct position as they say the sound.

Display **Picture Card** *mule* and have children identify the picture. Ask them which *u* sound they hear in *mule*, the long *u* sound, /yōo/, or the short *u* sound,

/ŭ/. Follow the same procedure with **Picture Cards** *bus, cube*.

Write *no* on the board. Remind children that two-letter words that end with *o* have the long *o* sound. Point to each letter and help children to blend, /n//ō/, nnnōō. Then write *note, tube,* and *mule*, pointing to the vowel-consonant-*e* pattern. Remind children that the *e* in this pattern is silent and the vowel sound is often long. Help children to use **Blending Routine 2** to blend each word. Example: have children say the sound for *n*, /n/, then the sound for long *o*, /ō/, and blend nnnōō. Then have them say the sound for *t*, /t/, and blend nnnōōt, *note*.

Practice

Point to the word *no* on the board. Display **Large Letter Cards** *g* and *s*. Have children choose a letter to place in front of *o* and read the new word. If they need help reading, have them blend continuously. Example: sssōō, *so*.

Follow the same procedure with *note* and the letters *t* and *v* (tote, vote), and *mule* and the letter *r* (rule).

Apply

Have partners look for words with long *o* and long *u* in **Phonics Library** story *Duke's Gift*. Have them read aloud each word and the sentence that contains it.

Monitoring Student Progress

If...	Then...
children need more practice with long *o* and long *u*,	• continue coached readings of the **Phonics Library** story *Duke's Gift* and have children read it at home. • have children read **I Love Reading Books**, Books 51–54.

CHALLENGE/EXTENSION: Long *o* (CV, CVC*e*) and Long *u* (CVC*e*)

Making Picture Cards

Have children brainstorm a list of long *o* and long *u* words. List the words on a chart. Then have children choose one long *o* and one long *u* word to write and illustrate on blank cards. Children can add their picture cards to the ones in the classroom. Possible words are *robe, globe, poke, hole, mole, pole, bone, cone, nose, rose, cube, tube*.

CHALLENGE

Cone and Cube Sort

Make a cone out of paper and use the same paper to cover an empty cube-shaped tissue box. Then give children a group of long *o* and long *u* word cards you have made: *joke, hole, cube, cone, robe, huge, mule, bone, use, cute, nose, tube, rope, vote, woke*. Have children sort the cards according to vowel sound and put them in the correct container.

Final Clusters *ft, lk, nt*

OBJECTIVES

- Associate the clusters *ft*, *lk*, and *nt* with the sounds they represent.
- Blend and read words ending with *ft*, *lk*, and *nt*.

Target Skill Trace

- Final Clusters *ft, lk, nt*, p. T34

Materials

- **Large Sound/Spelling Cards** *fish, tiger*; **Large Letter Cards** *f, k, l, n, t*; **Picture Cards** *ant, bell, milk, raft, run, scarf*; **Blending Routines Card 2**; **Word Cards** *raft, milk, ant*; **Phonics Library** story *Duke's Gift*; **I Love Reading Books,** Books 55–57

Teach

Display **Large Sound/Spelling Cards** *fish* and *tiger*. Remind children of the sound for *f*. Have them repeat it after you, /f/–/f/–/f/. Be sure children have their mouth in the correct position as they say the sound. Repeat the procedure for the letter *t*.

Use **Large Letter Cards** *f* and *t* to model how to blend /f/ and /t/. Hold the **Large Letter Cards** apart, and as you say /f/–/t/, move them together until they touch. Have children repeat /f/–/t/, *ffft*, as you move the cards next to each other a few times. Repeat this procedure for the clusters *lk* and *nt*.

Hold up **Picture Card** *raft* and ask children to identify the picture. Ask them what sounds they hear at the end of *raft*. (/f//t/) Repeat with **Picture Cards** *milk* (/l//k/) and *ant* (/n//t/).

Write the word *raft* on the chalkboard. Underline the *ft* and explain that the consonants *f* and *t* come together at the end of a word. Use **Blending Routine 2** to help children blend *raft*. Have them say the sound for *r*, /r/, then the sound for *a*, /ă/, then blend *rrrăă*. Have them say the sound for *f*, /f/, and blend *rrrăăfff*. Finally, have them say the sound for *t*, /t/, and blend *rrrăăffft*, *raft*. Then write *left* and *gift* on the board, underline the *ft,* and have children blend the words with you.

Repeat the procedure with the words *milk, elk,* and *silk* for *lk* and the words *ant, tent,* and *hunt* for *nt*.

Practice

Have three children hold **Picture Cards** *raft, milk,* and *ant*. Remind children that *raft* ends in /f//t/, *milk* ends in /l//k/, and *ant* ends in /n//t/. Give three other children **Word Cards** *raft, milk,* and *ant,* and have each child stand next to the child with the matching **Picture Card.**

Apply

Have partners work together to find words with *ft, lk,* and *nt* in the **Phonics Library** story *Duke's Gift.* Each time a child finds a word, the child should read it aloud and have his or her partner read the sentence that contains it.

Monitoring Student Progress

If . . .	Then . . .
children need more practice with final clusters *ft, lk,* and *nt,*	• continue coached readings of the **Phonics Library** story *Duke's Gift* and have children read it at home. • have children read **I Love Reading Books,** Books 55–57.

CHALLENGE/EXTENSION:
Final Clusters *ft, lk, nt*

Make a Match

Make word cards for the following words: *raft, left, milk, elk, mint, tent.* Put the cards in an empty milk carton. Then ask children to empty the carton and match the two *ft* words, the two *lk* words, and the two *nt* words.

mint   tent

CHALLENGE

Changing Words

Give children a copy of **Blackline Master 197**. Starting with the word *tent,* show children how to write a new word ending with *nt* on each line by changing one letter each time (*tint, mint, hint, hunt*).

te n t

ti

mi

hi

hu

Long *e* and Vowel Pairs *ee, ea*

OBJECTIVES

- Associate the long *e* sound with the letter *e* and the vowel pairs *ee, ea*.
- Blend and read words with the letter *e* and vowel pairs *ee, ea*.

Target Skill Trace

- Long *e* and Vowel Pairs *ee, ea*, pp. T114–T116

Materials

- **Large Sound/Spelling Card** *eagle*; **Picture Cards** *bed, feet, leaf, jeans, jeep, jet, leash, leg, peach, queen, seal, web*; **Word Cards** *feet, leaf, seal*; **Blending Routines Card 2**; **Phonics Library** story *Seal Beach*; **I Love Reading Books,** Books 58–61

Teach

Point to yourself and ask children to guess the word you are demonstrating. When someone has called out *me*, say the word and have children repeat it after you. Remind children that the sound at the end of *me* is the long *e* sound, /ē/.

Then have them say the long *e* sound after you, /ē/–/ē/–/ē/.

Hold up **Picture Card** *jeep* and ask children to identify the picture. Ask them which *e* sound they hear in *jeep*, the long *e* sound, /ē/, or the short *e* sound, /ĕ/. Follow the same procedure with **Picture Cards** *bed, queen, jeans, jet, leash, web, peach, leg,* and *seal*.

Hold up **Large Sound/Spelling Card** *eagle* and point out that the *e, ea,* and *ee* are three ways that the long *e* sound can be spelled. Have children say /ē/ as you point to each of the different sound/spellings again.

Write *he* on the board. Point out that the single *e* at the end of the word stands for the long *e* sound.

Use **Blending Routine 2** to help children blend the sounds in *he*. Have children say the sound for *h*, /h/, then the sound for long *e*, /ē/, and blend *hhhēēē, he*.

Display **Word Cards** *feet* and *leaf*. Remind children that the vowel pairs *ee* and *ea* usually stand for the long *e* sound.

Run your finger under the *ee* in *feet* and the *ea* in *leaf* and have children say the long *e* sound in both words. Then use **Blending Routine 2** to help them blend each word.

Practice

Distribute three self-stick notes with the letters *b, m,* and *w* written on them. Have children use their notes to place over the *h* in *he* and read each new word. (*be, me, we*)

Display **Word Card** *feet*. Distribute four self-stick notes with the letters *b, m, d,* and *l* written on them. Have children place their notes over the *f* or *t* in *feet* and read each new word. (*meet, beet, feed, feel*) If children need help reading, have them blend continuously. Example: *bēēēt, beet*.

Follow the same procedure with **Word Card** *seal* and the letters *t, r, h,* and *m*. (*seat, real, heal, meal, seam*)

Apply

Have partners look for words with long *e* and vowel pairs *ee* and *ea* in **Phonics Library** story *Seal Beach*. Record the words and have individuals underline the *e, ee,* and *ea* in each word, then read the word aloud.

Monitoring Student Progress

If . . .	Then . . .
children need more practice with long *e* or vowel pairs *ee* and *ea*,	- continue coached readings of the **Phonics Library** story *Seal Beach*, and have children read it at home. - have children read **I Love Reading Books,** Books 58–61.

CHALLENGE/EXTENSION:
Long *e* and Vowel Pairs *ee*, *ea*

Word Search

Hide word cards for long *e* (CV, CVCe) and vowel pairs *ee* and *ea* around the classroom. Ask children to find the cards and return to their seats. Then ask children to display their card, say the word, and tell what letters make the long *e* sound in their word.

me	leaf
peach	he
jeep	queen

CHALLENGE

Long *e* Tree

Draw or make a large tree with bare branches. Then have children write long *e* words on construction paper leaves using the CV pattern, the CVCe pattern, or vowel pairs *ee* and *ea*. Ask children to attach each leaf they write onto the tree. They should group words with the same vowel pattern or vowel pair on the same branch. Children can take turns reading the long *e* tree.

RETEACHING *(vertical tab)*

Vowel Pairs *ai, ay*

OBJECTIVES

- Associate the long *a* sound with the vowel pairs *ai, ay.*
- Blend and read words with vowel pairs *ai, ay.*

Target Skill Trace

- Vowel Pairs *ai, ay,* pp. T184–T186

Materials

- **Large Sound/Spelling Card** *acorn;* **Large Letter Cards** *d, h, m, p, r, s, v;* **Picture Cards** *bat, braid, cab, cat, chain, gray, hay, mat, tray;* **Word Cards** *braid, hay;* **Blending Routines Card 2; Phonics Library** story *Rain Day;* **I Love Reading Books,** Books 62–63

Teach

Hold up the **Large Sound/Spelling Card** *acorn,* and ask children to identify the picture. Remind them that the long *a* sound is the same as the letter name. Have children say the long *a* sound after you, /ā/–/ā/–/ā/. Be sure that children's mouths are in the correct position as they say the sound.

Display **Picture Card** *braid,* and ask children to identify it. Say *braid,* and ask children to repeat it after you. Ask them which *a* sound they hear in *braid,* the long *a* sound, /ā/, or the short *a* sound, /ă/. Follow the same procedure with **Picture Cards** *hay, cab, gray, bat, chain, cat, tray,* and *mat.*

Display **Word Cards** *braid* and *hay* next to the corresponding **Picture Cards.** Then hold up **Large Sound/Spelling Card** *acorn.* Point to the *ai* on the card and the *ai* in the word *braid* as you say /ā/ and have children repeat /ā/. Repeat this for the *ay* in *hay.* Tell children that *ai* and *ay* are two ways that the /ā/ sound can be spelled. Then help children to blend *hay* and *braid* using **Blending Routine 2.** Example: Have children say the sound for *h,* /h/, then the sound for *ay,* /ā/, and blend *hhhāāā, hay.*

Practice

Draw three boxes on the board as shown. Write *ai* in the middle box and *n* in the last box; display the **Letter Cards** *m, p, r,* and *v.* Tell children that you are putting two letters in one box to show that two letters stand for one sound.

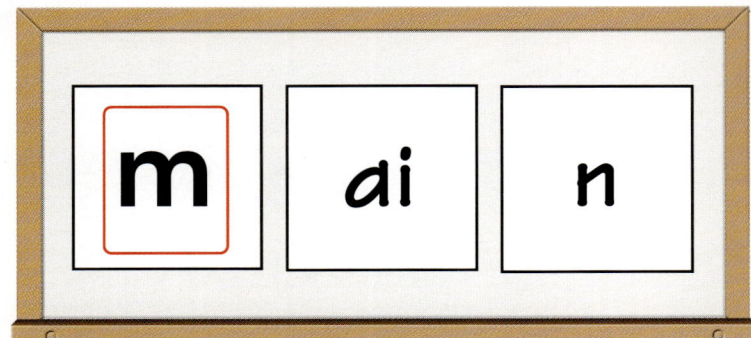

Have a child choose a letter to place in the first square and blend it continuously with *ai* to make a new word. Continue with the other **Letter Cards.** Follow the same procedure with *ay* and two boxes. Print *ay* in the last box. Have children use **Large Letter Cards** *s, d, h, p, m,* and *r* to make new words.

Apply

Have children look for words with vowel pairs *ai* and *ay* in **Phonics Library** story *Rain Day.* Each time they find a word, ask them to say it aloud so you can write it in one column on a chart. When the search is complete, have children read the chart.

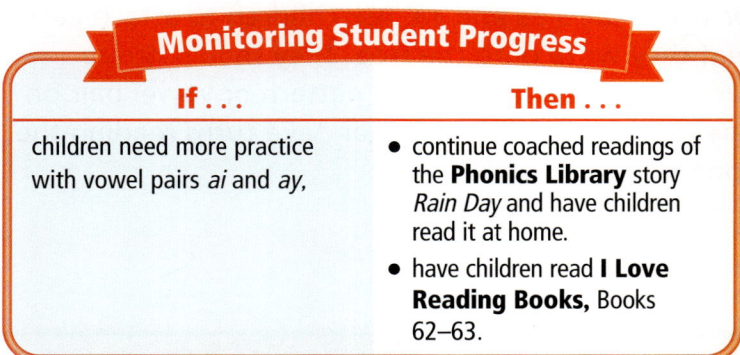

Monitoring Student Progress

If . . .	Then . . .
children need more practice with vowel pairs *ai* and *ay,*	• continue coached readings of the **Phonics Library** story *Rain Day* and have children read it at home. • have children read **I Love Reading Books,** Books 62–63.

CHALLENGE/EXTENSION:
Vowel Pairs *ai, ay*

A Rainy Day Umbrella

Draw an outline of a large umbrella on chart paper. Have children help you fill the umbrella with words that contain the vowel pairs *ay* and *ai*. Then have each child choose one *ai* or *ay* word to illustrate. Staple all the illustrations together to make a "Rainy Day" book.

CHALLENGE

A Train of Words

Have small groups of children brainstorm lists of words that contain the vowel pairs *ai* and *ay*. Have them create a train of *ai* and *ay* words by writing or illustrating each word on an index card cut in the shape of a train. Tape the cards together to make a train of *ai* and *ay* words.

CHALLENGE / EXTENSION

RETEACHING: High-Frequency Words

Words for Week 1

OBJECTIVES

- Read and write high-frequency words *morning, found, shout, by, out, show, climb.*

Target Skill Trace

- High-Frequency Words , p. T42

Materials

- **Letter Cards** *b, c, d, f, g, h, i, l, m, n, o, r, s, t, u, w, y*

Teach

Write the words *morning, found, shout, by, out, show,* and *climb* on the board. Point to each word as you read it aloud. Invite children to help you read the words aloud a second time.

Display the **Letter Cards** on the chalk tray. Ask children, *How many letters are in the word* found?

Draw five squares on the board.

Ask children to help spell the word *found.* Point to the word on the board and ask, *What letter comes first?* Instruct children to say the letter and draw it in the air. Ask a child to find the letter, write the letter in the first box on the board, and face the group holding the card. Repeat the procedure for the remaining letters, asking, *What letter comes next?* Have children stand side by side with the **Letter Cards** to spell the word *found.* Ask the group to read the word aloud together. Repeat the procedure for the remaining words.

Practice

Instruct children to write each high-frequency word on a large index card. Write the following sentences on the board:

> In the morning, I do not climb out of bed.
>
> I like to sleep as long as I can.
>
> Mom and Dad come by with a shout.
>
> "Show us you are up! We found you! It is time to go out!"

Read the sentences aloud and point to the words as you read. Next, read without pointing, and instruct children to raise their word cards when they hear those words in the sentences.

Apply

Have children write the sentences from the previous activity on sentence strips and illustrate them on large index cards. Then have children cut up the sentence strips so that they can rebuild the sentences. Have children exchange pictures with a partner and match the sentence strips to the pictures.

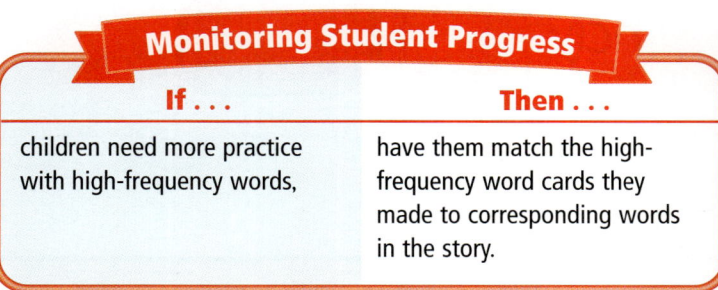

Monitoring Student Progress	
If . . .	**Then . . .**
children need more practice with high-frequency words,	have them match the high-frequency word cards they made to corresponding words in the story.

CHALLENGE/EXTENSION:
High-Frequency Words

A Pig in My Bed!

Write the following sentence starter on the board and have children complete it in as many ways as they can, using as many new words as they can.

> *If I found a pig in my bed,*

Possible answers include:

I would shout to get him out.
I would climb in and roll him out.
I would show my mom and dad.

When finished, have children read their sentences to see how many different endings they have.

CHALLENGE

Wake Up That Pig!

Ask children to write instructions that tell how to wake up a pig. Remind them of the importance of sequence in giving instructions. Encourage children to use as many new words in the instructions as they can.

RETEACHING: High-Frequency Words

Words for Week 2

OBJECTIVES

- Read and write high-frequency words *cow, table, now, door, there, through, horse, wall.*

Target Skill Trace

- High-Frequency Words, p. T124

Materials

- **Letter Cards** *a, b, c, d, e, e, g, h, l, l, n, o, o, r, s, t, u, w*

Teach

Write the words *cow, table, now, door, there, through, horse,* and *wall* on the board. Point to each word as you read it aloud. Invite children to help you read the words aloud a second time.

Display the **Letter Cards** on the chalk tray. Ask children, *How many letters are in the word* cow?

Draw three squares on the board.

Ask children to help spell *cow.* Point to the word on the board and ask, *What letter comes first?* Instruct children to say the letter and draw it in the air. Ask a child to find the letter among the letter cards, write the letter in the first box on the board, and face the group holding the card. Repeat the procedure for the remaining letters, asking, *What letter comes next?* Have children stand side by side with the **Letter Cards** to spell the word *cow.* Ask the group to read the word aloud together.

Repeat the procedure for the remaining words.

Practice

Instruct children to write each high-frequency word on a large index card. Write the following sentences on the board:

There is a cow on the table.

A horse has come through the door.

Now two cats climb up the wall.

As you read the sentences aloud, point to the words. Next, read without pointing, and instruct children to raise their word cards when they hear the corresponding words in the sentences.

Apply

Have children write the sentences on sentence strips and illustrate them on large index cards. Then direct children to cut up the sentence strips and rebuild the sentences. Have children exchange pictures with a partner and match the sentence strips to the pictures.

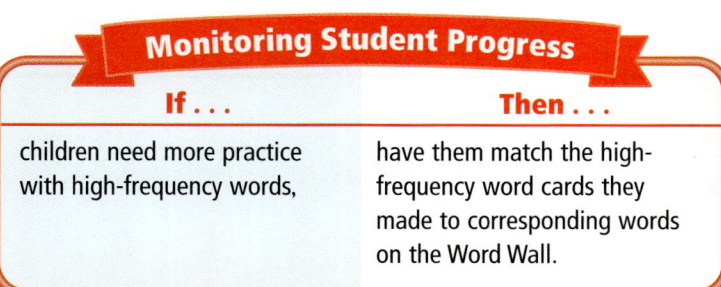

Monitoring Student Progress

If . . .	Then . . .
children need more practice with high-frequency words,	have them match the high-frequency word cards they made to corresponding words on the Word Wall.

CHALLENGE/EXTENSION:
High-Frequency Words

Sentence Frames

Have children complete the following sentence frames to tell a story. Encourage children to use as many new words in the sentences as they can. Then have them read their stories to a partner.

One day _____ knocked on the _____. _____ got up from the _____ to answer it. _____ was no one _____. Suddenly _____ walked _____ the door and _____.

CHALLENGE

Animal Rules

Have children write a list of rules for animals to follow in the house. You may also want to ask children to make signs for the rules. Encourage them to use as many new words in the rules as they can.

1. Do not lay eggs in the house.

2. Do not knock over lamps.

3. Never chase other animals in the house.

No laying eggs!

RETEACHING: High-Frequency Words

Words for Week 3

OBJECTIVES

- Read and write high-frequency words *been, far, forest, goes, hungry, soon, evening, near.*

Target Skill Trace

- High-Frequency Words, p. T194

Materials

- **Letter Cards** *a, b, e, e, f, g, h, i, n, n, o, o, r, s, t, u, v, y*

Teach

Write the words *been, far, forest, goes, hungry, soon, evening,* and *near* on the board. Point to each word as you read it aloud. Invite children to help you read the words aloud a second time.

Display the **Letter Cards** on the chalk tray. Ask children, *How many letters are in the word* far?

Draw three squares on the board.

Ask children to help spell the word *far.* Point to the word on the board and ask, *What letter comes first?* Instruct children to say the letter and draw it in the air. Ask a child to find the letter, write the letter in the first box on the board, and face the group holding the card. Repeat the procedure for the remaining letters asking, *What letter comes next?* Have children stand side by side with the letter cards to spell the word *far.* Ask the group to read the word aloud together.

Repeat the procedure for the remaining words.

Practice

Instruct children to write each high-frequency word on a large index card. Write the following sentences:

Soon it will be evening.
The family is hungry.
They have been far in the forest all day.
Will they be near home when the sun goes down?

Read the sentences aloud and point to the words as you read. Next, read without pointing, and instruct children to raise their word cards when they hear those words in the sentences.

Apply

Have children write the sentences from the previous activity on sentence strips and illustrate them on large index cards. Then have children cut up the sentence strips so that they can rebuild the sentences. Have children exchange pictures with a partner and match the sentence strips to the pictures.

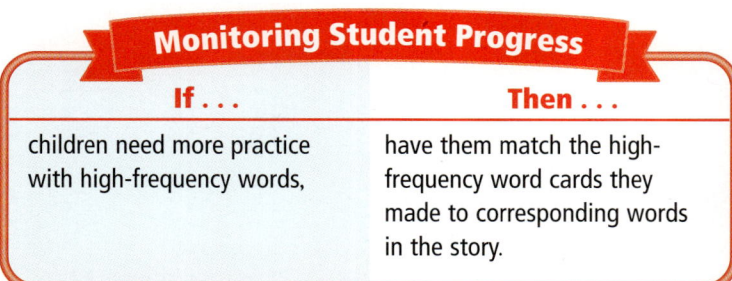

Monitoring Student Progress	
If . . .	**Then . . .**
children need more practice with high-frequency words,	have them match the high-frequency word cards they made to corresponding words in the story.

CHALLENGE/EXTENSION:
High-Frequency Words

Main Idea

Have children use the following main idea sentence to write three sentences with supporting details.

In the evening, hungry animals walk through the forest.

Encourage children to use as many new high-frequency words as they can. When finished, have them read their sentences in small groups.

CHALLENGE

Snake Book

Invite children to write stories about the snake in *Red-Eyed Tree Frog.* Ask them to include in the story what they think the snake does each night. Encourage children to use as many new words as they can in their stories. You might want to have children copy their finished stories onto construction paper snakes that can be folded into books.

To make the snake book: Instruct children to make three C-shaped cuts in a sheet of paper. For a longer snake, have children cut two pieces of paper. Direct children to lay the bands out in a row, alternating up and down. The snake should have wave-like curves. Have children glue the ends of the bands together, and when the glue dries, shape the head and tail with scissors. Children can write their stories on the snake. Display the snake as is, or fold it in a fan pattern to create a book.

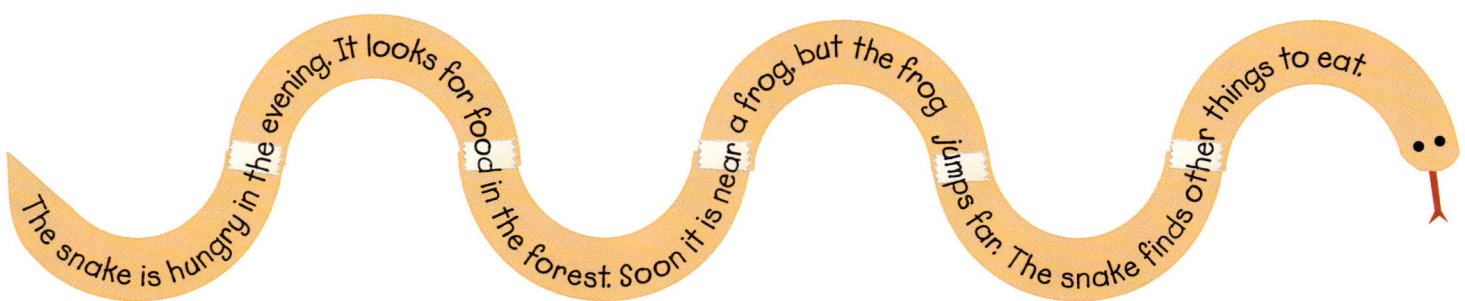

The snake is hungry in the evening. It looks for food in the forest. Soon it is near a frog, but the frog jumps far. The snake finds other things to eat.

RETEACHING: Comprehension Skills

Story Structure

Teach

Have children help plan a story about their class. Ask,

- *Who is in the story?*
- *Where and when does the story take place?*
- *What happens in the story?*
- *Is there a problem to solve?*

Explain to children that every story tells who is in the story, where and when the story takes place, and what happens. Explain that these parts of a story are called the *characters,* the *setting,* and the *plot.* Tell children that the plot often contains a problem to solve.

Practice

Begin a story map for *The Sleeping Pig.* Read aloud the first page of the story. Ask children to identify the setting and the characters. Ask them to tell what they know about the plot so far. Ask, *Is there a problem to solve?* Elicit further information about the plot, new characters, and new information about the setting, and complete the story map.

Story Map

Place: Watermelon Patch

Setting/Time: Morning

Characters: Celina, Mrs. Pig, Coyote

Problem: A pig is sleeping in the watermelon patch and won't wake up.

What happens:

1. Coyote howls to try to wake pig up.
2. ?
3. ?

Solution: ?

Apply

Have children use the story map to summarize the story. Record their ideas in a paragraph.

Help children to see how developing a story map and summarizing the story can help them to remember and understand what they read.

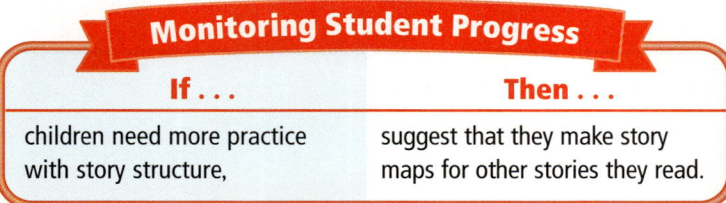

Monitoring Student Progress	
If . . .	Then . . .
children need more practice with story structure,	suggest that they make story maps for other stories they read.

CHALLENGE/EXTENSION: Story Structure

CHALLENGE

A New Ending

Ask children to change the ending of *The Sleeping Pig*. Have them write about a new character that figures out a way to wake up the sleeping pig in the watermelon patch. Invite children to share the new ending with the class or have them tape-record their new ending.

Story Problems

Have children write a math problem that is also a story. Instruct them to include characters, setting, and plot in their story problems. Children can write their story problems about buying and selling fruits and vegetables at a farm stand or about farm animals.

$$2 + 3 = 5$$

A Story Map

Have children work in pairs to complete a story map for another story about animals. You might want to have children read another animal story or use one they already know, such as *The Three Little Pigs* or *Little Red Riding Hood*.

CHALLENGE / EXTENSION

Noting Details

Teach

Invite children to look out a classroom window and describe an object that they see. It could be another building, a playground, or a tree. As they describe the object, draw their attention to small details. Children may say that a building is tall or that there are a lot of swings. Ask, *How many floors does the building have? How many swings are there? What shape are the leaves on the tree?* Invite children to tell what they learned about the object that they didn't know before. Explain that looking carefully at objects and noting details help us understand what we see, and also what we read.

Practice

Reread aloud *EEK! There's a Mouse in the House.* Elicit details from children about characters and what they do. Ask, *Why is the animal brought into the house?* and *What does the animal do in the house?* Record children's suggestions in a word web.

Point out that the child in the story invites animals into the house to solve a problem. Walk through the story with children and work together to complete a word web. Ask them if they think the animals are helping. Remind children that noting details helps us understand what we read.

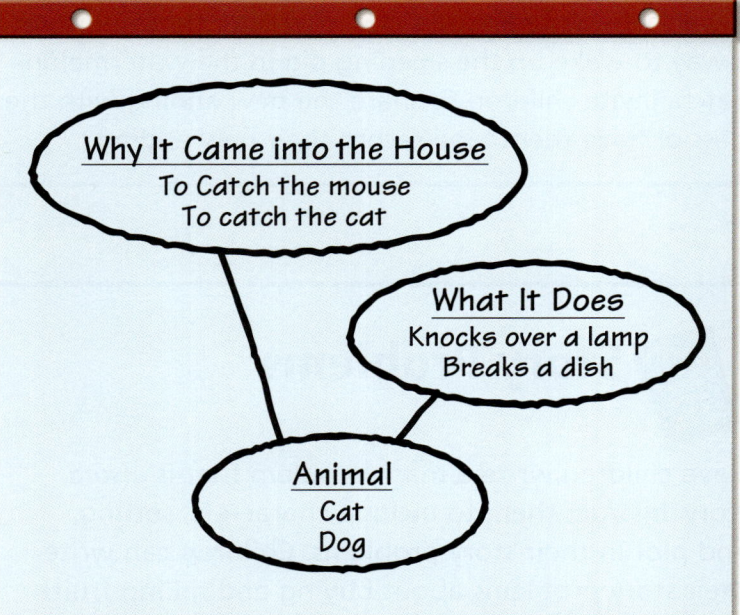

Apply

Have children reread the story, noting details that tell about time and place. Instruct children to look carefully at the pictures. When they are finished, have them draw and label a picture that describes the time and place of the story.

Monitoring Student Progress

If . . .	Then . . .
children need more practice with noting details,	suggest that they make a word web of details from other stories they read.

CHALLENGE/EXTENSION: Noting Details

Independent Activities

CHALLENGE

Visualizing Details

Have children listen to a story on tape. Direct them to visualize the story details as they listen. For example, what do they think the characters look like based on the description they hear?

You might want to replay the story several times. When finished, have children draw picture details to support the story they heard and compare their illustrations with those of a partner.

A Guessing Game

Explain that the author of *EEK! There's a Mouse in the House* provides many details about things in a house. Have partners play a guessing game. Explain that one child thinks of an object in a house, while the other child asks *yes* or *no* questions to try to guess what the object is. For example, a child might ask, *Is it in the*

kitchen? (Yes) *Do you cook with it?* (No), and so on. Explain to children that their questions should help them to identify more and more detail.

An Animal Chart

Explain to children that noting details is very important to scientists when they classify and categorize animals. Have children categorize the following animals in a chart based on which animals have feathers, which have scales, and which have fur: *mouse, cat, duck, rat, dog, fish, bird, hog, frog, cow, sheep, hen, pig, snake,* and *rabbit*. Children may want to illustrate their charts.

CHALLENGE/EXTENSION

RETEACHING: Comprehension Skills

Making Predictions

OBJECTIVES
- Use story details and personal knowledge to make predictions.

Target Skill Trace
- Making Predictions, pp. T218–219

Teach

Invite several children to dramatize the following action.

Tell the individuals, *Put your jackets on* and *Pack your bags.* Ask their classmates to tell what they think will happen next. Correct responses include they will leave the room and they will go home. Discuss why children think those events will follow.

Explain that we use what we already know from our experiences and clues from our environment to figure out what will happen next. When we tell what we think will happen next, we are making a prediction.

Practice

Read aloud the first three pages of *Red-Eyed Tree Frog.* Draw children's attention to important details such as *evening comes, some animals will soon go to sleep,* and *the red-eyed tree frog has been asleep all day.* Ask children to predict what they think will happen next, and why. If necessary, model making a prediction with the following Think Aloud.

Think Aloud *From the details I read in the story, I know that it is almost night and that some animals are going to sleep. I also know that the frog has been asleep all day. I know from my experience that after sleeping all day or all night it is time to wake up. I think that the frog will wake up soon.*

Continue reading aloud until page 202. Draw children's attention to the details *hungry boa snake* and *near the frog* on page 203. Ask children what they know about a hungry snake and what they can tell about it from the picture. Ask them to predict what will happen next. Explain to children that they used details from the story, and what they already know from their experience about hungry snakes.

Apply

Have children make predictions with a partner for the following parts of the story. Instruct children to explain how they make their predictions.

Pages 208 and 209: The frog sees a moth on a leaf. What will the frog do? (It will eat the moth.)

Page 211: The tree frog is no longer hungry. What will it do next? (It will go to sleep.)

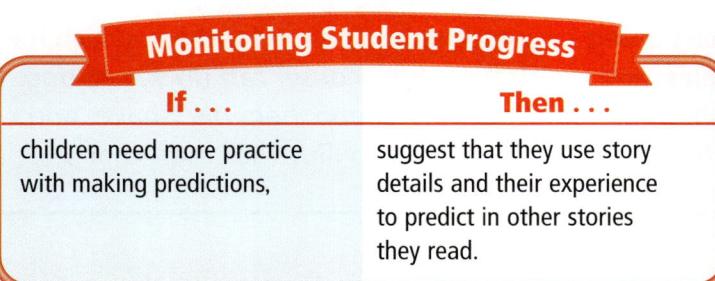

Monitoring Student Progress	
If . . .	**Then . . .**
children need more practice with making predictions,	suggest that they use story details and their experience to predict in other stories they read.

CHALLENGE/EXTENSION: Making Predictions

CHALLENGE

Safety Rules

The red-eyed tree frog in the story knows how to keep itself safe from poisonous caterpillars and boa snakes. Have children discuss some rules that are meant to keep them safe, and then have them illustrate predictions about what happens if the rule is not followed. You may want to provide the following rules for children to consider:

- No running.
- No diving.
- No bicycle riding on sidewalks.
- No skates allowed on the bus.
- Do not touch.
- Do not enter.

Number Patterns

Teach children the first three verses of the song *Ten Little Monkeys*.

Ten little monkeys jumping on the bed.
One fell off and bumped his head.
Mama called the doctor and the doctor said,
"No more monkeys jumping on the bed!"
Nine little monkeys jumping on the bed.
One fell off and bumped his head, etc.

Have children continue the song on their own, making predictions about what the next verse will be, based on the number pattern. Have children write the number pattern for the song and make up other number patterns. Encourage children to make up new songs using the patterns.

Drawing Predictions

Children can work with partners to make predictions with pictures. Instruct children to divide a piece of paper into four boxes and to draw a picture of sunrise in the first box and sunset in the second box. Direct children to draw pictures in the remaining boxes of what happens in a day after sunrise and after sunset.

For example, after sunset, children might predict that stars come out and people go to bed. The drawing would show stars in the sky and people asleep in bed. Display children's pictures for the class to see.

STUDY SKILL: Parts of a Book

OBJECTIVES

- Identify captions, headings, and index.
- Find captions and headings in books.

Materials

- Reading **Anthologies** *Here We Go!*, *Let's Be Friends*, and *Surprises*; Teacher's Edition for *Animal Adventures*; chapter books; social studies and science textbooks

Teach

Tell children that books have many parts that give readers information. In addition to the table of contents and glossary, some books include chapters, captions, or an index.

Chapters Use a chapter book of your choosing to point out where chapters begin, or turn to and hold up pages 111 and 117 in *Here We Go!* Remind children that the heading at the top of the pages tells readers when a new chapter begins in the story *Big Pig*.

Next, use *Let's Be Friends* or a book of your choosing to demonstrate where new sections begin in stories. The headings on pages 18, 21, 26, and 29 let readers know when they've reached a new section and will read about a different season, respectively, fall, winter, spring, and summer.

Captions Point to and read the captions in the social studies article *What Is a Desert?* on pages 156–157 of *Surprises*.

Tell children that some types of writing include photographs, diagrams, maps, or drawings. A caption is the text that accompanies the photo or illustration, and it gives readers more information about the photo or illustration. Sometimes a caption provides detailed information, and other times it identifies a place or photo.

Index Tell children that an index is found at the back of some books. An index lists, in alphabetical order, the topics that are included in a book and gives the page number(s) on which the information can be found. Show children the index at the back of the Teacher's Edition for *Animal Adventures,* and read aloud a couple of entries to demonstrate the type of information found in an index. Tell children that an index can be helpful if a reader wants to know whether a book has information on a particular topic.

Practice

Have children turn to pages 158–159 of *Surprises*. Have children identify the captions. Hold up a chapter book, such as a Frog and Toad book by Arnold Lobel. Call on children to locate chapters within the book. Then have children tell you where an index is located in a textbook. (at the back of the book)

Apply

Divide the class into small groups. Tell each group to find a variety of books with an index, chapters, and captions. Have groups share their findings with the class, pointing out the specific features in the books.

out

shout

show

by

climb

found

morning

Use for Theme 6, Week 1.

Word Wall Cards **R33**

table

there

through

wall

cow

door

horse

now

Use for Theme 6, Week 2.

goes

hungry

near

soon

been

evening

far

forest

Use for Theme 6, Week 3.

Word Wall Cards R35

Name _____

Word Search

Find and circle each word from the Word Box.

Word Box				
morning	found	long	out	shout
show	climb	her	by	more

b	y	d	k	p	s	l	o
f	s	m	h	e	r	o	a
s	h	o	w	b	z	n	t
m	o	r	n	i	n	g	p
r	u	e	c	l	i	m	b
l	t	f	o	u	n	d	m
y	m	r	u	l	j	a	r
p	s	o	t	e	b	n	k

Theme 6: **Animal Adventures**

Answer Key:
morning: row 4
show: row 3
found: row 6
climb: row 5
long: column 7
her: row 2
out: column 4
by: row 1
shout: column 2
more: column 3

Name _____

Rhyming Word Match

could	now	good	cow
give	wall	live	small
grow	door	show	more
light	through	right	blue

Answer Key:
could, good
give, live
grow, show
light, right
now, cow
wall, small
door, more
through, blue

Directions:
Have children cut out the word cards and place them face-down on a table. Then have pairs of children take turns turning over two cards at a time, trying to match rhyming words. If the words rhyme, the child keeps the cards and takes another turn. If the words do not rhyme, it is the other child's turn.

Theme 6: **Animal Adventures**

Name _____

Matching Opposites

far		morning
cold		take
evening		up
goes		full
hungry		big
down		stays
give		near
little		hot

Theme 6: **Animal Adventures**

Answer Key:
evening: morning
give: take
down: up
hungry: full
little: big
goes: stays
far: near
cold: hot

Directions:
Read the words with children. Then have children cut out the word cards and glue them next to the word with the opposite meaning.

Animal Song

1. Al - li - ga - tor, hedge - hog, ant - eat - er, bear,

Rat - tle - snake, buf - fa - lo, an - a - con - da, hare.

2. Bull - frog, wood - chuck, wol - ver - ine, goose,

Whip - poor - will, chip - munk, jack - al, moose.

3. Mud turtle, whale, glow-worm, bat,
   Salamander, snail, and Maltese cat.

4. Polecat, dog, wild otter, rat,
   Pelican, hog, dodo, and bat.

5. Eagle, kingeron, sheep, duck, and widgeon,
   Conger, armadillo, beaver, seal, pigeon.

6. Reindeer, blacksnake, ibex, nightingale,
   Martin, wild drake, crocodile, and quail.

7. House rat, toe rat, white bear, doe,
   Chickadee, peacock, bobolink, and crow.

Little Pig

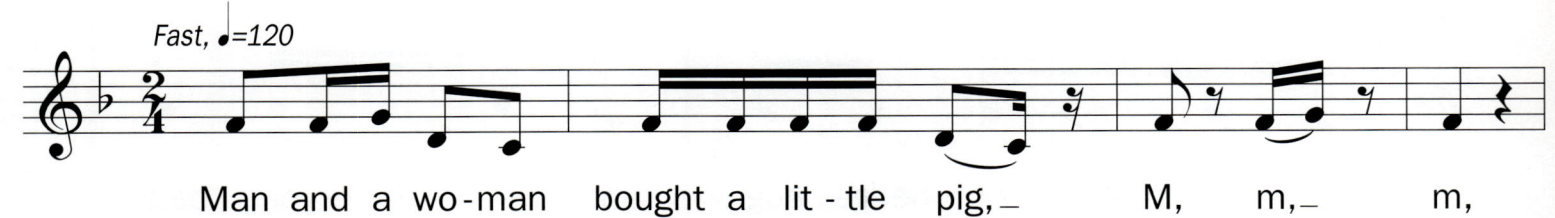

Man and a wo-man bought a lit-tle pig, — M, m,— m,

Man and a wo-man bought a lit-tle pig, Did-n't cost much, for it

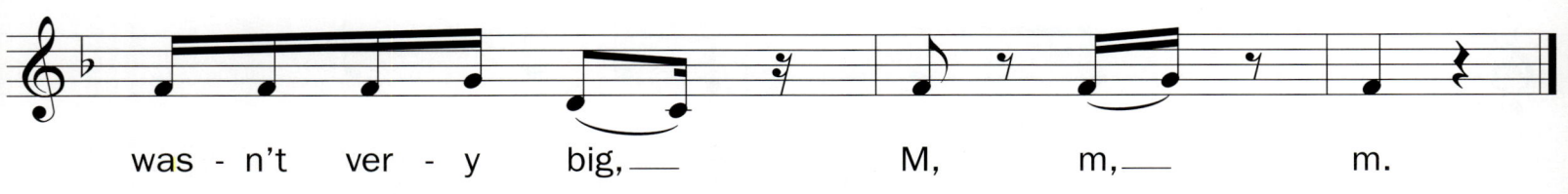

was-n't ver - y big, —— M, m,—— m.

WORD LIST

THEME 6, WEEK 1

Phonics Skills:
Long *o* and Long *u;* Final *ft, lk, nt*

High-Frequency Words:
by, climb, found, morning, out, shout, show

Day 1

Phonics Library: *Duke's Gift*

Phonics Practice Words: bone, Duke, Duke's, gift, holes, huge, hunts, left, no, plants, rose, **and,** back, best, checks, Dad, Dad's, dig, digs, **five,** got, has, hide, his, it's, **not,** place, prize, safe, this, up, yells

High-Frequency Words: *a,* for, he, more, right, the, to

Day 2

Phonics Library: *Legs Gets His Lunch*

Phonics Practice Words: ant, hole, hopes, huge, nose, plant, pokes, silk, **so,** soft, use, *and, at, big, can, catch, fat, get, gets, hides, his, in, is, it, last, Legs, log, lunch, shines, spin, spots, sun, then, up, web, wet, will*

High-Frequency Words: climb, out, *a,* he, small, the, to, where

Day 2; Day 3

Anthology: *The Sleeping Pig*

Phonics Practice Words: **go,** home, huge, left, lift, mule, nose, sulking, tune, use, went, whole, woke, *am, **and,** at, ate, bed, but, came, can, can't, did, didn't, fast, get, hop, **in, is,** it's, just, let, make, **not, on,** patch, pick, pig, rest, sing, snake, thanked, then, time, up, wake, will, wish, with, yes*
Challenge: push, sleeping

This list includes all words in Phonics Library and Anthology selections for Theme 6. Words in regular type apply skills for the week; words in italics apply previously taught skills; words in boldface type indicate high-frequency words that are now decodable. High-Frequency Words are practiced in Phonics Library and Anthology selections and in Practice Book and Word Wall activities; each is practiced at least six times in the week it is taught. Challenge words include some known phonics elements and some that are unfamiliar.

High-Frequency Words: by, climb, found, morning, out, shout, show, *a, do, does, for, good, her, here, how, I, know, look, me, my, of, one, pull, said, she, small, the, they, to, what, would, wouldn't, you*

Story Vocabulary: began, celebrate, Celina, coyote, cricket, howl, Mrs., rabbit, tail, watermelon, watermelons

Day 5

Phonics Library: *The Nest*

Phonics Practice Words: bent, broke, cute, home, huge, Jude, left, no, plant, Rose, silk, **so,** soft, spoke, went, **and,** *as, big, crack, egg, fine, get, had, hatch, hatching, his, **in, is,** it, it's, just, nest, then, this, time, will, yelled*

High-Frequency Words: by, found, morning, *a,* down, looks, one, said, the, to

THEME 6, WEEK 2

Phonics Skills:
Long *e;* Vowel Pairs *ee, ea*

High-Frequency Words:
cow, door, horse, now, table, there, through, wall

Day 1

Phonics Library: *Seal Beach*

Phonics Practice Words: beach, **eat,** feed, keeps, lead, sea, seal, seals, **see, sees, she,** steep, **these, we, and,** *at, back, can't, dive, fish, from, **is,** it, its, last, Mom, nap, pup, squid, steps, swim, take, that, them, this, up, wakes*

High-Frequency Words: her, I, looking, mother, **the,** to, walk

Day 2

Phonics Library: *Pete and Peach*

Phonics Practice Words: bee, creek, **green,** leap, **me,** Peach, Pete, **see, she, and,** *but, fine, grass, **in, is,** it, just, let's, run, sits, smells, that, this, wide, with, yells*

High-Frequency Words: cow, horse, wall, *a,* flower, **the**

Day 2; Day 3

Anthology: *EEK! There's a Mouse in the House*

Phonics Practice Words: eating, EEK, **he, me,** sheep, **and,** *big, but, cake, came, cat, catch, chase, dish, dog, eggs, fish, from, get, has, hen, hog, hole, **in, is,** kicked, knocked, lamp, make, mop, no, **on,** ran, rat, rid, scamp, send, sending, stop, that, them, then, with* **Challenge:** after, broken, dear, goodness, heavens, mistake, shoo, squeezed, stable, uh-oh, within, yarn

High-Frequency Words: cow, door, horse, now, table, there, through, wall, *a, all, for, her, house, more, my, of, once, out, over, room, shout, **the,** there's, to, walked, was*

Story Vocabulary: barn, dancing, elephant, laying, marched, mercy, mouse, tangled

Day 5

Phonics Library: *Gram's Huge Meal*

Phonics Practice Words: beans, **eat,** feast, **green, he,** leaned, meal, peas, real, **she, these,** treat, **and,** *big, black, came, fine, get, Gram, Gram's, grapes, his, huge, **in, is,** it, just, **long,** made, neck, **not, on,** Pops, set, spots, stuck, then, this, went, white, will, with, yum*

High-Frequency Words: cow, horse, now, table, *a,* right, said, to

THEME 6, WEEK 3

Phonics Skills:
Vowel Pairs *ai, ay*

High-Frequency Words:
been, evening, far, forest, goes, hungry, near, soon

Day 1

Phonics Library: *Rain Day*

Phonics Practice Words: day, may, **play, playing,** rain, tail, **and,** *dog, ducks, feet, frogs, **in,** it, **lake,** like, pond, **she, so,** splash, stamp, this, wags, **we,** wet, will*

High-Frequency Words: all, her, jumps, our, **the,** too

WORD LIST

Day 2

Phonics Library: *Cub's Long Day*

Phonics Practice Words: day, **play,** stain, tail, trail, waits, way, **and,** at, back, big, catch, cave, cub, cub's, deep, each, **eats,** face, feet, fish, gets, has, **he,** his, home, **in, is, long, on,** red, rests, run, stream, that, then, this, treats, up, wakes, when

High-Frequency Words: evening, forest, hungry, *a,* finds, little, **the,** to

Day 2; Day 3

Anthology: *Red-Eyed Tree Frog*

Phonics Practice Words: day, rain, wait, *an,* **and,** ant, as, branch, but, crunch, **eat,** flicks, frog, frogs, from, **go,** has, hops, **in, is,** it, its, **jump,** lands, leaf, moth, no, **not, on,** red, **see,** shuts, sleep, slips, snake, tastes, tree, up, wakes, will **Challenge:** air, along, another, asleep, climbs, longer, slithers, something

High-Frequency Words: been, evening, far, forest, goes, hungry, near, soon, *a,* all, away, comes, do, does, find, here, look, morning, onto, out, **the,** to, what

Story Vocabulary: boa, caterpillar, eyed, eyes, iguana, iguanas, katydid, macaw, moves, poisonous, tongue, toucan

Day 5

Phonics Library: *Jay's Trip*

Phonics Practice Words: bay, day, gray, Jay, Jay's, Kay, pail, sails, snail, way, **and,** at, beach, big, fine, from, gets, has, **he,** him, his, home, **in, is,** leaf, **long,** nap, **on,** plants, red, seen, sets, **she,** sleeps, takes, that, thinks, this, trees, trip, up, wakes, when, while

High-Frequency Words: evening, far, goes, near, soon, *a,* her, never, one, right, **the,** too

HIGH-FREQUENCY WORDS

Word	Taught as High-Frequency Word THEME/WEEK	Decodable THEME/WEEK	Word	Taught as High-Frequency Word THEME/WEEK	Decodable THEME/WEEK	Word	Taught as High-Frequency Word THEME/WEEK	Decodable THEME/WEEK
a	1/3	1/1	*climb	6/1	n/a	*girl	4/2	10/1
*able	10/3	n/a	cold	3/1	r/a	give	5/3	n/a
about	8/1	n/a	*color	3/3	r/a	go	1/1	6/1
*above	10/2	n/a	come	4/1	r/a	goes	6/3	n/a
*afraid	7/2	n/a	could	5/2	n/a	*gone	7/1	n/a
after	9/2	10/1	*cow	6/2	8/2	good	5/3	7/2
again	7/1	n/a	*dance	9/1	n/a	green	3/3	6/2
*against	10/2	n/a	*divide	10/1	n/a	grow	5/1	7/1
all	3/2	n/a	do	2/2	n/a	*happy	8/1	9/1
*already	10/2	n/a	does	2/3	n/a	*hard	7/1	10/2
*also	3/3	n/a	done	9/2	n/a	have	1/3	n/a
always	8/2	n/a	*door	6/2	n/a	he	2/3	6/2
and	1/2	5/2	down	4/3	8/2	*head	10/1	n/a
*animal	3/1	n/a	draw	8/1	9/3	*hear	4/3	n/a
any	7/2	n/a	eat	3/2	6/2	her	5/3	10/1
are	2/3	n/a	*edge	9/3	n/a	here	1/2	n/a
*arms	8/2	10/2	eight	8/2	n/a	hold	4/3	n/a
around	9/1	n/a	*else	9/1	n/a	*horse	6/2	10/1
away	2/3	n/a	*enough	9/3	n/a	*house	5/2	8/2
*baby	9/3	n/a	*evening	6/3	n/a	how	5/2	8/2
*bear	7/2	n/a	*ever	9/1	10/1	*hungry	6/3	n/a
because	8/1	n/a	every	3/2	n/a	hurt	4/3	10/1
been	6/3	n/a	*eye	10/3	n/a	I	2/2	2/2
before	9/2	n/a	fall	3/1	n/a	*idea	7/2	n/a
*began	10/1	n/a	*family	4/1	n/a	in	2/1	1/3
*begin	10/2	n/a	far	6/3	10/2	is	2/2	1/3
*bird	3/1	10/1	*father	4/1	n/a	jump	1/2	4/3
blue	3/3	7/3	find	1/3	n/a	kind	8/3	n/a
*body	8/2	n/a	first	3/2	10/1	know	4/2	7/1
both	7/1	n/a	five	2/1	5/3	laugh	10/1	n/a
*break	10/1	n/a	*flower	3/1	10/1	*learn	4/3	n/a
brown	3/3	8/2	fly	5/3	9/1	light	5/1	7/3
*build	7/3	n/a	*follow	7/2	8/2	like	3/3	5/3
*butter	8/3	10/1	for	2/2	10/1	little	5/3	n/a
buy	9/2	n/a	*forest	6/3	10/1	live	2/3	n/a
by	6/1	9/1	found	6/1	8/2	long	5/1	5/2
call	3/2	n/a	four	2/1	n/a	look	3/1	7/2
*car	4/3	10/2	*friend	4/2	n/a	*love	4/1	n/a
carry	8/3	9/1	full	3/1	n/a	many	3/3	n/a
*caught	10/2	n/a	funny	3/3	9/1	me	2/2	6/2
*children	4/1	n/a	*garden	9/3	10/2	*minute	10/2	n/a

THEME 6: Animal Adventures

Word	Taught as High-Frequency Word THEME/WEEK	Decodable THEME/WEEK	Word	Taught as High-Frequency Word THEME/WEEK	Decodable THEME/WEEK	Word	Taught as High-Frequency Word THEME/WEEK	Decodable THEME/WEEK
*more	5/1	10/1	*school	9/2	n/a	walk	4/3	n/a
*morning	6/1	10/1	*second	10/1	n/a	*wall	6/2	n/a
*most	7/2	n/a	see	3/1	6/2	want	7/1	n/a
*mother	4/1	n/a	seven	8/2	n/a	warm	8/2	n/a
my	2/2	9/1	shall	3/2	5/1	was	5/3	n/a
*near	6/3	n/a	*sharp	9/3	10/2	wash	9/2	n/a
never	3/2	n/a	she	4/2	6/2	*watched	9/3	n/a
not	1/2	2/1	*shoe[s]	7/3	n/a	*water	7/2	n/a
now	6/2	8/2	*shout	6/1	8/2	we	1/2	6/2
*ocean	9/1	n/a	show	6/1	7/1	*wear	7/3	n/a
of	3/1	n/a	sing	4/2	5/2	were	8/3	n/a
off	9/2	n/a	small	5/1	n/a	what	2/1	n/a
old	7/3	n/a	so	5/2	6/1	where	2/3	n/a
on	1/1	2/1	some	3/3	n/a	who	1/3	n/a
once	2/1	n/a	soon	6/3	7/3	why	3/2	9/1
one	1/3	n/a	start	7/3	10/2	work	8/3	n/a
only	9/3	n/a	*sure	10/1	n/a	*world	5/2	n/a
open	9/1	n/a	*table	6/2	n/a	would	4/3	n/a
or	7/1	10/1	*talk	9/1	n/a	write	4/2	5/3
*other	5/1	n/a	*tall	7/2	n/a	you	2/2	7/3
our	5/3	8/2	*teacher	8/1	10/1	your	4/1	n/a
out	6/1	8/2	the	1/1	6/2			
over	5/2	n/a	their	4/3	n/a			
own	5/2	7/1	there	6/2	n/a			
*paper	3/2	n/a	these	5/1	6/2			
*part	8/1	10/2	they	2/3	n/a			
*people	4/1	n/a	*though	9/1	n/a			
*person	8/3	n/a	*thoughts	10/3	n/a			
*picture	4/1	n/a	three	2/1	6/2			
*piece	7/3	n/a	*through	6/2	n/a			
play	4/2	6/3	*tiny	8/1	n/a			
*present	10/3	n/a	to	1/3	n/a			
pretty	9/2	n/a	today	4/2	n/a			
pull	2/3	n/a	together	9/3	n/a			
put	8/3	n/a	too	1/2	7/3			
read	4/2	6/2	try	5/3	9/1			
*ready	8/2	n/a	*turn	7/1	10/1			
right	5/1	7/3	two	2/1	n/a			
*room	5/1	7/3	under	7/3	10/1			
said	2/2	n/a	upon	2/1	n/a			
saw	8/3	9/3	very	7/3	n/a			

* Words from the 800 Base Words of Highest Frequency of Occurrence in the American Heritage Computerized Study of the Vocabulary of Published Materials Used in Public Schools. Words without asterisks are from the Dolch list.

High-Frequency Words **R45**

TECHNOLOGY RESOURCES

American Melody
P.O. Box 270
Guilford, CT 06437
800-220-5557
www.americanmelody.com

Audio Bookshelf
174 Prescott Hill Road
Northport, ME 04849
800-234-1713
www.audiobookshelf.com

Baker & Taylor
100 Business Center Drive
Pittsburgh, PA 15205
800-775-2600
www.btal.com

BDD Audio/Random House
400 Hohn Road
Westminster, MD 21157
800-733-3000

Big Kids Productions
1606 Dywer Ave.
Austin, TX 78704
800-477-7811
www.bigkidsvideo.com

Books on Tape
P.O. Box 25122
Santa Ana, CA 92799
800-541-5525
www.booksontape.com

Broderbund Company
1 Martha's Way
Hiawatha, IA 52233
www.broderbund.com

Filmic Archives
The Cinema Center
Botsford, CT 06404
800-366-1920
www.filmicarchives.com

Great White Dog Picture Company
10 Toon Lane
Lee, NH 03824
800-397-7641
www.greatwhitedog.com

HarperAudio
10 E. 53rd St.
New York, NY 10022
800-242-7737
www.harperaudio.com

Houghton Mifflin Company
222 Berkeley St.
Boston, MA 02116
800-225-3362

Informed Democracy
P.O. Box 67
Santa Cruz, CA 95063
800-827-0949

JEF Films
143 Hickory Hill Circle
Osterville, MA 02655
508-428-7198

Kimbo Educational
P.O. Box 477
Long Branch, NJ 07740
800-631-2187
www.kimboed.com

Library Video Co.
P.O. Box 580
Wynnewood, PA 19096
800-843-3620
www.libraryvideo.com

Listening Library
P.O. Box 25122
Santa Ana, CA 92799
800-541-5525
www.listeninglibrary.com

Live Oak Media
P.O. Box 652
Pine Plains, NY 12567
800-788-1121
www.liveoakmedia.com

Media Basics
Lighthouse Square
P.O. Box 449
Guilford, CT 06437
800-542-2505
www.mediabasicsvideo.com

Microsoft Corp.
One Microsoft Way
Redmond, WA 98052
800-426-9400
www.microsoft.com

National Geographic School Publishing
P.O. Box 10597
Des Moines, IA 50340
800-368-2728
www.nationalgeographic.com

New Kid Home Video
P.O. Box 10443
Beverly Hills, CA 90213
800-309-2392
www.NewKidhomevideo.com

Puffin Books
345 Hudson Street
New York, NY 10014
800-233-7364

Rainbow Educational Media
4540 Preslyn Drive
Raleigh, NC 27616
800-331-4047
www.rainbowedumedia.com

Recorded Books
270 Skipjack Road
Prince Frederick, MD 20678
800-638-1304
www.recordedbooks.com

Sony Wonder
Dist. by Professional Media Service
19122 S. Vermont Ave.
Gardena, CA 90248
800-223-7672
www.sonywonder.com

Spoken Arts
195 South White Rock Road
Holmes, NY 12531
800-326-4090
www.spokenartsmedia.com

SRA Media
220 E. Danieldale Rd.
DeSoto, TX 75115
800-843-8855
www.sra4kids.com

Sunburst Technology
1550 Executive Drive
Elgin, IL 60123
800-321-7511
www.sunburst.com

SVE & Churchill Media
6677 North Northwest Highway
Chicago, IL 60631
800-829-1900
www.svemedia.com

Tom Snyder Productions
80 Coolidge Hill Road
Watertown, MA 02472
800-342-0236
www.tomsnyder.com

Troll Communications
100 Corporate Drive
Mahwah, NJ 07430
800-526-5289
www.troll.com

Weston Woods
143 Main St.
Norwalk, CT 06851-1318
800-243-5020
www.scholastic.com/westonwood

PRONUNCIATION GUIDE

In this book some unfamiliar or hard-to-pronounce words are followed by respellings to help you say the words correctly. Use the key below to find examples of various sounds and their respellings. Note that in the respelled word, the syllable in capital letters is the one receiving the most stress.

Dictionary letter or mark		Respelled as	Example	Respelled word
ă	(pat)	a	basket	BAS-kiht
ā	(pay)	ay	came	kaym
âr	(care)	air	share	shair
ä	(father)	ah	barter	BAHR-tur
ch	(church)	ch	channel	CHAN-uhl
ĕ	(pet)	eh	test	tehst
ē	(bee)	ee	heap	heep
g	(gag)	g	goulash	GOO-lahsh
ĭ	(pit)	ih	liver	LIHV-ur
ī	(pie, by)	y	alive	uh-LYV
		eye	island	EYE-luhnd
îr	(hear)	eer	year	yeer
j	(judge)	j	germ	jurm
k	(kick, cat, pique)	k	liquid	LIHK-wihd
ŏ	(pot)	ah	otter	AHT-ur
ō	(toe)	oh	solo	SOH-loh
ô	(caught, paw)	aw	always	AWL-wayz
ôr	(for)	or	normal	NOR-muhl
oi	(noise)	oy	boiling	BOYL-ihng
o͝o	(took)	u	pull, wool	pul, wul
o͞o	(boot)	oo	bruise	brooz
ou	(out)	ow	pound	pownd
s	(sauce)	s	center	SEHN-tur
sh	(ship, dish)	sh	chagrin	shuh-GRIHN
ŭ	(cut)	uh	flood	fluhd
ûr	(urge, term, firm, word, heard)	ur	earth	urth
			bird	burd
z	(zebra, xylem)	z	cows	kowz
zh	(vision, pleasure, garage)	zh	decision	dih-SIHZH-uhn
ə	(about)	uh	around	uh-ROWND
	(item)	uh	broken	BROH-kuhn
	(edible)	uh	pencil	PEHN-suhl
	(gallop)	uh	connect	kuh-NEHKT
	(circus)	uh	focus	FOH-kuhs
ər	(butter)	ur	liter	LEE-tur

Glossary

Glossary

Visit **www.eduplace.com** for e • Glossary and e • Word Game.

A

anywhere
Anywhere means in any place. You can sit anywhere you like.

B

ball
A **ball** is something that is round. Miguel hit the **ball** with the bat.

barn
A **barn** is a kind of building on a farm. A farmer keeps his cows and pigs in the **barn**.

beautiful
Beautiful means very nice to look at or hear. Anna drew a picture of a **beautiful** rainbow.

began
To **begin** means to start. School **began** in September.

222

boa
A **boa** is a kind of snake. A **boa** can live in the rain forest.

C

caterpillar
A **caterpillar** is an insect that looks like a worm. A **caterpillar** will change into a butterfly.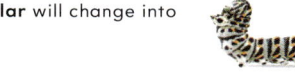

celebrate
To **celebrate** is to do something special for an event. We went to the park to **celebrate** my birthday.

convinced
To **convince** means to talk someone into something. I **convinced** my mother to let me go on the trip.

country
A **country** is a place where people live and share the same laws. There are many **countries** in the world.

223

coyote
A **coyote** is an animal that looks like a small wolf. The **coyote** didn't look much bigger than a dog.

cricket
A **cricket** is a small insect that looks like a grasshopper. Jamal saw the **cricket** jump.

D

dancing
To **dance** means to move your body to music. Jan and her friends like **dancing** at parties.

E

Earth
Earth is the planet we live on. **Earth** looks round when you see it from space.

easy
Easy means not hard to do. Riding my bike is **easy**.

224

elephant
An **elephant** is a very big animal with thick skin, big ears, and a long trunk. The **elephant** was the biggest animal in the circus.

eyes
Eyes are the parts of the body that let it see. The kitten closed its **eyes** and went to sleep.

F

fancy
Fancy means prettier or better than usual. We had a **fancy** cake at the party.

G

giant
Giant means much bigger than usual. Michael looked up at the **giant** tree.

225

H

heavy
Heavy means hard to lift. The box of toys was too **heavy** to carry.

hide
To **hide** something is to put it where nobody will see it. When I **hide**, my friends can't find me.

howl
To **howl** is to make a long cry like a dog, coyote, or wolf. My dog will **howl** when she's lonely.

I

iguana
An **iguana** is a kind of lizard. Tanya wanted an **iguana** for a pet.

inside
To be **inside** means to be in something. I'm staying **inside** the house because it's raining.

226

K

katydid
A **katydid** is a large green insect like a grasshopper. A **katydid** will rub its wings together to make a noise.

L

laying
To **lay** an egg is to make an egg. The hen was **laying** eggs in her nest.

M

macaw
A **macaw** is a large parrot. The **macaw** has a strong, curved beak.

marched
To **march** with someone is to take the same size steps at the same time. The band **marched** in the big parade.

mercy
To say **Mercy** is to show surprise. **Mercy!** That was a close call.

227

mouse
A **mouse** is a very small animal with a long tail, short fur, and sharp teeth. The **mouse** likes to eat cheese.

moves
To **move** is to go from one place to another. A bird **moves** from tree to tree by flying.

N

news
News is a story about things that are happening. My mother watches the **news** on television.

P

perfect
If something is **perfect**, it is just right. It was a **perfect** day for flying our kite.

plain
Plain means very simple. I put my lunch in a **plain** brown paper bag.

228

poisonous
A **poison** is something that can cause sickness or death. A rattlesnake is a **poisonous** animal.

R

rabbit
A **rabbit** is an animal with long ears and soft fur. A **rabbit** can hop very fast.

raining
To **rain** means to fall as drops of water. Get your umbrella because it's **raining**.

rough
Something that is **rough** does not feel even. The bumpy road was very **rough**.

S

smooth
Something that is **smooth** feels even and has no rough spots. The ice at the rink was very **smooth**.

229

special
Special means important and not like all the rest. Holidays and birthdays are special days.

street
A street is a road in a city or town. Sue lives on a busy street.

T

tail
A tail is part of an animal's body. Laura's dog wags its tail when it gets a treat.

tangled
Tangle means to be all mixed up. The kite's string got tangled in the tree.

tongue
The tongue is a part of the body inside the mouth. Your tongue helps you eat and speak.

toucan
A toucan is a colorful bird with a very long, large bill. Amy was excited to see a toucan flying in the rain forest.

town
A town is a place where people live and work. My town is smaller than a city.

W

wait
To wait means to stay someplace until something happens. We wait at the corner until the school bus comes.

watermelon
A watermelon is a big sweet fruit that is pink or red inside. Watermelon is a good snack in the summer.

weather
Weather is what it is like outside. Jim goes swimming in warm weather.

Acknowledgments

Acknowledgments

For each of the selections listed below, grateful acknowledgment is made for permission to excerpt and/or reprint original or copyrighted material, as follows:

Selections

EEK! There's a Mouse in the House, by Wong Herbert Yee. Copyright © 1992 by Wong Herbert Yee. Reprinted by permission of Houghton Mifflin Company. All rights reserved.

The Kite, by Alma Flor Ada, illustrated by Vivi Escrivá. Copyright © 1995 by Santillana USA Publishing Co., Inc. Reprinted by permission of the publisher.

Me on the Map, by Joan Sweeney, illustrated by Annette Cable. Text copyright © 1996 by Joan Sweeney. Illustrations copyright © 1996 by Annette Cable. Published by arrangement with Random House Children's Books, a division of Random House, Inc., New York, New York, U.S.A. All rights reserved.

Moving Day, by Robert Kalan, illustrated by Yossi Abolafia. Text copyright © 1996 by Robert Kalan. Illustrations copyright © 1996 by Yossi Abolafia. Reprinted by permission of HarperCollins Publishers.

Red-Eyed Tree Frog, by Joy Cowley, photographs by Nic Bishop, published by Scholastic Press, a division of Scholastic Inc. Text copyright © 1999 by Joy Cowley. Photographs copyright © 1999 by Nic Bishop. Reprinted by permission of Scholastic Inc.

Poetry

"A discovery" by Yayū, translated by Sylvia Cassedy and Kunihiro Suetake, from *Birds, Frogs and Moonlight*. Copyright © 1967 by Doubleday and Co. Reprinted by permission of Ellen Cassedy.

"A little egg," by Tina Anthony from *Miracles: Poems by Children of the English Speaking World*, edited by Richard Lewis. Copyright © 1966 by Richard Lewis. Used with permission of Richard Lewis.

"The Chipmunk" from *Zoo Doings*, by Jack Prelutsky. Copyright © 1983 by Jack Prelutsky. Reprinted by permission of HarperCollins Publishers.

"Morning Sun/Sol matutino" from *Laughing Tomatoes and Other Spring Poems/Jitomates risueños y otros poemas de primavera*, by Francisco X. Alarcón. Copyright © 1997 by Francisco Alarcón. Reprinted by permission of the publisher, Children's Book Press, San Francisco, CA.

"Quack, Quack!" from *Oh Say Can You Say?*, by Dr. Seuss. TM & Copyright © by Dr. Seuss Enterprises, L.P., 1979. Reprinted by permission of Random House Children's Books, a division of Random House, Inc.

"The Snake" from *Zoo Doings*, by Jack Prelutsky. Copyright © 1983 by Jack Prelutsky. Reprinted by permission of HarperCollins Publishers.

"The Toucan" from *Pyke's Poems*, by Pyke Johnson, Jr., published by Shorelands Publishing Company. Copyright © by Pyke Johnson, Jr. Reprinted by permission of the author.

"Turtle, turtle" from *The Sweet and Sour Animal Book*, by Langston Hughes. Copyright © 1994 (text) by Romana Bass & Arnold Rampersad, Administrators of the Estate of Langston Hughes. Used by permission of Oxford University Press, Inc., and Harold Ober Associates, Inc.

"Two Feet, Four Feet," by Ilo Orleans. Copyright © 1992 by Ilo Orleans. Reprinted by permission of Karen S. Solomon.

Illustration from *Waiting for Wings*, by Lois Ehlert, is depicted on the Focus on Poetry Table of Contents page. Copyright © 2001 by Lois Ehlert. Reprinted by permission of Harcourt, Inc.

Special thanks to the following teachers whose students' compositions appear as Student Writing Models: Cheryl Claxton, Florida; Patricia Kopay, Delaware; Susana Llanes, Michigan; Joan Rubens, Delaware; Nancy Schulten, Kentucky; Linda Wallis, California

Credits

Photography

3 (t) Navaswan/Taxi/Getty Images. (b) Siede Preis/PhotoDisc Green/Getty Images. 5,6 © Navaswan/Taxi/Getty Images. 7 (t) © PhotoDisc/Getty Images. (b) Tim Davis/Photo Researchers, Inc. 9,11 © Siede Preis/PhotoDisc Green/Getty Images. 12-13 (bkgd) From *Look-Alikes, Jr.* by Joan Steiner. Copyright © 1999 by Joan Steiner. Photography by Thomas Lindley. 15 (m) © Navaswan/Taxi/Getty Images. 16 (bkgd) © Georgette Douwma/Taxi/Getty Images. 43 (t) Courtesy William Morrow. 44 (l) © PhotoDisc/Getty Images. (r) Artville. 46 (c) CORBIS/Smart Westmoreland. (b) J.H. (Pete) Carmichael. 47 (t) Dave King/Dorling Kindersley. (b) J.H. (Pete) Carmichael. 48 NHPA/Anthony Bannister. 49 CORBIS/Annie Griffiths Belt. 54 (c) John Zieb/Mercury Pictures. (b) Courtesy Annette Cable. 54-5 (bkgd) © Charles O'Rear/Corbis. 82 (t) Chris Arend/Alaska Stock Images. (b) Rubberball Productions. 83 (t) Jean Chen/Stock Connection/PictureQuest. (b) Michael Dwyer/Stock Boston/PictureQuest. 84 (tl) Chris Arend/Alaska Stock Images. (tr) CORBIS/Galen Rowell. (bl) Garry Adams/ IndexStock. (br) Rubberball Productions. 85 (tl) CORBIS/The Purcell Team. (tr) Jean Chen/Stock Connection/PictureQuest. (bl) Michael Dwyer/Stock Boston/PictureQuest. (br) Christopher Morris/Black Star/PictureQuest. 88-9 (bkgd) © Zephyr Picture/ Index Stock Imagery/PictureQuest. 102 Courtesy Alma Flor Ada. 103 Courtesy Vivi Escrivá. 106-9 (bkgd) © PhotoDisc/Getty Images. 108 Lynda Richardson. 109 (c) Lawrence Migdale/Stock Boston. (b) Lynda Richardson. 114-5 © PhotoDisc/Getty Images. 116 Tim Davis/Stone/Getty Images.117 Paul Chauncey/CORBIS. 118 Laurie Rubin/The Image Bank/Getty Images. 120 Daniel J. Cox/Stone/Getty Images. 122-3 Tim Davis/Photo Researchers, Inc. 124-5 Frank Muscati/CORBIS. 126 John Lei/Stock Boston. 128-9 (bkgd) © Ariel Skelley/CORBIS. 129 (m) © Siede Preis/PhotoDisc Green/Getty Images. 132 (l) Courtesy Carmen Tafolla. (r) Paul Buck/Mercury Pictures. 132-3 (bkgd) Kathryn Kleinman/FoodPix/Getty Images. 153 Courtesy Rosario Valderrama. 156-7 © Jim Brandenburg/Minden Pictures. 156 (bl) © Carr Clifton/Minden Pictures. (br) © Jim Brandenburg/Minden Pictures. 157 (bl) Frans Lanting/Minden Pictures. (bm) Brian Stablyk/Stone/Getty Images. (br) Kerrick James/Stone/Getty Images. 158 (t) (m) (b) Frans Lanting/Minden Pictures. (br) © Jim Brandenburg/Minden Pictures. 159 Will & Deni McIntyre/Stone/Getty Images. 160 © PhotoDisc/Getty Images. 164-5 (bkgd) © Albert Normandin/Masterfile. 183 Courtesy Wong Herbert Yee. 186-7 Mike Johnson Marine Natural History Photography. 188 Corbis Royalty Free. 189 (t) CORBIS/ George McCarthy. (b) Robert Tyrrell Photography. 190 © Nic Bishop Photography. 192 (bkgd) © R. Watts/Premium/Panoramic Images. 215 (tl) © Terry Coles. (tr) Michael P.L. Fogden/ Bruce Coleman/PictureQuest. (bl) David Aubrey/CORBIS. (br) Courtesy Nic Bishop. 216 © PhotoDisc/Getty Images. 217 CORBIS/David A. Northcott. 218 Snake, 20th century. Niki de Saint-Phalle, b. 1930, French, painted polyester. 19 in height. Private Collection. Christie's Images, Inc. 219 CORBIS/Kevin Schafer. 222 © PhotoDisc/Getty Images. 223 Kim Taylor/Dorling Kindersley. 224 © PhotoDisc/Getty Images. 225 © PhotoDisc/Getty Images. 226 PhotoSpin. 227 (t) Artville. (b) © PhotoDisc/Getty Images. 228 © PhotoDisc/Getty Images. 229 © PhotoDisc/Getty Images. 231 (t) ©Frans Lanting/Minden Pictures. (b) Artville.

Assignment Photography

15, 45 (t), 53, 80, 105 © HMCo./Joel Benjamin. 111, 221 © HMCo./Michael Indresano Photography. 131, 163, 184 © HMCo./Michelle Joyce. 155, 185 © HMCo./Allan Landau.

Illustration

87 Toby Williams. 112-113 Lois Ehlert. 115-126 (borders) Eileen Hine. 130, 132, 133-154 Rosario Valderrama. 163, 184 Sherri Haab. 191 Mircea Catusanu. 217 Lizi Boyd.

232

To Mattachin and Hiroshige – two's company . . . S.G.

TWO'S COMPANY, by Shirley Greenway, photographs by Oxford Scientific Films. Text copyright © 1997 by Shirley Greenway. Photographs © 1997 by Oxford Scientific Films (and individual copyright holders). Created by White Cottage Children's Books, London, England. Reprinted by arrangement with Charlesbridge Publishing, Watertown, MA.

Photographer Credits: Title Page Steve Turner; Introduction Rudie Kuiter; 4–5 (tl) John Downer; (m) (r) Hans Reinhard/Okapia; 6–7 Tom McHugh/Photo Researchers; 8 (tl) Konrad Wothe; (r) Daniel J. Cox; 9 (r) G.A. Maclean; 10 (l) Alain Christof; (m) (r) David Thompson; 11 Phil Devries; 12 Bruce Davidson; 13 Anthony Bannister; 14–15 (tl) John Gerlach/Animals Animals; (bl) Michael W. Richards; (r) Miriam Austerman; 16–17 Howard Hall; 18 (tl) Daniel J. Cox; (r) Frank Schneidermeyer; 19 Michael Fogden; 20 (tl) Hans & Judy Beste; (r) Des & Jen Bartlett/Survival; 21 Kathie Atkinson; 22–23 G.I. Bernard; 24–25 (tl) Mickey Gibson/Animals Animals; (r) David Shale/Survival; 26 (tl) William Bacon/Photo Researchers; (r) Jeff Lepore/Photo Researchers; 27 Lon Lauker; 28 (tl) Steve Turner (r) William Paton/Survival; 29 Des & Jen Bartlett/Survival; 30 Dr. A.C. Twomey/Photo Researchers; 31 (l) Frank Schneidermeyer; (r) Tom McHugh/Photo Researchers.

Houghton Mifflin Edition, 2001
Copyright © 2001 by Houghton Mifflin Company. All rights reserved.

No part of this work may be reproduced or transmitted in any form or by any means, electronic or mechanical, including photocopying and recording, or by any information storage or retrieval system without the prior written permission of the copyright owner unless such copying is expressly permitted by federal copyright law. With the exception of non-profit transcription in Braille, Houghton Mifflin is not authorized to grant permission for further uses of this work. Permission must be obtained from the individual copyright owner as identified herein. Address requests for permission to make copies of Houghton Mifflin material to School Permissions, Houghton Mifflin Company, 222 Berkeley Street, Boston, MA 02116.

Printed in the U.S.A.

ISBN 0-618-06701-9
123456789-B-05 04 03 02 01 00

Index

Boldface page references indicate formal strategy and skill instruction.

Home-community connection. *See* Home-Community Connections *book.*

Home connection, *T37, T43, T81, T119, T125, T163, T189, T195, T235. See also* Home-Community Connections *book.*

Home-school connection. See Home-Community Connections *book.*

Illustrators of selections in Anthology
Bishop, Nic, *T211*
Valderamma, Rosario, *T57*
Yee, Herbert Wong, *T139*

Independent and recreational reading
suggestions for, *T6–T7, T29, T41, T61, T69, T77, T79–T81, T84–T87, T111, T123, T143, T151, T159, T161, T166–T169, T181, T193, T215, T223, T225, T231, T233–T235, T238–T241, R3–R11*
See also Reading modes.

Independent writing
daily writing prompt, *T29, T41, T61, T69, T77, T111, T123, T143, T151, T159, T181, T193, T215, T223, T231*
suggestions for, *T83, T165, T237*
See also Teacher's Resource Blackline Masters.

Individual needs, meeting. *See* Reaching All Learners.

Inferences, making
about characters' actions and feelings, *T202, T204*
from illustration, *T198*
See also Comprehension skills, cause and effect; Comprehension skills, generalizations, making.

Information skills. *See* Reference and study skills.

Journals, *T47, T63, T129, T145, T199, T217*

Knowledge, activating prior. *See* Background, building.

Language and usage. *See* Grammar and usage.

Language games, *T72, T73, T155, T156*

Language mechanics. *See* Mechanics, language.

Learning styles, activities employing alternate modalities to meet individual, *T62, T63, T144, T145, T216, T217. See also* Reaching All Learners.

Lesson plans
daily, *T22–T23, T104–T105, T174–T175*
Managing Flexible Groups, *T24–T25, T106–T107, T176–T177*

Lessons, specific
comprehension, **T64–T65, T146–T147, T218–T219**
decoding, **T35–T37, T79–T81, T117–T119, T187–T189, T233–T235**
grammar, **T67, T83, T149, T165, T221, T237**
high-frequency words, **T42–T43, T124–T125, T194–T195**
listening, speaking, viewing, **T39, T83, T121, T165, T191, T237**
phonics, **T32–T34, T114–T116, T184–T186**
spelling, **T38,** T58, T66, T74, T82, **T120,** T140, T148, T156, T164, **T190,** T212, T220, T228, T236
visual literacy, **T153**
vocabulary, **T45, T74, T127, T156, T197, T220, T228**
writing, **T121, T141, T191, T213, T239**

Leveled Bibliography, *T6–T7*

Leveled books
On My Way Practice Readers
Fox and Mule, R3
Real Wolf, The, R9
What Animal Is It?, R6
Theme Paperbacks
Fishing Bears, R5
Little Red Hen, The, R4
Trade books
Annie and the Wild Animals, R11
Every Autumn Comes the Bear, R7
Henry and Mudge and Annie's Perfect Pet, R8

vowel(s)
  long *a,* **T12,** *T150, T180, T214, T222*
  long *e (CV, CVCe), T12,* **T114,** *T122, T135, T226, R16–R17*
  long *i,* **T12, T72,** *T180, T222*
  long *o,* **T12, T26,** *T32–T33, T60, T142, T154, T180, T214, R12–R13*
  long *u,* **T12, T26,** *T32–T33, T52, T60, T76, T154, R12–R13*
  schwa, *T200*
  vowel pairs
    ai, ay, **T178, T184–T186,** *T192, T205, T230, R18–R19*
    ee, ea, T48, T116, T192, T227, R16
  See also Decoding skills; Spelling.

Phonics Library titles
  Cub's Long Day, T195
  Duke's Gift, T35–T37
  Gram's Huge Meal, T161–T163
  Jay's Trip, T233–T235
  Legs Gets His Lunch, T43
  Nest, The, T79–T81
  Pete and Peach, T125
  Rain Day, T187–T189
  Seal Beach, T117–T119

Phonological awareness. *See* Phonemic awareness.

Poetry
  "The Snake," by Jack Prelutsky, *T224*
  "The Toucan" by Pyke Johnson, Jr., *T225*

Predicting outcomes. *See* Comprehension skills.

Predictions
  from previewing, *T129, T199*
  reviewing, *T51, T57, T133, T206, T211, T232*

Previewing
  illustrations, *T47, T129, T178, T199*
  text, *T47, T129, T199*

Prewriting. *See* Reading-Writing Workshop, steps of; Writing skills, prewriting.

Print awareness. *See* Concepts of print.

Prior knowledge. *See* Background, building.

Process writing. *See* Reading-Writing Workshop; Writing skills.

Proofreading. *See* Reading-Writing Workshop, steps of; Writing skills, proofreading

Publishing. *See* Reading-Writing Workshop, steps of; Writing skills, publishing

Punctuation. *See* Concepts of print; Mechanics, language.

Purpose setting
  for reading, *T47, T70, T129, T152, T198, T224*

Questions, formulating, *T56,* **T128,** *T129, T131, T132, T133, T137, T138, T139, R3*

Reaching All Learners
  Challenge, *T50, T56, T58, T71, T132, T138, T140, T205, T210, T212, T225, R13, R15, R17, R19, R21, R23, R25, R27, R29, R31*
  English Language Learners, *T44, T46, T52, T56, T63, T70, T83, T121, T126, T128, T135, T145, T165, T191, T196, T198, T203, T204, T208, T237, R3, R6, R9*
  Extra Support, *T47, T50, T51, T54, T56, T63, T91, T129, T130, T132, T137, T138, T145, T152, T199, T202, T204, T205, T210, T224*
  On Level Students, *T50, T56, T71, T132, T138, T205, T210, T225*
  See also English Language Learners; Reteaching.

Read Alouds. *See* Teacher Read Alouds.

Reading fluency. *See* Fluency.

Reading log. *See* Journals.

Reading modes
  comprehension support, *T79, T161, T233*
  cooperative reading, *T51, T78, T133, T160, T161, T195, T206, T232*
  guiding comprehension. *See* Critical thinking.
  independent reading, *T161, T195, R3–R11*
  oral reading, *T37, T78, T79–T81, T81, T119, T160, T189, T232, T235*
  partner reading, *T79, T195, T235*
  teacher read aloud, *T30–T31, T112–T113, T182–T183*
  See also Rereading.

Reading strategies. *See* Strategies, reading.

Reading traits
  establishing comprehension, *T65, T147*
  realizing context, *T219*

Reading-Writing Workshop (process writing)
  conferencing, **T96**
  evaluating, **T98**
  reading as a writer, **T91**
  steps of
    drafting, **T94–T95**
    prewriting, **T92–T93**

  proofreading, **T97**
  publishing and sharing, **T98**
  revising, **T96**
  student model, **T90–T91**
  subjects
    description, **T88–T99**
  See also Writing skills.

Reference and study skills
  book, parts of a, *T71,* **R32**
  graphic sources. *See* Graphic information, interpreting.
  reference resources
    books, *T109*
    encyclopedia, *T109*
    magazines, *T109*

Rereading
  for comprehension, *T78, T139, T141, T160, T211, T232*
  orally, *T37, T78, T81, T119, T160, T189, T232, T235*
  with feeling and expression, *T37, T78, T81, T119, T160, T189, T232, T235*
  See also Fluency; Lesson plans, Managing Flexible Groups.

Research activities, *T109*

Resources. *See* Technology resources; Theme resources.

Responding to literature, options for
  discussion, *T50, T56, T84, T85, T86, T87, T132, T138, T144, T166, T167, T168, T169, T205, T210, T217, T238, T239, T240, T241, R3, R4, R5, R6, R7, R8, R9, R10, R11*
  Internet, *T63, T145, T217*
  personal response, *T63, T145, T217*
  writing, *T63, T145, T217*

Reteaching, *R12, R14, R16, R18, R20, R22, R24, R26, R28, R30, R32*

Retelling, *T40, T57, T64, T78, T83, T160, T165, T191, T232*

Revising. *See* Reading-Writing Workshop, steps of; Writing skills, revising.

Rhyme. *See* Phonemic awareness.

Routines
  daily, *T28–T29, T40–T41, T60–T61, T68–T69, T76–T77, T110–T111, T122–T123, T142–T143, T150–T151, T158–T159, T180–T181, T192–T193, T214–T215, T222–T223, T230–T231*
  daily message, *T28, T40, T60, T68, T76, T110, T122, T142, T150, T158, T180, T192, T214, T222, T230*
  instructional, *T11*
  management, *T10*

high-frequency words. *See* High-frequency
 words.
story vocabulary, *T44, T45, T48, T49, T52, T54,*
 T84, T85, T86, T87, T126, T127, T129, T132,
 T133, T134, T135, T137, T166, T167, T168,
 T169, T196, T197, T200, T203, T204, T205,
 T209, T238, T239, T240, T241
 See also Decoding skills.

Vocabulary skills
 alphabetical order to the first letter, **T66**
 See also Vocabulary, building; Vocabulary,
 selection.

Vowels. *See* Phonics; Spelling.

Word analysis. *See* Structural analysis;
 Vocabulary, building.

Word Wall, *T28, T40, T60, T68, T76, T110, T122,*
 T142, T150, T158, T180, T192, T214, T222, T230,
 R33

Writer's log. *See* Journals.

Writing activities and types
 book cover, *T179*
 class writing, *T121, T141*
 class summary, **T191, T213**
 cooperative writing. *See* Writing modes, interactive writing, shared writing.
 descriptions, *T13, T29, T61, T68, T77,* **T88–T99,**
 T111, T122, T143, T159, T179, T181, T193,
 T223, T231
 dreams, *T27, T77*
 independent. *See* Independent writing.
 instructions, *R21*
 journal, *T83, T165,*
 letters and cards, **T39, T59,** *T109, T237*
 list of chores, numbered, *T145*
 list of rules, *R23*
 persuasive writing, **T39, T59, T75**
 riddles, *T212, T216, T217*
 sentences, *T13, T26, T27, T71, T140, T223, T228*
 solution to problem, *T145, T151*
 story, *T41,* **T121, T141,** *T215, R25, R27*
 summary, **T191, T213, T229**
 See also Reading-Writing Workshop.

Writing as a process. *See* Reading-Writing
Workshop.

Writing conferences. *See* Reading-Writing
Workshop.

Writing modes
 descriptive, *T13, T29, T61, T68, T77,* **T88–T99,**
 T111, T122, T143, T159, T179, T181, T193,
 T223, T231
 expressive, *T27, T77*
 interactive writing, *T59, T141, T213*

narrative, *T41, T121, T141, T215, R25, R27*
 persuasive, *T39, T59, T75*
 shared writing, *T39, T121, T191*

Writing skills
 drafting
 answering a comprehension question, **T157**
 exact words, **T95**
 sensory language, **T94**
 topic sentence, *T75*
 formats. *See* Writing activities and types.
 prewriting
 brainstorming, *T75, T83, T94*
 choosing a topic, **T92**
 organizing and planning, **T93**
 proofreading
 writing sentences, **T97**
 publishing
 act out, *T121*
 Anansi big book, *T141*
 class book, *T98, T141, T165,*
 e-mail, **T98**
 read own writing, *T229*
 snake book, *R25*
 revising
 summary, *T229*
 See also Reading-Writing Workshop.

Writing traits
 conventions, *T99*
 ideas, *T89, T93, T99*
 organization, *T99*
 presentation, *T99*
 sentence fluency, *T99*
 voice, *T99*
 word choice, *T89, T95, T99*